South Asian Media Cultures

South Asian Media Cultures

Audiences, Representations, Contexts

Edited by
Shakuntala Banaji

ANTHEM PRESS
LONDON · NEW YORK · DELHI

Anthem Press
An imprint of Wimbledon Publishing Company
www.anthempress.com

This edition first published in UK and USA 2011
by ANTHEM PRESS
75-76 Blackfriars Road, London SE1 8HA, UK
or PO Box 9779, London SW19 7ZG, UK
and
244 Madison Ave. #116, New York, NY 10016, USA

© 2011 Shakuntala Banaji editorial matter and selection;
individual chapters © individual contributors

The moral right of the authors has been asserted.

All rights reserved. Without limiting the rights under copyright reserved above,
no part of this publication may be reproduced, stored or introduced into
a retrieval system, or transmitted, in any form or by any means
(electronic, mechanical, photocopying, recording or otherwise),
without the prior written permission of both the copyright
owner and the above publisher of this book.

British Library Cataloguing-in-Publication Data
A catalogue record for this book is available from the British Library.

Library of Congress Cataloging-in-Publication Data
The Library of Congress has cataloged the hardcover edition as follows:
South Asian media cultures : audiences, representations, contexts / edited by Shakuntala
Banaji.
p. cm.
Includes bibliographical references.
ISBN 978-1-84331-842-2 (hardcover : alk. paper) – ISBN 978-0-85728-955-1
(eBook : alk. paper)
1. Mass media–Social aspects–South Asia. 2. Mass media–Political aspects–South Asia.
I. Banaji, Shakuntala, 1971-
P92.S64S685 2010
302.230954–dc22
2010003805

ISBN-13: 978 0 85728 409 9 (Pbk)
ISBN-10: 0 85728 409 6 (Pbk)

This title is also available as an eBook.

For
Ammar Al-Ghabban, Mukul Mangalik, Rohini Hensman and Jairus Banaji,
whose imagination and integrity transcend disciplines and borders;
and
in memory of C. R. Hensman

CONTENTS

List of Illustrations ix

1. Introduction 1
   Shakuntala Banaji

Part One. Elaborating Audiences: Meaning, Use and Social Context

2. Talking Back to 'Bollywood': Hindi Commercial Cinema in North-East India 29
   Daisy Hasan

3. 'Adverts Make Me Want to Break the Television': Indian Children and their Audiovisual Media Environment in Three Contrasting Locations 51
   Shakuntala Banaji

4. Urdu for Image: Understanding Bangladeshi Cinema through its Theatres 73
   Lotte Hoek

5. Musical Media and Cosmopolitanisms in Nepal's Popular Music, 1950–2006 91
   Paul D. Greene

Part Two. Telling Texts: Media Discourse, Identity and Politics

6. Private Satellite Media and the Geo-Politics of Moderation in Pakistan 109
   Tahir H. Naqvi

7. Forgetting to Remember: The Privatisation of the Public, the Economisation of Hindutva, and the Medialisation of Genocide 123
   Britta Ohm

8. Myth – The National Form: *Mission Istanbul* and Muslim
   Representation in Hindi Popular Cinema   145
   Noorel Mecklai

9. A Peace of Soap: Representations of Peace and Conflict
   in Popular Teledramas in Sri Lanka   163
   Neluka Silva

10. Destigmatising Star Texts – Honour and Shame among Muslim
    Women in Pakistani Cinema   181
    Irna Qureshi

Part Three. Alternative Producers: The Articulation of (New) Media, Politics and Civic Participation

11. Through the Lens of a 'Branded Criminal': The Politics of   201
    Marginal Cinema in India
    Rashmi Sawhney

12. Pakistani Students' Uses of New Media to Construct
    a Narrative of Dissent   221
    Saman Talib

13. Expanding the Art of the Possible: Leveraging Citizen
    Journalism and User Generated Content (USG) for Peace
    in Sri Lanka   235
    Sanjana Hattotuwa

14. Conclusion   255
    Shakuntala Banaji

List of Contributors   263

LIST OF ILLUSTRATIONS

Figure 2.1	Manipuri film posters (courtesy of Daisy Hasan)	36
Figure 2.2	Manipuri films have replaced Bollywood in theatres in Imphal (courtesy of Daisy Hasan)	37
Figure 2.3	Manipuri film showing in a theatre in Imphal (courtesy of Daisy Hasan)	38
Figure 2.4	A cinema hall in Imphal screening a Manipuri film (courtesy of Daisy Hasan)	39
Figure 11.1	'Entrance to Chharanagar' (courtesy of P. Kerim Friedman)	204
Figure 11.2	Scene from *Ek Aur Balcony* ('One More Balcony') (courtesy of Budhan Theatre)	205
Figure 11.3	Scene from *Ek Aur Balcony* ('One More Balcony') (courtesy of Budhan Theatre)	205

Chapter One

INTRODUCTION[1]

Shakuntala Banaji

South Asia through the Lens of Totalising Events

Throughout this volume 'media cultures' refers to the complex interactions between particular audiences, their practices of meaning-making and use, and specific texts, representations, formats or media. It also refers to the interplay of politics, history and finance in the relationships between media producers and texts, ideologies and social contexts. The chapters collected here present a wide range of media cultures and associated cultural practices from across South Asia. At the same time they explain those cultures and practices through a set of historical, political and theoretical engagements that share many common elements. This might be, for instance, in relation to violence and peace, ethnic divisions and state responses or conflicts between supposed tradition and erstwhile modernity. Or it may be in relation to pleasure and learning, autonomy, morality and resistance on the part of marginalised peoples or highly controlled groups. All of these have been explored by the authors in their research, and practice, in the areas of media audiences, texts and contexts in South Asia. Before treading new ground, however, it is worth asking why the kind of approach taken in this volume is so necessary, and why now.

Several cohorts of university students in London, listing what came immediately to mind in relation to the five best known countries in the South Asian region[2], almost uniformly linked India to words such as 'vast', 'amazing', 'spiritual', 'Bollywood', 'non-violence', 'poverty', 'IT/call centres', 'large democracy' and 'beautiful', Pakistan to the phrases 'terrorism', 'Islam' and 'near Afghanistan', Sri Lanka to 'war' and 'honeymoons', Nepal to 'Mount Everest' and Bangladesh to a single phrase: 'always flooding'. When asked the same question, a similar group of university students in Bombay[3] responded in an almost identical manner, except that the vituperative list in relation to Pakistan was slightly more elaborate and that Nepal was seen as a 'honeymoon' destination. Stereotypes about most countries circulate widely in international settings, and so are not in and of themselves shocking. But for readers of this volume, the proximity of these countries to each other, their shared histories, languages, religions, cultures and traditions (both positive and negative) should make the stark differences in perception noteworthy. When asked what evidence they based these associations on, students either recanted or mentioned some form of media, the most common being photographs, television and newspapers. What gets shown or does not get shown, discussed or ignored by the national and international media with regard to South Asia, and the reasons or processes operating behind those decisions, evidently contributes to the construction of particular sets of meanings about South Asian nations and national identities.

Distinctive media events, for instance, can become points of departure for public interest in and understanding of contemporary political realities. A bomb attack, in Pakistan, on the Sri Lankan cricket team, supporters and staff by members of an (unknown) supposedly Islamist extremist group; the hostage-taking, arson and killing in Bombay, India in November 2008; the recent violent mutiny in Bangladesh[4]; video evidence, taken on a mobile phone, of a young woman in Pakistan being beaten with a whip while a crowd of men watch in seeming silence; the film *Slumdog Millionnaire* (2008) by the British Film-maker Danny Boyle. Even in diaspora, some of these media events actually make prime time viewing. Yet, events such as these are hardly representative of the cultures of media and politics in South Asia. Myriad everyday counterparts of these sensational events contribute to the fabric of life in South Asia. From the attention paid to regional radio broadcasts in vernacular languages through the uses of urban internet cafes to mass demonstrations against local dam-building projects filmed by locals on mobile phones, less spectacular activities and happenings are frequently ignored in academic, journalist and policy literature. Thus the morally complex, socially diverse, historical and political processes and contexts within which the events listed above are embedded take place largely out of sight. This situation is problematic for two reasons.

First, the history of the region comes to be read mainly or even solely within the sporadic, ideologically dangerous and/or simplistic frame of such internationally sensational events and the media discourses which surround them. One manifestation of this trend, both in journalism and in academic writing relating to South Asian media and politics, is the tendency to emphasise religious differences, conflicts and borders rather than both positive and negative civic solidarities and shared cultural trends. Second, large areas and aspects of media production, interpretation and use are discussed via highly simplistic frames of reference. Others are misrepresented (deliberately or unconsciously), suppressed or ignored. This may be seen in the lack of debate about learning, media and culture, and in misleading causal explanations about the relationship of media and media reception to politics in South Asia. Frequently the topic of popular culture and its relationship to politics appears limited to the realm of textual analyses of television news, film and other entertainment genres. India dominates the locale. Even more narrowly, anxieties about or celebrations of Indian popular cultural representations remain a key subject for much output on the politics and history of South Asian Media. Thus, for instance, advertising (consumerism) and sexual 'obscenity' are vocal concerns across the political spectrum but communal stereotypes and xenophobia are only occasionally discussed; equally, cultural imperialism and the 'westernization/corruption' of youth is a favoured topic, but increasing religious and political censorship or arbitrary suppression of media producers and products rarely merits legislation or prosecution. So how might those of us interested in South Asian media and cultures of reception and production more fruitfully approach this topic?

While there is some merit in embedding a discussion of media cultures within a context of enduring national political conflicts, this approach is problematic if it represents India as somehow successfully negotiating between 'modernity' and 'tradition' via its apparently vibrant democracy and neo-liberal economic conditions, while its neighbours are mired in religious fundamentalism, economic collapse, terrorism or separatist armed conflict. In particular, India should not be understood as a monolithic entity, as if its diversity of linguistic, religious and cultural inhabitants, its multiparty system and its local, regional and national elections equate to successful democracy. In light of the gaps in discussions about South Asian media identified earlier, one of the key aims of this collection is to address continuing interdisciplinary debates around the following questions: how and by which groups of media producers are historical and social events in South Asia being represented to South Asian audiences? In what ways are discourses on gender, nationalism, ethnicity or class being expressed by mainstream media texts across South Asia and how do different sections of the public negotiate meanings from these discourses? Who are some of the real people often conflated under the terms 'audience' or 'citizens' in different South Asian countries and can their media habits and interpretations be said to form distinct 'media cultures'? Which political themes and concerns are expressed across different media audiences *and* across borders in the subcontinent? And how should these issues be addressed by policy-makers?

In order to get a sense of how these questions might be grounded and inflected differently for each author, it is worth turning here, albeit briefly, to three interlinked areas: national political histories; media traditions and relationships to ruling elites; and cultural practices within groups whose relationships to media and politics in South Asia make up the 'media cultures' in this volume.

Shared Histories

To a certain extent, all historical overviews, however brief or extended, construct their subject in particular ways. This one is no exception, and runs the risk of positioning all South Asian history in relation to the arrival and departure of western colonial powers and the formation of distinct nation states. Given the preoccupation of a number of contributors to this volume with the idea of the role played by media and academia in the construction of history and memory or forgetting, this section should be read with the clear warning that it leaves out far more than it includes: notably the eclectic and complex pre-British period, when much of South Asia – and the princely states within it – developed for several centuries under a series of quite different and contrasting styles of Mughal rule (Habib 1963; Thapar 2005; Alam 2009; Guha 2009; Talbot 2009).

Colonial rule in all five countries (mainly by the British though also, in the cases of parts of India and Sri Lanka, by the Portuguese and the Dutch), decolonisation struggles and their aftermath offer a common framework for beginning to describe the political contexts of India, Pakistan, Bangladesh, Nepal and Sri Lanka. The introduction and indigenisation of newspapers and cinema both occurred in South Asia during colonial rule, while the conflicts between religious communities in India, Pakistan and Bangladesh, for instance, have often been attributed to British policies of 'divide and rule'. Although one does not get from a listing of historical events a sense of the way in which 'the event attaches itself with its tentacles into everyday life and folds itself into the recesses of the ordinary' (Das 2006, 1), later in the volume the social and cultural repercussions and significance of these events will become apparent, time and again, in the everyday narratives of media production, representation, interpretation and use.

Post 1948, India's historical imaginary has been dominated by the violence that occurred at and around the time of partition from Pakistan: the large-scale flight of Bengali Muslims into what was then East Pakistan and the reverse flight of many Hindus into West Bengal; the flight of millions of Sikhs and Hindus across the new border into India from Pakistan; the flight of millions of Muslims from India into (West) Pakistan; and the widespread, horrifying, violence of one community against another that left around a million dead and more than four million people displaced (Das 1990; Pandey 2001; Brass 2003; Talbot 2007). The physical and psychic scars left by the bereavement and the killing, the abduction of women and girls, the loss of children, rape by men of all communities against those from others, loss of property, livelihoods and life were never fully explored, discussed or reconciled in years following partition (Das 1990; 2006). Instead, these events have been replayed in novels and films on each side of the various borders with varying degrees of historical accuracy and have continued to simmer beneath the surface of everyday life in areas that were directly affected. They also frequently form the ostensible (and media perpetuated) rationale for ongoing tensions between Sikhs, Hindus and Muslims, even in areas that did not experience partition. Widespread unemployment, subsistence wages and – despite the various 'development plans' implemented post-independence – the continued control of resources, land, social and political power by a small minority of rural and urban elites, ensured that corruption became endemic across the country. Successive Indian governments, led by coalitions, or by one or other of the major parties[5], have done little to decrease the enormous gap between classes or to ease tensions between communities.

On the contrary, the last three decades have seen two Indian Prime Ministers from the same family assassinated for the perceived or actual role their governments' played in suppressing secessionist groups or struggles, as well as dozens of politicians implicated in voting scandals, widespread nepotism, the instigation of riots and aggressive far-Right Hindu nationalism. Further movements to secede from India – in Kashmir (Schofield 2003), by Sikhs in Punjab (Dos Santos 2007) and in Assam (Saikia 2005) to name but a few – have seen violent repression against local populations by the Indian army, leaving many hundreds of thousands of people dead or disappeared and destroying infrastructure in these regions. The persecution and execution of local journalists and other local media producers in India, the suppression of dissent within the local populations and the lack of reporting about atrocities taking place make the role of the national media all the more complex, and locate the mainstream fictional representations of these areas and their populations within complicated and often conflicting ideological networks.

Pakistan's history of political violence, coup d'etats and its succession of democratically elected presidents followed by military dictatorships is also well known: Ayub Khan's coup and his rule from 1958–69 was followed by Zulfikar Ali Bhutto's civilian government from 1972–77. Bhutto was then ousted by General Zia-ul-Haq, whose rule was accompanied by the increasing intrusion of religion into the polity and by the weakening of secular democratic forces. Corruption and censorship continued to thrive in the 1990s under the successive civilian governments of Benazir Bhutto and Nawaz Sharif. In 1999 General Pervez Musharraf came to power in another military coup. Ironically, although it ended in further censorship and dictatorial edicts, under Musharraf's nine-year regime, some semblance of secular ethos returned to parts of Pakistan and the country's media began to open up to a range of cultural interests. All through this turbulent half century, according to Shakil Rai Akhtar, Pakistan's dominant cultural ethos has remained 'parasitic landlordism' which is resilient despite 'Islam, modernism, democracy, socialism, some of the causes espoused by the different political leaders and regimes at different times' (2007, 213). Meanwhile, wars between India and Pakistan in 1965 over territory around the border, and in 1971–72 when India took East Pakistan's side over secession from West Pakistan (Marwah 1979), entrenched the hostility between the two countries as a mind-set in both fictional and non-fiction media texts (Mankekar 1999; Bharat and Kumar 2008).

Similarly, in Bangladesh, the violent struggle in the 1960s and early 1970s between the Bangla 'freedom fighters' and the West Pakistan army, which resulted in the creation of the state of Bangladesh in 1972 (Mookherjee 2006; Jahan 2004), were followed by armed resistance to the dominance of Bengali nationalism by, for instance, the people in the Chittagong hill tracts, who were neither Bengali speaking nor Muslim. Equally problematically, the stigmatization of women raped during the 1971 conflict and the disenfranchisement of hundreds of thousands of non-Bengali speaking residents from India and Pakistan meant that internal resentments and communal positionings were entrenched in the new Bangladesh. Although the nationalist narrative consolidated in Bangladesh around 1971 can be seen to have displaced the one of partition which still dominated in India and Pakistan, widespread corruption and political nepotism in the newly created Bangladesh, animosity towards India for its seeming interference in internal Bangladeshi affairs and growing poverty led to an extended period of political instability (Van Schendel 2009). Military coups, religious factionalism and dictatorial rule which included the intimidation, jailing and murder of journalists (Rahman 2004) and the closure of all but four of Bangladesh's state controlled newspapers in the immediate post-1971 era, have had a lasting effect on the development of the country's media (Rahman 2004, 8).

Detached geographically by its island status from the countries discussed so far, Sri Lanka's post-independence history followed a different but equally violent and discriminatory course. The two major parties in Sri Lanka – the United National Party (UNP) and Sri Lanka Freedom Party (SLFP) – have both used the issue of ethnic difference to bolster their electoral position. The first UNP government, which came to power after Independence in 1948, disenfranchised the poorer Upcountry Tamils, most of whom had been brought over by the British as indentured labourers (Jayawardena 2003). In 1956, the SLFP made 'Sinhala Only' its electoral platform. The passing of the Official Language Act was followed by large-scale anti-Tamil pogroms in 1958, which were brought under control only when the Governor-General declared a curfew and state of Emergency. The JVP uprising of largely unemployed Sinhalese youth in 1971 made it clear that these discriminatory measures did not solve the problems of the Sinhalese, yet in 1972 the Bandaranaike government enacted a new Constitution giving Buddhism a special place, entrenching Sinhala as the only official language, and removing protection for equal rights for minority communities (Wickramasinghe 2006). The consequence was the rise of Tamil militancy in the mid-1970s. This grew exponentially after J.R. Jayawardene of the UNP came to power in 1977, enacted a new Constitution and declared himself executive president. Increasingly serious anti-Tamil pogroms and use of the Prevention of Terrorism Act against hundreds of Tamil youth came to a head in the island-wide massacre of Tamils in 1983, which turned the conflict into a civil war. But Tamil militancy displayed the same totalitarian tendencies, with the LTTE wiping out rival militant groups as well as civilian critics, attacking Sinhalese civilians and carrying out massacres of Tamil-speaking Muslims in the East and ethnically cleansing the North of about 75,000 Muslims (Hoole 2001). Tamils under the jurisdiction of the LTTE suffered enormously too. A pass system kept them prisoners in LTTE-controlled territory, and children were forcibly conscripted. Recently, an enormously expanded Sri Lankan army has been responsible for the military and organisational demise of the LTTE, along with tens of thousands of Tamil civilians in a massacre of horrific brutality.[6] This has been accompanied by increasing state authoritarianism in the South, with journalists critical of the war or the regime being killed by government death squads (Hensman 2009).

The recent political history of Nepal is less overtly based around ethnic or religious conflict than that of its neighbours, but is similarly violent and unstable, and, underlying it, there certainly are similar practices of linguistic (pro-Nepali) and religious (pro-Hindu) discrimination. Ruled in a dictatorial fashion by an unelected Hindu King from the 1960s to 1990s (Whelpton 2005), opportunities to contest social and cultural identity within Nepal or for the national media to challenge any aspect of the political system publicly and consistently were limited. Even in the period since then, political murders, popular insurrection against the ruling elite and the widespread violence against local populations have kept much of the population in dire poverty and insecurity.

It is in this context of almost consecutive emergencies and wars for the past twenty-five years not in all five countries, but across the region, that the writers in this volume engage with the media landscape. But equally, no discussion of media, culture and politics in the region can afford to ignore the impact of social and cultural practices in relation to gender, ethnicity and religion. In the following section I set out in condensed form some of the key practices in relation to these intersecting identities that assume significance in the chapters to come.

Troubling Realities: Women, 'Minorities' and Human Rights

The erstwhile political manoeuvring around how to get the votes of each different religious, ethnic and caste group has often been a matter of debate, accusation and counter-accusation in the South Asian media. In fact, such scandals have often been more evident than the will of successive governments in the different countries to integrate each community under a common legal and political framework, to deliver not just basic needs such as water, shelter and food but also education, employment and civil rights. Additionally, while extensive poverty across swathes of both rural and urban India, Pakistan, Nepal and Bangladesh and more recently in Sri Lanka has ensured the effective curtailing of democracy for vast parts of the population, the overlapping of poverty and 'minority' status, and further discrimination against people from 'minority' languages and faiths or from supposedly lower castes and 'backward' ethnicities has further undermined claims to democratic governance in the South Asian region. Further, widespread religious or ethnic riots, amounting in many cases to pogroms against 'minority' communities, castes, linguistic or faith groups have been endemic across the region since the late 1940s but have tended to be misrepresented as outbursts of 'spontaneous' community hatred. In most cases, research and careful legal examination has identified various wings of the state in each country, from the police and the judiciary in some instances to cabinet ministers and the army in others, as perpetrators and/or instigators of the 'riots' or the ethnic cleansing (Basu et al 1991; Narula 2003; Van Schendel 2009). Despite this evidence, few of the instigators and perpetrators have ever been punished. In case after case a majority of the national press and broadcasters have either cooperated willingly in (mis)representing the situation as one of 'spontaneous and equal' rioting, or have been intimidated and co-opted into doing so.

In this situation, writing or speaking as if there is some equivalence between those *protected by* and those *targeted by* the state and politically motivated non-state actors has become one of the commonest functions of state sanctioned news outlets. Fiction formats, meanwhile, have tended to play upon notions of 'essential' difference between religious and linguistic groups or, occasionally, to argue that nationalism should transcend such partisan loyalties. This latter category of media text has tended to emphasise patriotism as a feature which is able to unite religious or ethnic groups against those in neighbouring South Asian countries.

While intersections of caste and class, language and religion, still dominate political realities, mediated communications and community psychology, gender norms and family relations play a major role in structuring the everyday lives of South Asians (Sen 1990; Kapadia 2002; Banaji 2006). In this sense, practices and experiences of gender discrimination and patriarchal family structures in South Asia (Chen et al 1981; Harriss and Watson 1987) though varying widely depending on class, location and community, could be said to be one of the most enduring and homogenous features of life in the subcontinent and even for many of its diaspora (Dasgupta 2005). Without wishing to play into some Western orientalist and essentialist misconceptions (Banaji 2009),[7] I think it is important for any collection examining South Asian diversity to note the range of discriminatory experiences that being female in South Asia might routinely entail. From cases where little girls as young as six years old are married off to middle aged men in locations across South Asia, through the still prevalent practices of female infanticide, bride-burning, dowry and the existence of religious law or religious personal codes that govern women's everyday lives, to the stoning, killing or violent public humiliation of women who are said to have transgressed public morality in some way, South Asian customs and practices offer plenty of examples of discrimination against women and girls (Jayawardena and de Alwis 1996; Sangari and Vaid 1996; Banerjee 2002) . Further, actual realities are often more complicated than the names of such practices might indicate in that gender-based strategies of control, violence and hierarchy cross over with issues related to caste, class or religion, leaving women and children in positions of multiple stigmatization and vulnerability (Zaman 1999; Niaz 2003; De Mel 2002).

Although it is certainly not the case that all women in South Asia suffer to the same degree, and while to a sizable minority of upper-class and upper-middle-class, highly educated, urban women, some of these issues might seem to reside in *another* South Asia, recent cases of women college students being attacked in Mangalore, India by right-wing Hindu chauvinist mobs[8] and the public whipping of a young woman in Swat, Pakistan[9] are reminders that only a fine invisible line, and the constant efforts of countless small feminist groups and women's organisations (Bhutalia 2002), separate those who live with such realities every day from those who do not. Additionally, as Tanika Sarkar and others remind us, in light of widespread support for anti-Muslim and anti-Christian violence by far-right Hindu women cadres (Sarkar 2001; Narula 2003), easy assumptions about women's non-participation in political violence need re-thinking.

While historiographers argue over the reliability of sources in some of the conflicts discussed, and about the extent to which inter-communal and/or cross border hostilities have been sustained as much for political and strategic purposes as in people's everyday lives, in the recent past, particularly from the 1990s onwards, a combination of geopolitical forces including the proliferation of nuclear weapons on either side of the India-Pakistan border aided by forces in the United States administration, the resurgence of a powerful Hindu nationalist middleclass in India and various militarist and Islamicist factions in Pakistan have brought South Asia to the brink of disaster (Raman 2004). Efforts to describe and understand commonalities between South Asian peoples are all the more urgent in this context. The previous section attempted to outline some of the most well known macro-political events and conflicts that have dominated modern histories of the region. In the next section, where I examine some of the issues arising out of the somewhat limited contemporary literature on cultural implications and contexts of South Asian Media,[10] these will be seen to have suffused the content and influenced the form of media output, control and change.

Nationalist Visions, Global Corporations, Alternative Voices

Regional variations in governance, infrastructure, discourse and social interaction, which were developed or suppressed strategically under colonial rule (Neild 1979), still persist in different guises in the post-colonial era. These continue to inflect people's identities, relationships and interactions with national, local and supra-national media formats and texts. The 'mediascape' (Appadurai 1990) in South Asia has in general been no exception to the pattern of patchy technologisation interlinked with vested interests that reproduce existing social structures and discourses across Asia and Africa. This has had multiple repercussions for media production. On the one hand, class and capital have continued in the hands of a small minority, who have tended also to control mass media technologies. Even under so-called democratically elected governments with commitments to media freedom, media outlets have been either controlled, co-opted or silenced by local landed elites, urban elites, warring factions or regional militias for ostensible reasons as diverse as propaganda and (supposedly) religious censorship. In some cases, entire national media systems may be treated as the private property of a ruling elite. For instance, writing a decade ago about key political events that unfolded in the media in Pakistan between 1970 and 1990, Rai Shakil Akhtar examines the manner and extent to which different regimes 'tried to manipulate, influence, pressurize, and control the process of political discourse' (2000, x) in Pakistan's media. He looks also at the ways in which Pakistan's recent political past, its 'cultural traditions', continued to shape and influence the structures of governance and political as well as social life, including the media. He seeks to explain why various forces, including the media and the intelligentsia, at one point or another, ally themselves with an anti-democratic ruling elite instead of with groups seeking 'change'. However, as India's situation testifies (Sonwalker 2001a and 2001b; Banerjee 2008), if these forces were less entrenched there is no guarantee that a highly democratic and egalitarian media situation would thrive. In fact, enduring even in this age of international digital and satellite media, a monolithic, culturally homogeneous, social development-orientated, patronising and partisan government-sponsored media system has been in evidence in each of these countries. The cultural ethos behind this system has, to a certain extent, shaped the output from and values of even notionally 'private' and/or independent print and broadcast media outlets (Senadhira 1996; Ohm 1999; Mankekar 1999; Akhtar 2000; Kharel 2001). Where individual journalists do not 'conform' to the demands of political actors, they are threatened, physically attacked and have their powers curtailed (Banerjee 2008; Khan 2011).

Since the collapse of the Soviet Union in the early 1990s, the confluence of 'modern' capitalist/neo-liberal economic policies with Party-political agendas and each different ruling elite's unique traditions have changed media output almost unrecognisably. The media systems, initially in Nepal and India, but now increasingly in Pakistan, Bangladesh and Sri Lanka too have 'opened up' to foreign channels and include a plethora of both fiction and non-fiction content from across South-Asia and around the world. Popular songs, images of war, fan websites, films, cartoons, documentaries and many more formats are routinely encountered in some parts of each of these countries, by those who have access to and/or can afford the technology (Brosius and Butcher 2001; Page and Crawley 2001; Waheed 2007; Mehta 2008).

Print, television and national film industries in some South Asian countries were harnessed in the post-independence period to the task of creating or binding viewers and citizens into shared national visions and projects which looked quite different in Nepal (Onta 2006; Wilmore 2008) and Bangladesh (Waheed 2007; Van Schendel 2009), for instance, and in India (Mitra 1996; Mankekar 1999) and Pakistan. Indigenous or local art forms from dance and music to theatre and poetry were and still are either suppressed, ignored or incorporated into 'popular' media formats depending on their orientation towards the national/ist project under particular regimes. This does not mean that they have been totally silenced, however, and many have continued to inform, entertain or cause controversy, albeit facilitated by different financial and technological conditions (Manuel 1993; Bharucha 2001).

Although North American and European conceptions of 'public service broadcasting' might be seriously misplaced in connection to government sponsored radio and television in India or Bangladesh or Pakistan (the 'public' itself being a hotly contested configuration), commercial media organisations and supposedly international sponsors do not straightforwardly equate to *neutral* and *free* media. Various sources testify that religious and cultural prejudices – the obsessive association of purity with women and modernity with men, the post facto, ahistorical justification of religious and ethnic violence (by majority communities) and a construction of 'nation' as associated with only particular ethnicities or religions – suffuse media products from government-controlled, international and independent media producers operating in post-liberalisation South Asia (Manuel 1993; Rajagopal 2001; Mankekar 1999; Akhtar 2000; Hoole 2001). And, as Michael Wilmore (2008) discusses eloquently in his book about Nepal's vibrant 'alternative' media scene, even so-called *alternative* producers and productions do not always map neatly onto categories such as 'progressive' or 'conservative', 'traditional' or 'modernising' or 'public-interest'. Cyber kiosks in rural India bringing 'ICT' to the rural masses may entrench the control of men and of rural landowning elites (Sreekumar 2007); watching the most sexist and ethnically monolithic representations of families in serials on television might provide women and children with a small measure of leisure time autonomy (Mankekar 1999).

Existing literature on South Asian media cultures such as work by Purnima Mankekar (op. cit.), Arvind Rajagopal (op. cit.) or Mark Whitaker (2006), suggest the important role that media plays in expressing national and proto-nationalist identities in the public sphere. Whittaker theorises the ways in which alternative and/or non-mainstream views (of history and politics) can gain space, initially, and then some form of legitimacy, even within contexts of extreme repression and/or fierce violent conflict between competing 'hegemonic' forces. He focuses in a quasi-ethnographic manner on the case of a now well-known Tamil nationalist website *TamilNet* and its rise to respectability on the world wide web. He contends that the internet's 'normative Habermasian presence [can act] as an alternative but proximate political landscape [and] provide a counter-context in which different possibilities can be displayed by people who would otherwise be constrained from speech, and who can now speak to audiences they would otherwise be unable to reach' (2006, 268). Highly problematically, he acknowledges, the website tended not to criticise the vicious excesses of the Tamil Tigers, but constructed a nationalist narrative that itself suppressed internal criticism, albeit in the language of supposedly neutral 'Western' media.

The framework of decentralisation of content and control offered by new satellite channels, the internet and new media, will be seen to be taken up by writers in this volume. It is precisely some of the complicated processes in relation to media meanings, technologies, representations and their significance in people's everyday lives which occur at the intersection of audiences, contexts, producers and texts that will get attention. But before turning to specific chapters, it is worth casting a brief glance over the methodologies that underpin the work in question.

Situating the Subject: Method and Identity in Cultural Studies

The academic writers' trade so often appears to construct a place for the writer that appears neutral, or at least approximates to a position of ideological neutrality in a landscape that is not easy to navigate in moral or political terms. Frequently academic texts are written as if 'anyone' could have been the writer. We, the writers, write as if anyone could have seen the same 'evidence'. We wish readers to assume that anyone could have drawn the same conclusions, as if all readers in whatever contexts, will share the same concerns and presuppositions. This neutral and mysterious position, however eloquently expressed, is a fiction. A point made elegantly by Robert Hodge and Gunter Kress (1988: 259) indicates that the process of beginning to make meaning, 'of entering into semiosis' as they put it, 'is for everyone a real and complex historical event, or rather a series of histories. These histories contribute different ideological traces to the set that comprises the adult ideological repertoire...'. In this view, all writers, however experienced and whatever their subject, are anchored within both individual repertoires and shared worldviews that have developed over years, and perhaps decades, in different cultural and social locations and different political contexts. These worldviews inflect academic meaning-making and writing as much as they do everyday conversation or mediated meanings. In this sense, the ways in which the writers in this volume collect and interpret their data, the methods they choose and believe in and the conclusions they draw are also subject to the inflections of their individual and shared social beliefs. It would be problematic to assume that the histories of South Asian politics, media production and conflict, the descriptions of mediated meaning-making and media use and the reflections on ways forward to media theory and activism are not linked to the places and spaces currently inhabited by each of the contributors. So, the histories will be partial, in both senses of the word. Despite this and because of the more overarching orientation towards a Cultural Studies model of media analysis, in its entirety, *South Asian Media Cultures* offers diverse insights into group-specific, national, local or regional case studies of media production and use.

Challenging the hegemony both of textual analysis and of large-scale quantitative survey research in relation to media in South Asia, the contributors in this volume utilise a diversity of primarily qualitative approaches to their subjects, from ethnography in the tradition of Shirley Brice-Heath and Brian Street (2008) to in-depth interviews with media users, audiences and producers, historical research and Narrative research (Shotter and Gergen 1989). Many of the contributors, writing from the interdisciplinary perspectives of Literature, Anthropology, Film and Media Studies, Sociology, Journalism, History and Social Psychology call upon a strong Cultural Studies tradition (for instance, Williams 1958/1981; Hall 1990; Storey 1996/2003; Buckingham 1993). As such, the longstanding tension between theories privileging 'textual' forces over the complexities of meaning, context and interpretation, and theories championing the 'activity' of readers or audiences is an ongoing concern. While this might be characterised crudely as a debate about 'structure' versus 'agency' (Tudor 1999, 16–17), and about textual effects – a debate that I feel has not been satisfactorily resolved anywhere in the social sciences to date – it is much more subtly explored here because of the importance given to history and context by all the contributors. Thus questions about the erstwhile effects of media texts are always about *particular* sets of representations and discourses circulating in *specific* communities, at *precise* historical moments, in *wider* political climates. The volume thus maintains a focus on media texts – and draws on textual analysis as a method – while remaining committed to an understanding of the historical and political contexts inflecting meaning, content, form and use.

From the General to the Particular: Case Studies in this Collection

Eschewing country-based or methodology-centric classifications, the chapters in this volume are organised around three themes that relate to the *uses and meanings, representations* and *political contexts of production* of media in Bangladesh, India, Nepal, Pakistan and Sri Lanka. The chapters in Section One (two to five) cohere broadly around audiences, meanings and social contexts, with a focus on the responses of complex but rarely surveyed social groups to specific media contexts, ideas, genres or texts; in Section Two (six to ten), claims about the connections between public perceptions of ethnic or gender identity and social action in the context of 'media discourse, identity and politics' will be interrogated; in Section Three (eleven to thirteen), the significance of media technologies both new and old for enabling alternative and bottom-up civic and political critiques to arise in situations of violent conflict or widespread political discrimination will be discussed. Here, an overview of chapters is offered based on connections between the overarching themes and concerns of the various writers.

Opening the collection, in chapter two, Daisy Hasan looks at the ways in which different marginalised tribal communities in the North-East of India are using media to 'talk back' to mainstream media or 'talk about' their local, tribal and regional identities. Hasan's chapter examines the impact of the Hindi commercial film industry on 'peripheral' cultures in India. As indicated in the exceedingly brief political history in previous sections, North-East India is home to diverse ethnic groups, which have historically never felt a part of mainstream India. The region is, in fact, caught up in several political conflicts with the Indian state. Today, however, Hindi commercial cinema is beginning to be accepted despite the fact that several political groups have banned the public from viewing Hindi films. The first part of Hasan's chapter discusses the ambivalent relationship of the region with Hindi cinema. The second part examines two locally produced films in the Khasi language of Meghalaya to show how local filmmakers are creatively appropriating a dominant genre to create their own nascent 'film industry'. Hasan concludes by exploring the political implications of this appropriation. She ends with a series of questions that will be addressed in several chapters: Does the dominance of Bollywood in the local imagination threaten indigenous peripheral cultures? Is this then a form of 'internal imperialism' or are people able to resist the 'ideology of the Hindi film'? And if so, how might this best be done? These are questions revisited from a different perspective by Rashmi Sawhney later in the collection.

My own research in chapter three pays attention to a small sample of an enormous, rarely surveyed and internally heterogeneous South Asian audience – children. The media environment surrounding middle-class children, even in small-town India, has altered almost unrecognizably in the last two decades. Millions of urban children can watch *Peppa Pig* or *Hanna Montana* dubbed in Hindi or in English or programmes in a number of vernacular languages; some have access to Japanese children's cartoons, Hollywood films, Hindi, Tamil, Malayalam, Bengali, Gujarati and Marathi films and serials, MTV-India and a host of other programmes from Disney to Nick Junior and local sponsors. However, discourses about children and mainstream media have remained fairly stagnant. These discourses tend to fall into one of two paradigms – a stridently protectionist one that sees most 'western' media products as dangerous and having negative effects on 'Indian' ethics and culture and hence on children; and one which views all developments as good because they somehow make India feel more 'modern' and economically competitive, thus giving advertisers or ideologues a larger market. While other positions do exist, these are rarely articulated publicly. Built around an interview-based study with several groups of Bombay children, three focus groups of children in Kerala, and a group of girls in the Himalayan foothills about their media viewing, this chapter explores the ways in which restricted television content in remote areas and the largely negative *effects debates* surrounding television viewing can and do work *against* the best interests of children and, in particular, against adolescent girls. The findings reveal children's critical negotiations of class, gender, ethnicity, regionalism and age in a fast-changing social context, and their attempts to remain loyal to their parents' perceived values while enjoying some leisure and learning outside the rigid context of school.

Taking cinema halls and their staff in Bangladesh and the histories and practices of viewing they testify to as her subject matter, in chapter four Lotte Hoek looks both at a stigmatised national cinema – the much maligned Bangladeshi commercial films – and at a stigmatised section of the Bangladeshi audience: young, working class, male viewers known as 'the Manna factor'. To her, in Bangladesh, the cinema hall is a powerful symbol of modernity, technology and urbanity. The Tosbir Mohol cinema hall in Jessore is a case in point. Its Urdu name, meaning 'image', harks back to the time when Bangladesh was part of Pakistan. The delicate wooden pillars holding the balcony date from the colonial era while the faded marble plaque inside the hall recounts its opening as a theatre in 1927 as Bisonath Sorkar Memorial Hall, in

Colonial India, patronised by the wealthy Hindu landowners who ruled Jessore. Hoek shows, firstly, how the place of the cinema hall in the cityscape, its architecture and the uses to which it is put, sheds new light on the history of film in Bangladesh. Secondly, she discusses how the fate of the theatres echoes national political transformations, as well as the interlocking of local and global political change. She contextualises this discussion by an initial sketching of the changes in the film industry in Bangladesh; the changing place of cinema in the public realm of the city; and the ways in which the national and global transformations have impacted the business of film exhibition in Bangladesh. Her chapter, therefore, shows how the industry's current concerns about satellite competition, a slide into 'obscenity' as well as a prevalence of action cinema can be better understood.

Focusing primarily on alternative circuits of media consumption and production but also on the negotiation of and relationship to Indian and international popular media, in chapter five, Paul Greene examines Nepali popular music in the post 1950s era, taking a detailed and thoughtful look at the transformation of indigenous musical forms, their distribution and audiences. Popular music throughout South Asia is often equated with or thought to revolve closely around the Indian film industry. Though the pull of Bollywood is substantial in Nepal, Greene argues, this characterisation does not adequately explain the variety of Nepal's popular musics, the course of their evolution, or the eclecticism and independence of thought and expression exercised by Nepalis. His chapter combines ethnographic data with a social and musical history of popular music in Nepal, 1950-2008, to paint a detailed portrait of music, meanings, and cultural scenes. During the 1950s, at state-sponsored Radio Nepal, *aadhunik gīt* ('modern song') and *lok gīt* ('folk song') emerged. These genres integrated elements from Western music – marked as 'modern' and 'developed' (*bikaasit*) in Nepali experience – together with distinctively Nepali melodies, instruments, and songtexts, to serve as vehicles of a modern Nepali subject position. Greene describes how the advent of affordable digital music recording and production technology in the 1990s accelerated the rise of Nepali pop: music created by and for urban young people primarily at universities, largely independent of both state-controlled and commercial media institutions. During the 2000s Nepal underwent a period of insurgency and conflict, during which the democratically-elected government was temporarily dissolved, and some songs emerged to voice resistance or call for change. Greene explores how a Nepali media culture has taken shape through a complex synergy between commercial mass media, Western influences, Bollywood, persistent Nepali aesthetics, and the eclecticism and creativity of Nepali musicians and listeners. To characterise this synergistic Nepali media culture, he invokes and develops the concept of *cosmopolitanism*, which may be glossed as a personal and cultural practice of thinking beyond the local, of living locally-situated lives in the friction of global encounters.

Looking at the media in Pakistan against the apparently paradoxical backdrop of dictatorship and liberalisation of producers and formats in chapter six, Tahir Naqvi examines a number of daytime talk shows and political news and views programmes aired in recent years via discussions with their producers. Domestic private satellite stations began to operate in Pakistan in the early part of the twenty-first century. Since 2001 thirty-five stations have commenced broadcasting from and to Pakistan (since most stations uplink their signal to Dubai). Pakistan is now awash in 24 hour news cycles, on-the-spot reporting, and an array of talk shows covering politics, health, religious affairs, celebrity lifestyles and so on. Naqvi argues that Pakistan's new channels are now at the forefront of mediating the shifting geo-political, democratic and cultural frontiers of the political. Alternating between overview and situated account, his chapter considers the medium's formative negotiation of what, in Pakistan, has come to be the increasingly militarized division of the body politic into moderate and extremist camps. The involvement of private satellite stations in producing and representing such distinctions, reveals, on the one hand, their obvious dependence on multinational advertising revenue. On the other hand, it reveals the secular liberal affinities of the Pakistani media's new elite, who conceive of themselves as working against real and possible threats of state censorship; in this light, they view the role of satellite television talk shows, for instance, as an emergent discursive vehicle for the elaboration of new and subjective visions of the national imaginary. In particular, the focus on a talk-show host's public negotiation of sexual and gender identity signals another central and contested domain in South Asia, and suggests the role media may play in shaping discourses in this arena. His chapter is thus illustrative of some of the continuing tensions and complexities in relation to the relationship between political elites and media elites in Pakistan today, and eschews easy critiques of apparently bourgeois and/or Islamic trends within programming.

Historically, a series of political discourses and media formats have been used to maintain widespread myths surrounding what Purnima Mankekar has dubbed the 'communalization of nationalism' (1999, 10). They have assisted in stigmatising both minority communities and those secular civil society actors working against the perpetuation of the myth of 'spontaneous' eruption of ethnic/religious intolerance and violence. On several occasions, these discourses and media formats are the subject of writers in this volume. In their respective chapters (seven and eight), Britta Ohm and Noorel Mecklai choose India as their locale, and focus on the ways in which both fiction films and television news have, in recent years, played with and into communal stereotypes of the Muslim as 'other', as 'terrorist' and as enemy to the Indian nation which, they suggest, is defined, in contrast, as cohesive, modern, democratic, and essentially *Hindu*.

Only a limited number of academic studies on Hindi cinema have dealt with 'communalism', what Mecklai calls 'the fundamental, founding discourse of the Indian nation'. To her, this silence extends as far as many discussions of films in virtual Bollywood fan communities, on which her chapter draws for audience attitudes. She argues further that as Hindi cinema became established in the early years of nationhood, the political value in cinema was perceived, and the project of nationalism emphasised, by the development of a film form that privileged Hindu identity through the use of mythic stories. Despite the obvious contradictions of Muslim stars playing Hindu heroes, or a greater part of the Hindi film talent – such as scriptwriters, musicians and production hands – being Muslims, Muslims were cast as 'outsiders', miscreants, or as violent gangsters, in short as anti-national, especially in the low budget 'B' grade films. But do the repercussions of the portrayal of Muslims affect public perceptions of the minority community and help to influence both sides towards a parochial politics? Mecklai's chapter draws attention to the politics of Muslim representation in Hindi cinema, arguing that the constant differentiation between the mythic (Hindu) hero and the 'other' as represented in Hindi cinema, might be one of various factors contributing to the continuing violence between Hindus and Muslims.

Remaining with the overt theme of anti-Muslim prejudice and its repercussions in India, Britta Ohm's work in chapter seven focuses on the intertwined relation between the increasing privatisation and commercialisation of news television in India and the representation of anti-minority violence in the context of the 2002 Gujarat pogrom. The state-sponsored anti-Muslim pogrom of Gujarat – governed since 2001 by the Hindu-nationalist Bharatiya Janata Party (BJP) under Chief Minister Narendra Modi – certainly represents the best-documented and most extensively reported communal violence in India. Implied in this is the paradox of a simultaneous democratisation and de-democratisation. It was, on the one hand, the first communal violence that has been classified by the UN as an attempted genocide and that was broadcast live within India both nationally and locally. On the other hand, it was also the instance of communal violence that provoked the least opposition in terms of resistance against the violence within the 'common-sense' public sphere. Rather, journalists, and especially television journalists, were confronted with massive opposition against any critical reporting and thus with a hitherto unprecedented sense of impotence and loss of authority. On the basis of ethnographic material gathered at the time amongst executives and journalists of leading national news channels, Ohm attempts to contextualise this complexity in terms of the transition of news television from an institution of public information into a medium that is seen by its viewers as having to be answerable to their private opinions, feelings, and religious sentiments, and the public discourse of 'blame displacement' led by India's Sangh parivar, the 'family' of Hindu-nationalist organisations. Pertinently, the chapter expands on the implications of the second re-election of Narendra Modi in the 2007 Assembly elections, the largely uncritical reporting of this victory, and the lack of impact that the *Tehelka* magazine's and website's exposure of leading Hindu nationalists as having been involved in the pogrom had on perceptions in the public sphere.

So, the contributors to this volume open up a seeming paradox: concurrent increases in apparent freedom of expression in the mainstream media around issues of discrimination are accompanied by a further entrenching of discriminatory and quasi-fascist ideologies in the public sphere. While some of the misogynist incidents and discriminatory practices discussed in the previous section find their way onto *YouTube*, onto satellite television channels, and into national or international newspapers, other gender-related aspects of media cultures may take more subtle and complex forms. Neluka Silva in chapter nine looks historically and socioculturally at different aspects of the continuing political violence in Sri Lanka and its reflection in or challenge by contemporary teledramas and their producers.

Since the introduction of the television serial *Dimuthu Muthu* in the early 1980s in Sri Lanka, the 'teledrama' as it is popularly known today, is one of the most popular cultural genres and is regarded as the principal form of family entertainment. Silva's chapter explores how popular culture in Sri Lanka has responded to political and popular discourses on conflict and peace. Through close readings of selected episodes from Sri Lankan teledramas *A9* and *Take This Road*, which have overtly pivoted around the ethnic conflict and the brief ceasefire agreement in Sri Lanka, she argues that a certain type of discourse governs political and public perceptions of the 'other' community in Sri Lanka. The teledramas become cases of the different kinds of quasi-communal but also gender-specific messages about peace and belonging, language and citizenship that have been circulated and have gained primacy in Sri Lanka. On the one hand, audience perceptions, interviews with prominent actors and directors on the imaging of war and peace in popular television are foregrounded, to suggest that the breakdown of the peace process and the return to full-scale armed conflict at the time of her research may be attributed partially to the unsustainable notions of peace that have become dominant across the media and civil society. On the other hand, the commercial and ideological constraints under which those wishing to construct popular but alternative representations of ethnic identity operate militate against sustained and sophisticated representations of gender or ethnicity in fiction formats on mainstream channels.

In chapter ten, Irna Qureshi takes the multiple stigmatization of Kanjar women who become actresses in Pakistani popular cinema as her topic. She explores the ways in which their *de-stigmatization* still turns on the oppression of women and the maintenance of myths about ethnic, caste and gender purity and honour. Hira Mandi is the vice district in Lahore. Many film actresses have had roots in Hira Mandi's 'lower class' Kanjar society, a morally outcast community of professional dancing girls and prostitutes. Wealthy Lahori men sometimes keep Kanjari mistresses, and dancing girls are often hired for weddings and private parties. As a number of 'Lollywood' directors have traditionally turned to Hira Mandi for new heroines, Kanjar women have regarded the film industry as an escape route from Hira Mandi as it has enabled them to gain respect through wealth and popularity. 'Kanjar' is a degrading ethnonym and a common term of abuse among Pakistanis, encompassing both a gender-specific derogatory reference and an ethnic appellation, thus similar to but not properly described by the English 'whore'. This taboo compels girls and young women from 'chaste' backgrounds to distance themselves from the film industry. It also encourages non-Kanjars to shun social links with Kanjars. After mapping the social context, this chapter describes how such taboos inflect both viewing practices and star personae.

Attempts by media producers and by citizen activists to use media to address some of these issues of inequality and discrimination – in an effort to build peace in conflict situations or to deliver human rights to those who have had theirs violated for generations – are also reflected in other chapters offered in this volume. Rashmi Sawhney, in chapter 11, takes up similar issues to those addressed by Qureshi about the role of mediated self-representation in changing national – and perhaps international – perceptions. Sawhney focuses on a marginal and stigmatised Indian community, the Chharas. She examines the ways in which their use of a non-popular genre for self-expression (in the context of the widely watched Hindi commercial cinema) might lead to further marginalisation of their artistic and political work. Images of Adivasis (Indian tribal communities) being displaced by the building of industries and dams have been regularly flashing across our television screens for the last twenty years, yet, media scholars have shown very little interest in this constituency either as producers or as audiences. Sawhney argues that, contrary to the mass media's favourite stereotype of the forest-inhabiting 'native', India's tribal communities exist in a complex constellation of modernities, both urban and rural, and that many of these communities have at least a nominal contact with media cultures. One such group, the Chharas of Ahmedabad, popularly branded as a criminal tribe, has made extensive use of street theatre and film in its activism for social and political rights. Based on the case of the Chharas and on the work and biography of director Dakxin Bajrange in particular, Sawhney's chapter explores issues around the politics of film production in India – how the means to production, subjectivity and speaking position, and agendas of advocacy influence the form and content of independent cinema. Further, this thread of her inquiry is framed against the backdrop of Hindi and Tamil commercial cinema's dominance of the Indian 'social imaginary', raising questions about the extent to which independent cinema can effect change, and the particular challenges this resistance on the part of audiences to viewing documentary films poses to historically disenfranchised groups in finding a cinematic language for self-representation.

Saman Talib, in chapter 12, looks at the conscious and motivated use of new digital media and communications such as mobile phone cameras, blogs and websites to create and maintain a cohesive and non-partisan movement against dictatorship and for democratic rights in Pakistan. Her chapter takes the form of a historical case-study following the events of 4 November 2007 when hundreds of students marched in political protest at a small, elite university, LUMS in Lahore, at the arrest of faculty members in the aftermath of the emergency declared by the then dictator, President Pervez Musharraf. Initially, she recounts, the movement seemed to be composed of a number of independent and unrelated individuals. However, over time, the formation of SACs, student action committees, the challenges faced by the students – the authoritarian response of the government to any public dissent; lack of mass media to approach; the mass-media blackout imposed by the regime; a need for anonymity; and the need to organise rapidly – and the availability of new media led to the widespread use of blogs, mobile phones and You Tube videos in the anti-emergency movement. The theoretical framework for Talib's study draws on concepts about youth political activism, particularly in urban areas, and the impacts of new media on civic engagement amongst youth, which is also currently a major issue of debate in North America, Europe and the Middle East (cf. Dahlgren 2007; Banaji 2008; Banaji and Buckingham 2010; Hands 2011). Her chapter adds both to understandings of the role of new media technologies in regional South Asian civic movements and to the international literature on youth civic engagement, which is currently somewhat lacking outside North American, European and Australian academia.

In the same national political context as Silva, and a similar media context to Talib, and again showing how deeply continuing violent conflict affects all aspects of civil society in a country, in chapter 13 Sanjana Hattotuwa meticulously unpicks the story of the growth of a Sri Lankan citizen-journalist website aimed at peace-building. The chapter paints a complex picture. The media in Sri Lanka appears diverse and multilingual with distribution and consumption of traditional media (e.g. TV, radio, print) spread over the island. Further examination reveals serious and growing challenges to impartial, accurate and responsible journalism. Journalists themselves rarely adhere to professional standards and ethics, or are often violently coerced into acting as supine, submissive agents of government propaganda. There is not a single newspaper in Sri Lanka that is in both Sinhala and Tamil. Most journalists themselves are monolingual. Lack of access to the embattled North and East and the stereotypes of the other result in biased, unprofessional reporting that fuels violent conflict. The overarching problems of a state riven by violent conflict, corruption, nepotism and the significant breakdown of democratic governance and human rights, especially in recent years, deeply inform the timbre of traditional media. It is a vicious symbiosis – media is both shaped by and shapes a violent public imagination. Hattotuwa's chapter, however, looks for points of change and hope. The potential of Web 2.0 and new media in general and citizen journalism, mobile phones and USG in particular (e.g. YouTube videos, blogs, SMS and mobile sites) suggests that content that critiques the *status quo*, authored by civil society, can play a constructive and increasingly significant role in peace-building and stronger democratic governance in Sri Lanka. Through a series of path-breaking examples encompassing text, video and audio content in English and the vernacular, produced for, disseminated through and archived on the web for PCs and mobile devices, Hattotuwa interrogates the potentials and pitfalls of web and Internet activism in a violent country. He argues that the greatest challenge lies not in the technology itself, but in the creation of a social and political movement – one fostered by citizen journalism and mediated through new media and new technology – that is able to maintain, in some small way, the hope of a just and lasting peace for all Sri Lankan citizens.

Finally, pulling out key strands from the contributions in this collection, the conclusion asks what lessons can be learnt by media educators, regulators and historians as well as students of Cultural Studies, Citizenship Education and Anthropology via such a situated focus on the contexts of media production and use in South Asia. In particular, can specific conclusions be drawn with regard to the role played by media products and processes in shaping, strengthening or undermining the contexts of discrimination and ethnic tension described? The conclusion reflects on these issues, and on the gaps and absences even in a collection spanning five countries and half a dozen media. It focuses on areas that need further research – such as the theorising of structure and agency debates with regard to media in South Asia, children's media cultures and cross-border media use – and on those that are particularly amenable to interdisciplinary approaches.

Notes

1 I owe thanks to Diane Carr and Rohini Hensman for close readings and helpful comments on this introduction.
2 The South Asian region also includes Bhutan and the Maldives, which will not be covered in this volume.
3 Throughout this volume the city will be named as Bombay rather than the now almost ubiquitous 'Mumbai'. This is a clear political choice in resistance to the

erasure of the history of secularism and solidarity in the city via the renaming of places by a succession of far-Right Marathi chauvinist regimes and its unquestioning adoption first by commercial organisations internationally and now even by many residents and academics. Contrary to what might be thought, Mumbai was not the 'original' name of the city.

4 See, for instance, 'Muslims not for Burning' at http://unheardvoice.net/blog/2009/04/16/muslim-bodies/ (accessed 2 May 2009).
5 The Congress Party and the Bharatiya Janata Party (BJP) being the current majority parties, but there are numerous others.
6 http://www.timesonline.co.uk/tol/news/world/asia/article6383449.ece (accessed 28 July 2011).
7 Unfortunately, not even feminists are immune to fantasies about the essential identities of women in non-Western nations, as debates over veiling, female genital mutilation and other atrocities suggest (cf. Banaji 2009).
8 http://www.nowpublic.com/world/stop-attacks-women-mangalore (accessed 2 May 2009).
9 http://www.timesonline.co.uk/tol/news/world/asia/article6022878.ece (accessed 2 May 2009).
10 Excluding only the growing and increasingly sophisticated literature on Indian cinemas.

References

Akhtar, R. S. (2000) *Media, Religion and Politics in Pakistan* Oxford, New York, New Delhi: Oxford University Press

Alam, M. (2009) 'The Mughals, the Sufi Shaikhs and the Formation of the Akbari Dispensation' in *Modern Asian Studies* (43) 1:135–174

Appadurai, A. (1990) 'Disjuncture and Difference in the Global Cultural Economy', *Public Culture* (2) 2: 1–24

Banaji, S. (2006) *Reading 'Bollywood': The Young Audience and Hindi Films*, Basingstoke: Palgrave Macmillan

────── (2008) 'The Trouble with Civic: A Snapshot of Young People's Civic and Political Engagements in Twenty-first Century Democracies' in *Journal of Youth Studies*, Volume 11, No. 5, October 2008: 543–60

────── (2009) '"Who are the Girls?": Reflections on ethnicity, culture, and the idea of "girlhood"' in *Feminist Media Studies*, (9) 1: 109–125

Banaji, S. and Buckingham, D. (2010) 'Young People, the Internet, and Civic Participation: An overview of key Findings from the Civicweb Project' in *International Journal of Learning and Media*, (2) 1: 10–19.

Banerjee, N. (2002) 'Between the Deveil and the Deep Blue Sea: Shrinking Options for Women in Contemporary India', in Kapadia, K. (ed.) *The Violence of Development: the Politics of Identity, Gender and Social Inequalities in India*, New York: Palgrave Macmillan, pp. 43–68

Basu, T., Datta, P., Sarkar, S., Sarka, T. and Sen, S. (1993) *Khaki Shorts Saffron Flags*, New Delhi: Orient Longman

Bharat, M. and Kumar, N. (2008) *Filming the Line of Control: The Indo-pak Relationship Through the Cinematic Lens*, New Delhi: Routledge

Bharucha, R. (2001) *The Politics of Cultural Practice: Thinking Through Theatre in an Age of Globalisation*, Oxford, New York, New Delhi: Oxford University Press

Bhutalia, U. (2002) 'Confrontation and Negotiation: The Women's Movement Responses to Violence Against Women', in Kapadia, K (ed.) (2002) *The violence of development: the politics of identity, gender and social inequalities in India*, New York: Palgrave Macmillan, 207–234

Brass, P. R. (2003) 'The partition of India and retributive genocide in the Punjab, 1946–47: means, methods, and purposes' in *Journal of Genocide Research (*2003), 5(1), 71–101

Brosius, C. and Butcher, M. (eds) (1999) *Image Journeys: audio-visual media and cultural change in India*, New Delhi, Thousands Oaks, London: SAGE

Brown, K. B. (2007) 'Did Aurangzeb Ban Music? Questions for the Historiography of his Reign' *Modern Asian Studies* 41, 1: 77–120

Chen, L. et al. (1981) 'Sex Bias in the Family Allocation of Food and Health Care in Rural Bangladesh' in *Population and Development Review*, Volume 7, Issue 1: 55–70

Dahlgren, P. (ed.) (2007) *Young Citizens and New Media: Learning for Democratic Participation*, London and New York: Routledge

Dasgupta, S. D. (2005) 'Women's Realities: Defining Violence Against Women by Immigration, Race and Class' in Sokolof, N. J. (ed.) Domestic Violence at the Margins: Readings on Race, Class and Culture, New Jersey: Rutgers University Press: 56–70

Das, V. (1990) *Mirrors of Violence: Communities, Riots and Survivors in South Asia* (ed.), Oxford: Oxford University Press

_____(2006) *Life and Words: Violence and the Descent into the Ordinary*, University of California Press

De Mel, N. (2002) 'Fractured Narratives: Notes on Women in Conflict in Sri Lanka and Pakistan', in *Development*, March 2002, Volume 45, Number 1, 99–104

Dos Santos, A. N. (2007) *Military Intervention and Secession in South Asia: The Cases of Bangladesh, Sri Lanka, Kashmir, and Punjab*, Praeger Security International, New York: Greenwood Publishing Group

Gajjala, R. (2006) 'Cyberethnography: Reading South Asian digital diasporas' in Landzelius, K. (ed.) (2006) *Native on the Net: Indigenous and Diasporic Peoples in the Virtual Age*, Oxford and New York: Routledge, 272–291

Guha, S. (2009) 'The Frontiers of Memory: What the Marathas Remembered of Vijayanagara' in *Modern Asian Studies* 43, 1: 269–288

Gunaratne, S. A. (1999) 'The Media in Asia: an Overview' in *Gazette*, Volume 61(3–4): 197–223

Habib, I. (1963) The Agrarian System of Mughal India 1556–1707, Bombay: Asia Publishing House

Hall, S. (1990) 'The Emergence of Cultural Studies and the Crisis of the Humanities' in *October*, No.53. Summer: 11–24

Hands, J. (2011) *@ is for Activism: Dissent, Resistance and Rebellion in a Digital Culture*. London: Pluto Press.

Harriss, B. and Watson, E. (1987) 'The Sex Ratio in South Asia' in J.H. Momsen and J.G. Townsend, (eds), *Geography of Gender in the Third World* New York: State University of New York Press

Heath, S. and Street, B. (2008) *Ethnography: Approaches to Language and Literacy*, New York: Teachers College Press

Hensman, R. (2009) 'Self-determination, Sovereignty and Democracy: The Reality Behind the Rhetoric in Sri Lanka,' in Benjamin, J. (ed), *Democratic Process, Foreign Policy and Human Rights in South Asia*, New Delhi: Indian Social Institute

Hodge, R. and Kress, G. (1988) Social Semiotics, Cambridge and Oxford: Polity Press

Hoole, R. (2001) *Sri Lanka: The Arrogance of Power – Myths, Decadence and Murder*, Colombo: UTHR-J

Jahan, R. (2004) 'Genocide in Bangladesh' in Totten, S. Parsons, W and Charny, I. (eds) *Century of Genocide: Critical Essays and Eyewitness Accounts*, London and New York: Routledge

Jayaprakash, Y. T. and Shoesmith, B. (2007) Community Radio and Development: Tribal Audiences in South India, in Community Media: International Perspectives, ed. Linda Fuller, New York: Palgrave Macmillan, 43–54

Jayawardena, K. and De Alwis, M. (2006) *Embodied Violence: Communalising Women's Sexuality in South Asia*, New Delhi: Kali For Women

Jayawardena, K. (2003) *Ethnic and Class Conflict in Sri Lanka*, Sanjiva Books, Colombo

Kapadia, K. (2002) *The Violence of Development: The Politics of Identity, Gender and Social Inequalities in India*, New York: Palgrave Macmillan

Khan, I. M. (2011) Pakistani Journalist Saleem Shezaad Found Dead. BBC News online, Islamabad. Online at http://www.bbc.co.uk/news/world-south-asia-13599172 (accessed 28 July 2011).

Kharel, P. (ed.) (2001) *Media Practices in Nepal*, Khatmandu: National Press Institute

Mankekar, P. (1999) *Screening Culture, Viewing Politics: An Ethnography of Television, Womanhood, and Nation in Postcolonial India*, Durham, North Carolina and London: Duke University Press

Manuel, P. (1993) *Cassette Culture: Popular Music and Technology in North India*, New Delhi, London, New York: Oxford University Press

Marwah, O. (1979) 'India's Military Intervention in East Pakistan 1971–1972' in *Modern Asian Studies*, Volume 13, Issue 4: 549–580

Mehta, N. (2008) *India on Television: How Satellite News Channels have Changed the Way We Think and Act*, New Delhi: Harper Collins

Menon, R. and Bhasin, K. (1996) 'Abducted Women, the state and questions of Honour: Three Perspectives on the Recovery Operation in Post-Partition India' in Jayawardena, K. and De Alwis, M. (eds) *Embodied Violence: Communalising Women's Sexuality in South Asia*, London: Zed Books, 1–31

Mookherjee, N. (2006) '"Remembering to Forget": Public Secrecy and Memory of Sexual Violence in Bangladesh' in *Journal of the Royal Anthropological Institute*, Volume 12, Issue 2: 433–450

Narula, S. (2003) 'Overlooked Danger – Hindu Nationalism in India', in *Harvard Human Rights Journal*, Volume 16, Spring 2003

Neild, S. M. (1979) 'Colonial Urbanism: The Development of Madras City in the Eighteenth and Nineteenth Centuries' in *Modern Asian Studies*, Volume 13, Issue 2: 217–246

Niaz, U. (2003) 'Violence Against Women in South Asian Countries' in *Archives of Women's Mental Health* 2003, 6:173–184

Ohm, B. (1999) 'Doordarshan: Representing the Nation's State' in Brosius, C. and Butcher, M. (eds) (1999) *Image Journeys: audio-visual media and cultural change in India*, New Delhi, Thousands Oaks, London: Sage, Pages 69–98

Onta, P. (2006) *Mass Media in Post-1990 Nepal*, Kathmandu: Chautari Books

Page, D. and Crawley, W. (2001) *Satellites over South Asia: Broadcasting, Culture and the Public Interest*, New Delhi, Thousand Oaks, London: Sage Publications

Pandey, G. (2001) *Remembering Partition: Violence, Nationalism, and History in India*, Cambridge: Cambridge University Press

Rajagopal, A. (2001) *Politics after Television. Hindu Nationalism and the Reshaping of the Public in India*, Cambridge: Cambridge University Press

Raman, J. S. (2004) *Flashpoint: how the U.S., India and Pakistan brought us to the brink of nuclear war*, Common Courage Press, 2004

Rahman, M. (2004) *The State of Media in Bangladesh*, Dhaka: NewsNetwork

Saikia, Y. (2005) *Assam and India: fragmented memories, cultural identity, and the Tai-Ahom struggle*, New Delhi: Permanent Black

Sangari, K. and Vaid. S. (1996) 'Institutions, Beliefs, Ideologies: Widow Immolation in Contemporary Rajasthan' in Jayawardena, K. and De Alwis, M. (eds) *Embodied Violence: Communalising Women's Sexuality in South Asia*, London: Zed Books, 240–296

Sarkar, T. (2001) *Hindu Wife, Hindu Nation : Community, Religion and Cultural Nationalism* New Delhi: Permanent Black

Schofield, V. (2003) *Kashmir in Conflict: India, Pakistan and the Unending War*, London: I.B. Tauris & Co.

Sen, A. (1990) 'More than 100 Million Women are Missing' The New York review of Books, Volume 37, No. 20, December 1990

Senadhira, S. (1996) *Under Siege: Mass Media in Sri Lanka*, New Delhi: Segment Books

Shotter, J. and Gergen, K. (eds) (1989) *Texts of Identity*, London, Newbury Park and New Delhi: Sage

Sonwalker, P. (2001a) 'Opposition to the Entry of the Foreign Press in India 1991–1995: The Hidden Agenda' *Modern Asian Studies*, Volume 35, Issue 03: 743–763

——— (2001b) 'India: Makings of Little Cultural/Media Imperialism?' in *International Communication Gazette*, 2001, Volume 63, Issue 6: 505–519

Sreekumar, T. T. (2007) 'Cyber kiosks and dilemmas of social inclusion in rural India' in *Media Culture and Society*, Volume 29, Issue 6: 869–889

Storey, J. (1996/2003) *Cultural Studies and the Study of Popular Culture*, Edinburgh UK: Edinburgh University Press

Talbot, C. (2009) 'Becoming Turk the Rajput Way: Conversion and Identity in an Indian Warrior Narrative' in *Modern Asian Studies* Volume 43, Issue 1: 211–243

Talbot, I. (2007) 'A Tale of Two Cities: The Aftermath of Partition for Lahore and Amritsar 1947–1957' in *Modern Asian Studies* , Volume 41, Issue 01: 151–185

Thapar, R. (2002) *Early India: From the Origins to AD 1300*, London: Allen Lane

——— (2005) *Somnatha: The Many Voices of a History*, London: Verso

Thusu, D. K. (2007) 'The "Murdochization" of news? The case of Star TV in India' in *Media, Culture and Society*, Volume 29, No. 4: 593–611

Tudor, A. (1999) *Decoding Culture: Subject and Method in Cultural Studies*, London, New York and New Delhi: SAGE

Van Schendel, W. (2009) *A History of Bangladesh*, Cambridge and New York: Cambridge University Press

Waheed, Z. H. (2007) 'Emergence of Satellite Television and Enigmatic Geo-Political Strategy of Bangladesh government' in *Bangladesh e-Journal of Sociology*. Volume 4, Issue 1. January 2007

Whelpton, J. (2005) *A History of Nepal*, Cambridge: Cambridge University Press

Whitaker, M. (2006) 'Internet *counter* counter-insurgency: *TamilNet.com* and ethnic conflict in Sri Lanka' in Landzelius, K. (ed.) *Native on the Net: Indigenous and Diasporic Peoples in the Virtual Age*, Oxford and New York: Routledge, 255–271

Wickramasinghe, N. (2006) *Sri Lanka in the Modern Age: A History of Contested Identities*, Honolulu: University of Hawai'i Press

Williams, R. (1958/1981) *Culture and Society*, New York: Columbia University Press

Wilmore, M. (2008) *Developing Alternative Media Traditions in Nepal*, Lanham USA and Plymouth, UK: Lexington Books

Zaman, H. (1999) 'Violence against women in Bangladesh: Issues and responses', *Women's Studies International Forum*, January 1999, Volume 22, Issue 1: 37–48

Part One

ELABORATING AUDIENCES: MEANING, USE AND SOCIAL CONTEXT

Chapter Two

TALKING BACK TO 'BOLLYWOOD': HINDI COMMERCIAL CINEMA IN NORTH-EAST INDIA

Daisy Hasan

Hindi Commercial Cinema and Popular Culture in North-East India

This chapter looks at the impact of the Hindi commercial film industry on 'peripheral' cultures in India. The Indian film industry – which comprises both 'Bollywood' (as the Hindi commercial film industry is becoming known) and regional film industries particularly in south India – is one of the largest film industries in the world. The industry puts out over a thousand films every year and a staggering audience of fourteen million people watch an Indian film every day (Bose 2006). Bollywood exerts considerable cultural influence in India as it often both mirrors and mocks Indian society. The reception of Bollywood (and of mainstream Indian popular culture which is dominated by the former) among peripheral and under represented cultures in North-East India, is the subject of this chapter. The chapter looks at the love-hate relationship towards Hindi popular and film culture that people in this region have. North-East India is home to diverse ethnic groups, who have historically never felt a part of mainstream India. The region is caught up in several political conflicts with the Indian state.[1] Most of these movements claim political autonomy, arguing that the distinct identities of people in the region entitle them to self-government and cultural freedom. Today, as satellite channels have proliferated in the region, Hindi commercial cinema is becoming extremely popular despite the fact that several political groups have banned such films. The first part of this chapter looks at the historical relationship between the Indian state and indigenous peoples of North-East India. Part two, which is based on in-depth interviews with film and video producers and their audiences,[2] examines locally produced films and other entertainment in Meghalaya and Manipur (states in

North-East India) to show how indigenous filmmakers creatively appropriate a dominant genre to create their own nascent 'film industry'. Audiences' views about the influence of Indian popular culture on local identity are discussed. The chapter ends by exploring the political implications of the appropriation of Bollywood. Does the dominance of Bollywood in the local imagination threaten peripheral indigenous cultures? Is this then a form of 'internal imperialism' or are people able to use mainland cinema and culture to further local identity 'projects'.

As elsewhere in the country, Hindi commercial cinema has an ubiquitous presence in North-East India and particularly in Shillong, the cosmopolitan capital city of Meghalaya. There are well-entrenched film theatres here and film music can be heard playing from numerous shops, restaurants and taxis. Video libraries that loan Hindi films have multiplied in recent years. Satellite channels showing mainstream Indian entertainment and Hindi films have also grown phenomenally since the early 1990s. FM radio channels – the latest addition to contemporary media – also devote a lot of space to Hindi film songs. The easy availability of India's popular cinema does not, however, mean that people in this region have a comfortable relationship with it. Existing literature on this subject is sparse. Sonwalkar's (2001) study of the 'little cultural imperialisms' exercised by dominant national cultures in the global south is illuminating. Appraisals of local cinema, in particular Hasan and Bhartiya (2001), and of cultural policing in the region in general Bhartiya (2007) have also illuminated the issue to some extent although it still remains an under researched area. To understand the region's unease with Hindi cinema and popular culture it is important to look at the historical cultural relationship that has existed between mainstream India and its North-Eastern periphery.

The Cultural Assimilation of Indigenous Peoples in Post-Colonial India

Spotting the North-Eastern region of the country on the map of India is not the easiest of tasks. In most maps it is depicted as an amorphous mass of territory, tenuously connected to mainland India by what is often called a 'chicken neck corridor' of land which, at its widest, is no more than forty kilometres. This fragile link with the rest of India has played a significant role in determining the region's history. The perceived difference between people in the hills and those in the plains has had important political and cultural implications for the way in which 'hill' or indigenous peoples relate to the rest of India. While the plains of Assam are regarded by some historians and by most national politicians as part of a mainstream 'Indic' and Sanskritic cultural tradition, the hills are seen as having been more susceptible to cultural influences from Southeast Asia. One of the main factors which distinguishes the hill people from those in the plains is the fact that they follow the Christian faith spread by Christian missions which were patronised by the British administration and allowed to work in the hills in the nineteenth century.³

India's first Prime Minister, Jawaharlal Nehru, is often described as having had a 'vision' for North-East India. He was opposed to the economic or social coercion of indigenous people into the national mainstream and wanted to ensure their cultural freedom. National perspectives on the region were, at the time of India's independence in 1947, greatly indebted to the influential writings of the anthropologist and folklorist Verrier Elwin. As an advisor to the government on the administration of tribal areas, Elwin advocated a policy of 'integration not imposition' for indigenous societies (Rustomji 1998: 56).⁴ His championing of self-governance in these areas influenced Indian policy on the matter.⁵ While Nehru and Elwin recognised the cultural autonomy of the region, it was politically imperative at the time to build a national cultural identity at the cost of regional affiliations. Even as the Indian state made political concessions to regional groups it adopted a deeply centralised cultural policy aimed at forging a pan-Indian national identity. Culture was thought to be an important marker of national identity. 'Indian culture' and 'tradition' had been powerfully invoked in nationalist struggles against imperial domination and orientalist perspectives on Indian society (Ganesh and Thakkar 2005, 21). Once independence was attained, the state made a self conscious effort to build on this (reinvented) cultural identity that subsumed regional differences. Hence the slogan – 'Unity in Diversity'. Policies were usually aimed at advancing the state's understanding of a composite Indian culture rather than reflecting local cultural understandings. While the rhetoric of an Indian national identity was 'deeply meaningful to educated classes' in North India, it did not carry the same weight in other regions which had strong indigenous cultures (Rajagopal 2001, 22). National policies tended to isolate and make a fetish of regional cultures. The indigenous cultures of North-East India were patronised and presented as a glowing example of India's ethnic plurality. While the intention behind India's national cultural policies was to bring local cultures into national prominence, promoting them through museums, archives, and later through the centralised mass media, which perpetuated a culture of 'gazing' at indigenous peoples, led to cultural stereotypes.

Cultural policy in post-independent India tended to classify the cultures of the North-East as 'folk' – a term which suggested that they had little contemporary relevance and their chief value lay in symbolising a past 'tribal' heritage that now had to be preserved. Cultural critics have pointed out that, in theoretical discussions about culture, 'folk' was placed at the lower end of the scale, the top of which was occupied by classical or high (usually Indic) culture.

Such categorisation fed national perceptions of indigenous cultures as backward and obscured the interconnections between 'folk', 'popular' and 'classical' traditions that actually existed in India (Ganesh and Thakkar 2005, 22). The indigenous elite also played an important role in projecting a 'tribal' identity to the rest of the nation. Since the Indian state had granted political privileges to various groups in the region on the basis of their ethnicity, ethnic identity came to be seen as something that could be used strategically to bargain with the Indian state for political and cultural concessions. The 'Nehru/Elwin policies', though unsuccessfully implemented, had created considerable legitimacy for the cultural expression of ethnic identities (Taylor 2002, 19). Indigenous elites, therefore, played up national stereotypes of themselves as backward or even 'primitive.' Thus both central administrators and peripheral elites colluded in discussing and representing societies of North-East India in these terms. But even as folk culture was thought to be underdeveloped, it was appropriated by the market and refashioned as 'ethnic chic' meant to appeal to a niche (and elite) group. By being alternately denigrated and romanticized, the indigenous cultures of North-East India lost much of their dynamism and political potential. National broadcasting and films greatly added to this loss.

Representations of 'Tribals' and 'Terrorism' in Hindi Films

Hindi commercial cinema, especially in the 1950s and 1960s, which often colluded with the post-colonial Indian state's agenda for development and modernization, adopted the perspectives of the centre on tribal cultures treating them as '...Other – "backward", "violent", "underdeveloped", "tribal" in the worst sense' (Taylor 2002, 2). At the same time tribal cultures were also viewed in several films as '... close to nature, isolated from the enervations of modernity...carrying in local artistic traditions a non-reflective but powerful creativity that expresses some essential, primitive, timeless humanity' (op. cit., 2). Films that depicted indigenous peoples made little effort to contextualise these cultures allowing the same 'mumbo-jumbo' chanting characters, wearing a parody of indigenous costumes to stand for diverse ethnicities. For instance, the 1972 film *Yeh Gulistan Hamara* depicts, but does not identify, a tribal community living on the Indo-China border. A song in the film (Mera Naam Aao) was considered particularly offensive to the Ao community in Nagaland and subsequently withdrawn from the film. While Bollywood 'borrow[s] indiscriminately from the classical and the folk...' (Nandy 1998) and 'adivasi' cultures of other parts of India have been shown in several films, North-East India has hardly ever found a place in mainstream Hindi cinema. The political turmoil in several states of North-East India has only recently begun, sparingly, to lend itself to film plots especially since there have been a spate of terrorist films in the 1990s depicting '...separatist insurgencies...bomb blasts, religious riots, high level kidnappings, and hijackings' (Ganti 2004, 41). These include *Dil Se* (1998) and *Tango Charlie* (2005). However, the focus of these films has remained on the prowess and patriotism of the North Indian male protagonist (Shah Rukh Khan plays Amarkanth – an All India Radio executive in *Dil Se* and Bobby Deol plays Sepoy Tarun Chauhan – Tango Charlie – in the film of the same name). These films have either misrepresented the various 'insurgencies' in the regions or glossed over the region's political discontent[6] and cultural nuances. This attitude has alienated some sections of people in the region from Hindi cinema even as it has managed to seduce others.

Policing Bollywood and Mainstream Indian Culture in North-East India

The overt nationalism and patriotism of Hindi films have little resonance for separatist groups that are culturally and politically at odds with the idea of being a part of India. Films that depict wealthy, upper caste, North Indian, Hindu families showing them conduct detailed Vedic rituals and weddings thus '"presenting a nostalgic vision of 'Indian culture' and 'family values'"' (Ganti ibid., 51) have been thought to be far too 'foreign' for local tastes. The raunchy song-and-dance sequences of contemporary Hindi films have also been frowned upon by cultural groups who 'police' local cultural consumption. Bhartiya (2007, 417) writes

> in Manipur, Bollywood films and Hindi film music are banned by all 32 groups of the revolutionary brigade. The ban is implemented on the grounds of the revolutionary claim that Bollywood is having a bad influence on Manipuri youth and culture. The ban is also supposed to help the cause of Manipuri cinema and culture.

Digital Cinema: Fallout of the Ban on Hindi Commercial Cinema in Manipur

A research trip to Imphal in 2007 revealed that filmmakers in Manipur have been quick to exploit easily available audio-visual technology. Describing the situation after the ban on Hindi films called by 'underground' organisations, a filmmaker[7] said 'all the cinemas were shut down for three years...then the digital revolution came. People started making music videos...the album thing was major in Manipur.' Ironically, such music videos were also banned for corrupting local culture. To circumvent the ban on music videos filmmakers started including them as part of longer feature films. At the same time many filmmakers started making films on important social issues in Manipur. Commercial and documentary films in Manipur are flourishing as a result. As digital technologies were used to make these films, the 'digital cinema' movement came about. A freelance filmmaker[8] who has been making films about HIV and AIDS since 2001 and of late assisting a reputed director, remarked, 'Manipur has become a pioneer of digital film movement all over India.' Filmmakers work with digital cameras and capture cards and make most films on HDV, a high definition video format. Feature films are also made on HDV and are transferred to celluloid through a process of reverse tele-cine. There are a number of homegrown studios in Imphal that make good use of various computer-based film editing programmes (Yumnam 2007). These films are supported by organizations like the United Nations Office on Drugs and Crime (UNODC), Public Service Broadcasting Trust (PSBT), Doordarshan (DD) and even the British Broadcasting Corporation (BBC). They are watched through film festival circuits, as well as on national television if funded by DD or other broadcasters. They are also uploaded on the internet and exchanged through informal technological circuits in Manipur.

Filmmakers are usually trained graduates from institutions such as the Satyajit Ray Film and Television Institute of India (SRFTII) and Xaviers Institute of Communication (XIC). Some are young directors apprenticed to more established filmmakers like Leichil Luwang who has been assisting the reputed Manipuri director, Ningthouja Lancha since 2000 and is now a trained and experienced filmmaker. Haobam Paban Kumar, a SRFTII graduate, started by assisting Aribam Shyam Sharma, one of the most well-known directors of Manipur, before venturing out on his own with digital films. Sunzu Bachaspatimayum, who graduated from XIC and worked with Wadia films in Bombay making advertisements for a while, returned to Manipur when the AIDS crisis hit the state. Finding that "in Manipur you can't hope to make money through only films as it is very far flung...not much companies are here...no ads...", he turned to news, working, initially, for Asian News International (ANI) and then as a freelance producer for the University Grants Commission's (UGC's) Consortium for Educational Communication and for the Audio Visual Research Centre in Manipur. Other filmmakers also confessed that they have to resort to different professions to sustain their filmmaking. Doordarshan has funded and commissioned many digital documentaries but as a filmmaker put it 'Doordarshan is very limited. They still believe in the narration, voice of god documentaries.'[9] Yet some distinguished films have also been commissioned by Doordarshan such as *Nongdi Tarak-Khidare* which was included in the Indian panorama section in IFFI in Goa in 2004.

Telling stories through film is seen as a way to circumvent the problems of 'telling the real things in the real format which is tough to do in Manipur', as one established director[10] put it. He observed that the distinction between documentary and short films is becoming blurred as filmmakers have found it easier to fictionalise real events in the constrained political situation in Manipur. Manipur's various pressing problems and social trends[11] are being documented on film. Films have dealt with issues like the Kuki and Naga ethnic cleansing ('*Nongdi Tarak-Khidare*' or 'But it Never Rains', 2004, and '*Masangtheigi Mang*' or 'The Dream', 2000–2001, directed by Ningthouja Lancha), the suffering of women caught up in the conflict ('Soldiers of Sarong', 2003, directed by Prof. Lokendro, 'Living in Manipur', 2002, directed by Sunzu Bachaspatimayum[12] and 'AFSPA, 1958', 2005, directed by Haobam Paban Kumar), children in conflict ('Innocent Guns', forthcoming, directed by Sunzu Bachaspatimayum) and the handloom industry ('Thread of Life', 2000–2001, directed by Sunzu Bachaspatimayum). The AIDS crisis in Manipur ('Rude Awakening', 1995 and '*Shingnaba*' or 'Challenge', forthcoming, directed by Sunzu Bachaspatimayum) and the use of drugs ('Punish' directed by Leichil Luwang, 2007) have, and continue to be, documented on film. Many of these films are path breaking and have been widely acclaimed. Ningthouja Lancha's feature films have done exceedingly well both in Manipur and outside the state. His most recent film, 'Mami Shami'[13] (2008), a love story set against the militancy in the state, has been acclaimed for being entertaining while making a break from the more flippant commercial cinema in Manipur (Phanjoubam 2009). In 'Real', directed by Leichil Luwang, for the first time in the history of Manipur, seven young men and women publicly admitted that they were HIV positive. The film is archived in the Museum of Modern Arts in New York and was screened there in 2005. 'AFSPA, 1958' directed by Paban Kumar won the Critic's award at the Bombay International Film Festival and was also critically acclaimed at other international film festivals (Yumnam 2007).

Filmmakers are, however, often frustrated when it comes to distributing these films locally, for though some films are shown on the local channel and are screened in theatres, there are complications with such displays. One filmmaker[14] described the situation thus:

> In Manipur you are not allowed to show digital films in theatres in municipality areas. So for every film every week, they take permission from the District Commissioner. Video does not come under the Cinematographers Act. You can show it in video parlours but not in theatres. But what is happening in Manipur is all the theatres are showing digital films and the textures, everything is different.

As far as markets for these films go filmmakers are alert to the possibilities of marketing them within the region as well as creating international markets and talk ambitiously about their craft.

Commercial Cinema in Manipur

While many believe that the commercial film industry in Manipur has also flourished because of the ban on Hindi films, the commercial cinema in Manipur is still heavily derivative of Bollywood. Talking about the popularity of Bollywood in Manipur, a filmmaker[15] remarked, 'In Manipur … people grow on Hindustani music…they love Hindi songs…and then…you're told not to watch…and ironically these Manipuri digital films are doing exactly the same thing…they are just a take off from Bollywood or the South films…we have song sequences…more singing and dancing around the trees…and all the stories are centered on love lives…'.

Doren (2006) also writes that in Manipur local film directors follow the Bollywood 'formula' and films abound with song and dance sequences, melodrama and the gloss of Hindi commercial cinema. 'Originality, local culture or social themes are rare in Manipuri [commercial] cinema today', he

Figure 2.1. Manipuri film posters (courtesy of Daisy Hasan)

laments and then adds dramatically, 'Bollywood reign (sic) supreme. Amitabh Bachhan (sic) hasn't left Manipur' (ibid., 1). Films typical of this genre include, among many others, 'Thawanmichakna Kenkhrabada' (When the Star Falls 2002), directed by Kishorekumar, which tells the love story of the rich 'outsider', Jiten, who falls in love with a disabled singer, Meera, when he visits Manipur during his university vacation. The couple are married, but when Jiten returns to Pune to complete his studies, Meera, unable to bear the ill treatment by her in-laws, returns to her own home. Her parents-in-law only acknowledge their ill-treatment of Meera when their own daughter is disabled in an accident. The film's climax is achieved when Jiten and Meera are reunited after a long separation.[16] More talked about and better directed commercial films include '*Lakhipurgi Lakhipyari*'[17], 2008, directed by Surjakanta, '*Basantagi Nonganlamdai*'[18] (Part 1, 2 and 3), 2006–2008, directed by Teskishore and '*Meera Memcha*'[19], 2008 directed by Mohindro. Speaking about these films, critic and film juror, Bimol Akoijam, (2008) writes, 'the directors of these films should be commended for their handling of the story, actors and the cinematic craft'.

While filmmakers working in the documentary and short film genre oppose the blanket ban on Hindi films, they are, more often than not, suspicious if not openly critical of Manipur's flourishing commercial film industry.

Figure 2.2. Manipuri films have replaced Bollywood in theatres in Imphal (courtesy of Daisy Hasan)

Figure 2.3. Manipuri film showing in a theatre in Imphal (courtesy of Daisy Hasan)

A filmmaker[20] commented, 'we don't like to borrow methods...from anywhere in the world. We should develop our own...'. Commenting on Manipuri commercial cinema, he went on to say, 'Commercial films are a very G grade or D grade copy of Bollywood. I think we should change the concept of entertainment. We should entertain people according to our conditions... in Manipur we need certain lyrical stories.' It is also felt that the

Figure 2.4. A cinema hall in Imphal screening a Manipuri film (courtesy of Daisy Hasan)

film industry in Manipur needs 'a certain kind of intellectualization...we should make films to express ourselves.'

Commercial films in Manipur have also had to contend with censorship in the form of the recently set up Film Forum[21] which has been instrumental in banning music videos and some films. Talking about the ban a filmmaker[22] said 'the reason for this ban is that the videos are claimed to be showing culture in a defamatory way.' Speaking about the rationale for the Forum, a member[23] said:

> We have different threats and different pressures both from the militants and from the state. So we feel that anything which negates our moral values... we need certain ramifications (sic) in the film itself. We are trying to have a genre of our own...like Korean movies...it should be very realistic. They can exaggerate...it can be a melodrama but it should not try to challenge our mores and values.

Filmmakers are asked to submit their scripts for scrutiny to the Forum and edited versions are also scrutinised. This is a way of pre-empting other 'illegal' or underground organisations from calling blanket bans on digital films. While some filmmakers do not agree with the Forum they feel that it has been accepted because of 'the situation in Manipur. Because otherwise anybody can ban your film'.[24]

Khasi Commercial Cinema

In Shillong the 'Bombaiya' idiom in which local film directors have begun to make Khasi films has caused embarrassment in some quarters. The embarrassment comes from discovering secret longings for things 'Indian' in a culture that has implicitly if not explicitly adhered to political grafitti like 'We are Khasis by blood. Indians by accident.' This belief makes people express concerns about Indian popular culture – '...Western and Hindi music have become a habit which is hard to take away. Ever since a child is born he only hears Hindi or English songs...only Khasi dance festivals have traditional music...people are not proud of Khasi culture... our identity is deteriorating...'[25] The 'accident' with Indian popular culture, however, continues as cricket matches gain more popularity[26] and Khasi songs thinly disguised in Hindi film tunes blare out of taxis and local tea shops. The danger of a numerically insignificant community getting absorbed into a pan-Indian, homogeneous culture ever stalks political ideologues and groups anxious to preserve the 'authenticity', real or imagined, of indigenous cultures (Hasan and Bhartiya 2001).

Bollywood as Inspiration for Khasi Films

Despite the cultural vigilance exercised by political groups, local film producers in Meghalaya derive their cultural inspiration not only from American and European or Far Eastern film and music channels but also from Bollywood.

In Shillong, having been discouraged by the ostensible lack of demand for local music and films, a Khasi director[27] claimed that he conducted a market survey and found that people would only buy Khasi albums if they were 'directly translated from Hindi to Khasi.' When he made his own Khasi music album he spent twice the amount on publicity and found it selling like 'hot cakes in town.' Talking about the reasons for this success, he said, 'in Shillong the music market is divided into so many categories...so I combined everything into one album. I made the singer sing some Khasi songs in a very Arabic style...with lots of Latin instruments in-between...and the beats were all Khasi...and that has really clicked...'. Having once worked as an assistant director in the Hindi film industry in Bombay, this director has also attempted the reverse – introducing Khasi folk music into Hindi songs – and thus feels that 'fusion' is a two way process. He has not, however, felt obliged to introduce elements of Khasi culture either in the form of music or dress if, as he put it, 'the script [does] not demand it.' Similarly another upcoming Khasi film director[28] said that he would only make films that reflected Khasi culture if he got good scripts. 'Otherwise I'll go for commercial movies...'. Referring to his first film – *Lano Kane Ka Meit Kan Shai*[29] – he confessed that it 'is a bit Hindi...you know villains and drugs ...with songs and all...but we can't help it...if we are making commercially we have to make those kind of movies.'

Khasi directors refute the purist position adopted by some sections of Khasi society who perceive local entertainment as cultural 'kitsch' that corrupts 'authentic' Khasi culture. A director responded to the charge that 'people from the media... and other singers' were making about his work being 'like Bollywood...', by saying that 'what is important is it's selling...and if they've compared my stuff with Bollywood I take it as a compliment. Bollywood is not a small thing...'[30] He went on to say that his critics wanted Khasi films to be 'very much western...they don't talk about Khasi culture...they talk about western... but I believe that whatever hits your ears first – whether its Hindi, Telegu, Tamil or Khasi – is what matters. Sometimes even I don't like what I'm doing... but I have to do it because people like it...'. Another director similarly declared that he actually never watched 'Hindi movies'. He continued, 'I like Hollywood. But the problem here is the Khasi audience watch Hindi kind of movies...if we think commercially then I have to make Hindi kind of movies... that's the problem... we have to make compromises...'. These directors, however, do not think that imitation spoils the culture:

> ...compare the scene here – what is selling more...English or Hindi cassettes? It's Hindi. In town people say we listen to English songs but in reality they hardly listen...the dominant demand is for Hindi films...you can make it out from the video-hire and cassette shops...the moment any

new movie comes...they start showing the trailers and people start asking for it.[31]

The easy availability of relatively cheap video technology in the last decade has made Khasi films and entertainment possible in a way that was not feasible before.[32] A study of seven music videos[33] made by director Pradip Kurbah's production company, Sonarishi Arts, showed that he employs highly stylised visual techniques which appear to be inspired by a variety of popular cultural sources not least the song and dance sequences of Hindi films. The themes of the videos vary around the boy-meets-girl plots seen commonly in Hindi films and music videos. The actors are, however, considerably younger than their Bollywood counterparts and at times appear unconvincing or self conscious. In the 1990s the film *Ka Mon Ba Jwat*, a Bollywood style Khasi film directed by Pradip Kurbah and produced by Pomu Das created much interest and encouraged others to take up the medium. Bobby Chyme is a relatively new entrant and his film *Lano Kane Ka Meit Kan Shai* makes an interesting study in tracing the influences of Hindi commercial cinema on the nascent Khasi film 'industry.' The plot of *Lano Kane Ka Meit Kan Shai* is a fairly recognizable one from Bollywood films – the well intentioned protagonist (Ban) turns into a killer when he accidentally stumbles upon a drug dealing and smuggling racket, is blackmailed to keep silent and finds his family murdered when he refuses to obey. The film opens with a verse from the venerated Khasi poet So So Tham[34] and uses entirely local settings (perhaps necessitated by the budget). However, the director introduces elements that are obviously derived from Hindi films, such as the Hindi-speaking villain and his comic sidekick, the love songs, and subplots based on coincidences. Hollywood-inspired sequences also make an occasional appearance such as the depiction of the 'bad guys' who kidnap Ban's daughter and eventually kill him. Interestingly, the film ends with the death of the hero; the audience is left with an image of the two women in the film walking away with Ban's daughter. This appears to be an affirmation of the matrilineal values upheld in Khasi society, which holds women in high esteem. The film, therefore, combines several cultural strands and yet manages to remain a uniquely Khasi film.

Contemporary commercial entertainment in the North-East, then, appears to combine several popular cultural influences strategically. The indigenous film and music industry is arguably flourishing, but people also appear inclined to accept mainland Indian popular culture, most prominently, Hindi films and music. The work and attitudes of local media and film producers, dwelt upon above, hint at the way in which indigenous cultures have been able to reinvent themselves using the cultural 'impositions' of Indian popular culture (particularly Bollywood) to their advantage.

Bollywood and its Audiences in North-East India

Though audiences in the North-East have historically been apathetic towards Hindi cultural entertainment on television, the more engrossing serials on channels like STAR Plus and Hindi films on movie channels have made viewers better attuned to mainstream Indian culture.[35] Young male audiences are, however, careful to state that Hindi entertainment on private satellite channels is 'only for girls'[36] This gendered division of television content is endorsed by the 'girls' themselves, as women interviewees admitted that the STAR Plus 'saas-bahu'[37] serials were a major source of entertainment for them, despite the fact that they did not understand Hindi perfectly. While viewers are also inclined towards local and global entertainment and translate Western media texts in order to find solutions to their local problems and to fulfil personal needs, national programmes remain in the reckoning through these Hindi serials and films on Indian television channels.

Given that the predominant sense of being a Khasi or Manipuri is anchored in a traditional, premodern past some audiences feel that there is a real threat to indigenous ways of life from mainstream Indian culture. Khasi culture is under siege today. In the urban sphere we can see the influence of western culture and in the rural segment it is the mainland Indian culture that has influenced Khasi culture...'[38] Satellite television is primarily blamed for this cultural onslaught. While it is conceded that '...Khasi culture has a sense of its own which is why it could survive the onslaught of different cultures at different points in its history,' there is a perception in some quarters that it is '...under a lot of pressure today because of the invasion of satellite television.'[39]

Though a large number of respondents take a more cautious view about the extent to which the popularity of television translates into a change in patterns of community life – '...our system is such that the boys would rather hang out on the streets with their friends rather than watch TV with their sisters... TV is the woman's space....the locality is the boys' space...'[40] – some argue that changes in social life can be directly traced to the 'influence' of television and film. A certain kind of 'rebellious behaviour' encountered among teenagers in schools is believed to have a lot to do with television. Others feel that satellite television has led to the creation of 'urban yuppies who talk in a certain language and think in a certain way. The fashion here strongly reflects what is there on the TV and films.'[41] Another interviewee lamented the fact that '...In today's generation very few youths are aware of the heritage... the traditional folklore and few identify themselves with that culture...rather there is a profound sense of dissociation ...that is worrying...it means that people have disowned their roots. There is a decline in cultural activities... it is these that reflect the greatness of a culture and language.'[42]

This argument, as mentioned above, is most commonly proffered by members of political and cultural organisations seeking to mobilise people in the name of a rigidly defined and bounded ethnic identity for political and cultural gain. Others do not entirely believe that 'there is a danger of local identities being wiped out...'[43] and a large number of young people interviewed disagreed with the idea that the prevalence of mainstream Indian culture has made fundamental changes in their social behaviour and identity. The adoption of a dominant culture, as one interviewee put it, is seen as 'a question of personal choice. 'We are not imposed (sic) to do it...it depends on your own personal interest...'[44] Most interviewees, therefore, refused to give in to the moral panic that has accompanied the spread of Bollywood in the region. Though it is admitted that the entry and spread of popular films and media cannot be stopped people argue that '...we have to analyse what we see. Take it with a pinch of salt at times.'[45]

A large number of respondents in my study argued that despite what some people believe, there is no threat in accepting that they are a part of India. 'Indigenous culture and Indian or western culture are not antagonistic. I am an Indian because Hynniewtrep is in India.[46] We want to survive with dignity and contribute to the rest of India and the world.'[47] A Khasi politician and former student union president[48] pointed out that 'today the Khasi intelligentsia has reacted against this sort of cultural militancy because they know that you can't ram culture down a person's throat. So to that extent a cultural movement should be based more on convincing people that a lot of things are worthwhile in one's own culture. It doesn't have to take the form of banning Hindi movies...'.

This rejection of extremist positions on the question of identity has made people more open to viewing Hindi films. Despite a strong resistance to mainstream Indian cultural entertainment from some quarters of society, satellite television has popularised Hindi film songs, soaps and 'infotainment' to an unprecedented degree. This has led to a revision of earlier (antagonistic) positions adopted on the issue of indigenous cultural assimilation with mainstream India. Though, as pointed out above, most audiences are careful to state that they would not like Khasi television to imitate the Hindi channels, yet most people also confess to a liking for Hindi entertainment. As one respondent put it – '...I must say that for the urban Khasi, we have always enjoyed Hindi movies...'[49] The ban on Hindi films initiated by extremist cultural organizations in the North-East is hence seen by respondents as 'the voice of the minority,' which is 'not going to work.'[50] In Manipur the ban on the consumption of Bollywood has been subverted by the informal networks of distribution or what is less salubriously known as the 'black market'. These circuits allow people to watch pirated CDs and DVDs of Hindi films which are sneaked into Manipur from India's metropolitan cities or even from across the Indo-Chinese border (Doren 2006).

The popularity of Hindi entertainment in rural Meghalaya is often cited as an example of resistance to cultural policing. It is felt that though the promotion of Hindi through the state-owned media was 'not accepted earlier,' yet the liberalised media and Bollywood have popularised the national language and culture through media forms to such an extent that '...in the villages people now hold competitions in Hindi film dance and music...'[51] This acceptance of Hindi cultural entertainment has admittedly not gone down well uniformly. Lamenting the 'adulteration' of traditional Khasi music one respondent complained that though he loved listening to Khasi music, the kind available in the market was 'embarrassing. You get those Hindi tunes... and they are so popular and sell like hot cakes in rural areas...'[52] Others feel that Khasis have accepted Hindi entertainment for a very long time while feigning public indifference if not outright aversion to it – 'They listen without even understanding...how many of them really understand. It's just the sentiment... like Chinese food is very popular in Shillong but I don't know how many Khasi people can use chopsticks ... (laughs). That means we are accepting new cultures...just the easy part. We don't want to trouble ourselves...'[53] Yet others have made strategic use of the popularity of Hindi entertainment so that speaking about an effort to organise a show of traditional songs and dances an interviewee confessed that because '...the audience [for traditional performances] is so sparse...we add something popular...something 'filmi'... and then the audience comes in droves. So ...in that way there's a kind of integration I think...in an indirect way with the rest of the country....'[54] Local societies, therefore, appear to have dealt with the 'invasion' of Indian popular culture by assimilating an indigenous cultural identity with an Indian political one. A traditional head remarked that, 'rural people love Hindi films...that is not a problem...I advise my children to learn Hindi...it's important because I'm living in India...I am a part of India...'[55]

Conclusion

Bollywood and Indian popular culture more generally provoke complex reactions among people on India's periphery, exciting and embarrassing their consumers depending upon their understanding of indigenous cultural identity and their relationship with the rest of India. It is, of course, evident that these marginal cultures cannot be swamped by India's dominant film culture as 'militant' cultural organisations would have us believe. On the contrary, it is reasonable to argue that local audiences strategically take on multiple identities, which enable them to relate to Indian popular culture without eroding their sense of being either Khasi or Manipuri or Mizo. Viewing and imitating Bollywood is accommodated as part of the fluid cultural practices of modern societies in the region. Indian popular culture is seen by the majority of people in this region as not necessarily alien or invasive but as inevitable. In so far as it is possible to talk about a consensus then, the way forward for local cultures appears to lie in their modernisation and 'fusion' with popular cultural forms both from India and abroad.

Commercial films are a step in this direction. Local directors and media entrepreneurs, as mentioned above, appear to strategically combine several cultural strands popularised through satellite television. Bollywood, in particular, has arguably reinvigorated the indigenous film and music industry. It has simultaneously encouraged people to accept mainland Indian popular culture and thus become more comfortable with the 'idea of India'. The 'discourse' of film and entertainment producers, dwelt upon in this chapter, hints at the way in which indigenous culture has been able to reinvent itself using the cultural 'impositions' of mainland India to its advantage. The local media, then, has been able to achieve a balance between lobbying for 'tradition' and participating in 'modernity.' The indigenous media plays an important role in negotiating, or simply put, making sense of, social life at a time of historical change (Rajagopal 2000, 294). This media has responded creatively to Bollywood and producers are looking for opportunities to graft declining traditions and contemporary social concerns[56] onto these more popular narratives. If Hindi commercial cinema has viewed and represented the region in largely pre-modern and orientalist terms, local producers today appear to be 'talking back' to Bollywood by playing its own game of hybridity and borrowing for cultural survival.

Notes

1. The region saw and continues to see the following major conflicts between political groups and the central government: 1) the conflict in Nagaland and the adjacent parts of Manipur; 2) the Meitei conflict in the Imphal Valley; 3) the Bodo conflict in Lower Assam; 4) The conflict waged by the United Liberation Front of Assam (ULFA) in mainland Assam; 5) The Hynniewtrep National Liberation Council (HNLC) conflict in Meghalaya and 6) the conflict waged by the National Liberation Front of Tripura (NLFT) in Tripura (Verghese, 1996: 7).
2. These interviews were part of a broader research project that surveyed the influence of satellite television in the region. The research was conducted between December 2003 and July 2004, and again during August 2007.
3. A two third majority of Meiteis, who are Vaishnavite Hindus, inhabit most of the valley in Manipur along with Muslim settlers from Bengal and other ethnic groups like the Kukis and Nagas. These latter are also predominantly Christian.
4. As a member on various committees relating to 'tribal' affairs, Elwin advised the government on the administration of what was then known as the North-East Frontier Agency (NEFA) now the state of Arunachal Pradesh.
5. Elwin outlined his approach to the region in three books. These included *A New Deal for Tribal India, Democracy in NEFA,* and *Philosophy of NEFA*.

6 *Tango Charlie* depicted the Bodo movement in Assam in a derogatory manner and its director was subsequently obliged to publicly apologise to the movement's members. See http://movies.dcealumni.com/archives/bodo-community-angry-with-tango-charlie/
7 Sunzu Bachaspatimayum. Interviewed in Imphal, August 2007.
8 Leichil Luwang. Interviewed in Imphal, August 2007.
9 Haobam Paban Kumar. Interviewed in Imphal, August 2007. Others have felt harassed by the broadcaster's style of interviewing. A filmmaker, Leichil Luwang, said 'I just applied once, as a director in 2006. There is no room for very serious filmmaker like me. They were asking the producer and me about lights. If they are going to ask me about the lights what's the use of me and the producer to get inside the interview hall. It would be better if they called the interview for our lighting designers.' Haobam Paban Kumar also presented the seamy underside of film commissions in DDK-Imphal when he said 'lots of people are pressuring… they are asking money from them. So, they have to go to Guwahati for the interview…lots of quotas. Some banned organisations, they are asking for quotas in the amount of film being commissioned'.
10 Ningthouja Lancha. Interviewed in Imphal, August 2007.
11 Apart from being reported in the regional versions of papers like 'The Telegraph' (http://www.telegraphindia.com/section/northeast/index.jsp), reportage and editorial commentary on events in Manipur regularly feature in 'The Imphal Free Press' (http://ifp.co.in/) edited by Pradip Phanjoubam (who was interviewed by this researcher) and online news magazines like 'E-Pao' (http://www.e-pao.net/) and 'Kangla Online' (http://www.kanglaonline.com/) all of which were consulted during the period of this research.
12 For more films directed and produced by Sunzu Bachaspatimayum, see his web page:- http://bachaspatimayumsunzu.tripod.com
13 'Mami Shami' refers to something that is shadowy or obscure.
14 Haobam Paban.
15 Sunzu Bachaspatimayum. Interviewed in Imphal, August 2007.
16 http://www.epao.net/epSubPageExtractor.asp?src=reviews.movies.thawanmichakna
17 Lakhipurgi is a place in Silchar, Assam. Lakhipyari is the name of a person.
18 'The Dawn of Basant'. 'Basant' is the name of a season but can also be used as a person's name.
19 'Meera Memcha' is the name of a girl.
20 Ningthouja Lancha.
21 The Film Forum has six member organisations including the Producers Association, the Exhibitors Association, the Cine Exhibitors Association of Manipur (AMEC), the All Manipur Video Filmmakers and Producers Association, the All Manipur Film Producers Association and the Cine Artists and Technicians Association (CATA). Two representatives from each of these organisations make up the forum.
22 Haobam Paban.
23 Ningthouja Lancha.
24 Haobam Paban.
25 "Khasi Audio Albums – Original and Traditional", (Peitngor Cable News, 21 March 2004).
26 Cricket, the nation's favourite sport, has historically not been as popular as football in the region.
27 Pradip Kurbah. Interviewed in Shillong on 12 June 2004. Director, Pradip Kurbah's first Khasi film *'Ka Mon Ba Jwat'* was not initially screened in cinema halls in Meghalaya

because of a conflict with the state government over entertainment tax. The dispute was resolved and the film screened in September 2005.
28 Bobby Chyme. Interviewed in Shillong on 13 June 2004.
29 *Lano Kane Ka Meit Kan Shai*, (When will this night turn into light?) was Bobby Chyme's first Khasi film released in 2004.
30 Pradip Kurbah.
31 Ibid.
32 Khasi films have rarely been made in the past. Until the early 1990s, the only Khasi film was 'Manik Rytong' – a 1984 national award winning film directed by Ardhendu Bhattacharya which was based on a Khasi legend (Hasan et al. 2001).
33 The music videos included 'Mynsiem' (Mynsiem, in this context, refers to the heart), 'Uff! Ka Jingieit' (Oh! Love!), 'Nga Ieid Iaphi' (I love you), 'Senorita', 'Jingkyrmen', 'Daphishisha' and 'Dur Bhabriew' (Beautiful picture).
34 'Sei Ka Bor te kum ki briew / Wat trei tang ban ioh ka bam / Hynrei artad ruh ban kiew/ Na ki kyrdan jong ka nam/ La phi rit bor la phi tlot / Jar Jar la phi dei ban iam / Ei ba ong ba phim la kot/ Sha ka kyrteng bad ka nam' (Bring out the strength in every man/ Don't work only to feed yourself/ Work also to raise yourself/ to reach the zenith of progress/ Even if you are small or weak/ even if you have to cry softly to yourself/ who says you cannot read books/ your name and title will live on.)
35 See Note 2.
36 Undergraduate student. Interviewed on 26 March 2004.
37 The saas-bahu (mother-in-law and daughter-in-law) serials on STAR Plus are immensely popular soap operas that have enabled the channel to retain its market lead in an increasingly competitive entertainment television market. The stories dwell on the lives of well-to-do North Indian women negotiating their roles as 'traditional' housewives and mothers and their own urge for personal fulfilment and more liberated 'modern' lifestyles. Media critic, Sevanti Ninan, believes that STAR Plus is targeting viewers located in smaller Indian towns whose aspirations for material prosperity is both encouraged by and imaginatively fulfilled through the affluence projected in these serials. (http://www.hindu.com/thehindu/mag/2002/07/14/stories/2002071400030300.htm) (accessed 3 May 2008)
38 Minister of Sports and Youth Affairs. Interviewed on 9 April 2004.
39 Ibid.
40 College Lecturer. Interviewed on 19 March 2004.
41 Director, Indigenous Women's Resource Centre. Interviewed on 1 April 2004.
42 Minister of Sports and Youth Affairs.
43 College Lecturer. Interviewed on 19 March 2004.
44 Call centre trainer. Interviewed on 26 March 2004.
45 Convenor, Mait Shaphrang Movement. Interviewed on 19 March 2004.
46 Hynniewtrep refers to the mythical seven huts part of the sixteen huts (Khadhynriew trep) where Khasis are believed to have originally resided. These huts were part of a cosmic order. The seven huts were ordained to preside over the earth. The appropriation of the term 'Hynniewtrep' by the Hynniewtrep Liberation Council (HNLC) suggests that they seek to liberate the Khasi people and re-establish ties with a sacred community of Khasis. (http://khasi.ws/spiritual_roots.htm) (accessed 3 August 2008)
47 Convenor, Mait Shaphrang Movement.
48 Interviewed, 9 April 2004.
49 Director, Indigenous Women's Resource Centre. Interviewed on 1 April 2004.
50 Ibid.

51 Retd. College Lecturer. Interviewed on 29 March, 2004.
52 Transmission Executive, All India Radio, Shillong. Interviewed on 21 April 2004.
53 Columnist with the Meghalaya Guardian. Interviewed on 9 April 2004.
54 Additional District Magistrate, West Khasi Hills. Interviewed on 4 April, 2004.
55 Khasi Priestess and Queen of Hima Khyriem. Interviewed on 24 April, 2004.
56 For instance, the recent film *Hep*, directed by Pradip Kurbah and released in 2006 addresses drug addiction in Meghalaya.

References

Akoijam, A.B. (2009) 'Manipuri Cinema: Nursing the Pain of Transition and Murky Life', *Kangla Online* http://www.kanglaonline.com/index.php?template=kshow&kid=1113 Date (accessed 17 January 2009)

―――― (2008) 'Manipuri Cinema: Festival and Beyond', *E-Rang* http://e-pao.org/erang/Reviews/Manipuri_cinema_Festival_and_beyond.php (accessed 14 January 2009)

Bhartiya, T. (2007) 'Liberal Nightmares: A Manual of North-Eastern Dreams', *Sarai Reader 07 Turbulence*, Delhi: Centre for the Study of Developing Societies. 413–421 http://www.sarai.net/publications/readers/06-turbulence (accessed 25 April 2007)

Bose, M. (2006) *Bollywood: A History*, Gloucestershire: Tempus Publishing

Doren, O. (2006) 'Has Amitabh Bachchan left Manipur?' www.e-pao.net/epSubPageSelector.asp?src=Has_A... (accessed 20 July 2007)

Ganesh, K. and U. Thakkar (2005) *Culture and the Making of Identity in Contemporary India*, New Delhi: Sage Publications

Ganti, T. (2004) *Bollywood: A Guidebook to Popular Hindi Cinema*, London: Routledge

Hasan, D. and Bhartiya, T. (2001) 'A Short and Incomplete Guide to Khasi Cinema' in *The Express Magazine of The Indian Express*, 8 July 2000

Nandy, A. (1983) *The Intimate Enemy; Loss and Recovery of Self under Colonialism*, New Delhi: Oxford University Press

Nandy, A. (1998) (ed.) *The Secret Politics of Our Desires: Innocence, Culpability and Indian Popular Cinema*, London: Zed Books, 157–207

Mangang, R. (2009) 'Helloy: Between conscious and sub-consciousness', *E-Pao* http://www.google.co.uk/searchhl=en&q=names+of+commercial+Manipuri+films&start=20&sa=N (accessed 17 January 2009)

Phanjoubam, P. (2009) 'Mami Sami: Fascinating Struggles of Individuals in a Tormenting Time', *Kangla Online* http://www.kanglaonline.com/index.php?template=kshow&kid=1116 (accessed 17 January 2009)

Rajagopal, A. (2000) 'Mediating Modernity; Theorizing Reception in a Non-Western Society', in J. Curran and M. Park (eds) *Dewesternizing Media Studies*, London and New York: Routledge, 293–302

Rajagopal, A. (2001) *Politics after Television: Religious Nationalism and the Reshaping of the Indian Public*, Cambridge: Cambridge University Press

Rustomji, N. K. (1988) *Verrier Elwin and India's North-Eastern Borderlands*, Shillong: North-Eastern Hill University Publications

Sonwalkar, P. (2001) 'India: Makings of Little Cultural/Media Imperialism?' in *Gazette: The International Journal for Communication Studies* Volume 63, Issue 6: 505–519

Taylor, B. (2002) 'Public Folklore, Nation-Building, and Regional Others: Comparing Appalachian USA and North-East India' in *Indian Folklore Research Journal* 1: 1–27

The Shillong Times (2006) 'Hep – Contemporary Khasi movie with compelling social message' *The Shillong Times,* 11 September 2006

Verghese, B.G. (1996) *India's North-East Resurgent; Ethnicity, Insurgency, Governance, Development,* New Delhi: Centre for Policy Research and Konark Publishers

Yumnam, R. (2007) *Imphalwood Deep focus on Manipuri Cinema* http://manipuri-cinema.blogspot.com/2007_06_01_archive.html (accessed 17 January 2009)

Chapter Three

'ADVERTS MAKE ME WANT TO BREAK THE TELEVISION': INDIAN CHILDREN AND THEIR AUDIOVISUAL MEDIA ENVIRONMENT IN THREE CONTRASTING LOCATIONS

Shakuntala Banaji

Introduction: 'Indian' Children, 'Global' Media?

The media environment surrounding children in a metropolis like Bombay, India has altered almost unrecognisably in the last two decades. Despite the introduction of hundreds of cable and satellite channels and broadband internet into many middle and some lower middle-class homes, however, discourses about children and media have remained surprisingly stagnant. These discourses tend to fall into one of two paradigms. The first is an effects paradigm, which focuses on content in either a negative or a positive manner. Instances include the protectionist stance that sees most Western media products as dangerous and having negative effects on 'Indian values', or the argument that the liberalising of the Indian media economy has brought about changes in content that challenge sexist and other negative attitudes. The second paradigm posits content as irrelevant. It views all innovations in the Indian media and communications environment as socially beneficial because they, apparently, make India more modern and competitive. While a host of other positions exist amongst parents and young people, these are rarely articulated publicly. The voices that get most coverage in the public sphere are usually those calling for censorship and/or technological skills development. Complexity is seen as problematic, and hence sidestepped.

Built around a small-scale interview-based study with Bombay children (aged between 9 and 12) about their film and television viewing and their experiences with ICTs at school and in the home over a period of four years, a focus group of girls (aged between 10 and 12) in a village (Barsu) in the Himalayan foothills[1] and a larger focus group study with children (aged between 10 and 14) in a small town (Palakkad) in Kerala[2], this chapter[3] aims to disentangle some of the rhetoric about values, global skills and ethnic identity from the diverse realities of children and young people's media, family and social experiences in contemporary Indian settings.

Researching the Child Audience

Surveying literature on the Media environment of children in India over the past three decades (Noorani 1978, Behl 1988; Yadava and Reddi 1988; Bajoria 2004, N Bhaskara Rao 2005, Joseph 2005, Kaur and Singh 2006) several issues come to the fore. The content of Hindi films (Banaji 2006), debates about the effects of media representations (Unnikrishnan and Bajpai 1996, Varghese 2008), technological differences between urban and rural areas (Dugger 2000; Arora 2007) and income differences between strata of the population have usually been the subjects of social research. More recently, the burgeoning of ICTs and mobile communications and the advent of digital satellite television stations have been debated, both in academia and within the media themselves. Again, in this regard, one strand of research has concentrated on the supposed impacts of 'cultural globalisation'. These have been thought to be brought about through first nationalist and then international (also called Western) programming and the internet on the 'Indian' life-style and 'psyche' (Johnson 2001; Jensen and Oster 2007). Another strand, which fits into a more economic paradigm, has either celebrated the entry of India into the global 'knowledge economy' or described and decried the slow pace of take-up of ICTs in particular areas and sectors. While children figure occasionally in both these types of discussions as adjuncts to adults, or as the 'next generation of the global workforce' and as 'quick' learners with little need for systematic tuition when it comes to ICTs (Mitra and Rana 2001), they most frequently do so in a completely generalised and peripheral manner, with no attempt made to distinguish between their needs and concerns based on class, region, locality, gender or any other feature. In fact, so little has been made of the child audience in India, except by commercial corporations, that although there is a Children's Film society of India, there is no known body with oversight of – or responsibility for rating – output available to children on television. Discussions in coming sections aim, at least partially, to indicate why this imbalance needs to be addressed.

Methods and Sample

Researching with children in any setting can be tricky, particularly in relation to issues that might cause conflict between the interviewees and their parents. Ethically the imperative not to harm vulnerable research subjects is of paramount importance in these instances. For this reason, the researchers needed to be people who were trusted both by the children and by their parents, in the first instance, and, in the second, who would ensure confidentiality in relation to particular details of the young people's life experiences even if questioned on this score by parents. Much has been written elsewhere about the role of the researcher who is both insider and outsider in particular research situations (cf. Kauffman 1994; Wong 1995). In two cases in the present study, Bombay and Palakkad, the researchers were known to several of the children in the focus groups prior to data collection, through local school or neighbourhood channels. Recruiting new children was never a problem as there were numerous volunteers. However, establishing rapport and trust were key criteria when conducting the groups, and efforts were made by the researchers to reduce the relationship of power experienced by the children via the use of non-classroom settings for the interviews, food, and humour, as well as maintaining confidentiality from parents. In all cases, an effort was made to ensure a balance of genders and some homogeneity in ages, although in the Barsu sample the selection was based on pragmatic criteria (for instance, the boys chose not to volunteer because they felt shy talking to a woman researcher; older girls were followed by younger siblings) and in Palakkad on friendship groups.

Language is often crucial when conducting research with children in India. The Bombay interviews were conducted in Hindi and English. Responses were in English, Hindi and Gujarati and have been translated to give as near a feel as possible to the colloquialisms routinely used by the children. For example, the phrase 'too much' in Bombay English means 'wonderful' or 'very much' as well as 'an excess'. The phrase 'English movies' refers not to British-made films but to any films in English; thus mainly Hollywood films. The Barsu focus group was conducted in Hindi and responses were in Pahadi and Hindi. The Palakkad interviews were conducted in Malayalam[4].

Selecting excerpts from discussions for analysis also entailed making decisions about which aspects of the children's media-related talk were more and which less relevant. Consequently, much of their discussion about educational settings, schools and homework as well as about leisure, gender and friendship is missing here. Similarly, given the repetition of themes in the Bombay and Palakkad focus groups, only one of each is quoted from here. The picture built up is necessarily fragmentary but nevertheless tries to do justice to the richness and depth of the children's original testimonies. In this vein, where possible, the same children have been quoted on several occasions, to follow through and link their ideas and opinions. There is no claim made here to 'representativeness' on the part of any of the groups of children. However, there is a significant way in which the ideas and opinions voiced by the specific children here can be seen to inform debates around children and media in India more widely, and to provide frames of reference that help in offsetting, assessing and/or understanding some of the current debates in literature on the subject.

Bombay: The Cutting-Edge Audience?

The lower-middleclass children (aged between 9 and 12) interviewed in the Bombay study have, unsurprisingly, the most diverse experience of media among the three groups. Most of them have been on the internet, especially in the past three years, looking up sporting websites, playing games on Disney and Fox Kids, downloading or listening to music or looking up information for school, and some have occasional but unfettered access to broadband or dial-up connections and computers while their parents are at work during the daytime, and when they are alone at home looking after younger siblings. Computers, which are uniformly situated in communal spaces, are seen as necessary by their parents for skilling them for the modern economy, and hence especially the boys but even the girls are encouraged to do some work on the computer every day.

Television (with cable and/or VCDs and DVDs) remains, by and large and with the exception of trips with friends to the cinema, the favourite form of entertainment, with everyone in the sample agreeing that they love to watch television, especially unsupervised.

> **Dhiren, 11**: If we are alone with friends, then we can laugh more: I can share the jokes with them; we can talk about it. Sometimes there are very funny things that are not that clean [vulgarities, innuendo] in the film or programme and we can talk about it.
> **Chirag, 11**: Cartoon movies I prefer to watch with my friends, Hindi movies with my mom, English [British and American] movies with my dad. I don't like English movies.
> **Sheetal, 11**: I prefer watching all movies and playing games online with my friends only, not my parents at all. So that we can have a good laugh out of it, especially of some corruption [innuendo, sexual sequences] is there, we can have a good laugh out of it.

The children introduce a moral discourse into the interview unprompted – referring to 'things that are not that clean' but which they find amusing, and to 'corruption' (a word said in English). They are explicit that such sequences and jokes in films and programmes are impossible to enjoy when parents are around and explain (see below) their parents' reasons for disliking their viewing of such material.

The kinds of programmes watched here in this crowded lower-middleclass inner city neighbourhood vary widely from a plethora of Hindi films, chat-shows, comedy programmes and serials such as *Dhoom Machao Dhoom*[5] (some with quite adult scenes and themes) to films in English (especially ones like *The Mummy* and the *Harry Potter* series), and dubbed American, Canadian and Japanese programmes: *Peppa Pig*, *Dora the Explorer* and the Indian version of *Sesame Street* appealing to younger siblings, while *Hannah Montana*, *Drake and Josh*, *That's So Raven* and *The Suite Life of Zach and Cody* are favourites with the tween girls. The boys claim to prefer to watch sport, especially cricket, and always films. Fights with younger siblings about viewing time are routine and usually lost by the older children. Apart from the fact that Hindi 'family serials' are generally despised as containing 'too much crying', there is little here that might not be encountered in discussions with urban children across the globe. But further probing revealed different contexts of viewing and responses to aspects of the programmes:

> **Interviewer**: This word 'corruption' – what do you mean by it?
> **Sheethal, 11**: Silly things – *come on* you understand – couples, silly faces, flirting...
> **Chirag, 11**: bad words, teasing...
> **Interviewer**: You enjoy that with your friends but you can't watch with your parents?
> **Sheetal, 11 and Heena, 11**: Never.
> **Jeev, 12:** Never.
> **Interviewer:** Why?
> **Jeev, 12:** Parents think that we too are becoming like the corruption, thinking in that way.
> **Sheetal, 11:** 'Good girls don't watch bad things', my mom would say. And I don't want to watch such things with my father. I already get enough lectures about "time-wasting".
> **Heena, 11:** It is boring for her to listen to the lectures from her parents about why is this not good, why is that a bad thing to watch. Better they don't know what she watches (all laugh). *I* don't watch such things because I don't enjoy them (interviewee's emphasis).

There was some shuffling and jostling at this construction by one girl of the other as transgressive while she herself is 'rule abiding' and if space permitted much could be written about such constitutive tactics on the part of children in their discussions of media and each other's viewing habits.

All the children in Bombay talked knowledgably about aspects of older teenage culture (both Western and Indian) and spoke in a sophisticated manner about issues as diverse as relationships, sex (which caused some shyness and much hilarity), potential careers, bullying, advertising, fashion, national identity, managing money and adolescent crushes. Children's television viewing, however, was said to be generally viewed by parents as a waste of time or even dangerous. It was variously understood to be seen by parents to compete with doing housework, looking after younger siblings and playing outdoors. It was also suggested by some of the children that their parents thought it was teaching them 'foreign values' and encouraging them 'to behave disrespectfully and selfishly like Western teenagers'. However, the most overwhelming complaint reported was that their parents thought it made the children *lazy* about their homework. All the Bombay children interviewed – including those not quoted here – were routinely expected to study for five hours every day in addition to the time they spent at school. This was confirmed by all the parents and teachers I spoke with, before and after focus groups. The findings about their television viewing, based on the children's descriptions of their parents' attitudes, are also consistent with the findings of Kavitha Cardoza's study in 1999 with Bangalore parents about their feelings towards and regulation of their children's television viewing (Cardoza 2002).

In this battle over whether leisure time was permitted and what it should be filled with, the children viewed advertising as their enemy in that it ruined the content of programmes, extended programmes which should have been short so that parents got more angry or so that they did not get the satisfaction of viewing an entire film. Their responses are uniform:

Dhiren, 11: I hate the adverts. They make me want to break the television!
Chirag, 11: (simultaneous) Extremely irritated. They make me so annoyed.
Jeev, 12: I too hate them. They are stupid (in Hindi – *a waste of time*).
Sheetal, 11: (simultaneous) Extremely irritated and frustrated. They interrupt our programme and the story, and then it's such a long time for them to go. Yesterday there was a advertise break of half an hour!
Heena, 11: And they come again and again, stupid adverts. All these stupid things to make thin, to make fair... [they sing jingles and make fun of the ads].
Jeev, 12: And if you leave the room then suddenly the film will come on again! It is *sooo* annoying.
Interviewer: If someone said that you could have a channel without adverts then you would say...?
All: Yes, Please! Yaar [Friend]! Because adverts are *really* boring.

Interviewer: So, why don't you ask for this?
Sheetal, 11: We don't only want one channel!
Dhiren, 11: The government only wants profit, the companies wants profit, so we children can never get rid of the adverts if we want our programmes.
Chirag, 11: Even if we pay the government for one children's channel with no adverts, there will still be so many that have them. But I would still like to have that one channel.

Here, notably, the children's keen sense of the ways in which capitalist logic currently structures leisure and interferes with viewing pleasure suggests an interest in and nascent media literacy that could and should be given space within an educational curriculum. There are differences of opinion too, about the value of non-commercial channels for children, with a clear preference expressed for the fiction content of commercial channels but minus the advertisements. Questions about regulation and control in this seemingly internationally and commercially saturated media environment prompted me to ask how they would react if they were confined to viewing programmes specifically targeted at a child audience. Their responses were categorical.

Sheetal, 11: I would kick the television. I would be so upset. We are growing up. There are so many things we like to watch. I like to see how teenagers in other countries behave, how people in America and Japan live with each other. I like to see music programmes from everywhere and sometimes horror movies. It makes me think much more than my school books. The TV can teach different things that our teachers don't know. Could you see all this just on children's shows? By our age we may be children, but this does not mean that we should only watch baby stuff.
Heena, 11: I would like to be able to choose to watch both cartoons and adults films if I want. I like both of these *too* much.
Chirag, 11: I would accept it. It's okay. Whatever our parents tell us to watch is for our own good.
Dhiren, 11: I would find a way to watch Adults (A/18 Rated) films. Sometimes our parents don't know what we are watching and sometimes they let us watch with them without realising. Children's programmes are also good, but adult programmes are also exciting. I know about a lot of stuff about foreign countries and about the government from watching Hindi films and talk shows and the news. And we see about boy-girl stuff (laugher).
Sheetal, 11: I would buy a VCD and watch it by myself. I would go on You Tube and watch clips of my favourite shows. Especially Harry Potter films.

Chirag, 11: We learn things from Hindi movies. Even the ones meant for those older than us. What is the point of only watching little kids' programmes?

Dhiren, 11: Like *Lagaan* – it teaches about how we should accept everyone: that makes us stronger. We should not be against someone because of who they are. Their religion or where they come from. And *Chak-De* India is about overcoming our differences, every girl, from every part of India is able to give something to help the team win.

Jeev, 12: Like *Ta Ra Rum Pum*; It tells about the dangers of taking loans, what can happen if we take loans and then we cannot pay and how we should not tell lies. [general agreement] It was a very good movie. And it has children in it.

Chirag, 11: I've seen it [TRRP] four times. So has my little brother. He's *four* [voice emphatic, as if that clinches it].

In this extended excerpt, the children develop multilayered rationales for viewing 'grown-up' content and not being confined to the equivalent of a children's curriculum on television. Learning about diversity and social cohesion, a clearly adult-sanctioned pedagogic message, is one of the primary lessons they refer to learning from Hindi films. However, although they mainly refer to fiction formats such as films, at points they mention the news, factual programmes and talk shows. Evidence collected previously (Banaji and Al-Ghabban 2006) suggests that these are formats often watched with and framed for children by their parents. Indeed, Sheetal's statement that horror films, music videos and television in general make her 'think much more than [her] school books' is crucial in underlining the potential pedagogic role in stimulating imagination and providing what is seen as 'relevant' knowledge in a society where school text-books are frequently devoid of either. Thus, despite the fact that pre-marital relationships are not sanctioned in any of the households and that the children will probably not be marrying until they have finished college, there is an evident interest in viewing around this theme, as there is in popular music of all kinds and in the acquisition of mobile phones and video cameras. This is a finding which again connects these Bombay children to children and young people in studies about similar topics in North America and Europe (Buckingham and Bragg 2004; Banaji 2006) These children are all set to become teenagers in a media environment that can quite plausibly be called 'international' and has most certainly been affected by digital convergence. They are not typical Indian children precisely because, as the following case-studies suggest, there is no such thing as a 'typical' Indian child.

Barsu: Heroic Identifications

Barsu was selected for this study because it provided not just a rural location but also for its seeming inaccessibility, which might be thought to militate against the common use of the latest information and communication technologies. It is in the foothills of the Himalayas at a height of approximately 7500 feet but unlike Katmandu, discussed by Paul Greene (in chapter five of this volume) for its urban youth music scene, Barsu is not frequented by Western tourists. It is, however, on a route popular with trekkers as it is surrounded by Himalayan peaks and the nearest town and district capital is Uttarkashi, which is about 40 kilometres away. Uttarakhand's state capital, Dehradun, is 250 kilometres of climbing mountain roads away, thus making the village fairly inaccessible to 'townies', and the capital more so to villagers. On the estimation of a long-time resident, Barsu has about 800 inhabitants. It is a single-religion, single-caste village. Most families are related to most other families in some way, and intermarriage is not allowed inside the village. Agriculture and cattle rearing are the main occupations. Several of the boys and men work as guides or porters when climbers pass through the village. Most children attend the local primary school and some move on to the secondary school further down the mountainside. For higher education, if and when this is an option, they have to go to Uttarkashi. Some boys from the village do go to college, but it is, apparently, extremely rare for girls to have that opportunity.

The focus group analysed here took place with six girls, aged 10 to 12. The family of one of the 10-year-olds did not own a television and she watched TV at her cousin's home. The channels they mentioned receiving were: Star TV and Star Utsav, Zee Smile, Doordarshan National, DD Sports and the Disney Channel. Most of them do not seem to come into conflict with their parents about the amount of time spent viewing but, having finished housework, watch whatever is on at home, which tends to be Hindi serials.

> **Interviewer:** Why do you like watching serials?
> **Minni, 12**: We like watching programmes about love, conflict. They tell you that love is good, and how to be good.
> **Interviewer:** Tell me about some characters you like in these serials.
> **Saira, 11**: Prerna in Kasauti! She is the bahu (daughter-in-law) and is very good. She looks after the family and loves everyone.
> **Interviewer:** Do you get any Ghadhwali channels? Or any programmes on Doordarshan that are set in your area or about your stories – like set in the mountains or in Uttaranchal or Gadhwal?
> **Gita, 10**: No. We get DD (the local channel) but we don't watch it very much.

> **Interviewer:** You said you watch *Sai Baba* – Do you watch anything else?
> **Gita, 10:** We watch *Ramayan* and *Mahabharat* on Star Utsav.
> **Interviewer:** Who is your favourite character there?
> **Gita, 10:** Ram. We really like him. [Others nod].

Again the children introduce a moral discourse about 'goodness' and 'love' very early into discussions of their preferred viewing. Unlike the children in Bombay who have a host of both adult and child stars to identify with, most of these children express a penchant for morally upstanding adult characters like the daugher-in-law Prerna in a Hindi serial, and mythological representations like the God Ram in the serialised version of the *Ramayana*. They represent their own television viewing as a way in which they learn about 'idealised' social relations quite outside the everyday sphere of their normal lives, akin to the discussions of devotional serials in Gillespie's work on British-Asian viewing of the *Mahabharata* (1993). Here there is little additional banter about relationships, or talk about audiovisual content dealing with romance and real life. While this may partly be due to shyness and to the fact they do not know the researcher particularly well, it is also reflective of their restricted viewing experience. Ironically, in this rural context, real representations of the women in each household would show independent working mothers, often running entire households for years while men labour in the pastures or down in the cities on the plains. Even Hindi films would have more chance of representing their circumstances occasionally or in an idealised form; but, as this next excerpt shows, they have little chance of viewing films.

> **Interviewer:** When you're watching TV is there anything that makes you feel shy?
> [They all turn away and try to hide their faces. Long pause.]
> **Minni, 12:** We don't like it when in some songs women take off their clothes or when they wear too little. You know. [long pause].
> **Interviewer:** Does anyone try to stop you from watching those programmes?
> **Saira, 11:** Yes. Our parents. The older people. Yes, they do.
> **Minni, 12:** I get up and go out of the room when there is something I know they don't like. [...]
> **Interviewer:** Do you ever go out to see films in a cinema?
> **Girls all:** No. Never.

Here the discourses of moral disapproval in relation to representations of women on television voiced by the children coincide closely with what they think to be their parents' views. It is not easy to discern whether these girls would be more exploratory about their viewing given greater privacy, but it is certain that they are highly sensitised to any romantic or sexual content by the overt disapproval of their elders. Additionally, although some of the Gadhwali girls enjoy some freedom in terms of being allowed to watch television if their contribution to family chores and school work has been accepted or is shared between a large number of siblings, what they actually get to watch is limited both in terms of type of media and of television format compared to what was described in the Bombay sample.

Most interestingly, they watch virtually no content that in any way reflects or relates to their own everyday lives, to their community in the mountains, to children or to their local dialect. Also crucially, these girls, like the children in Bombay and in Palakkad (see next section), are skilled at finding pedagogic justifications for a leisure pursuit frowned on as 'time-wasting' by some adults. It is also evident, however, that the actual learning which can take place from entertainment and popular media – as is amply demonstrated by the children in Bombay – is constricted in this case by the limited range of content viewed. The lack of anything related to their local life, to education or to childhood and the experience of children, whether in other settings (as may be seen in Hindi films) or from similar backgrounds to themselves, is deeply problematic, in circumstances where most houses now do have access to television but not all the children have access to secondary and higher education.

Palakkad: Language, Learning and Leisure

This focus group consists of four boys and four girls aged between 11 and 14. These children are from a rural area, and are studying in 7th to 10th grades in a small Kerala town. They volunteered for the focus groups because of their interest in and access to television, with a variety of channels watched such as Sun TV (Tamil), Sun Music (Tamil), Kairali TV (Malayalam), Doordarshan, Animal Planet, Star Movies, Star Utsav (Hindi), HBO, Pogo, Cartoon Network, Star Cricket, Surya (Malayalam) and Asianet (Malayalam). To put their viewing in context, most of the other children in the classes attended by these children do not have access to television in their homes and are, in fact, from such impoverished families that even radio, the primary medium available to them, is sometimes absent and the mid-day meal provided by the school is the incentive that persuades their parents to send them to the school on a regular basis for part of the year. Most of the children in this cohort hail from labouring families, and many themselves contribute to the (incredibly small) household incomes via their labour, both in the fields and as domestic servants or carers.

Parental feelings about television viewing here tended to concentrate on it in a binary manner – Malayalam content, which is generally permissible and may be watched with elders, and 'other language content', which is described primarily as a waste of time and potentially by a small number of parents as a corrupting influence. Internationally, there exists a vast literature on children, parents and television, and on parental regulation of children's television viewing, within which this discussion might usefully be located given the time. Buckingham (1993, 107–109) discusses some of the findings from previous research into parental attitudes vis-à-vis their children's viewing habits. He notes that in some instances there are gaps between what parents say they do to regulate their children's viewing the accounts given by children. There are also often notable discrepancies between the rational arguments for or against viewing given by parents to middle-class academic interviewers and their own actual practices (and possibly feelings) with regard to television. Susan Grieshaber (1989) has suggested that 'the discourse surrounding children's viewing of television is part of a much broader range of discourses which are used to normalize and regulate parenting' (in Buckingham 1993, 109). These discourses are inflected by class, location and culture (Rydin 2003, Sjoberg 2003), all of which are key features in this study, and by the homogeneity or heterogeneity of the local cultural contexts in which the children and parents reside. The children in Palakkad appear to circumvent the proscription of viewing in other languages either by going to watch out of their parents' sight (which is not so difficult given that parents are often engaged in manual labour for upto fourteen hours per day) or by stressing the educative potentials of the medium, where parents are understood as being open to such rhetorics. Language, however, is the distinguishing feature of generational viewing, in that the children are willing to watch and attracted by a diversity of languages including Hindi, English and Tamil.

> **Anju, 14:** I watch Tamil and Hindi television mostly with my brother. Mother and father also join us if we are watching Malayalam.
> **Vijay, 12:** My parents watch only Malayalam programs. But I enjoy many programs in English and Hindi. We all sit together and watch Malayalam films and other programs. They don't allow me to watch Hindi or Tamil film songs as they say the scenes are often not suitable for children. But I insist on watching if the songs are really good! I'm not bothered about what's shown in the scenes, I enjoy the music.
> **Interviewer:** How do your parents react to that?
> **Vijay, 12:** When I was little they used to scold me for switching on such programs. Most of the new songs in Hindi and Tamil have vulgarly dressed actors and bad scenes. I switch off the TV if it's really bad, otherwise watch. But when I have to watch other language movies, like in Hindi or English, I go to my uncle's house. I like watching Hindi movies. [...] I learn... a lot of Hindi words and usages from that.

'ADVERTS MAKE ME WANT TO BREAK THE TELEVISION'   63

> **Interviewer:** Why do you go around to all your relatives' houses to watch TV, when you have the facility at home?
> **Vijay, 12:** My parents don't watch TV much. They scold me. They don't understand English or Hindi, nor can they enjoy the programs that I enjoy. I enjoy watching quiz programs, and animated movies. But they are not interested, so I go to other houses to watch them.
> **Bindu, 13:** I watch TV mostly with my younger sister. My whole family sits together at night to see programs. [Adults] will leave the place if we are watching Hindi programs. Otherwise they would sit in front of the TV and talk and talk and I won't be able to hear anything! I like to enjoy the Hindi programmes by myself and to learn from them about life. My family feels that I am learning the language, so they do not scold.

Two striking themes in this exchange are the complexity of learning and its embeddedness in leisure viewing – 'learning about life' is seen as an appropriate reason for viewing Hindi films, but learning the language is the reason acceptable to parents. Clearly pleasures are not acceptable reasons for leisure viewing in non-vernacular languages. The second is the lack of a peer culture in this setting for discussing and commenting on the programmes. Because so many of the children in the school do not have access to television at all, and because the few who do tend to watch quite different programmes in a variety of languages often not understood by everyone, television viewing for these children is quite a private and almost secret activity, sometimes but not always shared with a sibling.

The theme of getting embarrassed or becoming uncomfortable was picked up from their initial responses to questions about what programmes they liked to watch and stated explicitly by the researcher. This was done with a view to understanding how these working-class Malayali children perceived their own development in relation to the pedagogic potential of television and the social context of family life. Interestingly, gender does not seem to play an enormous role in differentiating either parental expectations or children's responses at this stage as both the boys and girls respond in the same ways.

> **Interviewer:** Have you ever felt uncomfortable due to something that you watched on television?
> **Chirag, 13:** Very often, when I am sitting with my parents and watching some film song, I feel very embarrassed when the scene changes to *vulgarity*. Many advertisements make me feel the same way. [...] I leave the room. Or my parents soon switch off the Television.
> **Leela, 11:** Many film scenes and dressings of heroines make me feel embarrassed to sit and watch. I leave the room if my parents are present.

Vijaya, 12: I too feel uncomfortable watching poorly dressed women in films and advertisements. I either change the channel or leave the room.
Dipu, 13: I would change the channel.
Vijay, 12: At times while watching some really educative program, like a program on AIDS – suddenly they show images of how the disease spreads, I feel very uncomfortable sitting there and watching with parents though it's very informative.
Anju, 14: Vulgar scenes in movies and some advertisements make me feel uncomfortable. I leave the room when it happens. [*Becoming shy*] We are not supposed to see such things.
Interviewer: Why?
Vijaya, 12: What would my parents think if they see me watching that? On my own – I could continue to watch.
Vijay, 12: They would not like us to watch. They are responsible for our upbringing. We might want to know more. But they think they know what we should not know.

The children's reactions in the early part of this segment are clearly as much to their parents' presence at the time of viewing as to the content of the programmes they describe. Something about the combination of the two in these circumstances produces intense discomfort and, sometimes, outright censorship on the part of parents who switch off the set or self-censorship on the part of the children who change the channel or leave the room. Here, like many of the UK children in Buckingham and Bragg's study *Young People, Sex and the Media* (2004, 70), there is an 'ideological dilemma' (Billig et al. 1988) evident: although these children wish to support their parents' decisions about what they can and cannot watch, and are themselves embarrassed to go on viewing anything with vague references to sex while in parental company, they also experience a growing wish to find out more, and to participate in viewing that is slightly transgressive. In fact, both children and parents in this village setting appear to be negotiating this ideological dilemma as suggested in the discussion of parental regulation of children's viewing in the previous section. This leads Vijay, a 12 year old boy, to watch programmes he feels might draw parental censure only when he visits relatives homes and can watch unobserved, but not at his own house, despite the presence there of a television. It also leads some of the others to leave the room when their parents happen to be present and scenes depicting the body, sexuality or romance of any kind appear in televised advertisements, programmes or films. This disavowing behaviour occurs partly to convince parents that children have no desire to view such sequences and can be trusted alone with the television and partly because the discomfort of communal viewing in such cases causes too much embarrassment.

Awareness that some of the 12 and 13-year-old girls are only a few years away from their marriages to much older men[6] must, however, cause their responses to be read within a different frame from those of the children in Bombay. Given the lack of sex education in their formal schooling, the taboo on speaking seriously about this subject with or in front of adults, the absence of books on the subject and lack of internet within the community, their situation is clearly one in which the only knowledge gleaned with regard to sex and sexuality is likely to come randomly from older peers, television or occasional magazines. If this too is still censored by parents or self-censored because of embarrassment on their part, one implication is that some children might be more endangered by the lack of access to a variety of media and particularly the lack of sensitive representations of sex and sexuality than they would be by unsupervised access. This is clearly a claim that would be hotly disputed by those who are concerned primarily about what they see as the deleterious effects of media representations of sex on young people. However, I maintain, contexts of viewing can make all the difference. In India, and particularly in families and locales where girls and young people are 'married' in adolescence or sent to work alongside adults, the 'harmful' effects that might be thought to ensue from media viewing of films and programmes for adults need to be balanced against the dangers of uneducated, unsafe and/or non-consensual sexual encounters at an early age and an overall lack of autonomy and leisure.

Lessons for Research and Pedagogy

Participating in the adult world in many ways – for instance through their domestic and agricultural labour; the proximity of marriage for some of the girls; and by growing literacy and language skills which will help the family in official situations – most of the school-aged children in Palakkad and in Barsu are not expected to enjoy leisure time media unless it is viewed alongside adults. At least in Palakkad, they therefore have to resort to subterfuge – or to fake or even real pedagogic justifications – in order to gain any privacy in which to engage pleasurably with television. Clearly, simply having dedicated children's channels in local languages will not ease this tension for such children, although it might help younger members of their families.

The children in Palakkad are evidently keen to experience aspects of India that are not completely linked to the local context of Malayalam channels that their families might be able to watch and respond to. They use the notion of learning other languages – English, Tamil, Hindi – to access programmes and formats not available in the vernacular and this again begins to separate them from the older members of their families, while making them feel more connected to the rest of India and giving them skills that might serve them well outside the local context of daily poverty and unskilled labour that they inhabit. Additionally, in the case of the children in Barsu, regional politics in broadcasting means that representations of their own lives, language and concerns on television do not exist. These children are triply absent from the televised public sphere either fictional or non-fictional: because of their location, because of their status as children and because of their class.

In other locales and contexts – for instance the lower-middle class families in Bombay – childhood is treated as a distinct phase by parents, and children are apprentice citizens, whose duty it is to become highly educated in order to fulfil the supposed demands of adult life – marriage, supporting parents and financial independence. The children in these households are used, in most cases, to more freedom within the home than their peers in other settings: and outside, they actually get to go to the cinema and enjoy unsupervised viewing. However, they are also seen to be in need of greater protection and supervision – from 'outside' influences, from 'bad' peers, from the media – particularly television, as well as from their own 'laziness' and media viewing which is understood by parents and many teachers to be a direct challenge to education and educational opportunity. The concept of leisure time for children, while acknowledged by adults with a certain level of income, is not popular or encouraged. However, because many parents work outside the home and do not actually have the time to preside over every aspect of their children's daily life in such lower-middleclass city settings, many of these children have the most diverse media environment across the country and make use of the internet, dvds, vcds and satellite television to access, enjoy and discuss a wide range of commercial media formats produced both in India and other countries and aimed both at children and adults.

But what do the foregoing case-studies teach us about the linkages between class, locale and children as a media public in India? Connecting the three cases, the issue of 'child labour' looms large in the sense that almost none of the children lives what would be considered to be a 'typical' western childhood[7]: the lower-middleclass city girls care for babies and younger children alone for significant periods of each day and also have heavy study schedules in preparation for their entry into a twentyfirst century labour market. The village children in the mountains and in the small southern town labour in the fields, looking after livestock, carrying loads and doing domestic work in addition to school work. Class and location are evidently issues both in relation to the types of media technologies and texts at their disposal – from mobile phones and broadband in one setting to radio or television in the others – making generalisations about developmental stages in the use of technologies and in meaning-making quite misleading. In Bombay, children as young as four are going to the cinema regularly and wielding the remote control or taking photographs on their parents' mobile phones. In Palakkad and Barsu, most of the children have never been to the cinema let alone sat unsupervised at a computer connected to the internet.

In some cases, calls for censorship of children's media use precede even the advent of technology to a community; and discussions of the negative pedagogic and social implications of so many Indian children's lack of access to a range of leisure media and to media education are rare indeed. This final section explores some possible ways of theorising children's media viewing and the public sphere in a country encompassing widely differing political and social contexts of childhood.

Conclusion: Indian Children, Media and the Public Sphere

In the opening sections of her argument that the 'invention of children as consumers brought down the walls between childhood and adulthood' (2005, 163) in many countries and particularly in rhetorical constructions of childhood, Jyotsna Kapur directs us to consider two peculiarities of children's predicament. First, because of their physical vulnerability in a society marked by inequality, '[i]n spite of the aggressive corporate move to construct children as autonomous sovereign consumers, children are the most likely to be exploited in the market and susceptible to violence in the family' (ibid., 42). And second, one of 'history's dialectics' as she puts it, 'childhood, itself an invention of modernity, [is often] also imagined as its antidote, as an unchanging state that exist[s] outside time, as if in another country entirely' (ibid., 45). Kapur points to a dialectical relationship between childhood and adulthood, mediated by various aspects of capitalist society such as consumer practices, the family and the media. The case-studies in this chapter strongly support this view, further suggesting that the rhetorical constructions of childhood as a period of vulnerability and innocence might serve some children well in some contexts if applied to aspects of their lives, while harming and stifling others if applied to areas in which they might conceivably display independence and autonomy.

In the collection *Studies in Modern Childhood*, the editor, Jens Qvortrup writes about the 'Varieties of Childhood' (2005, 1–20). This discussion moves historically from assorted modern calls for 'child-free zones' in European public spaces backwards to the Arièsian vision of children's representation in medieval and post-medieval society, where children were present physically but childhood was not acknowledged (Ariès 1962, 398 in Qvortrup, 2005, 2). It situates the present reification of childhood in some parts of Western society by tracing the origins and symbolic significance of the idea. In this view, lacking cohesion as a conceptual category or group in medieval society, children were part of public life – but *not as children*. Rather, their presence and participation in that society as part of a labour force signified the invisibility of childhood. Reflecting on the interesting historical change that has taken place in many cultures with regard to children's presence in the public sphere, Qvortrup writes, 'children in modern society basically belong to the private family which is portrayed as a "Haven in a Heartless world"... . In this sense children have historically experienced a movement from visibility – as small adults in open local communities – to invisibility in public spaces in a modernity which is characterised by much more freedom and democracy and in this sense, openness' (2005, 2). Thus, as he explains, somewhere between the individualising modernity of the call for 'child-free' public spaces and the 'pre-modern' non-existence of childhood, the notion of the 'child' came to prominence and a variety of disciplines openly dedicated themselves to the study of children. Though the child now gained far more prominence in some ways than in the pre-modern social circumstances outlined and 'the much larger likelihood for survival increased the attention to and protection of the child', who was seen as increasingly vulnerable, paradoxically, apparently, 'children were denied the kind, amount and scope of participation that they were previously granted' (2005, 3). In Qvortrup's analysis, changing modes of production further reduced the need for children as a small adult workforce, and they were increasingly confined to a private sphere of family (as possessions or an investment for the future to be nurtured) and school, where their 'labour' as learners was demanded, sometimes vehemently, but with no tangible or (financial) rewards.

Though described in a particularly stark way that strips it of the softening rhetoric about caring and protection, this complex situation described above will be familiar from various accounts of middleclass family life even in urban areas in places like India. But it needs to be pushed to its logical conclusion to give a sense of what many Indian children experience on a daily basis: what effects did the new discourses of 'protection' and 'vulnerability' have on children's lives? The link between acknowledging children's vulnerability and exercising authority in supposed efforts to protect them has been made on various occasions in this chapter – in Palakkad the censorship of material about sexuality and relationships on television; in Bombay the discourse of 'laziness' which castigates media use – by the things children discuss in relation to school, family, work and television viewing.

In India, contexts (including amongst the children interviewed here) exist where below-minimum wage child labour is the norm, children contribute their labour or even their bodies to 'family' upkeep without remuneration and without any say in the family's future. This makes assertions about their 'participation' in the public sphere *via their labour* highly dubious. Child labour and child marriage do not equal 'participation' or guarantee any autonomy. Likewise, in India the rhetorics of 'protection' and 'education' are often linked, in practice, to increasing control over children's leisure. In this sense, the children whose parents cannot be present to 'protect' them at all times, speak with and display the greatest sense of their own autonomy and efficacy.

Just as there are discourses locating children in a matrix of arguments about (economic) development and (cultural) authenticity, Olsen (2003) notes that research related to children frequently positions them as always and only 'developing through ages and stages' (2003, 19), in the process of being socialised, never quite fully formed. He argues, 'this developing child discourse tends to treat children's use of the media as a learning process in which children gradually gain experience and competence according to their age' (2003, 19). The case studies in this chapter, which have shown a variety of 10–14 year old children in India in very different geographic and economic circumstances discussing their media and leisure pursuits, casts further doubt on the strongly psychological developmentalist position that Olsen critiques. Instead, the situation in India, as discussed in this chapter, suggests that children and childhood do not inhabit a single recognizable social context that can be theorised using a single psychosocial frame. In some locales and circumstances children still exist in conditions little different from those in medieval Europe, and 'childhood' itself does not seem to be particularly relevant either as a phase or as an ideology. Here children work, are married, contribute to household income through their labour appear in the 'public sphere' in this context. However, they have no control over what they do or do not get to learn at school and are allowed virtually no 'participation' in the public sphere in which they appear. Access to media is limited by class status but, where it exists, forms one of the only areas in which children can attempt to exercise autonomy.

The strength of the children's feelings about the kinds of things they can learn from unfettered access to television and the internet is undeniable. However, currently, parents are not trusted to understand or explain much of what is viewed, and in many cases are completely removed from the sphere of what their children are viewing. Thus a number of Indian parents, whose concerns are frequently completely genuine, often both critique media use unjustly and miss the most problematic aspects of the texts available to their children. Seeing oneself and one's contexts and concerns represented is by no means straightforward, or an end in itself. Nevertheless as theorist bell hooks reminds us in her study of black women viewers talking back to Hollywood (hooks 1999) being absent, excised from or misrepresented in media texts can also have profound and damaging consequences. While the testimony of the child audiences in this chapter make the dual case for dedicated, regional and vernacular children's channels and for media education in India all the more pressing, the absence, nationally and internationally, of plausible representations of real Indian children and their diverse life circumstances is an issue that can and should be addressed even without legislation by media producers across the globe.

Notes

1 The data in Barsu was gathered by Dr. Leena Kumarappan, a trained teacher and researcher.
2 The data in Palakkad was gathered by Chitra Kumarappan, a trained teacher and local resident liked by the children.
3 I am grateful to David Buckingham for encouraging me to pursue this project and for his careful critique of the first draft of this chapter; I owe thanks also to Rashmi Sawhney for reading and commenting on the final version, and for confirming my insights.
4 The complexity of multi-sited research in India is much increased by the vast number of languages and dialects spoken – according to the 2001 Census, 29 languages are spoken by more than a million native speakers in India while there are over a hundred languages and dialects spoken by under a hundred thousand.
5 The story of four young girls who come together to form a band 'against all odds'.
6 The researcher in Kerala has noted that while official statistics across the state for child marriage are lower than those country-wide, many of her female students – the classmates of those interviewed in the focus groups – leave school (unwillingly) at the age of fourteen or fifteen to be married off. NGOs and Human Rights organisations continue to protest against the practice with little support from government. http://infochangeindia.org/20070201244/Children/Features/CSOs-demand-a-more-comprehensive-child-marriage-bill.html (accessed 8 March 2009).
7 If indeed there is such a thing.

References

Arora, P. (2007) 'The ICT laboratory: Analysis of computers in public high schools in rural India' in *AACE Journal*, Volume 15, Issue 1: 57–72
Bajoria, J. (2004) 'Disney launches India TV channels', Friday 17 December 2004, available at http://news.bbc.co.uk/1/hi/world/south_asia/4104089.stm, (accessed 7 April 2009)
Banaji, S. (2006) *Reading 'Bollywood': The Young Audience and Hindi Film*, Basingstoke: Plagrave-Macmillan
Banaji, S. and Al-Ghabban, A. (2006) '"Neutrality comes from inside us": Indian and British-Asian Perspectives on Television News "After September 11"' in *Journal of Ethnic and Migration Studies* June 2006, Volume 32. Issue 3: 1005–1026
Behl, N. (ed.) (1988) 'Equalizing status: Television and Tradition in an Indian Village' in *World Families Watch Television* (ed.) James Lull, Newbury Park/Beverly Hills/London/New Delhi: Sage, 136–157
Billig, M., Condor, S., Edwards, D., Gane, M., Middleton, D., Radley, A.R. (1988) *Ideological Dilemmas*, London: Sage Publications
'Biskut Badshah? For Millions of Indian Children, That Means "Cookie Monster"' interview with Rosenfeld, creator of *Sesame Street* and the Indian version, 'Galli, galli, sim, sim' January 10, 2008 in India Knowledge@Wharton online at http://knowledge.wharton.upenn.edu/india/article.cfm?articleid=4249 (accessed 7 September 2008)
Buckingham, D. (1993) 'Boy's Talk: Television and the Policing of Masculinity' in Buckingham, D. (ed.) *Reading Audiences: Young People and the Media*, Manchester: Manchester University Press, 89–115
―――. Buckingham, D. (1993b) *Children Talking Television: the Making of Television Literacy*, London, UK and Bristol PA USA: The Falmer Press

———. & Bragg, S. (2004) *Young People, Sex, and the Media: The Facts of Life?* Basingstoke: Palgrave Macmillan

Cardoza, K. (2002) 'Parental control over children's television viewing in India', in *Contemporary South Asia*, Volume 11, Issue 2: 135–161

Dugger, C. (2000) 'India's Unwired Villages Mired in the Distant Past', *The New York Times*, Technology section, March 19th 2000, online at http://query.nytimes.com/gst/full page.html?res=9C0CEEDC133AF93AA25750C0A9669C8B63 (accessed 7 March 2009)

Gillespie, M. (1993) 'The *Mahabharata*: from Sanskrit to sacred soap. A case study of the reception of two contemporary televisual versions' in Buckingham, D. (ed) *Reading Audiences: Young People and the Media*, Manchester: Manchester University Press: 48–73

Grieshaber, S. (1989) 'A Pilot Study of Areas of Parent and Child Conflict', Paper presented at the *International Conference on Early Education and Development*, Hong Kong, July 31–August 4, 1989

hooks, b. (1999) 'The Oppositional Gaze: Black Female Spectators' in *Black Looks: Race and Representation*, London: Turnaround: 115–131

Jensen, R. and Oster, E. (2007) 'The Power of TV: Cable Television and Women's Status in India', NBER Working Paper No. 13305, Issued in August 2007, available at http://www.nber.org/papers/w13305, 1–53. (Last accessed 7 March 2009)

Johnson, K. (2001) 'Media and social change: the modernizing influences of television in rural India' *Media, Culture & Society* 2001, Volume 23: 147–169

Joseph, A. (2005) 'Where have all the children gone? in *India Together*, 8 August 2005, online at http://www.indiatogether.org/2005/aug/ajo-children.htm (accessed 7 September 2008) NP

Kapur, J. (2005) *Coining for Capital: Movies, Marketing and the Transformation of Childhood*, New Jersey/New Brunswick/London: Reuters University Press

Kaufmann, K. S. (1994) 'The Insider/Outsider Dilemma: Field Experience of a White Researcher "Getting In" A Poor Black Community' *Nursing Research*. Volume 43, No. 3:179–183, May/June 1994

Kaur, P. and Singh, R. (2006) 'Children in family purchase decision making in India and the West: a review' *Academy of Marketing Science Review*, Volume 2006, No. 8: 1–31

Mitra S. and Rana, V. (2001) 'Children and the Internet: experiments with minimally invasive education in India' in the *British Journal of Educational Technology* Volume 32, No 2: 221–232

N. Bhaskara Rao (2005) 'Wither Children's Television in India?', *The Tribune*, online edition, Chandigarh, Sunday, 26 June 2005, at http://www.tribuneindia.com/2005/20050626/edit.htm#5 (accessed 7 September 2008)

Noorani, H. (1978) 'Children and Television in India' in *Phaedrus*, Spring 1978, Volume 5, Issue 1: 34–36

Olsen, J. (2003) 'Why do we study children's media use the way we do?: Discussions on Methodological Reflexivity' in Rydin, I (ed.) (2003) *Media Fascinations: Perspectives on Young People's Meaning Making*, Goteborg University Press: Nordicom, 15–29

Qvortrup, J. (2005) 'Varieties of Childhood' in Qvortrup, J. (ed.) *Studies in Modern Childhood: Society Agency Culture*, Basingstoke: Palgrave Macmillan, 1–20

Rydin, I. (ed) (2003) *Media Fascinations: Perspectives on Young People's Meaning Making*, Goteborg University Press: Nordicom

Seghal, R. (2007) 'CEOs demand more comprehensive child marriage bill', Infochange India, February 2007, http://infochangeindia.org/20070201244/Children/Features/

CSOs-demand-a-more-comprehensive-child-marriage-bill.html (accessed 25th November 2008)

Sjoberg, U. (2003) 'Making Sense of Screen-based Media: The Uses and Readings of Television, Computer Games and the Internet among Swedish Young People' in Rydin I. (ed.) (2003) *Media Fascinations: Perspectives on Young People's Meaning Making*, Goteborg University Press: Nordicom, pp. 147–164

'Turner launches new TV channel for children', *The Times of India* online edition, 25 Nov 2003, at http://timesofindia.indiatimes.com/articleshow/301748.cms, (accessed 7 September 2008)

Unnikrishnan, N. and Bajpai, S. (1996) *The Impact of Television Advertising on Children*, Thousand Oaks, CA: SAGE

Varghese, T. M. (2008) 'Role of TV in increasing Violence among Children' in E-Magazine of the NGO SHARP, *School Health in India*, Volume X, July–September 2008, available at http://www.schoolindia.org/article/violence_x.htm, (accessed 7 September 2008)

Wong, D. E. (1995) 'Challenges Confronting the Researcher/Teacher: Conflicts of Purpose and Conduct' *Educational Researcher*, Volume 24, Issue 3: 22–28

Yadava, J. S. and Reddi, U. (1988) 'In the Midst of Diversity: Television in Urban Indian Homes' in (ed.) James Lull, *World Families Watch Television*, Newbury Park/Beverly Hills/London/New Delhi: Sage, 116–135

Chapter Four

URDU FOR IMAGE: UNDERSTANDING BANGLADESHI CINEMA THROUGH ITS THEATRES

Lotte Hoek

Introduction

'*Tasveer* is an Urdu word,' said Aziz, the assistant manager at Tosbir Mohol cinema hall. He explained the unfamiliar word that gave the theatre its name: *Tosbir Mohol*, or Picture Palace. It was written in bold Bengali letters, transliterating the *tasveer* to *tosbir*, over the entrance of the small cinema hall in Jessore. I had traveled to the district town to witness the screening of a Bangladeshi action film. I had been studying the production and consumption of this film, that I call *Mintu the Murderer*, for nearly a year. After many months of production, it was during Eid 2005 that the film was finally released. One of the theatres in which it opened was Tosbir Mohol in Jessore. For two weeks, *Mintu the Murderer* competed there with the offerings at the four rival Jessore cinema halls: Chitra, Nirala, Monihar, and Manushi.

In this chapter I will give an account of contemporary Bangladeshi cinema written from the perspective of the cinema halls in a single Bangladeshi city. Film studies throughout South Asia is generally deeply committed to textual studies (Raju 2006; Gazdar 1997; Gopalan 2002), so much so that the question of representation comes to overshadow questions of audience and the contexts of production and consumption (Hughes 2003). In this chapter, I approach contemporary Bangladeshi cinema through the theatres of Jessore. Ethnographic data from these halls yields new insights about contemporary Bangladeshi cinema. I argue, firstly, that the built space of the cinema (Larkin 2008) memorises the history of cinema in Jessore in a manner that is different from common views of Bangladeshi film history. My account illustrates historical continuities where radical rupture is often imagined, and highlights the links between transformations in public life and visual culture. Secondly, I suggest that common assumptions about the decline of contemporary Bangladeshi cinema need to be rethought on the basis of empirical evidence from the cinema halls at a distance from Dhaka. To argue these points, I narrate several research experiences in Jessore in November 2005.

Tosbir Mohol – B. Sirkar Memorial Hall, circa 1927

Mintu the Murderer had been simultaneously released in twenty different cinema halls in regional capitals spread across the country. Released on the occasion of Eid-ul-Fitr, the film had not premiered in any of the Dhaka cinema halls. The film aimed for a *mofussil* audience, the core constituency of the contemporary Bangladesh film industry. *Mintu the Murderer* opened in places such as Feni, Satkhira and Jessore. The small town audiences came out in strong numbers to see this cheaply produced action movie. While Dhaka-based critics and film buffs lamented the decline of the film industry, in the *mofussil*, *Mintu the Murderer* did brisk business. The film belied the dark predictions of scholars of Bangladeshi cinema who consider the industry to be in crisis (Nasreen and Haq 2008). In the south-west of Bangladesh, the town of Jessore counts just over one million inhabitants spread over 25 square kilometers and has five cinema halls. Jessore municipality was established in 1864. Tosbir Mohol is its oldest cinema hall and it was here that *Mintu the Murderer* opened. The hall's outward appearance belied its age. The theatre consists of a cement building with a tin roof, a newer section containing two offices built to its side. Along its boundary walls, small shops sell tea and snacks.

Inside the courtyard, during one of my visits, an elderly man wearing a faded lungi sat on a wooden bench. In his hand he held a stack of plastic chips, each of which was numbered. 'I look after the bicycles, four Taka per bike,' he said by way of introduction. Behind him bicycles were tightly stacked together, many of them decorated with pictures of Bangladeshi film actresses. Motioning me to sit down, he disappeared up a flight of steps. He returned with a young man wearing a shirt and pants.

The young man needed no invitation for conversation. 'Aziz', he offered unprompted, 'my brother-in-law owns the cinema hall. I've been working here as his assistant for about three years.' He talked about the cinema hall and his job. He preferred the work at the cinema hall to the work he used to do in a construction company. 'This is much more relaxed', he explained, 'I can go home for lunch in the afternoons.' As he spoke about the pleasures of his job, the 12:30 pm show ended. Spectators streamed into the small courtyard, momentarily setting the tranquil quad aflutter with activity. 'Come,' said Aziz, 'I'll show you something.'

We entered the empty cinema hall. 'Turn up the light', Aziz shouted. Above the balcony shrouded in darkness, a light bulb shone through a small window. Behind the window the projectionist responded to Aziz. As the lights came on, the dusty cinema hall came into relief. The floor sloped up towards the back. At the front, wooden benches were set before a low wooden fence. The seats had seen better days and the bare concrete of the walls added to the general sense of dilapidation. The theatre's most peculiar feature were the delicate wooden pillars which carried the balcony, on which another few rows of seats were placed. 'See this', said Aziz. He pushed aside a heavy curtain that framed the screen. Hidden beneath the thick black fabric was a white marble plaque, inscribed with black English letters. It commemorated the opening of the hall in 1927 as the B. Sirkar Memorial Hall. The white marble plaque read:

Erected in memory of
Babu Bisveswar Sirkar
Of
Jatrapur (Jessore)
By
Messrs. B. Sirkar and Sons
'Guinea House'
Calcutta.
1927

'In the English time this was a theatre and a library', explained Aziz. 'B. Sirkar was a big Hindu *zamindar* in that time.' I looked around again. The hall was indeed a theatre. The stage was still intact, now providing a space for the screen. The design of the slim pillars and the trellis along the balcony did seem anachronistic and out of place in the cement shell of the theatre. The time of the wealthy Hindu *zamindars* of colonial East Bengal and its theatre performances lay buried deep inside Tosbir Mohol.

Brian Larkin has argued of Nigerian cinema halls that "[e]ncoded in the physical space of the theater, in the dirty bricks and broken lights, and in the walls that divide the arena, are traces of history of colonial rule and colonial urbanism' (2008, 145). Larkin suggests that the infrastructure of the cinema shapes the social practices within it. Similarly, Stephen Hughes has suggested that government practices of cinema regulation have been formative of exhibition practices and the experience in the cinema halls in early twentieth century Tamil Nadu (2000). As in India, the Cinematograph Act of 1918 provides the basis for contemporary Bangladeshi cinema legislation. Much of this act remains un-amended in the present-day Cinematograph Act in Bangladesh. Seemingly insignificant practices in the cinema halls, such as the peculiar practice of snack vendors banging glass bottles of soft drinks together in the theatres, creating a piercing noise, can be traced back to article 12 of the Cinematograph act which states 'No shouting for Howking/Sale' (*sic.*, Government of Bangladesh, undated). Possibly instituted to craft an ideal silent auditorium, article 12 might have had unforeseen consequences. In a variety of ways, the colonial era continues to shape the context of Bangladeshi cinema exhibition. While standard histories of Bangladeshi cinema tend to skip over colonial times as a formative period in Bangladeshi cinema (Hayat 1987), in the everyday practice of film exhibition and consumption this continuity is more palpable.

Those colonial roots need to be teased out as they are not immediately visible in the landscape of Bangladeshi *mofussil* towns. Architecturally, little remains of the colonial times in the rural hinterland of the colonial capital Kolkata. Dhaka itself only has the faintest of colonial remains, located mainly within the university area and surrounding churches. Partly, this is due to the city planning and building (Ashraf 1989). Older remains disappear under newer manifestations. However, the minimal visual remnants of colonial times are also due to national narratives which frame Bangladesh through the events of its national independence rather than the century preceding it. The colonial and Pakistan era have been relegated beyond the significant formative moment of the Bangladeshi nation-state. Tosbir Mohol, however, carries within it explicit signs of the earlier history of cinema in Bangladesh. The name commemorates the significance of Urdu in Jessore before 1971. Its internal structure betrays the colonial past and whispers about former hierarchies of power in rural Bengal.

I asked Aziz how *Mintu the Murderer* was doing. 'On Eid business was good,' he said. The film's producer had recouped his investment within the first week of the screening of *Mintu the Murderer*. For Tosbir Mohol, which had been offered the film on a 'percentage basis', the income from *Mintu the Murderer* was only 40 percent of the money made off ticket sales. 'Now it has slowed down,' Aziz continued, 'The film doesn't really have a good storyline. But there were songs and dances, the audience was satisfied.' I asked why they chose *Mintu the Murderer*. 'On the basis of the title,' said Aziz, 'then we looked at the casting, whose film it was and whether it had action.' *Mintu the Murderer* had not done as well as it could have done. 'There was a lot of competition from *Jail Theke Bolchi*,' said Aziz about the film shown at rival cinema hall Monihar (see below). For the theatre it was necessary to gather in as many spectators as possible during the second week of Mintu's Eid run. Spectators for the 3:30 pm screening were finding a place to sit on the benches. *Mintu the Murderer* had drawn a modest audience. At the start of the screening, the balcony was almost empty while the floor seats housed a couple of dozen spectators. It was the last day of *Mintu the Murderer*'s screening in Jessore. We watched the screening and noticed that an extra song had been included amongst the reels.

The greatest selling point of Bangladeshi action movies is the inclusion of uncertified sexually suggestive as well as sexually explicit material among the reels of certified movies (Hoek 2006). They can be compared to American exploitation movies (Schaefer 1999). Film producers make short reels of such material during the production process of a film but do not submit this to the Bangladesh Board of Film Censors. This preemptive cutting gives the scenes their name: 'cut-pieces'. Such clips are spliced into a film when producers consider it necessary to make a film more attractive to audiences and when they have ensured that the conditions in a particular cinema hall are amenable.

At Jessore's Tosbir Mohol during my observation, a song performed by the actress Jenny was included among the reels. This song was not submitted to the Censor Board and therefore constituted illegal material. However, despite the song's slightly suggestive lyrics, 'come close, I have news for you', and Jenny's provocative postures, the audience at Tosbir Mohol seemed uninterested in Jenny's song. The Censor Board concerns itself greatly with the 'effects' uncensored material might have on its audiences, and newspapers feature many articles about the role of cut-pieces in the decay of the industry. This particular cut-piece, however, was not explicit and garnered little response. Jenny's flowing white costume revealed less than the shorts and cropped top worn by the Indian actress Rimi Sen in the choreography to the song 'Shikdum' of the Bollywood film *Dhoom* (Sanjay Gadhvi 2004), of which Jenny's song was a cover[1]. The song could everywhere be seen on television and the songwriters for *Mintu the Murderer* had cleverly adapted the song. While colonial India was buried deep inside the hall's architecture, on screen the proximity and dominance of contemporary India was undeniable.

Chitra – Bengal Talkies, 1952

Like Tosbir Mohol, the Chitra cinema hall dates from colonial times and its name means 'Picture'. While *tasveer* is Urdu for picture, *chitra* is its Bengali equivalent. The cinema hall has changed names many times since its opening in British times. The theatre's previous projectionist had still screened silent movies. In 1953, the year after the language movement (Van Schendel 2009, 109–115), the hall had been renamed 'Bengal Talkies'. But the talking movies of Chitra would hardly all have been in Bengali that year. In 1952, the year that student protests in Dhaka against making Urdu the state language of Pakistan were violently beaten down, six films were released in Pakistan. One of these was in Punjabi, the other five in Urdu (Gazdar 1997, 244). That year, Chitra screened mainly foreign movies, a fair number of which would have been Bengali talkies from Indian West-Bengal.

In 2005, as in Pakistan times, Chitra vied with the Nirala hall, two streets further down on Horinath Dotto Lane. Both halls were in the heart of Jessore town and dated back to a pre-partition era. Their histories are similar. 'The hall was owned by Hindus who left at Partition,' said the projectionist at Chitra, 'They exchanged their theatre.' Nirala was similarly swapped. According to the manager of Nirala, the cinema hall had been called Modhu Chokro then. 'They just placed an add in the newspaper,' he said, 'and exchanged it for a similar cinema hall on the other side.' Many theatres had changed hands in that manner at Partition. 'They weren't Bengalis,' said the elderly projectionist at Chitra, 'The new owners of Nirala screened mainly Urdu films.' The projectionist slowly led the way up the narrow stairs to the projection room of Chitra. Bengal Talkies, he underscored, had always been in Bengali hands. During the 1960s, both halls would have screened many Urdu films, from both East and West Pakistan, as well as Bengali and Hindi/Urdu films from India.

The infrastructure for filmmaking in East Pakistan was consolidated in the late 1950s. The East Pakistan Film Development Corporation (EPFDC) was set up by the Film Development Corporation Act of 1957 after a bill proposing a government backed film studio in East Pakistan was passed (Hayat 1987, 58). The 'Dacca Studio', or EPFDC, was set up by the provincial government to support the film industry in East Pakistan. It provided the first formal infrastructure for filmmaking in East Pakistan. Both Urdu and Bengali language features were made, and they competed in East and West Pakistan with Indian films in Hindi and Bengali. Only after the India-Pakistan war of 1965 was foreign cinema banned from the Pakistani cinema halls, in an attempt to keep out Indian cinema. Six years later, the war of 1971 resulted in the additional banning of Pakistani features from Bangladeshi halls.

This moment of national 'birth' has erased much of the pre-1971 past in the analysis of Bangladeshi cinema. Aziz from Tosbir Mohol gave a standard account of the pre-1971 cinema past. 'In 1950 it [Tosbir Mohol] was rented out to Iqbal Nonani the father of the present owner,' said Aziz, 'He named it 'Tosbir Mohol'.' I was then that I asked him what it meant. 'Tosbir means picture in Urdu,' he said, 'in those times it was mainly Indian films that were shown here, films in Urdu. Since 1971 it has been films made in Dhaka.' Such standard stories postulate a clean break at 1971. Even accounts that attempt to complicate the teleological narrative that leads effortlessly up to a thoroughly national Bangladeshi cinema, remain marred in sketching the Bengali films made in the 1950s and 1960s as the natural predecessors to Bangladeshi cinema. Both Alamgir Kabir (1979) and Zakir Hossain Raju (2001), among the most critical of commentators, refrain from discussing the plentiful popular Urdu features that were made in Dhaka during these decades. Similarly, the accounts of Pakistani cinema largely neglect the discussion of East Pakistani Bengali cinema. Mushtaq Gazdar, in his overview of Pakistani cinema, discusses at length only those features from East Pakistan that were in Urdu and notes that 'a number of significant Urdu ventures from Dhaka took the Lahore and Karachi based production houses by surprise' (1997, 104).

The production numbers for the 1960s show a more varied picture. Many filmmakers in East Pakistan directed films in Urdu as well as Bengali rather than exclusively shooting in a single language. Zahir Raihan's record illustrates this. In 1970 Raihan made his famous *Jibon Theke Neya* that indicted the dictatorship of Ayub Khan in 'the first filming expression to the rising tide of Bengali nationalism that became the living spirit behind the War of National Liberation less than a year later' (Kabir 1979, 45). The film barely escaped a government ban. In 1971 he made the documentary *Stop Genocide* (1971) together with Alamgir Kabir on behalf of the *Bangladesh Liberation Council of the Intelligentsia* and was active behind Mukti Bahini lines to rethink the shape of the film industry (Kabir 1979, 48–50). Before the year was out Zahir Raihan was dead, allegedly murdered as he searched for his brother who had disappeared, together with many prominent intellectuals, on the eve of Pakistan's surrender. Raihan's towering presence in Bangladeshi cinematic history is inflected by a staunchly nationalist rhetoric within everyday parlance in the film industry. The lab at the FDC in Dhaka is called the Zahir Raihan Laboratory and a marble plaque commemorates his life in film. However, during the 1960s, Zahir Raihan made six films, four of which were in Bengali and two in Urdu. The dividing lines between Bengali and Urdu in East Pakistan were not as clear as retrospectively suggested.

In 1970, the year before the independence war, prominent Bengali Pakistani actors and filmmakers were making films in Urdu at the 'Dacca Studio'. This is generally considered surprising, as Zakir Hossain Raju suggests: 'later in the 1960s both Khan and Dosani made Urdu films in the Dhaka studios, films which directly go against the essence of Bengali nationalism' (2001). In 1970 over 100 films were made in Pakistan. Gazdar counts 114 films released in Pakistan that year, of which 26 were made in East Pakistan. The records of the Bangladesh Film Producers Distributors Association (BFPDA), as well as Alamgir Kabir (1979), list 41 films produced and released from Dhaka[2]. Gazdar counts four films made from Dhaka in Urdu (1997, 266–9), Kabir counts only two (1979, 45). That year film director Mustafiz made three films, one in Urdu (*Payel*), one in Bengali (*Eki Angey Eto Rup*) and one mixed Bengali-Urdu (*Bablu*), all from the EPFDC. *Payel* featured Razzak and Shabana, two Bengali actors commonly associated with the 'golden age' of Bengali cinema. This mythical era is longingly referred to as the lost utopian period of 'good' Bengali cinema and retrospectively postulated as the time when films were 'healthy' and cinema halls 'clean'. As Syed Badrul Ahsan writes: 'Ask any movie buff. And the chances are that he will tell you that movies made in the 1960s and till the mid-1970s were perhaps the best that this nation has had to offer' (Ahsan 2005). The Urdu film *Payel* was made at the height of this period, with beloved Bengali actors of the era. Razzak and Shabana featured in both Bengali and Urdu films before 1971 and strictly Bengali films afterwards. Similarly, Mustafiz largely made Urdu features in the 1960s while from 1971 he directed only Bengali films. Judging from this, it can be concluded that the 1960s did not constitute the decade for the slow emergence and expansion of a Bengali artistic elite within the film industry who struggled against their Urdu speaking competitors. Rather, with the changing political climate Bengali directors and actors start to move slowly away from making Urdu cinema[3].

At the top of Chitra, a narrow room housed a single projector, angled down towards the auditorium that could hold 510 spectators. 'The projector is a Westrex, from Pakistan,' the projectionist explained, 'it's from 1965.' The year of the India-Pakistan war spelled the banning of Indian and other foreign films from the Pakistani cinema halls like Chitra. This did not apply to the equipment, however. 'The sound system is Indian,' said the projectionist, 'from Gunjan.' The Indian company Gunjan PA Systems made public address systems and its equipment amplified the Bangladeshi films that were screened at Chitra. The measures aimed to protect the Bangladeshi film industry from foreign competition had not included the reliance on foreign technology. The elderly projectionist at Chitra maintained the machinery himself. There was no money for replacement of the old and failing projector.

Despite the official protection for the cinema halls, piracy, satellite television and cheap technologies of reproduction have left the old cinema halls struggling. 'We make a loss every month,' the projectionist said, 'We are so much behind on pay that we didn't get an Eid release.' Rather than screen an expensive newly released film during Eid, Chitra had been forced to take on a film that had been released earlier and had been screening around the country for some time. Although Nirala had invested in an Eid release, it still did not manage to break even during the only time in the year that cinema halls across the country were 'house full'. 'We didn't make a profit on *Bandha*,' said Nirala's manager, 'we're four months behind on pay and make a loss of over a *lakh* per month.' The costs of the cinema hall's maintenance were countenanced by income from the owner's chicken farm. The protective measures from 1965 could no longer protect the film industry from foreign competition in the form of pirated DVDs. Yet it also denied cinema halls like Chitra the option of reverting to the pre-1965 practice of screening popular Indian films. While the Pakistani period is systematically erased from accounts of the Bangladeshi film industry, it is legislation dating from Pakistani times that appears to be hurting the theatre business today.

Monihar, 1986

The design of the Monihar cinema hall was worthy of the Bangladeshi James Bond, Masud Rana. The modernist architecture of the hall, with its abstract beige and ochre wall decorations and heavy wooden paneling, form the ideal backdrop to the adventures of the suave counterintelligence spy. Upon entering the cinema hall, visitors are faced by a large artwork in wooden relief. To the right is a fountain, its pool decorated with mosaic tiles. Around it, a ramp swerves up to the second floor in a majestic curve. Coloured lights illuminated the powerful beam of water as it reached up to the second floor, where heavy brown doors open into an auditorium that could hold 1430 spectators. The spacious landing was decorated with framed portraits of Bangladeshi film stars. Bright afternoon light decorates the walls with abstract coloured shapes as it shines through the stained glass windows. The counter opposite the auditorium doors sells snacks, books and magazines. The novels describing the adventures of Masud Rana, Bangladeshi spy extraordinaire, stand amidst Islamic romance novels, volumes of poetry by Kazi Nuzrul Islam and Rabindranath Tagore, film magazines as well as American Playboy.

'The opening film was *Johny*', said Mithu, owner of Monihar. He flipped through the pages of the photoalbum. *Johny* was the smash-hit action movie released in 1983 which consolidated the fame of actor Sohel Rana. The actor had become famous for debuting as the super-spy Masud Rana in the epynomous film adapted from the novels. 'Look,' Mithu says as he found the page, 'see all the women? All the seats were filled.' The black and white photograph was taken when the hall opened in 1986. Mithu pointed to the pictures of the building of the hall. They show paddy fields, amidst which the huge building was being erected. Today Monihar sits in the middle of town, and all the long-distance buses stop outside its gate, providing a steady stream of patrons. Hotels have sprung up around it. Jessore has enveloped the hall.

We entered a small but stylish apartment built on the top floor of the cinema hall. The beds were covered with plastic and sheets drape wooden furniture. 'Whenever we have a stage show, this is where the actors stay,' explained Mithu, 'everyone has slept in these beds!' He listed all the famous Bangladeshi film stars that have graced the hall with their presence over the years. I asked who had been there last. 'Riaz and Purnima,' said Mithu, 'when *Moner Majhe Tumi* opened here.' The stars had addressed the packed auditorium. On those occasions even the large Monihar was 'house full'. Subsequently, the film ('You're In My Heart', Motiur Rahman Panu 2003) had run for six consecutive weeks at Monihar. 'Only *Beder Meye Josna* ['Gypsy Girl Josna', T.H. Bakul 1989] did better,' recounts Mithu, 'it ran for ten weeks at steady profit.' Both were love stories that continued to be in circulation in Bangladesh in the beginning of the twenty-first century.

While the 1960s and 1970s are eulogized as the glorious era of Bangladeshi cinema, it was the 1980s that saw a feverish expansion of the Bangladeshi film industry. Production numbers shot up (from 47 in 1980 to 89 in 1989) and genres diversified. It was a decade of growth and prosperity for the cinema. Elaborate cinema halls built for massive capacity in a strikingly modernist style, such as Monihar, are architectural landmarks in many district towns of Bangladesh. These entertainment palaces were built to display the fast-paced action flicks that started to progressively replace the social movies of the previous decades. This transformation in the film industry (towards action genres and an expanding audience outside the big cities) coincided with major economic restructuring in Bangladesh. After the de-nationalisation of the economy in the late 1970s, the New Industrial Policy (NIP) of 1982 prioritised economic liberalization, export production and foreign aid (Feldman 2002, 229). New money entered the country and some of it found its way into the film industry. A new vision of progress translated itself into action movies. Middleclass drawing-rooms were progressively replaced by bars and foreign hotels in the films. Bangladesh cinema was now ready for Masud Rana, the sauve, worldy and high-tech spy trained by Bangladesh Counter-Intelligence. These signs of a new era of progress in the movies were paralleled by the design of the cinema halls that housed them, such as Monihar.

During my visit, I asked Mithu which film had done well recently at Monihar. He shook his head. Success is rare. '*Noya Mastan* did well,' he said, 'we made a good profit off that.' The film ('New Gangster', Opurbo-Rana 2005) is an action film associated with cut-pieces. It was a success throughout the country but had quickly run into trouble with the Censor Board. '*Jail Theke Bolchi* did alright,' said Mithu. They had picked the film ('Speaking from Jail', Malek Afsari 2005) as Monihar's Eid feature. Unlike the choices of Nirala, Tosbir Mohol and Chitra, this film was considered a 'healthy' (*sushthodhara*) movie. It was an action film featuring many of the B actors that populated films like *Mintu the Murderer*, but a crucial difference lay in its protagonist-producer, the superstar Bangladeshi film hero Manna. Unexpectedly deceased in 2008, the star had dominated early twenty-first century Bangladeshi cinema. He had become famous for a spate of action-packed angry-young-man flicks. Branching out into film production, *Jail Theke Bolchi* was his first attempt at acting and producing simultaneously. For Mithu it had been a good choice: 'We made almost sixty thousand Taka profit in the first week.'

Manna and his *Jail Theke Bolchchi* illustrate the transformed place of cinema in Bangladesh as effectively as the dried up fountain in the elaborate entry hall of Monihar. Manna's picture was not up on the walls nor did Mithu name him among the illustrious film personalities to have graced the private apartment on top of Monihar. Manna had steadily worked through the mid-1990s until he shot to fame in 1999 when he starred in Kazi Hayat's melodramatic action movie *Ammajan* ('The Mother', Kazi Hayat; see Raju 2006). He dominated Bangladeshi action cinema for almost a decade. His sudden death in 2008 shocked his substantial fanbase and brought an astonishing number of people onto the streets of Dhaka. In a perceptive article, Rumi Ahmed suggests that the national media expressed surprise at the spontaneous mobilisation of thousands of working class youth because of a 'collective failure to understand the pulse or even identify a big and energetic but vulnerable section of our society' (Ahmed 2008). Ahmed credits this unrecognised but large part of the young population for recent and seemingly spontaneous political movements in Bangladesh, such as the Phulbari protests against open pit coal mining in northern Bangladesh. Ahmed can only effectively name this large and amorphous part of the population by attaching the name of the film actor Manna to it. Calling them 'the Manna factor', Ahmed signals their distance from the political and cultural mainstream of Bangladeshi society (who largely ignore Bangladeshi cinema and its stars like Manna), as well as their massive numbers (who account for Manna's tremendous popularity and the continuing viability of Bangladeshi cinema). Rather than the *mofussil* middle class readership of the Masud Rana novels that populated the cinema halls in the 1980s, Monihar now was forced to cater to 'the Manna factor'. The actor Manna was the new film star, the inheritor of the stage shows, able to command a massive rural and semi-urban audience that constituted the main addressee of the twenty-first century Bangladeshi cinema. He was not celebrated as an actor in the way his predecessor Sohel Rana was, nor did he command the respect of the audience that populated the photographs of Monihar's opening shows. Even after his sudden death in 2008, it is Manna who embodies the condition of contemporary Bangladeshi cinema.

The struggling management of Monihar cinema hall let the fountain stand dry. It barely filled even parts of its massive auditorium by screening a film produced by, and starring, the action superstar it didn't acknowledge among its framed portraits. The modernist palace was crumbling. The soft tones of the abstract wall designs were further hushed by the loud colours of the film posters announcing upcoming attractions. The suave days of Masud Rana and elaborate stage shows had passed. Now it was the Manna factor that determined the fate of a cinema hall. Without Manna, Monihar would not have made a profit during Eid 2005.

Manushi, 2005

'They say Manna sent the journalists after *Mintu the Murderer*,' confided the usher at Manushi cinema hall. 'Manna knows that Shiplu's films always draw a massive audience. He tried to stop *Mintu the Murderer* from being released simultaneously with *Jail Theke Bolchi* because he was afraid his films wouldn't be able to handle the competition.' We walked up the stairs to the small office on the first floor. Both the entry hall and the first floor landing were empty, the walls bare. Only in one corner small film posters had been taped to the wall in a tidy row. Except for the doors to the auditorium, the entire building was whitewashed bricks and cement. To describe Manushi as sparsely decorated would be an understatement.

The usher led the way to a small office on the first floor where Manushi's manager sat with two colleagues. They corroborated the story. Manna had done his best to delay the release of *Mintu the Murderer* so that his own *Jail Theke Bolchi* had a better chance of big Eid box office profits. 'When he didn't succeed in delaying the release, he went even further.' My interlocutor leaned in closely as he asked me the rhetorical question: 'Why do you think journalists have been giving *Mintu the Murderer* so much attention?' Since the release of *Mintu the Murderer*, journalists of two major newspapers had written repeatedly about the 'obscenity' (*oshlilota*) of *Mintu the Murderer*. The journalists had indicted the film for containing uncertified scenes and illegal sexually explicit material. Eventually, these accusations would lead to the banning of *Mintu the Murderer* six weeks after its Eid 2005 release (Hoek forthcoming).

The manager of Manushi cinema hall could afford to speculate about the fate of the Eid releases in Jessore. The cinema hall on the outskirt of the town had not taken on a new film that Eid. In fact, the hall never showed first run movies, only second run. Such films had already screened in the main cities and towns before they started a second round at reduced rates. The austere building, without the embellishments of Monihar nor the historical resonances of Tosbir Mohol and Chitra, reflected the business sense of its managers. They kept investment low by relying on the tried and true recipe of second run action films, did not waste money on unnecessary luxuries such as decorative lighting or seating inside the theater lobby. There was not even a counter for snacks in the hall. It was a sober shell around a second hand film projector. Unlike the other cinema halls in Jessore, Manushi was making a profit.

The existence of Manushi cinema hall belies many common ideas about contemporary Bangladeshi cinema. Not only are most accounts tainted by a deep nostalgia, there is a general sense that the cinema halls are dying. Nasreen and Haq write that while many cinema halls are being torn down, 'it is said that in the past ten years no new cinema halls have opened' except for an expensive Dhaka Cineplex (2008, 155). However, Manushi opened in 2005 and it is likely not the only second run hall to have opened its doors in smaller towns around the country. I would argue that the reason why halls such as Manushi get overlooked by scholars and journalists is that they do not live up to the expectations these authors have of a 'proper' cinephiles' cinema hall. Nasreen and Haq write:

> Once upon a time, cinema halls were a quotidian companion. A social area. A regular meeting place. ... Those silver screens of the cinema halls are now ashen because 'glorious' cinema no longer plays on those screens. (2005, 154, my translation)

Manushi did not constitute a social area or regular meeting space. It had no soft sofas for pleasant chitchat or cold soft drinks in the interval. Its screen was neither ashen nor golden but in use five times a day. Nonetheless, it was not taken into consideration as a sign of the liveliness of contemporary Bangladeshi cinema.

The lament over lost golden screens coincides with a general despair over the apparent loss of artistry and vision within the industry (Ahsan 2005). It is part of a larger discursive field that laments the state of contemporary Bangladesh, expressed diversely in concerns over intractable political conflicts, the lack of mechanisms of power transfer, the widening disparity between rich and poor, and the anger over the apparent impunity with which war criminals and gangsters commit their crimes (see Mookherjee 2007). In terms of the cinema, a similar rhetoric laments a lost vision of progress and cultural self-sufficiency within the Bangladesh film industry. It sees only ashen screens and dilapidation.

How did Manushi manage in such dire times? Without hesitation the manager explained: 'Nowadays, Bengali film has taken over from English movies in providing pornography. People have seen the English ones; they're bored with that. Now the Bangla ones can provide something new and interesting. If it wasn't for the cut-pieces, people wouldn't come.' The vast majority of the films released in 2005 were B-quality action movies such as *Mintu the Murderer*. Only a limited budget would make it possible for the producer to recoup the investment. The audience was drawn neither by spectacular special effects nor by major stars. Instead, films like *Mintu the Murderer* drew crowds through their cut-pieces. I regard cut-pieces as a direct response to the spread of satellite television and film piracy that bypass the measures that had protected the film industry (Hoek 2006). In 2005, the films certain of a profit were cheaply produced action films that were rumoured to contain cut-pieces. It was no wonder that Manna had been concerned about the fate of his *Jail Theke Bolchi* when released simultaneously with *Mintu the Murderer*. The manager of Manushi laughed, with a little luck, he would be able to screen *Mintu the Murderer* in a year's time and make a profit of its second run.

Tosbir Mohol, 2005

Tosbir Mohol seemed transformed from the day before. The bicycle shed was completely filled. Stacked tightly together, images of famous Dhaka actresses peeped out between the pedals. Outside the gate a long row of rickshaws sat idle, waiting for the return of their drivers. My companion and I had returned to talk to the manager of the cinema hall. The bicycle guard sent us through, up the stairs. The manager's small office was dominated by a massive desk. Behind it sat a middle-aged man with a long beard. Three younger men sat around and addressed the manager as *guru*. 'We enjoy his company,' said one of them, who introduced himself as a journalist, 'he has a lot of knowledge.' Mr. Kashem, the manager, smiled. 'My learning comes from my *pir* [saint],' he said, 'I am his *murid* [follower].' I asked how long he has been a devotee to his *pir*. 'As you get older you become more concerned,' Mr. Kashem said by way of answer, 'you become concerned with religion and the next life.' Large colour posters of Mecca and Medina as well as Quranic scripture were pinned to the walls. I asked what his *pir*'s position on the cinema was. 'Cinema is not irreligious,' he replied. 'Cinema is not only about nakedness. It is about happiness, sadness, family life, it makes people laugh and cry.' Asking him about his own involvement in cinema, he returned to 1971. 'It was war but I still needed to earn,' he recounted, 'I was trained as an electrician. I couldn't find any work. They needed someone to help in the Nirala cinema hall nearby. I started working with the projectionist. In 1985 I joined Tosbir. I have been here ever since.' I suggested the business has changed much since then. 'The bane of the industry,' he said decisively, 'are dishes, discs and bombs. Too much competition, too little security.' I asked whether the cinema halls were unsafe. 'We had a threat this Eid,' he said, 'we take it very seriously. Not so long ago there was an explosion in a Satkhira hall.' The police station in Jessore aided in security. 'There's always one police officer at the hall,' Aziz had explained, 'they bring the scanner. Everyone who wants to see a film needs to be scanned.' 'But people still come?' I ventured. 'There isn't much other entertainment,' replied Mr. Khasem, 'and the rich don't come any more, only the poor.'

Leaving Mr. Kashem to theological discussions, we descended back towards the cinema hall. Before leaving we decided to have another quick look inside the hall where the evening feature was well underway. Taking the back door we entered the auditorium. This time the hall was packed. Around the delicate colonial pillars young men sat on the floor. Along the walls men were standing. 'Oh Tiny,' said a female American voice. On the screen a close up of an erect white penis cut to a medium shot of a blowjob. The American porn movie seemed to date from the eighties, judging from the hairstyles of the protagonists. At least 500 men were gathered in the space that officially held 400 seats. The audience in the hall was completely quiet.

The presence of Tiny on a Bangladeshi cinema screen was less unlikely than it might seem. Parallel with movies such as *Mintu the Murderer*, Chinese action movies dubbed into English and American pornographic feature films circulated in the Bangladeshi cinema halls in 2005. In Dhaka such features were rare, but outside the city cinema halls often screen such films on a double bill with foreign martial arts films. S.V Srinivas notes a similar circulation in what he terms the B-circuit in Andhra Pradesh, India (2003, 45). Martial arts movies and sex films share the same space of circulation both in Bangladesh and India.

Before we could find out what would become of Tiny and his lover, a guard came into the hall. 'Come, come,' he insisted, 'this is not for you.' Flustered, he ushered us out of the hall. 'Come again soon and stay in Jessore!' waved the bicycle guard as we passed through the gate of Tosbir Mohol and tumbled out onto the street laughing.

Conclusion

The life of contemporary Bangladeshi cinema plays itself out in the cinema halls in towns around the country. Not only is the main addressee of Dhakai films thought to reside in the *mofussil*, it is the material presence of the one thousand theatres that shapes exhibition and consumption of the cinema. Along town streets and in rural landscapes, theatres give visual form to the cinema beyond the film text. The historical experience of cinema in what is today Bangladesh is commemorated by these architecturally distinct structures that dot the landscape. Brian Larkin has suggested that '[o]bjects that were once new and symbolized modern life but whose historical moment has passed become inadvertent but dense signifiers of transformations in social structure' (2008, 125). Even when not directly visible, the complex history of East Bengal's cinema lies within its theatres, and the social life of film projection and consumption makes tangible social transformations in Bangladesh. The theatres are pregnant with previous eras while still embracing the new.

In this chapter, I have visited the cinema halls of Jessore to come to an understanding of contemporary Bangladeshi cinema. I encountered its history underway. Cinema has changed drastically over the years. While some have written its obituary, the 100 films released in Bangladesh in 2005 strongly suggest that this may be premature. The film industry in Bangladesh has, however, seen significant changes over the last decades. The cinema halls of Jessore are not witness to a fading industry. On the contrary, the experience in these theatres pinpoints exactly the consolidation of action cinema in Bangladesh, its reliance on exploitation techniques such as cut-pieces, shifting sources of patronage, new uses of distribution networks and a new aesthetic in theatre design. It is from within the cinema halls of towns such as Jessore that the contemporary film industry in Bangladesh springs most sharply into view.

Notes

1 *Dhoom*'s song Shikdum was itself a cover of the song Sikidim by Turkish singer Tarkan.
2 At least 13 of these films are unaccounted for by Gazdar, while two films (one in Urdu and one in Bengali) are dated differently by the BFPDA. The BFPDA does not list 2 films that Gazdar indicates as being made from Dhaka, and two more films from East Pakistan in 1970 are neither accounted for by Gazdar nor the BFPDA but are listed in Alamgir Kabir's *Film in Bangladesh* (1979). It may be concluded that the record on film releases in Pakistan is inconclusive.
3 Similarly, those films which are credited with a distinctive place within the emergence of Bangladeshi cinema may look differently when seen from an all-Pakistan perspective. The film *Rupban* (1965) generally thought to have opened the rural market for cinema in East Bengal and quintessentially Bengali because based the popular theatre genre of *jatra*. But in 1966, *Rupban* was remade in East Pakistan by its famed Bengali director Salahuddin in an Urdu version!

References

Ahmed, R. (2008) 'The Manna factor' in *The Daily Star* 23 December 2008
Ahsan, S. B. (2005) 'Of movies, of old story lines' in *New Age* 6 October 2005
Ashraf, K. K. (1989) 'Muzharul Islam, Kahn and Architecture in Bangladesh' in *Worldview: Perspectives on Architecture And Urbanism From Around the Globe* [Online] <http://worldview cities.org/dhaka/islam.html> (accessed 15 October 2007)
Feldman, S. (2002) 'NGOs and Civil Society: (Un)stated contradictions' in R. Jahan (ed.) *Bangladesh: Promise and Performance*, Dhaka: University Press Limited
Gazdar, M. (1997) *Pakistan Cinema 1947–1997*, Oxford: Oxford University Press
Gopalan, L. (2002) *Cinema of Interruptions: Action Genres in Contemporary Indian Cinema*, New Delhi: Oxford University Press
Government of the People's Republic of Bangladesh, *A manual on Censorship of Films Act, Rules and Code with amendments; Cinematograph Act and Rules, with amendments; Films Clubs Registration & Regulation Act & Rules and various Notifications, Orders etc*, Dhaka: Ministry of Information, undated
Hayat, A. (1987) *Bangladesher Chalachitro Itihash*, [The History of Bangladeshi Cinema] Dhaka: BFDC
Hoek, L. (2006) 'The Mysterious Whereabouts of the Cut-Pieces: Dodging the Film Censors in Bangladesh' in *IIAS Newsletter* Issue 42:18–19
———, (2008) 'Cut-Pieces: Obscenity and the Cinema in Bangladesh', PhD dissertation, University of Amsterdam
Hoek, L. (forthcoming) 'Unstable Celluloid: Film Projection and the Cinema Audience in Bangladesh' in *BioScope: South Asian Screen Studies* Volume 1, Issue 1
Hughes, S. P. (2002) 'Policing Silent Film Exhibition in Colonial South India', in Ravi S. Vasudevan (ed.) *Making Meaning in Indian Cinema*, New Delhi: Oxford University Press
———, (2003) 'Pride of Place', in *Seminar*, 525 <http://www.india-seminar.com/2003/525/525%20stephen%20p.%20hughes.htm> (accessed 2 March 2009)
Kabir, A. (1979) *Film in Bangladesh*, Dhaka: Bangla Academy
Larkin, B. (2008) *Signal and Noise: Media, Infrastructure, and Urban Culture in Nigeria*, Durham and London: Duke University Press

Mookherjee, N. (2007) 'The 'Dead and Their Double Duties': Mourning, Melancholia, and the Martyred Intellectual Memorials in Bangladesh' in *Space and Culture*, Volume 10, Issue 2: 271–291

Nasreen, G. and Haq, F. (2008) *Bangladesher Chalochchitra Shilpo: Sangkote Janosangskriti* [The Film Industry of Bangladesh: Popular Culture in Crisis], Dhaka: Shrabon Prokashoni

Raju, Z. H. (2000) 'National cinema and the beginning of film history in/of Bangladesh', in *Screening the Past*, Issue 11 http://www.latrobe.edu.au/screeningthepast/firstrelease/fr1100/rzfr11d.htm (accessed 26 July 2007)

———. (2006) 'Bangladesh: Native and Nationalist', in Anne Tereska Ciecko (ed.), *Contemporary Asian Cinema: Popular Culture in a Global Frame*, Oxford and New York: Berg

Schaefer, E. (1999) *'Bold! Daring! Shocking! True!': A History of Exploitation Films, 1919–1959*, Durham and London: Duke University Press

Van Schendel, W. (2009) *A History of Bangladesh*, Cambridge: Cambridge University Press

Srinivas, S.V. (2003) 'Hong Kong Action Film in the Indian B circuit', in *Inter-Asia Cultural Studies*, Volume 4, Issue 1: 40–62

Chapter Five

MUSICAL MEDIA AND COSMOPOLITANISMS IN NEPAL'S POPULAR MUSIC, 1950–2006

Paul D. Greene

In the literature on South Asian popular music, topics such as the Indian film industry, nationalism, and modernism tend to loom large. Writings often centre around binary oppositions, such as modernity edging out tradition, nationalism competing with regionalism, India's culture dominating over its neighbours, and Western culture replacing South Asian culture. While I agree with a number of the insights that follow from such binary models, I would suggest that these oppositions do not always draw out the full complexity and multiplicity of relations among local and translocal processes, traditions, identities and genres in Nepal. For even the most patently nationalistic Nepali music may contain within itself the seeds of a subsequent cultural movement that celebrates the West or India. Likewise, self-consciously Western-influenced expressions can become vehicles of Nepali national pride. To model the eclecticism and creativity that Nepali musicians and listeners exercise through their popular music calls for more subtle and sophisticated analytic tools.

In this chapter I combine ethnographic data with a social and musical history in an account of popular music in Nepal, 1950–2006, organised around a theme of *cosmopolitanism*. By invoking cosmopolitanism, I am not proposing that popular songs are treatises on the global community of human beings, or on cultural diversity. What I am proposing is that as Nepali popular songs draw together Nepali and non-Nepali musical elements and symbols, they inspire, among other things, various ways of thinking and feeling about and beyond the local. Musicians and listeners of different genres position themselves in complex and shifting ways vis-à-vis local and translocal, simultaneously constructing Nepali-ness and Nepali cosmopolitanisms. Music is considered as part of a history involving democracy movements, globalisation, change, and a Maoist insurgency. In the shifting musical forms I find that a sense of local Nepali culture is variously celebrated, memorialised, or erased, and that attitudes toward the West and toward India range from celebratory to obsessive to anxious.

The concept and term cosmopolitanism, in Western intellectual history, can be traced back to Stoic thought, subsequently elaborated in the Enlightenment by Emmanuel Kant and others. Kant's cosmopolitanism is a universalist perspective that involves an awareness and appreciation of many cultures, together with an idealisation of a universal human community that transcends them. In this conception there ultimately can be only one cosmopolitanism, in that there can be only one universal human community. Such a conception generally leads to mutually exclusive binary oppositions: such as between cosmopolitanism on the one hand, and nationalisms and regionalisms on the other. Contemporary social theorists call for a more complex model. As Briggs (2005) points out, presuming binary opposition leads one analytically to 'purify' constructions of both the local and the cosmopolitan, such that local cultures tend to be viewed as particular, static and essentialised, and 'the cosmopolitan' tends to be thought of as universal and free of any particular cultural bias. But there are and have been throughout human history many ways to model transcendent human communities, or more generally ways in which peoples of different cultures can or should interrelate. In short, there are many cosmopolitanisms, each rooted in its own local cultural history.

Pollock et al (2000) gloss cosmopolitanisms, in the plural, as various ways of thinking and feeling beyond the local, and this is the approach I take. They consider ways in which various historically- and culturally-situated individuals and groups think and feel beyond the local. This chapter likewise takes stock not only of cosmopolitanisms—attitudes toward cultures beyond the local, as evident in music—but also of nationalisms, because these likewise involve constructions of local and translocal. Since it is my goal to get beyond binary oppositions, such as cosmopolitanism versus nationalism, I probe cosmopolitan aspects of music designed to serve nationalist agendas, and vice versa.

One important factor in any construction of cosmopolitanism or nationalism in Nepal is the country's cultural diversity. Mountain ranges have kept peoples separate and allowed much cultural diversity to persist. In the Himalayan region along the northern stretch of Nepal can be found Buddhist groups related to Tibetans, such as the Manangs, Lopas, Sherpas and Tamangs. In the East are the Rais and Limbus, whose languages are part of the Tibeto-Burman family. Western, central and southern Nepal are inhabited by primarily Hindu groups: the Gurungs, Magars, Khas, Thakalis and Gorkhas. And the Newars, of the Kathmandu Valley, are originally a Tibeto-Burman people who practice both Hinduism and Buddhism, and have undergone centuries of mutual cultural influence with India. No single ethnic group comprises a majority, and the national language, Nepali, is a second language to most Nepalis.

The challenges of regional and cultural diversity have been complicated by uneven processes of globalisation. Nepal's cities – primarily Kathmandu and Pokhara – have been centres of education, international commerce, tourism, and contact with Western culture: processes which have powerfully transformed the wealth and cultural lives of city-dwellers. Rural Nepal has in many respects been marginalised from both the cultural impacts and economic benefits of globalisation. A disjuncture between urban and rural has been growing, and this has greatly shaped Nepal's social history and music.

Sociocultural analysis presented in this chapter draws on field projects I conducted in Nepal in 1999, 2000, 2001, and winter 2002–03. Research included both structured and unstructured interviews with over 200 people, primarily students in Kathmandu schools who listened to Nepali musics. I also interviewed musicians and record company executives, and visited shopping centres where popular music was sold or played. My general method in unstructured listener interviews was to start conversations about music, and then to follow the conversations as they moved to topics of identity, youth culture and politics. Sometimes I played specific pieces of Nepali music to help start these conversations. Using music as an entry point, I sought to trace out some of the common processes through which Nepalis constructed and imagined their social worlds. This chapter also draws on historical information published in Greene and Rajkarnikar (2001/2006).

Aadhunik Giit, Lok Giit, and Nepali Nationalism: 1950s through 70s

In 1951, the Rana regime, an absolute monarchy, was overpowered and rule restored to King Tribhuvan, who struggled with the elected government for control of the country. The 1950s through the 1970s were marked by a growing democracy movement. In the early 1950s the Rana policy of banning mass media from Nepal was reversed, and a rapid transformation took place (Liechty 1997; Grandin 1989, 113). The initial impact was a sudden proliferation of Indian films and film songs. Hindi is understandable in Nepal, so the film songs circulated rapidly. In addition, the state-sponsored Radio Nepal was founded, and it became a vehicle of creation and promotion of a distinctly Nepali popular music. Also, starting in 1961, the Ratna Recording Trust began to produce phonograph records of Nepali popular music. The national government actively promoted the national language, Nepali. Radio Nepal and Ratna Recording circulated Nepali songs, and musicians who worked there laboured, among other things, to advance a sense of Nepali nationalism. It was in this context that the musics of *aadhunik gīt* and *lok gīt* were cultivated. Another development in Nepali popular music came in 1973, when the Royal Nepal Film Corporation began to make films, inspired by the Indian film industry. Sambhujit Baskota emerged as the leading Nepali film Music Director, and he composed in a wide variety of folk, classical, Western, and modern Nepali styles.

At first, Nepali musicians at Radio Nepal performed and produced Indian 'light classical' genres of *ghazal* and *thumri*. Musicians such as Master Ratna Das Prakash, Amber Gurung and Nati Kazi drew together elements of Indian light classical music, Nepali folk songs, and Western harmonies, to develop a new, often sentimental genre which came to be known as *aadhunik gīt* ('modern song') (Grandin 1989, 116). *Aadhunik gīt* became Nepal's leading popular music, and it remains very popular today. The primary audience of *aadhunik gīt* was older, educated, urban music listeners.

Aadhunik gīt fused together Nepali, Indian and Western musical elements in a seamless, harmonious fashion. Grandin (1989, 120) finds that 'the borrowing of foreign (Indian and Western) music resources does not contradict the Nepaliness of the songs.' He cites Amber Gurung, a pioneer of *aadhunik gīt* who in 1972 found it 'striking' that *aadhunik gīt* dresses up a song's Nepali-styled melody 'modernly to look so new yet retaining all its national charm.' The vocal melody referenced Nepaliness in its melodic character and through use of the Nepali language; and the orchestral instrumentation and use of chords indexed the West and therewith modernity. A tinge of Indian classical (Hindustani) sophistication was audible in *gamak* slides, melodic suggestions of Indian ragas, and occasional use of Hindustani instruments such as sitar, tambura, and so on. These elements were merged smoothly together, effectively to gloss over musical contrasts between the original styles. *Aadhunik gīt* differed from, for example, Nepali remixes, in which stylistic contrasts remained patent (see below). Gurung's remark articulates particularly well what I found in interviews with listeners: that *aadhunik gīt* was experienced as the song of the modern Nepal, in which Nepali nationalism, Western modernity and Indian sophistication were in harmony. *Aadhunik gīt* was a distinctly Nepali music that bore trappings of sophistication from India and the West: prestigious cultural pillars and emblems of modernity. Because *aadhunik gīt* tended to be limited specifically to Indian and Western musical borrowings, it lacked the openness and cultural breadth that properly characterises cosmopolitanism, as the term is generally used. What it projected was a particular nationalism: one encouraged by the government and shared by urban, educated Nepalis of the period.

There was a sense in which the Nepaliness of *aadhunik gīt* took priority over its Western or Indian elements. For in traditional and popular Nepali modes of listening, melody – especially vocal melody – is almost always heard as paramount, and harmony and instrumentation are secondary. This is evident in

Gurung's remark above, and also in the fact that, in *aadhunik giit*, the song-texts and melodies were always composed first and chords were added later. The creative process resembled that of the North Indian film song, as documented by Manuel (1988), in which vocal melody was likewise primary. In this sense, the 'modern Nepal' constructed by *aadhunik giit* thus prioritised Nepaliness over Westernness and Indianness, through the primacy of the melody over its accompaniment. Western and Indian elements were thus enhancements of primarily Nepali expressions.

Lok giit ('folk song'), which also emerged in the 1950s, took as its basis actual songs from Nepal's villages, with song-texts translated from regional languages into Nepali. The vocal line was accompanied by a combination of Nepali and Western instruments: *baansurii* (flute), *maadal* (drum), *saarangi* (fiddle), guitar, violin and mandolin (Henderson 2003). More recently, electric guitars and Western rock drumsets have been added. *Lok giit* singers were typically either folksong collectors – such as Dharma Raj Thapa and Kumar Basnet – who travelled around Nepal to collect and then sing the songs at Radio Nepal, or members of distinctive Nepali ethnic or caste communities, such as Jhalakman Gandharwa. Since the 1960s, Kumar Basnet has been the most frequently recorded *lok giit* singer. The vocal line of *lok giit* carried a great sense of authenticity and connectedness to rural Nepal. But in many respects *lok giit* advanced much the same agenda as *aadhunik giit*, in that it also presented itself as the music of a modern Nepal. Likewise, the vocal line was harmoniously blended with Western musical elements, and listeners placed the same priority on the distinctively Nepali vocal line.

Although these genres were largely nationalist in function, it is important also to note cosmopolitan aspects and potentials within them. For in musically constructing a modern Nepal, the forms also reinforced the (secondary) value of both Indian classical culture and Western culture. This set the stage for future developments, for example, remixes in the 1990s, in which Nepalis imitated an Indian pop trend; and the thrash metal scene of the 2000s, in which young Nepalis adopted and clung tenaciously to a Western-originated identity as metalheads.

Democracy, Globalisation and Nepali Pop: 1980s and 90s

During the 1950s through 70s, the government exercised considerable influence in shaping popular music. But starting in the 1980s, young people played increasingly influential roles as pioneers, musicians and consumers. A new popular genre called *Nepali pop* was cultivated, not at state-sponsored Radio Nepal, but independently by urban young people, and came to serve as a vehicle of new, broader cosmopolitan sensibilities. This development was preceded by two decades in which Western popular music grew in influence. Beginning in the 1960s, Nepal became a haven for Western tourists and trekkers. First the area of 'Freak Street,' and then the Thamel neighbourhood became tourist districts in Kathmandu. Merchants sensed that there was a market for selling Western popular music to tourists, and young urban Nepalis also began to purchase the music (Henderson 1999). During the 1980s a number of private FM radio stations took to the air in Nepal, and they increasingly played Western songs. And with the advent of satellite television in the late 1980s, MTV brought Western pop into Nepali homes to an unprecedented extent.

The 1980s and 90s was a period of tremendous change. Nepal's democracy movement gained momentum, and in 1990 the king relinquished power to the elected government. More people went to school. In schools, young people[1] came together from throughout Nepal and from outside, to an unprecedented extent. Young Nepalis interacted with colleagues who had studied in Europe and North America. My interviews revealed that young Nepalis experienced a greater diversity of cultural influences than did their parents, and through their friendships they cultivated a broad cultural understanding. A cosmopolitan Nepali urban youth culture emerged, centred around student life, and this was to become the primary fan base of Nepali pop. Students' lives were filled with technologies of Western origin: cameras, computers, and Internet cafés. State development programs, schoolbooks, and programs on television and radio and reinforced an ideology of progress toward a modern Nepal characterised by technology, education and wealth (Pigg 1992). Liechty (1995, 169) describes the expansion of 'consumer modernity' among young people in Kathmandu: identifying the self in material terms, necessitating the ongoing purchase of 'modern' commodities. Young people also described new freedoms they enjoyed: to roam widely around the cities, to date, and ultimately to choose one's own spouse, rather than have parents arrange marriages.

Inspired by the music they were increasingly hearing, young people purchased rock instruments and learned to perform Western popular musics themselves. Cover bands formed, such as Wrathchild, Crisscross, Chimpanzees, the Elegance, Prism, and Next, performing concerts in English (Greene and Henderson 2003). Then young urban Nepalis began to write their own songs using Western instruments, in Western styles, but now in the Nepali language. This was called Nepali pop. Nepali pop also gained impetus from the simultaneous and parallel developments of Indipop – pop musics of India and its diaspora, such as Asha Bhosle, Alisha Chinai and Colonial Cousins.

Nepali pop musicians self-consciously embraced Westernised musics, identities, and lifeways. In fact, a pioneer group was called The Influence, a reference to the fact that the band saw itself as thoroughly Westernized, singing about contemporary urban lifeways that were thoroughly influenced by the

West and by modernisation (Phuyal 1998). The Influence became a musical symbol of a new, inescapable Western influence which many urban young Nepalis increasingly experienced daily. Nepali pop bands, like Indus Syangbo, Crossroads, Sparsha and The Elegance, primarily produced music on audio cassette; only a few products were distributed on CD. A few bands worked with Music Nepal; most worked out the financing of their own productions through a combination of their own resources and financial arrangements with music stores, which then sold the albums. By the 1990s, Nepali pop was beginning to make appreciable sales: up to five thousand units. This indicates that some bands had a significant, but not international, following, comparable to that of a successful, local underground band in North America or Europe.

Unlike the earlier popular musics, Nepali pop was fairly strongly associated with the upper and middle class. Zeepee, anchor of *Music+*, Nepal TV's leading Nepali pop program, found that the popularity of Nepali pop extended from the upper class down as far as the lower middle class. David Henderson goes further, finding a substantial following for Nepali pop among lower-class city dwellers (personal communication). Evidently for these fans, Nepali pop was a means culturally of identifying with the middle or upper middle classes (cf. Liechty 1995 on *Teen* magazine), and in this sense the genre retained a class identity that was perhaps more narrow than its actual appeal.

As Yubakar Raj Rajkarnikar, editor of Nepal's leading popular-culture magazine, *Wave*, told me, none of the distinct musical styles in Nepali pop triggered the formation of a subculture, until around 1999. Urban young people generally listened to every Nepali pop style, exhibiting broadly cosmopolitan sensibilities. In comparison to *aadhunik gīt* and *lok gīt*, Nepali pop represented a deepening and broadening of the ways in which Nepalis thought and felt beyond the local. Whereas *aadhunik gīt* presented a Nepali modernism supplemented by Western sophistication, young Nepali pop listeners thought of themselves as deeply influenced by the West: a shift signalled by The Influence in its music and name. Cultural identity became more hybrid, complex, and sometimes uncertain or exploratory.

Lok Pop and Remixes: Rural-Urban Tension in the 1990s

Whereas Nepali pop was generally identified as Western-influenced and urban, in 1993 began *lok pop* ('folk pop'), a Nepali pop subgenre that was identified with Nepal's rural cultural groups. In order to understand the growing popularity of *lok pop*, one must reflect on the symbolism of 'the folk' and 'the rural' in Nepali experience and imagination. For Nepalis, including urban Nepalis, the primary consumers of *lok pop*, not only celebrated the West and the modern; they simultaneously and to varying degrees lionised the Nepali village as a symbol or guarantor of Nepal as a distinct nation. Nepalis did not want to become a province of India, nor did they wish to become a 'nation of make-believe Americans' (Appadurai 1990, 3). In this sense, mountains and rural Nepal, as pictured on currency, newspapers (e.g., *Himal*—'Mountain') and government seals functioned as emblems of Nepal as one's *own* place, emblems of Nepaliness through which Nepal could remain distinct. Similarly, mountains were sometimes invoked in songs as signs of Nepaliness.

At the same time, as described above, state development programs, education, consumer modernity, and globalisation oriented Nepalis toward cities as centres of the modern Nepal. Therefore, representations of 'the folk,' including those in *lok pop*, were caught up in a tension between two competing orientations: on the one hand Nepalis looked to the rural folk to guarantee their Nepaliness, while on the other they aspired to more modern, Westernised, technology-enhanced lifeways. 'Unity through diversity' was a common slogan of Nepali modernity in the 1990s and early 2000s that attempted to draw together the two orientations. But the two goals often became mutually contradictory, simultaneously pulling Nepalis in opposite directions (Greene 2003). And in many ways, accelerating processes of global capitalism sharpened distinctions between city and village as they also redefined both. The processes and tensions described here contributed to the heightened violence and insurgency of the 2000s, which was in many respects a rural-urban conflict (Hutt 2004, 17).

Lok pop owed its initial popularity to the efforts of Nepathya, a Pokhara-based band that formed in 1990. Nepathya got its start covering Western popular music, and then turned to writing their own music in Nepali. To Nepali listeners Nepathya's music offered a 'tastier flavour, for their compositions are a fusion of Western music and our folk music' (*Wave* 1996). But unlike *lok güt*, *lok pop* rarely retained entire melodies from actual folksongs. Its folk 'flavour' was due to particular scales and melodic figures, words from Nepal's ethnic languages inserted into the primarily Nepali-language song-texts, and narratives about village life. Typical song-texts concerned journeys through the mountains, memories of rural culture, love for a village girl, village festivals, and village families. Nepathya became the first Nepali pop band to sell 100,000 units. Other *lok pop* bands followed, including Madhyana, Kandara, Nizzer, Deurali, Pokhareli, Manoj Shrestha, Bro-Sis, Vagabond and Mongolian Hearts. By 2000 *lok pop* was the best selling Nepali pop subgenre, according to music store vendors I interviewed.

Lok pop presented a new approach or attitude toward Nepaliness vis-à-vis influences from beyond, in that it presented Nepali traditional culture as receding, fading, disappearing (Greene 2003). This was accomplished through a number of expressive techniques. Rustic scenes and village life were presented in song-texts as memories. In music videos, rural scenes were presented as flashbacks, separated from the 'present' by a video dissolve. Melodic and studio-produced echo effects enhanced a sense of the receding nature of folk cultures. Ironically, *lok pop* in effect memorialised traditional cultures that actually continued: despite erosions due to Westernisation, capitalisation and modernisation, Nepal's alpine cultures and traditional musics have persisted. *Lok pop* therefore offered the Nepali music listener a new, nostalgic way to reflect on Nepal and its relationship to outside influences. This was a new way to think and feel about and beyond the local.

In contrast, other Nepali pop genres more conspicuously celebrated the new, the modern and the Western. One such genre was remixes, which became popular in Kathmandu in the late 1990s. A remix is a setting of a familiar song to a prominent, danceable beat, typically from international electronic dance music, often including a shifting accompanimental montage of musical styles. Nepali remixes combined passages and snippets of, for example, Nepali folksongs, Western dance beats, rap, Hindustani instrumental music, Tibetan *dung chen* trumpets, reggae, and rhythm & blues. The remix practice originated in 1970s North American disco, in which DJs and musicians produced extended dance versions of familiar songs to offer the crowd a variety of familiar, danceable music. Remixing spread to India and its diaspora during the 90s, and DJs and MCs remixed Punjabi *bhangra* folksongs, Bollywood songs from the past and present, and other genres, for use in a growing Indian urban dance craze. Indian remixes entered the Kathmandu music market around 1995. In Nepal, remixes were marked as distinctly high-tech music, and functioned as sonic icons of technology. In fact, images of sound studios were pictured in cassette album sleeves.

Whereas in North America and India remixes emerged in conjunction with DJ dance culture, in Nepal remixes were first made in sound studios, starting around 1993, and thereafter became popular in discotheques. After resisting discotheque culture, city authorities allowed discotheques legally to open in 1997. Initially, most featured Western popular music, but DJs increasingly also began to spin Nepali pop and remixes.

Nepalis I spoke to traced the remix trend not only to India but also to a more general practice of making 'mix music.' Mix music was a general term for music, such as remixes, which involved juxtapositions and layerings of stylistically contrasting musics, such that the distinctions and differences between them were patent. *Lok gīt* singer Kumar Basnet considered some of his reworkings of traditional folksongs in the mid 1990s to be early mix music, in that they layered Nepali folksongs over Western rock and pop accompaniments (although in his songs stylistic contrasts tended to be musically smoothed over). The first album of Nepali remixes, *Mega Mix*, was compiled by Brazesh Khanal and released in 1998. This was followed by remix albums of Nepali film songs and folksongs. In contrast with India, most Nepali remix albums were not created by DJs but instead by record companies. A few pop groups, like the Rock Yogis, 1974 AD, and Robin 'n' Looza also made them.

One important aspect of mix music was that when it incorporated Western and other musical styles, the precise timbres, rhythms, and tunings of sound bites of both foreign pop and indigenous music were reproduced more precisely than ever before. For example, as noted above, *lok gīt* employed some of the instrumentation of rock music, and early Nepali pop self-consciously incorporated Western styles, but in these musics it was not so crucial exactly to reproduce the original timbres or subtle aspects of performativity such as swing, or blue notes. This more timbrally and aurally precise mode of musical borrowing was facilitated by new studio technologies, such as samplers and tone modules, which allowed the specific sounds of a heavy metal guitar or a reggae beat to be incorporated. Until 1992, studio recording in Nepal had been mostly limited to four tracks or fewer; but with the global release of the Alesis ADAT, an affordable digital multitrack recording technology, sound studios suddenly had the unprecedented facility to record, copy, and mix multiple layers and styles of music. In the 2000s, hard disk recording technology was introduced, enabling a recording engineer or musician to use a computer to do multitrack recording, sampling, mixing and effects processing with unprecedented efficiency and facility.

Mix music reflected a general cultural climate of accelerated musical circulation. Radios, cassette players and CD players proliferated in the 1990s, and in the 2000s the Internet played a growing role in music dissemination. In places such as Thamel, snippets of Western, Nepali, Indian, and other musics resounded from countless sources, and were heard all jumbled together in the streets, hotels and restaurants. The musical montage-like quality of remixes, with contrasting styles abruptly juxtaposed, was related, in the experience of Nepalis, to urban soundscapes of the 1990s.

Contrasting musics remained largely unintegrated in mix music, their bristling distinctions and contradictions clearly audible, instead of smoothed over as in the fusions of *aadhunik gīt*. There was often no pretence in mix music that the styles were unified; in fact, musical contrasts and distinctions were celebrated. In this regard, mix music brought to mind not only urban soundscapes but also the general, dynamic, high-tech, multicultural world in which young urban Nepalis found themselves. One young man I spoke to put it this way:

> Change is good. Not that we completely adopt your culture, but we like it. Change is good. People these days can't stay in one place for even half an hour. We get lost listening to the same music for some time. ... I, for example, can't sit in one place for a while. I must move to many places. This

is for teens – they can't stay in one place. Elderly people are compelled to stay in one place ... Teenage life is like riding a motorbike through a city.

Many students experienced culture shock as they moved back and forth between student life and traditional family life, for example, and remixes musically reflected this experience (for more, see Greene 2001/2005). As the contrasting, juxtaposed styles brought to mind different cultural worlds, they also inspired a cosmopolitan reflection on the new multicultural lifeways that Nepali students were preparing themselves for. I found that the cosmopolitanism was 'unsettled' in the sense that, in their experience, the music presented no musical resolution or integration of the Nepali cultures and the non-Nepali ones. It was left to the listener to contemplate and explore the contradictory and ever-shifting world of turn-of-the-century urban Nepal (Greene 2001/2005).

Maoist Insurgency and Heavy Metal in the 2000s

During the 2000s Nepal underwent a period of strife and conflict. The Communist Party of Nepal (Maoist) began an insurgency in 1996 that increased in violence, involving armed conflicts and bombings of private and governmental targets. Maoists ordered *bandh*s: complete shutdowns of all workplaces and schools for days or weeks at a time. Anyone violating a *bandh* faced the threat of Maoist violence. As violence increased during the 2000s the daily presence of the police and the military increased. The Maoists promised to meet the cultural and economic needs of rural Nepalis, who increasingly joined their cause. On 1 June 2001 a multiple homicide took the lives of ten members of Nepal's royal family. The details of the incident remain unknown. King Gyanendra, crowned following the tragedy, declared that the elected government had failed effectively to handle the growing Maoist crisis. On 1 February 2005, he dissolved the government and assumed direct executive powers. Freedom of the press was suspended, and numerous protests against the King followed. The 2000s, up until 2006, were for most Nepalis a period of tremendous violence, anxiety and political uncertainty. Over 12,000 people were killed (Hutt 2004; BBC 2008).

In this context, popular music rarely critiqued the government or political situation explicitly, nor did it call for social change in specific ways. However, many songs voiced frustration, anger and alarm in general ways that, for many, reflected and embodied an affective response to the unfolding political calamity. Nepali heavy metal became one such music.

The history of Nepali heavy metal began in the 1980s, well before the insurgency began. Since the early 1980s, Western heavy metal and hard rock were quite popular and sold well in Kathmandu, particularly Metallica,

AC/DC, Iron Maiden, Led Zeppelin, Aerosmith, Def Leppard, and Guns 'n' Roses. Nepali bands like Wrathchild covered Western metal in live performances. The first band to produce a heavy metal album in Nepali was Cobweb, in 1993. Although Cobweb incorporated the overdriven guitars, loud volume and dynamic stage presence distinctive of heavy metal, they also retained a sweet, polished vocal style common in Nepali pop. Their music did not at first inspire the creation of what could be called a metalhead subculture (Greene 2001/2005).

But within a few years Nepal's heavy metal music and scene evolved. In 1997, Stash began to produce music with the intent to 'prove that it is possible to record an album with Nepali heavy metal songs' with the 'shrieking, hard-hitting styles' of Anthrax, Metallica and Iron Maiden. Though Stash's music had limited popularity, other bands followed, such as Mile Stone and Grease. In 1996, Dristhy formed, comprised of Nepalis living in Omaha, USA. Their goal was to set excerpts from the *Bhagavad Gita* concerning war to heavy metal (*Wave* 1999).

In the music of Dristhy, UgraKarma, X-Mantra, and others, a strong musical influence specifically from international thrash metal became evident. Distinctive features included rapid rhythm guitar figuration, downtuned and heavily distorted guitar sounds, use of double bass kick drums, absence or shortening of guitar solos, and significantly, the use of low-pitched, growled vocals. X-Mantra band members told me that only approximately five percent of their listeners could understand their song-texts, because of their growled vocal quality. To fully understand the impact of this musical development, one must consider it against the backdrop of the popular and traditional musical aesthetics cultivated for five decades in Nepal. For in folksongs, devotional songs, *aadhunik güt, lok güt* and most forms of Nepali pop, a pervasive aesthetic emerged in which primary emphasis was placed on the clarity and expressive power of the vocal line. This entrenched aesthetic became a foil against which Nepali thrash metal rebelled. In fact, when Dristhy was interviewed by *Wave* magazine (1999) they were asked to explain themselves.

An enthusiastic subculture emerged of young Nepalis, primarily middle-class males, age 15–22. These metalheads filled their lives with both Nepali and Western metal, participated in Internet metalhead communities, and read international metal fanzines.[2] To them, the music inspired a powerful translocal identification, in which their identity as metalheads often transcended their connection to the local (Greene, forthcoming). Whereas The Influence sought to cultivate a modern, westernized identity that was nonetheless also distinctly Nepali, in Nepali metal the Western identification was even stronger. Many Nepali metalheads expressed a greater sense of connectedness to metal fans in other countries than to non-metalhead Nepalis.

Nepal's thrash metal scene departed from expectations in other ways as well. Song-texts concerning death, corpses, suicide, and bloody warfare shocked and puzzled mainstream listeners. In some of the song-texts of UgraKarma were vivid descriptions of dark feelings and of violence, and even nihilistic, blasphemous, and anti-Hindu statements. UgraKarma band members explained to me that they were not against Hinduism as a whole, but actually against specific Hindu practices. For fans, the new heavy metal resonated on a deep, personal level, inspiring powerful affective experiences that helped them grapple with a wide variety of intense personal frustrations: with tradition, Hinduism, family and Nepali politics. One young metal fan told me:

> We want to scold the family, scold the politicians. ... Love tragedy is also a problem. If your love partner betrays you then that will make you angry for your whole life. ... We have deep feelings. If you feel this way how you can do it [sing] in a soft voice? Such emotion should be loud. In loud voice we want to lose control, just say anything and not have a fear. (quoted from Greene forthcoming)

I found that heavy metal in Nepal, as elsewhere, involved and celebrated tropes of rebellion and transgression, as perhaps definitive features of the music. As Walser argues (1993), the rush of power that many fans experienced in the music was a power to break out of confining musical and cultural expectations and limitations. And this experience of power was related directly to the way in which the music was made. For example, the heavily distorted guitar, an emblematic sound quality of the genre, was the audible result of deliberately overdriving a preamp, or other sound transmission device. The resulting clipped sound waves thus indexed a sonic expression so powerful that it overflowed the limitations of the means of its own transmission. Such a powerful musical channel overflow, enhanced by shouted or growled vocals and by the music's sheer volume, resonated with the generally transgressive nature of heavy metal. At many levels, heavy metal has always symbolically rebelled against or transgressed aesthetic, cultural, and religious norms, boundaries, and limitations. In Nepal, song-texts blasphemed against Hinduism and scolded national heroes, thereby transgressing limits of what was acceptable in daily life. I found that Nepali metalheads not only identified themselves tenaciously with international metal culture, but that the music itself also gave them a sense of transgressively bursting out of the local, which reinforced this transcendent identification. Participating in the scene was an emotionally, musically, and culturally expansive experience, and this expansion was powerful and accompanied by violent imagery and loud, distorted sound. As a way of thinking and feeling beyond the local it was unique.

This chapter recounts some of the complex and creative ways in which Nepal's popular music has evolved, responding to both local and translocal processes and influences. I think it illustrates that binary opposition models are not always the best analytic tools. For example, 'Westernisation versus tradition' does not adequately characterise the subtle ways in which *lok pop* musicians invoked the *idea* of 'Westernisation,' and anxiety about it, to inspire a nostalgic Nepali subject position in which, I argue, folk tradition was prematurely memorialised. Here, a way of thinking and feeling about Westernisation was at least as important as Westernisation itself. While at first glance Nepali remixes might appear to be a simple matter of Nepali trends following Indian ones, closer examination reveals ways in which Nepalis also related remixes to earlier Nepali musics and to their increasingly multi-musical, cacophonous urban soundscapes. Such complexities and subtleties could be obscured by binary opposition models. In the Nepali cosmopolitanisms surveyed in this chapter, 'the West,' 'India,' and 'Nepal' operated not only as influences but also as shifting signifiers: leitmotivs that were invoked, thought about, felt about, and refunctioned over the decades to serve various processes of identity-formation, in response to shifting sociopolitical realities.

Subsequent to my last field project in 2003, King Gyanendra returned power to the elected government. In 2006 a peace accord with the Maoists was negotiated, and the government reorganised itself as the Federal Democratic Republic of Nepal. There has been a tremendous reduction of violence and significant progress toward lasting peace and stability. It remains to be seen what new musics are emerging in this new political environment, and what new ways of thinking and feeling about and beyond the local they may inspire and embody. I would predict that young Nepalis will continue to play an important role in shaping popular music, as they have since the 1980s. And even as Indian and Western musical circulation continue to accelerate in Nepal, it seems certain that Nepalis will continue to find creative ways to construct and project distinctively Nepali identities in their music. There will continue to be a distinct Nepali contribution to the media culture of South Asia, though it is difficult to predict what form or forms it will take.

Notes

1 In this chapter, 'young people' (*ketaaketiiharu*: see Liechty 1995, 179) refers mostly to teenagers, but also includes older people in school, unmarried, and not yet settled on a career. The phase comes to an end with family and career responsibilities, in the twenties or early thirties.
2 E.g., http://heavymetalsource.com/; http://thegauntlet.com; http://www.asiandeath.com (accessed 9 October 2008).

References

Appadurai, A. (1990) 'Disjuncture and Difference in the Global Cultural Economy' in *Public Culture* Volume 2, Issue 2: 1–24

BBC (2008) 'Nepal.' http://news.bbc.co.uk/2/hi/south_asia/country_profiles/1166 502.stm, (accessed 17 January 2009)

Briggs, C. L. (2005) 'Genealogies of Race and Culture and the Failure of Vernacular Cosmopolitanisms: rereading Franz Boas and W.E.B. Du Bois.' *Public Culture* Volume 17, Issue 1: 75–100

Grandin, I. (1989) *Music and Media in Local Life: Music Practice in a Newar Neighbourhood in Nepal*, Linkoeping, Sweden: Linkoeping University Dept. of Communication Studies.

Greene, P. (2001) 'Mixed Messages: Unsettled Cosmopolitanisms in Nepali Pop.' *Popular Music* 20(2): 169–87. Reprinted in *Wired for Sound: Engineering and Technologies in Sonic Cultures* (eds) Paul D. Greene and Thomas Porcello. Middletown, CT: Wesleyan UP, 2005. 198–221

―――― (2003) 'Nepal's *Lok Pop* Music: Representations of the Folk, Tropes of Memory, and Studio Technologies.' *Asian Music* Volume 34, Issue 1: 43–65

―――― (Forthcoming) 'Electronic and Affective Overdrive: Tropes of Transgression in Nepali Heavy Metal.' In *Metal Rules the Globe* (eds) Jeremy Wallach, Harris M. Berger, and Paul D. Greene

―――― and Rajkarnikar, Y. R. (2001) 'Echoes in the Valleys: A Social History of Nepali Pop in Nepal's Urban Youth Culture, 1985–2000' (*Wave* 63:16–18, 21). Reprinted and enhanced in *Echo: A Music-Centered Journal* 7(1). http://www.echo.ucla.edu (2006)

―――― and Henderson, D. (2003) 'At the Crossroads of Languages, Musics, and Emotions in Kathmandu.' In *Global Pop, Local Language*. (Eds) Harris M. Berger and Michael Thomas Carroll. Jackson: University Press of Mississippi, 87–108

Henderson, D. (1999) 'The Sound of the City (Kathmandu Remix)' ASPAC paper, June 18.

―――― (2003) ''Who Needs the Folk?' A Nepali Remodeling Project' in *Asian Music* 34 (1): 19–42

Hutt, M. (2004) 'Introduction: Monarchy, Democracy and Maoism in Nepal' In Michael Hutt (ed.) *Himalayan People's War: Nepal's Maoist Rebellion*, Bloomington: Indiana University Press, 1–20

Liechty, M. (1995) 'Media, Markets, and Modernization: Youth Identities and the Experience of Modernity in Kathmandu, Nepal' in (eds) Vered Amit-Talai and Helena Wulff *Youth Cultures: A Cross-Cultural Perspective*, New York: Routledge, 166–201

―――― (1997) '"Selective Exclusion": Foreigners, Foreignness and Foreign Goods in Modern Nepali History.' *Studies in Nepali History and Society* 2 (1): 5–68

Manuel, P. (1988) *Popular Musics of the Non-Western World*, Oxford/New York/Toronto/New Delhi: Oxford University Press

Phuyal, S. S. (1998) 'The Influence: It's in the Name.' *Wave* 28 (April): 36

Pigg, S. L. (1992) 'Inventing Social Categories through Place: Social Representations and Development in Nepal.' *Comparative Studies of Society and History* 34(3): 491–513

Pollock, S., Bhabha, H. K., Breckenridge, C. A. and Chakrabarty, D. (2000) 'Cosmopolitanisms' in *Public Culture* 12(3): 577–89

Walser, R. (1993) *Running with the Devil: Power, Gender, and Madness in Heavy Metal Music*, Hanover: Wesleyan University Press

Wave (1996) 'Nepathya: The Village Pop Singers.' *Wave* 7 (Jan.): 29

Wave (1999) 'Dristhy.' *Wave* 41 (Aug.): 21

Part Two

TELLING TEXTS: MEDIA DISCOURSE, IDENTITY AND POLITICS

Chapter Six

PRIVATE SATELLITE MEDIA AND THE GEO-POLITICS OF MODERATION IN PAKISTAN

Tahir H. Naqvi

Pakistan's first private satellite television station began transmission at the end of the previous decade. Since 2001, 35 stations have begun broadcasting to and from Pakistan[1], a relative mania of tertiary sector investment that capitalised on the domestic hunger for news in the wake of the events of 11 September. The American invasion of Afghanistan; the meteoric boom of Pakistan's stock market; the murder of the Wall Street Journal reporter Daniel Pearl; a series of suicide attacks targeting Karachi's areas of international investment and tourism; and, the 2002 general elections which secured the military-presidency of General Pervez Musharraf and unprecedented parliamentary gains for the country's Islamist parties: it is in the lack of any coherent connection between local 'events' that their shared relation to a wider and complex conjuncture becomes apparent.

If uncertainty is a governing feature of political and social existence in Pakistan, the craving for official and unofficial news is one of its most apparent symptoms. As such, the growth of private television stations has been a largely news-driven phenomenon, while soundings of praise and disquiet about the effects of this 'new media' on the political consciousness of the 'average Pakistani' is underscored by the lack of information on the changing opinions and preferences of consumers of this media. Despite the current lack of marketing and audience-based research, the country is awash in 24-hour news cycles, on-the-spot reporting, and a diverse array of talk shows covering politics, health, religious affairs, and the private lives of political and cultural celebrities[2]. Political talk shows in particular have pushed the boundaries of familiar and permissible political discourse set during the era of state-controlled television (Pakistan TV) by bringing the various affinities and capacities of the parliamentary elite into more frequent and effective relief. A lawyer I know who is based in Karachi described this recent shift in the political form and content of news when he observed that 'until these stations came, all we knew of politicians was either the emotionalism of the rally or the formality of the print interview. Now they talk, they respond, you hear them reasoning, and to be honest, they sound more reasonable than people would have expected'[3].

Against a recent past of state-control and censorship of electronic media, deregulation has reconfigured and expanded the material and symbolic circuits of politics, participation and publicity. As a consequence, the new private stations are regarded as a key emerging broker of cultural, economic and political freedoms linked to globalisation. What complicates any easy equation of media deregulation with democratisation in Pakistan, as I describe in more detail below, is the fact that the country's most decisive deregulation policies were enacted outside legislative-parliamentary channels during the military government of General Pervez Musharraf (1999–2008).

For their part, Pakistan's 'new' stations have been at the forefront of entrenching consumerism: through high production-value advertisements for multinational products, the rise of youth as the dominant marketing demographic, or the eclipse of state-run 'social-realist' dramas by the global tele-novella form. Indeed, it is an open secret that the country's most profitable private stations actively drew upon the model of Indian, and to a lesser extent, Gulf stations, when devising their own network brands. Furthermore, executives and programmers in Pakistan's private stations today confront similar conflicts between the democratising and consumerist effects of deregulation. This may take the form a lamentational rhetoric about 'giving in' to sensationalism or unease about the growing influence advertisers and ownership over news programming and creative content.

My aim in this chapter is not to insist upon the derivative or exceptional nature of media deregulation in Pakistan (an encompassing arena that includes domestic FM radio and transnational circuits of marketing, production, and reception). Instead, my analysis will tack a position between the derivative, specific and singular dimensions of Pakistan's private television industry in order account for the role it has come to play in redefining the political and cultural frontiers of what we might call the 'national imagination'. It is not the discrepancy between democratic and consumer imaginaries of freedom that lends Pakistan's private media industry its salience, I argue, but the uneasy entanglement of these imaginaries with geo-political and extra-constitutional forms of power.

The first part of this chapter situates the deregulation of the media industry in the context of neo-liberal and martial logics of reform and rule. In the second part I consider the medium's formative negotiation of what, in Pakistan, has come to be an increasingly militarised division of the body politic into 'moderate' and 'extremist' Muslim camps. I examine certain situated practices through which Pakistan's private media stations – an institutional constellation in which I include owners, producers, journalists and creative talent – fold the geo-political distinction between moderate and extremist Islam into consumerist and political imaginaries of sovereignty. As a concept, moderation articulates the friction between capitalist and geo-political relations of power and difference. News and entertainment figures on Pakistan's private stations are therefore able to resist, appropriate and reconfigure the discourse of moderation in response to the limits and possibilities it presents for remaking Muslim nationality and selfhood within an emerging conjuncture.

The Nation's CEO: Neo-liberal Dictatorship and the Politics of Deregulation

Soon after waging the October 1999 military coup that removed the elected government of Nawaz Sharif from power [4], Pakistan's Chief of Army Staff, General Pervez Musharraf, remarked that in contrast to previous leaders, he would govern as the nation's 'CEO'. Between the 1999 coup and the American invasion of Afghanistan in 2001, Musharraf maintained a measure of global (and to a lesser degree, domestic) legitimacy by projecting himself as a committed and competent proponent of neo-liberal reforms. Prior to the coup, a string of elected governments throughout the 1990s sought, with disastrous results, to reconcile popular[5] demands for economic redistribution with landed elite control of the civil-political process and structural adjustment policies set in place by multilateral lending agencies such as the IMF and World Bank. During the previous dictatorship of General Zia ul-Haq (1977–1988) Pakistan enjoyed stature and largesse as a 'frontline' state during the Afghan-Soviet war; this, in addition to the Gulf remittance boom provided urban and rural Pakistanis a material and psychological buffer against the onset of 'privatization' policies by Zia's government in the 1980s. By the early nineties, however, elected civilian governments were left to deal with the outfall of declining levels of American economic and military aid and waning migrant-labor demand from the Gulf states. A larger crisis of transparency ensued. The inability of elected regimes to implement effective policies of economic redistribution set the conditions for more informal channels of patronage and enrichment. The post-cold war surfeit in light weaponry combined with the onset of neo-liberal conditionalities to transform the democratising narrative of the 1990s into one of a 'lost decade' mired by corruption, party violence and ineffective governance at all levels.

The narrative of civil-political breakdown outlined above illustrates the enduring nexus between Pakistan's macro-economic, geo-political, and domestic political environment. In his self-proclaimed role as the nation's 'Chief Executive Officer', Musharraf implemented Pakistan's existing structural adjustment conditionalities with an unprecedented literalism that resulted in the largest increase in the rate of inequality during the tenure of a sitting government. The regime was also responsible for deepening and rationalising the country's financial sector through a series of reforms that offset the income gap among the middle-classes through the expansion of consumer credit.

The political violence and malfeasance of the previous decade bolstered the regime's argument that it alone was capable of shepherding Pakistan's much awaited entry into the global market[6]. Such propositions suggest another incarnation of Musharraf-as-CEO: a neo-liberal dictator who bypassed legislative-deliberative channels with the implicit backing of Pakistan's industrial and commercial bourgeoisie. Indeed, at an early stage, political talk shows were at the forefront of introducing this pro-Musharraf elite and its cultural politics to the wider Pakistani public. On 6 September 2002 'BBC Question Time Pakistan', a political talk show conducted in English by Harvard-trained lawyer Mahreen Khan, invited Musharraf to field questions from a hand-picked audience comprised of Karachi's cultural and economic elite. Musharraf appeared on the program in casual Western attire and exuded the part of a modern secular leader, thus carefully distinguishing his persona from the orthodox piety of the country's previous military ruler. A female audience member in her mid-twenties exemplified the supportive mood of the audience at the time when she candidly posed to the General why it was the case that the country's banned parliamentary parties had to be reinstated. Why, mused the questioner, could Musharraf not rule Pakistan forever?

At one level, this mediated staging of benevolent dictatorship points to the predicament of de-politicisation evident among urban middle-class adults who were raised during the Islamising dictatorship of General ul-Haq. Coming of age during the lost decade of the nineties, the educated middle-class segment of this generation believes that while General Zia lacked the ideological inclination to integrate Pakistan into the global cultural economy, the elected governments of the nineties failed to do because they lacked the political capacity. Musharraf's decision to support America's campaign against al-Qaeda and the Taliban in Afghanistan emboldened his domestic self-positioning as a button-down proponent of secular liberal ideals. This image appealed to a segment of the Pakistani elite and urban middle-class who were anxious to parley Pakistan's geo-strategic position into a source of national and personal enrichment.

By creating Pakistan's first licensing and regulatory body for private electronic media in 2002[7], Musharraf briefly secured the belief that his government encouraged the free flow of information and open criticism. According to its first

Chairman Mian Mohmmad Javed, the Pakistan Electronic Media Regulation Authority's (PEMRA) aim was to 'provide the private sector a transparent and level legal infrastructure without the traditional red-tapism' (quoted in January 2003[8]). Expanding the number of Pakistani channels would, in Javed's view, offer a national-cultural bulwark against the numerous European, Arab, and (most especially) Indian stations that had been available in Pakistan since the late 1990s through locally owned cable providers. Moreover, PEMRA's approach to media deregulation is aligned with strategies put in place by multi-lateral lending institutions such as the World Bank. The Bank's 2002 *World Development Report* asserts that '[r]ivalry among firms in the media industry ensures a broader range of social and political views and greater incentives for demand-driven reporting. With such information, voters, consumers, and investors are less likely to be exposed to abuse in economic and political markets, and minority views— including those of the poor—are more likely to be represented' (2002, 189). The report's blurring of the logics of consumption and democratisation is worth noting here. The belief that media deregulation could have the described effects on the Pakistani polity, however, is complicated by the fact that PEMRA was created through military ordinance.

The Musharraf regime's deregulation strategy tacked a careful position between expanding consumer choice, promoting 'open' criticism of the government and envisioning media as technology of political pacification. As one Karachi-based marketer for a major private station observed, by being more pleasurable to watch than their state-run counterpart, the new stations had the unintended consequence of keeping people (underemployed males especially) off the streets. This instrumental conception of the role of media, one may argue, points to the regime's effort to articulate capitalist and authoritarian logics of citizen-making by casting both liberalisation and democratisation in gradualist terms as objects of 'reform'. As such, the regime's aim was not to stifle political consciousness so much as manage it by merging it with the sedentary and visual pleasures of consumerism.

As profit-making enterprises that rely upon advertising revenue, Pakistan's private stations operate according to an understanding that news and entertainment programming is a consumer good. An equally urgent awareness exists, however, among executives and creative talent alike that the new channels are at the forefront of mediating social, political and cultural fissions within the national body politic that state-run television had steadfastly ignored[9]. By contrast, private stations are increasingly caught between seeking the greatest possible market share and offering a distinctive network brand that feeds into existing social divisions. A number of stations executives I spoke with during the course of fieldwork acknowledged the primary role of owners in molding a station's implicit sectarian, political, and class orientation.

Notwithstanding the depoliticising objectives of the state, deregulation created unparalleled opportunities for the production and circulation of unofficial meanings. This is evidenced by the introduction of novel news formats such as the call-in political talk show and real-time broadcast and reporting of breaking stories. A brief yet crucial period ensued in the first half of this decade whereby private stations showed signs of conformity to the norms of Pakistan's perennial discourse of 'controlled democracy'. Although elected representatives of Musharraf's 'king's party' were often taken to task on the new political shows, most shows studiously avoided discussion on the legitimacy or legality of Musharraf's coup. This environment of mutual détente began to dissolve, however, in the wake of Musharraf's attempt to seek a constitutional mandate for his presidency, which would ultimately require a decision from the Supreme Court.

The events leading to and following the dismissal of Pakistan's Chief Justice Iftikhar Chaudhry in March 2007 reveal the underlying fragility of the regime's approach to deregulation. Although Chaudhry was removed from office by Musharraf on charges of corruption, it is public knowledge that the regime regarded him as an 'activist judge' who was not afraid to question the overextension of executive power. Such perceptions grew in intensity when it became apparent that the Supreme Court would have to adjudicate on the legality of Musharraf's attempt to (re)-assume the presidency through parliamentary channels.

In many ways, the removal of the Chief Justice introduced new actors and energies to the ongoing struggle for full democratic sovereignty. While previous mass movements against military dictatorship were spearheaded by parliamentary forces, the 'lawyer's movement' in support of Chaudhry represented a professional segment of civil society which had remained relatively aloof from displays of political resistance. Indeed, the media's coverage of the movement was not only substantive but offered many Pakistanis their first moving images of police brutality against male and female citizens. If such abuses were acknowledged in the past, the onset of rapid response reporting transformed the moral and temporal topography of political violence by irreversibly re-casting the viewing audience as witnesses.

On 3 November 2007, President Musharraf suspended Pakistan's constitution and declared a state of emergency in an effort to stifle widespread opposition to his unilateral removal of the Chief Justice, (which by this time had snowballed into a campaign for Musharraf's ouster). The regime's response was swift and forceful, and the legal fraternity and the new stations were singled out. Stations were banned from airing politically sensitive shows, such as GEO TV's popular and controversial call-in political talk show *Mere Mutabiq with Dr. Shahid Masood*, and in a number of cases were taken off the air entirely. The emergency introduced curbs on the expression of the media through a series of amendments to the PEMRA ordinance that barred publishing or broadcasting of 'anything which defames or brings into ridicule the head of state, or members of the armed forces, or executive, legislative or judicial organ of the state' (pemra.gov.pk). This included a ban on live broadcasts of political events. What is more, these amendments remained in force after the state of emergency was lifted on 15 December 2007. Musharraf's rationale for imposing censorship was a familiar merging of geopolitical crisis with praetorian political strategy. The media, he observed in a statement to the nation, showed a lack of 'responsibility' and was inciting terrorism through negative and sensationalist reporting. After experiencing threats and violent suppression by the regime, a number of stations assumed an open, survivalist stance of resistance against the Musharraf presidency.

Mediating Moderation

Musharraf's commitment to neo-liberal reforms, his assertion of having 'created' a free private media industry, and his decision to collude with the United States in the War on Terror can be placed within a larger imaginary of 'Enlightened Moderation'. Writing in the *Washington Post*, Musharraf described Enlightened Moderation as a response to crises and failures throughout the Muslim world and Pakistan in particular, that had culminated, in his view, in the events of 11 September. He observed that, 'It is not Islam as a religion that has created militancy and extremism but rather political disputes that have led to antagonism among the Muslim masses ... What we need is introspection. Who are we, what do we as Muslims stand for, where are we going, where should we be headed and how can we reach it? The answers to these questions are the Muslim part of Enlightened Moderation' (*Washington Post* 1 June 2004, p. A23). Musharraf attributed the rise of Islamicist terrorism to the general unwillingness of the world's Muslims to 'learn and acquire from others' and 'raise ourselves up by individual achievement and collective socioeconomic emancipation' (ibid.).

In a general sense, the discourse of Enlightened Moderation upholds the possibility of creating a modern (rational, flexible, historical) interpretation of religious scripture that nurtures personal conviction and supports the individual and collective integration of Muslims into a global liberal political order. For radical secular writers, such as Sam Harris (2005), moderation signifies an acknowledgment of religious identity that consequently fails to provide an effective response to the literalism and violence of militant Islamic fundamentalism. A more subtle critique of the discourse of religious moderation is found in a recent essay by the anthropologist Saba Mahmood

(2006). For Mahmood, it is moderation's normative attention to forms of religious interpretation that defines its secular character. Here, secularism does not represent the separation of religion from public life but rather functions as a normative regime that 'reshape[s] the form [religion] takes, the subjectivities it endorses, and the epistemological claims it can make. The effectiveness of such a totalizing project necessarily depends upon transforming the religious domain through a variety of reforms and state injunctions' (Mahmood 2006, 326). Writing against the dominant liberal theoretical construction of tolerance as a rational expression of moral individualism, Wendy Brown makes a similar argument about the liberal conception of tolerance. According to her view, tolerance must be addressed critically as a 'mode of late modern governmentality' that 'produces and positions subjects, orchestrates meanings and practices of identity, marks bodies, and conditions political subjectivities' (Brown 2008, 4). For Mahmood and for Brown, the secularising production of subjects of moderation and tolerance is not limited to the production of laws or the practice of state power. Its rationalities and asymmetries can be produced by non-state institutions and actors as well, such as the new private satellite stations we are concerned with in this chapter.

Pakistan's contemporary discourse of Muslim moderation can be traced to nineteenth and twentieth century Indian projects of elite Muslim religious reform, to the political crisis of military state authoritarianism, and to the geo-political crisis of Pakistan's role as a 'frontline state' in the prosecution of American imperial wars in Central Asia. The Musharraf regime's discourse of Enlightened Moderation signified less of a revolutionary contribution to existing theological strains of modernist reform found throughout the postcolonial Muslim world than an attempt to reconcile the disjuncture between the state's participation in the War on Terror and its desire to integrate Pakistan into the global capitalist system. Within this militarised field of globalisation, the discourse of moderation exists to fulfill its binary opposite. An empty signifier, moderation has been effective in marking 'extremists' (an equally ambiguous category in practice) as illiberal 'others' who can be killed or disappeared with impunity by the Pakistani state[10]. What is new about the current geo-political moment is the role of martial sovereign power in privileging this binary over other, more established official nationalist distinctions, such as the division between loyal Muslim national subjects and 'bad' ethno-provincial subjects (the latter have long been regarded by the military and bureaucratic arms of the postcolonial state as the principle threat to Pakistan's national integrity)[11]. Focusing on political talk shows and religious and cultural entertainment programs, I consider how in the process of constructing a 'national' audience, Pakistan's private stations engage, resist and redefine the official geo-politics of moderation.

Nusrat Javed, co-host of 'Pakistan Speaks', a daily call-in news program on Aaj TV, reflected on the cultural and political ambiguity of the official subject of moderation in a program devoted to Maulana Fazlullah, a religious leader who had set up a 'parallel government' in dozens of villages throughout the Northern region of Swat in 2007. Javed, who is one of Pakistan's most respected and outspoken senior journalists, took issue with the opinion expressed by a female caller that the women of Swat would naturally suffer under and oppose Fazlullah's plan to impose a strict form of *shar'ia* (religious) law in the region. In what I understand to be a political rather than moral invective, Javed responded that if 'what is meant by Enlightened Moderation in Islam is the right of women to wear low cut dresses, attend elegant parties and hold long stemmed glass then it clearly has no meaning for these young girls in Swat'. I wish to suggest that Javed's comment was less a critique of secular moderation than an attempt to draw attention to its political and ethical ambiguity within national discourse. His use of gendered and sensuous imagery does not suggest the inherent moral depravity of moderate Muslims; rather it points to the moral and political crisis that ensues when religious moderation is instrumentally deployed to bolster arguments for military intervention. Javed's comments anticipated a rush of televised commentary before the November 2007 emergency on whether enlightened moderation was a sovereign discourse of religious reform or the ideological armature of a military-comprador state.

Like many postcolonial Muslim-majority societies, the democratisation of religious knowledge in Pakistan has occurred in response to the bureaucratic interventions of the postcolonial state, the rise of mass literacy, and increased access of urban middle and lower middle-class citizens to a variety of religious media – ranging from cassette sermons, to printed resources, and of course, official and unofficial televised programs on religious affairs (see Eikelman and Anderson 1999, Hirschkind 2006). Scholars of religious media in the Muslim world observe how such processes have led to the 'objectification' of the Islamic tradition while simultaneously engendering a more autonomous practice and subject of Muslim piety whose dependence on religious experts has diminished.

Pakistan's largest private stations maintain a distinctively secular and progressive approach to programming. The offices of GEO TV were stormed on 30 January 2005 by Islamist activists after it aired an investigative report on child abuse and incest[12]. Similar Islamist grumblings have also been heard around the question of indecency, but have not amounted to much. Of the nearly 35 stations which operate in Pakistan, not one explicitly claims to be the voice of the religious right, for reasons, which speak less to the lack of will or capital than to the limits of media deregulation in an era of multinational capitalism and secular military government.

This orientation has not led to the absence of religious programming, but its careful reconfiguration into a consumer good and conduit for the dissemination of modernist theological perspectives. A young executive at one of the country's newest stations told me that 'without *quality* religious content, there is no point in starting up a satellite venture'. Stations like GEO negotiate the demand for religious content among the middle-class by gravitating towards hosts with modernist and non-sectarian orientations, such as Amir Liaquat, the dandyish former minister of state for religious affairs who moderates the popular call-in show 'Alim Online' where callers receive advice from a Sunni and a Shia member of the clergy. *Alim Online* has made Liaquat one of Pakistan's top celebrities, known for his sonorous voice, sartorial adventurism, and an ability to be moved to tears by the grace of God. Such qualities are both an effect and cause of his celebrity. Liaquat's persona has been critical to the success of the show, as well to GEO's effectiveness in transforming religious programming from an instrument of pedagogy to a more user-driven form 'infotainment'.

Fair and Lovely

I turn now to the case of Ali Saleem, who first gained attention for his impeccable impersonation of Benazir Bhutto on GEO TV's political satire program *Hum Sub Umeed Seh Hei* (a play on words meaning either 'we are hopeful' or 'we are pregnant'). More recently, he has gained notoriety for his role as the female host of the *Late Night with Begum Nawawish Ali Show*, which has been hailed in the international media for pushing cultural and religious boundaries in a 'conservative' Muslim society such as Pakistan. In what follows, I describe how the ambiguity between Saleem's on and off-screen *persona* speaks to emergent connections between publicity, sexuality and moderation in the new media arena.

Saleem migrated to the Aaj (Today) network in 2006, and was given his own talk show. In contrast to GEO's approach to programming and aesthetics, which simultaneously caters to the constructs the urban middle-classes as a self-sufficient benchmark of the nation's moral and aesthetic sensibilities, the Aaj network represents a decidedly 'aspirational'[13] or voyeuristic network brand. More specifically Aaj celebrates, and provides a primer for, the possibility of mobility into an elite universe stereotypically associated with progressive social mores, English, and sober and discerning taste. As I noted above, the creation of niche stations is integral to the experience of the cultural economy of media deregulation as the proliferation of choice. What is salient about such stations, I argue, is that the apparent exclusivity of their programming content does not oblige the viewer to assume the position of subaltern at the moment of reception (see Rajagopal 2001).

The *Late Show with Begum Nawish* is at once a parody of, and biographical statement on, the preoccupations of Pakistan's English-speaking elite. The character of the Begum is the widow of a retired army colonel and diplomat who has seen the world and is unashamedly available. Ali Saleem, who is the child of a retired army officer and is well connected in Karachi's social circles, discussed his source of inspiration for Begum Nawish in an interview in the English monthly *Newsline*. When asked if he was a female impersonator Ali replied, 'No. Begum Nawazish Ali is me, something I have dreamt of since childhood. The Begum is an expression of me as a woman. She is a socialite, very sweet yet bitchy'. In another interview Saleem describes the show's format from the perspective of producer: 'We decided to create a larger-than-life character to host a talk show where the host would be flirtatious and look good so she would be on a strong footing with her guests ... She can intimidate her guests and break through their tough exteriors to reach the inner person that he or she is.' (*Newsline.com.pk* January 2006).

Late Night plays upon the intimate *mis-en-scene* of the Oprah Winfrey show, whose production values are now firmly a part of the global mediascape. It combines diffused and warm lighting and privileges the body and affect of the female host as the means for arriving at the personal authenticity of its guests. The desire for and dangers of publicity within Pakistan's new media circuits are illustrated in part by the fact that the Begum's guest list, which has included celebrities from film and television as well top political figures (such as stalwarts from the Pakistan People's Party, and a retired supreme court judge who ran for president in 2007 and appeared on the show with his wife). No one is immune from the Begum's ribaldry and thinly veiled advances, however, which is often deftly woven into political commentary. Certain guests, such as Bollywood mega-director Mahesh Bhatt, have taken immense pleasure in the Begum's *jouissance*, while Karachi's former Islamist mayor insisted after his appearance on the show that he had no idea the Begum was actually man.

It follows that the achievement of the show's irony does not ensue from the Begum's failure to fulfil the codes of elite femininity, which are accomplished by Ali with tremendous vocal and bodily poise. Indeed, much of the pleasure of reception unfolds in anticipating the possible counter-advances or unravelling of the shows *male* guests. Like India, Pakistan has a vibrant *hijra* (male eunuch, third-sex) community whose public transgression of everyday codes of male heteronormative behaviour is neither celebrated nor suppressed by the society at large. Moreover, *hijras* often engage in the public performance of an imagined female sexuality that can be enjoyed by men without the accusation of homosexuality. For his part, Saleem shuns the title of *hijra* or female impersonator: the Begum is an 'expression' of Saleem, who has recently acknowledged his bi-sexuality. What ensues during the Begum's interviews with her male guests, I contend, is a structure of feeling, in which the existing *and* emergent contours of Pakistani popular culture enter into a kind of dialogue. The Begum's sexuality and candor only achieves significance in relation to Ali's performance of a certain class intellect, and it this combination that compels the show's male guests to speak beyond the dominant masculinist register of the public declamation.

This process of displacement brings us to the question of Ali's understanding of his character as an expression of moderate Muslim and feminist agency. For Ali, Begum Nawazish 'represents the aspiration of all Pakistanis who want a modern, progressive Pakistan'; her international acclaim has made her 'the face of an enlightened, moderate Pakistan.' – this, 'at a time when our country is tainted by images of [Islamic terrorism] happening around the world and suicide bombers …' Ali, who situates the impetus for Begum Nawazish in his life long desire to be a woman, insists the show is 'about empowering women psychologically. I am trying to show people that there is no difference between men and women. I have no gender bias.'

Ali has suggested that his use of 'drag' on the show has enabled him to 'get away with a lot' in terms of his performance of sexuality. Indeed, one can read Ali's statements through the lens of both paternalism and elite-liberal feminism. The sexual ambivalence he performs allows him to effectively embody both stances, I would argue, since each assumes the average Pakistani woman lacks the consciousness to express their desire in the domestic and public arena. For critics and fans alike, the show's exemplification of a possible moderate politics in Pakistan manifest less in the character of Begum herself than in the sexual ambivalence of Ali, who disseminates the character as both an 'impersonation' to be consumed and a comfortable extension of his libidinal self. Ali is well aware of how the ambiguity surrounding his sexual identity has played a crucial role in the show's phenomenal success. He recently starred in his own reality-based program in which he searches – this time without sari and makeup – for his future bride.

Conclusion

Pakistan's private stations form an important new ground for the staging of political, religious and capitalist modernity. As I have argued, the form this modernity takes involves a complex dialectic of the local and the global, in which the latter is framed by the competing consequences of neo-liberal reform and the global war on terror. The state-led discourse of Enlightened Moderation signified an attempt to reconcile these competing political imperatives of modernity and sovereignty for a nation-state and a region that, as I write this conclusion, is poised to eclipse Iraq as the United State's new central theatre of war. A larger study will address in more detail how viewers, producers and marketers appropriate and resist what I wish to call the *geo-politics of moderation*. The aim of this chapter has been to outline some of the key features of this emergent conjuncture of capitalist, nationalist and state representation, one which continues to seek hegemony after the ouster of Musharraf from power and the return of civilian-led democracy in 2008.

That the new stations seek to mediate moderation does not point to either the unity or dominance of the Pakistani or American state as entities with the exclusive capacity to define the moral or cultural terrain of moderation. At the level of public culture and the everyday a more plural and subtle set of discourses operate on the relation between politics and religion. These complicate any state-based attempt to frame moderation as the natural and compliant stance of Pakistan's 'silent majority'. While the new stations resemble the state to the extent that they do not feel compelled to represent this complexity, I argue that they differ from the state-based approach by conceiving of moderation in more substantive terms as a cultural politics that is integral to commercial success. In this sense, the new stations have assigned the geo-politics of moderation a certain kind of political and personal force, one that evokes a sense of societal transformation without the official burden of guarantees.

Notes

1. I use 'to' since a number of stations uplink their domestic signal to Dubai for transmission.
2. GEO TV, launched in 2001, is currently Pakistan's most watched private satellite station, followed by ARY and AAJ TV. Indus TV, which launched a news and music channel in 1999, holds the distinction of being the first private station.
3. Private conversation, Lahore Pakistan, 3 March 2002.
4. For a detailed account of the events of the 1999 military coup see http://news.bbc.co.uk/2/hi/south_asia/475195.stm (accessed 10 January 2009).
5. Pakistan returned to civilian rule in 1988, following the third military dictatorship of General Zia ul-Haq. Zia waged a coup against the government of Pakistan's first popularly elected Prime Minister (Z.A. Bhutto) in 1977.
6. An early example of this argument is Musharraf's first address to the nation following the October 1999 coup. See http://news.bbc.co.uk/2/hi/world/monitoring/477829.stm for a complete transcript. (accessed 10 January 2009)
7. See http://www.pemra.gov.pk
8. http://www.internews.org.pk/files/media-law-bulletin-issue-i.pdf (accessed 10 January 2009).
9. This observation is based on a series of interviews conducted with marketing executives from Express News and two leading advertising agencies.
10. See http://www.amnesty.org/en/news-and-updates/report/denying-the-undeniable-enforced-disappearances-in-pakistan-20080723. (accessed 10 January 2009)
11. See Ahmad, F. (1998) *Ethnicity and Politics in Pakistan*. Karachi: Oxford University Press.
12. http://www.internews.org/pubs/pakistan/pakistan_media_report_2005-05.shtm (accessed 10 January 2009).
13. Mazzarrella (2004).

References

Ahmad, F. (1998) *Ethnicity and Politics in Pakistan*, Karachi: Oxford University Press
Brown, W. (2008) *Regulating Aversion: Tolerance in the Age of Identity and Empire*, Princeton USA: Princeton University Press
Eickelman, D. F. and Anderson, J.W. (1999) (eds) *New Media in the Muslim World: The Emerging Public Sphere*, Bloomington: Indiana University Press
Harris, S. (2005) *The End of Faith: Religion, Terror, and the Future of Reason*, New York: W.W. Norton
Hirschkind, C. (2006) *The Ethical Soundscape: Cassette Sermons and Islamic Counterpublics (Cultures of History)*, New York: Colombia University Press
Islam, R. (2002) *World Development Report 2002: Building Institutions for Markets*, New York: Oxford University Press
Mahmood, S. (2006) 'Secularism, Hermeneutics, and Empire: The Politics of Islamic Reformation' In *Public Culture*, 18(2): 323–34
Mazzarrella, W. (2004) *Shovelling Smoke: Advertising and Globalization in Contemporary India*, Durham: Duke University Press
Rajagopal, A. (2001) *Politics after Television: Hindu Nationalism and the Reshaping of the Public in India*, London: Cambridge University Press

Chapter Seven

FORGETTING TO REMEMBER: THE PRIVATISATION OF THE PUBLIC, THE ECONOMISATION OF HINDUTVA AND THE MEDIALISATION OF GENOCIDE

Britta Ohm

On 8 December 2007, anchorwoman Barkha Dutt from the English-language section of the private Indian national news broadcaster NDTV (New Delhi Television, that was until 2003 *Star News*, part of Rupert Murdoch's transnational News Corporation) had a very interesting article published in the *Hindustan Times*. Dated two weeks before Narendra Modi's second electoral triumph as Chief Minister of the state of Gujarat was made public, it was – in the last phase of the election campaign – concerned with the media's positioning vi-à-vis the infamous yet highly popular regional leader of the Hindu nationalist BJP (Bharatiya Janata Party). The controversy around Modi arises from his personal and administrative support for the systematic killing of well over 2000 Muslims between March and May 2002, the investigation of which has been largely thwarted but which is basically beyond doubt[1]. Publicisation of the controversy is closely linked to the national, and particularly the English-language media, that often took a scandalised and highly critical stance towards Modi at the time; and again when the Gujarat electorate confirmed Modi in office in December 2002. In her article written five years later, Dutt analyses the personality cult that grew in intervening years around the Chief Minister in Gujarat. She considers it reminiscent of a 'monsters' ball', that has pushed aside the dominance of traditional party hierarchies in the state. Pointing out the 'tragic irony of today's Gujarat', namely that 'a Modi-centric attack [by the media, B.O.] that dwells on the state-sponsored violence of 2002 only seems to rally public opinion around him', Dutt concludes that in order 'to ensure the future of Gujarat, we can no longer remain prisoners of the past'[2].

Barkha Dutt has, over the years, attracted substantial criticism for her reporting from various fronts, and was accused of 'secular shrillness'[3] and of betraying the cause of Kashmiri pundits[4] as well as of over-the-top nationalism (in the context of the Kargil war in 1999) and, indeed, of soft-peddling *Hindutva* (politically organised Hindu-ness). Yet, Dutt has generally been careful not to display overt sympathies for Hindu nationalism and the BJP. The unwillingness of NDTV to succumb to the pro right-wing editorial intervention typical of Rupert Murdoch[5] (and a post-Gujarat legal initiative introduced by the central BJP-government and meant to hit English-language, 'secular' news television rather than News Corporation) in 2003 eased Mudoch's decision to part with the company and to set up his own, far less critical, Hindi news channel. In contrast to numerous other journalists and media outfits, Dutt cannot thus be overtly associated with BJP Hindutva rhetoric which, right from the pogrom onward, downplayed its character and implications, and has since then employed the 'enough-is-enough' argument that urges citizens, particularly in their avatar as consumers, to look ahead and to not waste time always looking back. Yet, Dutt's proposal marks a decisive turning point regarding traditional 'leftist-liberal secular' journalistic practise in India: precisely in order to be able to move, in a long-term perspective, into a presumably better, non-'Modi-fied' future, she suggests that one should *not* remember and critically acclaim the dead, name the culprits or continue to demand justice for the victims but, on the contrary, *forget* about all of that.

How can such an advocacy by a vocal journalist of forgetting rather than remembrance with regard to the most organised and merciless communal violence India has witnessed since Independence – and the first that the UN have classified as an attempted genocide – be understood and construed? What sort of 'realism' and what political rationale is at work when, in a formal democracy like India, journalists consider actual and potential victims to be 'safer' when the media refrains from recalling their plight and from reporting on the ongoing extremity of their marginalisation?

Communal Violence, Economic Liberalisation and Electoral Crisis

Dutt's proposition merely indicates a larger discursive shift in the national mainstream media over the past decade that essentially signifies a crisis. It is underscored by the overall ultimately uncritical coverage of Modi's second foreseeable electoral victory: now, in contrast to his first victory in December 2002, being attributed largely not to extreme Hindutva but to 'successful development' and *suraj* (good governance)[6].

Different from analysis that identifies the pogrom merely with the *breakdown* of law and order and state *failure* in Gujarat (cf. Yagnik and Sheth 2005, 282) and assumptions that see the 'free media' and Hindu nationalism as 'two walls of a canyon' (Jeffrey 2001, 41), deemed to have a merely antagonistic or contradictory relationship, I argue in this chapter that this discursive shift is an expression of the parallel and interrelated rise of Hindutva and the media to prominent, and indeed reality-generating positions in Indian society in the context of economic liberalisation policies. They both had a democratising and empowering function vis-à-vis the Congress state, leading, in the particular case of Gujarat, to the calculated *establishment* of a new, post-democratic and potentially post-global understanding and practise of governance that re-defines law and order according to effective exclusion of minorities and that impacts mainstream media coverage – rather than the other way round – without directly censoring or subjugating it.

Scholars have for long emphasised Hindu nationalism's basically 'soft' approach (Zavos 2000) that consistently avoids typically authoritarian actions like a coup-d'état (Jaffrelot 2001, Dutt and Girdner 2000) and that aided its close abiding by democratic rules (Ghosh 1999) and its 'undeserved' democratising impact vis-à-vis the paternalism, elitism, non-transparency and hierarchical organisation of the prior Congress-state with its didactic national principles of Nehruvian secular democracy and socialism (Hansen 1999). What is crucial, however, is that Modi could buttress and profit from a particular electoral crisis in the larger Indian context. It took shape with the watershed of the destruction of the 1528-built Babri mosque in the town of Ayodhya, in the state of Uttar Pradesh, through militant *kar sevaks* (Hindu nationalist volunteers) in 1992 and the ensuing violence in large parts of the country, including Gujarat, but particularly in Bombay.

Until then communal violence, overwhelmingly against Muslims and commonly under the narrative of 'Muslim aggression'[7] had been an ever-repetitive occurrence, generally implying some involvement of the state and used as electoral strategies by political parties (Akbar 1988/2003, Brass 2003). Governments, i.e. mainly the Congress party, thus got elected *despite* their involvement or because they were seen to have eventually *contained* the violence. In 1992, however, the central Congress government under Narasimha Rao, as much as the Congress state government of Maharashtra (Bombay), let the destruction of the Babri mosque in Ayodhya, and the ensuing assaults in Bombay itself, unfold largely without taking the measures it could have applied (cf. Eckert 2003, 117). One significant factor behind this rather obvious lack of interference in the anti-Muslim violence in 1992/93 was the importance of the Muslim votebank for an increasingly ailing Congress. This turned on the macabre – and, as far as the Muslim voters were concerned, illogical – calculation that the unhindered agency of Hindu nationalists would amply demonstrate their destructive inclinations and underline that the Congress was the only political force in India that could ensure secular democracy and the protection of minorities.

Thus the choice, for voters, was between obvious but ideologically passive supporters of the violence for their own gains (the Congress) and ideologically and performatively active – and thus, in a way, more 'transparent' – instigators and organisers of the violence (the *Sangh parivar*, the 'family' of Hindu nationalist organisations, including the BJP) in the pursuit of a *Hindu rashtra* (nation of Hindus). The following general elections in 1996 just about[8] brought to power India's first non-Congress coalition-government under the centre-left United Front, which indicated the preference of a 'third way' in the demands for decentralisation and a 'democratising of democracy' (Ohm 1999: 88). This was only an interlude, though, in the ascendance of BJP-led coalitions, which was also signified by the growing acceptance of communal violence (i.e. anti-Muslim violence) particularly amongst the middle classes. This violence slowly, albeit not wholly, shifted from the long-common justification of 'teaching the Muslims a lesson' (in subservience to Hindus and the Congress-state) towards an increasingly unconcealed and hatred-laden 'finish them off once and for all' rhetoric. This transition was closely linked to growing social insecurities and economic demands under an increasingly fast-paced liberalisation policy and globalisation (Datta 2003, Fernandes 2006, Hasan 2003). Particularly in the course of the recession towards the beginning of the new millennium, the BJP profited from demands for reduced economic and social state intervention (i.e. in the form of employment reservations for lower castes and Adivasis that affect upper caste dominance) and from rising expectations of effective governance in terms of property-enlargement, political and cultural stability and state security. All of this took an additional leap following India's Kargil war against Pakistan, 09/11, and the dubious supposed terrorist attack on the Indian parliament in December 2001[9].

Re-Defining Democracy, Empowerment and Freedom of Expression: Controversial Genocide and the Libera(lisa)tion of the Media

It is against this backdrop, in which violence was successively transferred from electoral strategy into electoral behaviour, that Narendra Modi – in the particular context of Gujarat, one of India's younger and fastest growing states that has featured particularly strong and largely caste-induced conflicts over the redistribution of economic and political resources (cf. Vasavi 2002; Yagnik and

Sheth 2005, 252; Shani 2007, 140) – has managed to upset, to some extent, the genealogy of authoritarian rulers, who often refuse to vacate the positions they have attained with increasingly non-democratic, suppressive means. In a move not uncommon in Indian politics, Modi was installed in October 2001 as Chief Minister of Gujarat by the national BJP leadership as 'a defender of the Hindu Faith' (Shani 2007, 181); he was a mere replacement of the local elections-losing Keshubhai Patel, a classic Hindu hardliner, whose government was viewed as non-performing in the desired sense[10]. The organisation and orchestration of the pogrom just four months later was a vital element in proving Modi's performative power in terms of creating a *Hindu sangathan* (unity of Hindus) by rallying high- as well as low-caste Hindus and Adivasis behind a common cause in an economically tense situation and thus generating the base for his democratic confirmation in office through an already highly communalised electorate.

The very fact that the systematic butchering of co-citizens was – even in the larger national domain – *controversial* in the first place and that Modi's being elected could *thrive* on a pogrom, underlines the inclusion of basic ethical standards that usually reside above political negotiation into the realm of popular democratic discourse and electoral behaviour. Accounting, in particular, for today's Gujarat but also for the larger post-Congress Indian context (Corbridge and Harriss 2001), it stands in contrast to the self-evidence of humane shock and outrage that overall still characterised reactions to the brutality of the Bombay riots a decade earlier[11] (no matter how much certain citizens had basically been in favour of 'teaching the Muslims a lesson' (Hansen 2001, 127). At the same time is it intrinsically implicated in the dramatically changed scope and position of the media as the foremost reflectors as well as generators of this change.

Crucially, the advance of Hindutva entailed a redefinition of democracy from the defining power of a political majority that protects the legal rights of minorities towards a cultural-religious (communal) majority that goes by sheer numbers and that betrays an inherent proclivity to market mechanisms. 'Empowerment' thus meant not the strengthening of the disadvantaged in a social, legal and political sense but the ontological appropriation of that position through a – middle class-led – Hindu majority against the so-called 'secular suppression' (and hypocrisy) of the previous Congress state. The parallel rise of the media, on the other hand, and their increasing transnationalisation, economic liberalisation and commercialisation since the early 1990s, was embedded in an understanding of democratisation and empowerment as signifying a lifting of restrictions on freedom of expression. This was particularly the case for television. While the press had always enjoyed a legally protected freedom, television had as a key instrument of developmental politics for decades, essentially unconstitutionally, been monopolised and controlled by the state, which had systematically censored coverage of communal violence. During the Bombay riots in 1992/93 television was only just in course of being released from that restraint and hardly had a chance, yet, to report on the violence, let alone on the absence of agency of the Congress government. The international wing of the BBC was the main TV reporting station, its pictures of the Babri mosque's destruction and triumphant kar sevaks being for the first time directly relayed to Indian audiences via satellite and cable, and evoking maybe subliminally ambiguous but, in the public discourse, still largely horrified reactions. The anti-Muslim violence of 1992/93 was thus the first communal carnage in India that was represented on television (that too, mainly to a limited group of metropolitan viewers), making its dimensions immediately graphic in a way that newspapers never could and that the state had rendered invisible. Meanwhile, its reporting through the BBC was part of a democratising and transnationalising process vis-à-vis the undemocratic broadcasting policy of the Congress-governments (Ohm 2001). The appreciation of an unprecedented freedom of expression on the part of quickly evolving Indian electronic and digital media but also of the booming newspaper market in various Indian languages (Jeffrey 2001, Ninan 2007), and an increased aversion against anything to do with state intervention overrode even the consciousness of an increasing vacuum of coherent democratic legislation that would protect especially electronic journalistic work (the first draft of a Convergence Bill was shelved in 2003, while the last draft of a Broadcasting Bill lapsed in 2006).

The different readings of democracy and empowerment by Hindutva and the newly liberalised media were thus willy-nilly walking common ground in their critique of the Congress-state, precariously uniting an interpretation of suppression in terms of 'Western-based' secularism and anti-majoritanism with an interpretation in terms of democracy and freedom of expression. It was precisely the Gujarat pogrom of 2002, however, that became a key event in demonstrating to the media that their understanding of 'freedom of expression' was not shared by audiences to the degree they assumed. When the violence erupted, many journalists took for granted not merely the same level of shock and outrage amongst the Indian population as was evinced in 1992/93. They also expected to be able to report far more directly and critically than ten years earlier, especially given that in this instance the active rather than passive involvement of the BJP-state government in the anti-Muslim pogrom was unmistakable from the very beginning. What soon became palpable, however, was, first of all, that the empowerment of audiences vis-à-vis government-controlled information in an acute situation such as the pogrom was expressed not in a greater claim for investigative coverage but in a pronounced rejection of mass media as a source of authoritative, or even reliable information; and in a certain panic at the idea of being manipulated. In the context of a now rating-dependent commercial television this translated into an understanding of a 'majority audience' that resonated with the majoritarian Hindutva definition. 'Empowerment' meant an increased demand for the answerability of the media to 'Hindu sentiment' rather than an acceptance of their being committed to 'the greater common good'. 'Freedom of expression', on the other hand, entailed the 'freedom' to support the violence openly and to 'speak out' not against the pogrom but against Muslims. While it was thus a supposedly liberated and liberalised media that *made* the pogrom publicly controversial, journalists were confronted with yet new and unexpected limitations in their work, expressed particularly in the outrage of readers, viewers and users not against the *violence* but against their *reporting* of the violence. This reporting was often attacked as 'biased' (pro-Muslim, anti-Hindu, anti-Gujarat), 'elitist' (pro-Congress), and 'counterproductive' (in terms of instigating the violence or 'blowing it out of proportion')[12]. This accounted particularly for comments about the English-language media, and re-emphasised their traditional invocation by the Sangh parivar as the 'secular' post-colonial adversary and as being 'culturally alienated' and unable to grasp 'the voice of the people' (Rajagopal 2001). As Barkha Dutt put it in an interview with the author a year after the pogrom-coverage and a few months after the first election of Narendra Modi:

> In this country the English language media used to have a potency record we were proud of, and suddenly it saw that a campaign it did not lead consciously but how our conscience made us see the story, made no difference. It absolutely made no difference. If your aim was to try and shock your reader, your viewer, you had failed, you had essentially failed. [...] I was flooded with hate-mails abusing me as being anti-Hindu. Some were even suspecting I was a Muslim in disguise. It was absurd. (20 April 2003)

Thus a reverse reification of the old 'communication gap' (Ohm 1999) between government-controlled television and an underchallenged, belittled and non-receptive audience was inscribed in the reformulation of 'freedom of expression' through empowered audiences: audiences' demands and readings were manifold and strengthened vis-à-vis the shrinking authority of the reporting journalist under commercialised conditions. Precariously, it was just this empowerment which enhanced the impression of internal democracy in India and minimised international alarm as well as the interest of non-Indian media in the pogrom. The assessment that this was 'just another riot' and an internal Indian matter, enforced by the BJP, was buttressed precisely by the coverage of the situation by professional Indian – rather than foreign – journalists.

In an intensified but reversed scenario from the 1992/93 violence, the Gujarat pogrom thus became the first attempted, and eventually electorally rewarded, genocide on a global scale that was broadcast live by competing and uncensored TV stations from the same country. On the one hand, this made the most merciless communal violence the most meticulously documented in India ever. On the other hand, this generated not merely a tolerance for (as under Congress-governments) but also a vindication of the perpetrators.

The form of discourse that enabled this paradox is characterised by semantic reversals and re-interpretations of modern terminology rather than by open ideological and structural antagonism – such as the discernable abolishment of democracy. It underlines the intrinsic modernism of Hindutva and the Sangh parivar and tallies with what Rancière (2002) has called 'dis-agreement', describing the conflict between 'the one who says 'white' and the one who also says 'white' but who absolutely does not mean the same thing' (translation mine). The following sections will briefly expand on three salient aspects of this 'Modi-fication' of democratic discourse in the particular context of the pogrom: the construction of the nondescript 'outsider' and the reverse readings of democratic law, the interpretability of imagery and the call for 'neutrality' of the media, all of which, in effect, rendered well-researched accusations against Modi, 'Gujarat' and the Sangh parivar inconsequential. Particularly, they underline the medialised, rather than merely mediated, character of the violence. A recent term more common in the German language analysis of media and based on Marshall McLuhan, medialisation describes the increasing merging of mediated representations and social and political reality: true is thus what appears in the media, and the media themselves become the generators and creators of reality (Imhof 2006; Krotz 2001).

Gujarati Nationalism against 'Outsiders': Re-Interpreting Critique and Law

A basic preliminary to as well as the ultimate outcome of the pogrom was the solidification of 'Gujarati pride' as part of a specific electoral mobilisation. In this context, quite beyond the rejection by their audiences, it would be very misleading to think that Indian journalists were just able to go about their job in covering the violence and were not impeded, influenced or threatened. In actual fact, the case was quite the opposite (see below)[13], underscoring the clear anti-democratic conditions in the situation. What was different from comparative scenarios, however, were the ways in which these impediments were legitimised. They indicated the renewed centrality of the (regional) state that enforces nationalistic fervour less through authoritarian and disciplinarian measures such as compulsion and censorship than through a skilful generation of definitional power 'in the name of the people' over conventional meanings within a democratic and media-oriented setting.

The conventional rhetorical line, that the violence represented an uncontrollable outbreak of 'Hindu anger' against "Muslim aggression', toed by the Modi government and various Sangh parivar-outfits, was conveniently topped up in the still-immediate post-09/11 atmosphere with unfettered rhetoric about 'Islamic jihad'[14] and inserted India swiftly into the new global paradigm, in which 'riot control [...] becomes part of 'war against terrorism" (Ahmad 2003, 22). A crucial additive to this intensified narrative of retaliation became the construction of supposed 'outsiders', who were to blame for the escalation of the violence. An essential(ist) entity in the generation of conservative nationalism as well as an indicator of the impulse to shelter crimes against humanity from outside investigation, the nondescript and opaque figure of the 'outsider' had to step in on behalf of Muslims, who were accused of instigating the violence, but who were existing in a situation of such escalating anti-Muslim violence that it was increasingly difficult to identify them with the role of perpetrators. The undeniable totality of the violence, moreover, seemed clearly to exceed a merely defensive 'Hindu anger', so that, in order not to compromise the official narrative, the responsibility for the aggression had to be relegated to non-specified 'outsiders', making the complementary 'insiders', who were to be protected from all accusations, commensurate with the Gujarati Hindus.

As far as the unimaginably brutal crimes against Muslim men, women, children, housing and property were concerned (Dayal 2002; Patel, Padgaonkar and Verghese 2002; PUCL 2003; Varadarajan 2002), when the media asked in various localities who could be named as culprits, in an attempt to purge the self of any involvement, the (barbaric) 'outsider' was pointed out. The same pattern of the acute empowerment of Gujarati nationalism could be observed on a more general level, when it came to criticism of the Modi government or open condemnations of Hindu aggression from any organisation or person 'inside' or 'outside' Gujarat. This provoked not merely the accusation of treason, but an actual disentitlement to being Gujarati and resulted in reprimands about wilfully discrediting, and about understanding nothing about Gujarat, respectively. This mystification of a Gujarat that follows its own rules and is, precisely because of that, way ahead of other Indian states and particularly of the politically corrupt capital, Delhi, could (in this case on the national news channel *Aaj Tak*) be reinforced repeatedly by Modi, thus relying on, as well as vindicating, a majority of supporters in the state: 'You have an ethos in Gujarat which you just don't have in Delhi'.[15]

Within the context of this neo-cultural mystification was the figure of the (ignorant, ill-meaning) 'outsider" most pointedly represented in the non-Gujarati media. This accounted in toto for the national, but particularly the

English language media. As there existed no legal possibility but also no real inclination of sustainably censoring them, they were accused of thoroughly misreading the situation, i.e. of distorted reporting, misrepresentation, sensationalism (see below) and hence of communal instigation and irresponsibility. Thus, instead of being able to confront Modi with his actions, they became an indispensable part of a concerted discourse, in which the Chief Minister played them off against the – largely sympathetic – local vernacular 'insider' media. Modi personally wrote recommendation letters to editors of Gujarati newspapers like *Sandesh*, which featured headlines such as 'Avenge Blood with Blood' (28 February 2002) and 'Hindus Beware: Haj Pilgrims Return with Deadly Plans to Attack' (5 March 2002)[16], thanking them for playing a 'decisive role as a link between the people and the government' and congratulating them on having 'served humanity in a big way' by supporting the government in 'trying its level best to restore peace'[17]. While Modi did thus not have to force considerable parts of the local media into subservience but could encourage existing support, the 'serving of humanity' and 'restoration of peace' did not, as conventional readings would have it, relate to compassionate or critical reporting and the active termination of the violence but rather to the instigation to kill more Muslims with the consent of the 'majority'. Woven into the 'othering' of the national media was, on the other hand, a certain language-dependent hierarchy, with greater support for the new majority-identified 'Gujarat' being expected of Hindi-language media like *Aaj Tak*. The effect of this definitional design was that Modi and other Sangh parivar outfits brought themselves into the position of *forgiving* Aaj Tak's critique, because, even though vernacular and 'home-grown', it could be disparaged as being still too influenced by the logic of English language media to know better and to defend its vernacular solidarity appropriately. The same 'forgiveness' was consequently not bestowed upon *Star News*, with Barkha Dutt as one of the head reporters on location, whose coverage was most directly pointing to the salient role of the government in organising the violence, the suffering of the victims and to Modi's denial of responsibility.

In taking full advantage of his rights as Chief Minister, Modi brought into force a Gujarat-wide prohibition on the dissemination of Star News by cable operators for one day by way of a warning. The decision was justified by 'the provocative reporting methods used'[18] and rested opportunistically on the employment of one of the few existing legal regulations in the television business, The Cable Television Networks (Regulation) Act, 1995. Paragraph 19, Chapter V explicitly legalises the administrative power 'to, by order, prohibit any cable operator from transmitting or retransmitting any particular programme, if it is likely to promote, on grounds of religion, race, language, caste or community or any other ground whatsoever, disharmony or feelings of enmity, hatred or ill will between different religious, racial, linguistic or regional groups or castes or communities or which is likely to disturb public tranquillity' (in Iyer 2000, 138). The 'disturbance of public tranquillity' thus did not correspond to the organisation of anti-minority violence but to the alarmed coverage about it. What could be read as a foresighted governmental measure to avoid unnecessary further protest and escalation (supposedly due to critical reporting) was actually a move to conceal ongoing atrocities against Muslims and to further unite and empower (Hindu) Gujaratis against 'outsiders'.[19] Modi's declaration of 'normalcy' in May 2002, immediately after the final calming down of the acute violence through special army forces worked accordingly. 'Normalcy' was commensurate not with the rehabilitation of victims but with the prompt closure of refugee camps, leaving around 200,000 Gujarati Muslim citizens, the unwanted 'outsiders inside', simply to their fate after having driven them from their homes. Officially not registered as displaced, and to a considerable percentage not even acknowledged to still exist, because the replacement of their burnt or lost voter-ID and ration cards has been systematically withheld (Ohm 2007), these 'outsider' citizens and their 'truth' were thus not only swiftly removed from the electoral process but were also systematically rendered a non-happening for the media without an obvious or substantial alteration of the apparent democratic framework.[20]

The Medialisation of Violence and the Interpretability of Images and Terminology

It is this context that made the pogrom a palpable and specific dimension of medialisation and privatisation. This accounted not merely for the largely private economic character of the mainstream reporting mass media, their dependency on ratings, and their re-definition by audiences as being publicly answerable to feelings and demands that had been declared private in the Congress-state, i.e. particularly to 'Hindu sentiment'. It showed as well in the strong private appropriation of different new digital media (mobile phones, Mini DV-cameras, the Internet and e-mail) by non-governmental agents competing for definitional power. Rioters and members of the Sangh parivar employed new media extensively in *organising and coordinating* the violence as much as those (like filmmakers, students, researchers etc.) who had, in addition to TV stations, come out in unprecedented numbers to *critically document* the events on their own initiative viewed them as new 'technologies of witnessing' (McLagan 2006). The concentration of media on the spot, and especially the quantity of *visual* evidence produced, thus said nothing any more about the democratic containment of the situation and spelt no hope for the victims in the sense that their situation would become known and eventually provoke consequences in their favour. Rather they highlighted that media are no more 'mediators' or representatives of an 'outer' reality but have – literally – become both creators and signifiers of realities, including violent realities.

As much as the same media technologies, albeit with extremely different intentions, were used at the same time in the same situation, the images produced were themselves, naturally, often identical and evoked an enhanced importance of textual contextualisation, framing and interpretation. This was further complicated by the fact that even a term like 'Hindutva laboratory' (referring to the particular preconditions in Gujarat made fruitful by the Sangh parivar in unfolding their vision of Indian society) was, for instance, used by the Sangh parivar and by Modi with pride in their accomplishment. It was employed, meanwhile, by critics in terms of a horror scenario that has become reality. The resulting space for critics to connect to larger audiences through commonly shared meanings or to mediate a viable counter-reality and, particularly, of artists to create works that 'speak for themselves' was grossly minimised, and stood thus in ironic contrast to the manifold increase in availability and mobility of media equipment. This led a number of concerned filmmakers – whose hesitation resembled an 'inner exile' of invisibility and speechlessness – to refrain from entering the discourse at all for fear of exposing their works to unnecessary attack or lending them to what *they* would define as misrepresentation (Wolf 2007).

Overall, however, TV-journalists reporting from Gujarat did not have the choice of retreating into oblivion, as they were sent there to do their job. The account of an *Aaj Tak* reporter underlines that their physical endangerment was in an unprecedented way related to the medialised character of the pogrom and consequently also to the battle over the very command of the medium:

> You almost get killed. You have mobs throwing stones at you. It's very amazing because when we landed there, people shook our hands, even took pictures, wanted autographs, because they had seen Aaj Tak or knew about Aaj Tak, and then we went into this place and they said, yaya, come and shoot this, come and shoot this, but suddenly it started that they were taking pictures which could be, you know, which may harm us [in the sense of documenting that they were filming in an 'anti-Hindu'/'pro-minority' way, B.O.]. And then suddenly they turned round, you know, and those very people started throwing stones at us, beating up the cameraperson, beating me up, taking away our wallets and... chasing us, they were like looters, you know. [...] It were the very same people. [...] It was a terrible time, because they were storming the house. And you could hear that their number was growing. And, you know, we just didn't know how to react, I mean, when you were in the room, you wondered, why should I be in

the room? Why should I run away from them? You know? I'm a reporter.
Why am I behaving like a coward? (Interview with the author, 22 April 2003)

The disbelief and bewilderment over the sudden meaninglessness of his profession and the reversal of his status from interpretative authority to bereft fugitive is here most graphically predicated upon the demanding appropriation of the medium through prospective audiences who claim the power over its representations. However, the account also carries another message that turns this reversal of power around again, so to speak, (even if at the cost of the journalist). The *Aaj Tak*-team, precariously poised at the threshold between 'vernacular' and 'outsider', was first welcomed, encouraged and directed in its work ('shoot this') in the obvious expectation of its supportive stance towards the 'just violence'. From one second to another, however, 'the very same people' apparently became acutely aware that 'the very same image' did not inherently subscribe to their 'defense of Gujarat' but might well serve to document their crimes. This instant transformation from boasting self-confidence to fear of consequences that is intrinsically linked to the medialised character of the pogrom speaks of the inherent risk that remains when a discourse is not simply suppressed but, on the contrary, pushed forward without ethical barriers. As Susan Sontag has so aptly observed: '[a]ll photographs wait to be explained or falsified by their captions' (2004, 10). Her contention, however, that pictures of the atrocities of war and the horrors of violence can not only stimulate the repudiation of war but 'also foster greater militancy' (ibid.) still derives from the 'normality' of repulsion and ethical condemnation. In the case of Gujarat this 'normality' was already shaken and compromised.

The Call for 'Neutrality': Impartial Media in a Partial State

Regarding the larger Indian context and the national audiences, it thus comes not as a surprise that an appeal for restraint and 'neutrality' on the part of the national media was salient in the Sangh parivar rhetoric. The reading of images and terminology had become an immediate matter of the power of numbers in terms of audience ratings as much as of a 'Hindu majority', and the pro-pogrom, or at least not explicitly anti-pogrom atmosphere during the violence made interpretations in favour of the Sangh parivar more likely. Different from objectivity, however, neutrality implies not merely an utmost openness to multiple readings but also a 'balanced view' with regard to 'both sides' involved. In this sense the call of the Sangh parivar also explicitly referred to a 'lack of balance' as far as the representation of 'the other side', i.e. the 'Muslim violence', in the 'communal tragedy' was concerned and was thus speaking of the 'danger' of the overall critical reporting still finding too many approving readers. Brought forward mainly by the national BJP-leadership, particularly by then Prime Minister Atal Behari Vajpayee and Home Minister L.K. Advani, the appeal betrayed the particular media-savvyness of the Sangh parivar in displaying a 'moral' concern that subtly supported the Modi-government's discourse 'inside' Gujarat.

Playing to the difficulties faced by Indian society in dealing with the speed of an unprecedented media-ubiquity since the late 1990s, and using growing concerns over hype and sensationalism, Vajpayee called the (critical) media-coverage 'exaggerated' and 'not constructive'[21]. This allusion reversed the logical conclusion that 'they cannot all be wrong' in their outrage into the – under democratic conditions even more plausible – postulation that 'they cannot all be right'. Following this same pattern, the BJP-close India First Foundation pointed out in its report precisely that 'media became an active participant rather than an independent observer', which overshadowed the literal 'invention' of the pogrom with the help of the wide-ranging employment of media through the Sangh parivar itself. This also made the medialisation and emotionalising of the coverage merely an act of critical reporting. The supposed 'lack of balance and impartiality' was attributed to the historically contingent fact that 'for most of the young TV journalists like the channels they represent, this probably was the first time that they were covering such an enormous tragedy' and 'channels and journalists got carried away'[22]. What thus passed for a concerned yet understanding governmental reprimand was actually the insidious de-legitimising of critical reporting by equating it with sensationalism, naïvety and underdeveloped professionalism (that could, moreover, easily be attributed to the long-standing control of television under the Congress).

For his part, L.K. Advani, whose highly media-oriented 10,000km *rath yatra* from Somnath in Gujarat to Ayodhya in 1990 had left hundreds of smaller Hindu-Muslim riots in its trail, was particularly critical of the tendency in the coverage to openly name, for the first time, Muslims as the targeted victims. Demanding to 'take lessons from the American coverage of 11 September' he suggested that 'sometimes, speaking the truth may not be an act of responsibility'[23]. This analogy is indeed quite fantastic, as it proposed that the US and India, i.e. Gujarat, had been subject to a comparable act of Islamist terrorism. In the context of Gujarat the suggestion that some noble restraint on the part of the media in the display of victims might mitigate the violence was actually quite clearly a call for the denial of Muslim victimhood. Reversing the relation between attacker and attacked, the analogy obscured that in the case of 9/11, despite being for the first time exposed to the world as vulnerable (which in itself marks an indirect appropriation of image production through the attackers), the attacked US had still had full command over their media in the course of the event. In the long run, this entailed, also, the conscious denial of the visibility of American casualties (civil or military) as an act of proving strength, if not immortality. In the case of the Gujarati Muslims, on the other hand, the display of their mutilated bodies and burnt livelihoods, even if difficult to distinguish from mere sensationalism, was at least *also* a signifier of complete powerlessness and a call for responsibility to be taken.

This discursive intervention by the BJP-leadership, i.e. the Indian state leadership at the time, made clear to many journalists that they could not count on much support 'outside' Gujarat either and that it was less their position than the ground beneath their feet that was shifting, re-arranging the parameters of their work without much of their doing. In contrast to objective reporting, calls for 'neutrality' and a 'balanced view' are irreconcilable with violence against minorities and particularly with genocidal violence, because they can only work to conceal it. While thus the demand to also try and report on the 'other side' in the so-called 'war on terror' betrays indeed a quest for objective journalism, the appeal in the context of the Gujarat 'Hindu-Muslim violence' enforced an imagined equal polarisation and effectively faded out that there *was* no other side.

Conclusions

The ground has shifted for good, it seems. Both in the general elections of 2004 – that were a fiasco for the BJP and brought to power the first Congress-led coalition – and in the Gujarat Assembly elections of 2007, 'Gujarat' remained largely a taboo topic in the sense that Barkha Dutt had indicated in her pre-election article. The main reason for this is that the re-election of the Congress at the centre (by a narrow margin) had little to do with a post-pogrom change of opinion regarding the Sangh parivar's responsibility but much to do with the BJP-led coalition not delivering on the promised economic improvement of the poorer sections of society (Roy/Wallace 2007). Especially amongst the upwardly mobile it was precisely this failure which reinforced Modi's leadership and Gujarat's aura as a future model for India, because Modi seemed to have delivered, where the national BJP clearly had not. Skilfully playing out the democratic deficiencies of the Congress-state and dissolving, with the help of the larger Sangh parivar, the meaning of images and terms like 'democracy', 'majority', 'empowerment', 'freedom of expression', 'responsibility', 'security', 'law and order', 'development' and objectivity, Modi could under the specific historical conditions in Gujarat go considerably further than the national BJP in other states as far as the introduction of a new economic-political paradigm is concerned. The result is the establishment of a post-Congress and post-democratic rule that can be said to represent 'neoliberal good governance' as opposed to historical 'leftist democratization' (Dembowski 2001). The 'Modi-fied' system stands for a triumphant disproof of the old political argument that Hindutva can only raise emotions and generate destructive agency but fails as soon as elementary questions of food, shelter and secured incomes arise. Fundamentally re-defining 'development' away from 'economic democracy' (cf. Frank 2001, Yagnik and Sheth 2005, 273), Modi has multiplied the number of ready national and international investors in the state relying on the absence of labour laws and workers' rights, which in turn fuels exceptional growth rates and systematic economic favouritism towards the Hindu majority.

Crucially, this entails the 'overcoming' of the 'communal problem' through the 'undoing' of Muslims, i.e. their consistent and institutionalised exclusion from access to legal and political systems as well as from representation and economic resources. Given the totality of the intimidation and marginalisation, it was not surprising that the 2007 election-campaign did not 'require' the organisation of violence, buttressing assessments from newspaper readers like 'The security machinery has proved effective, and law and order in the state is one of the best in the country. The country needs leaders like Modi who are forward-looking and not like the Leftists who are nothing but a case of the tail wagging the dog'[24]. If we understand 'globalisation' as the increasing dissolution of borders, growing interaction, connectivity and syncretism, Modi stands for a post-global scenario that fosters, in accordance with 'global post-global' tendencies, a religionisation of poverty, exclusion and protest, and makes plausible the argument that India would have no economic problems were the Muslims not there or were they everywhere ready to accept their status as second-class citizens.

As far as the media are concerned, the growing solidification and legitimacy of Modi-governance has helped to transfer the de-legitimising, rather than merely silencing, of critique into proof of the shifted understanding of democracy. In November 2007 the *Tehelka* magazine published first-hand, on-the-record accounts of perpetrators of the 2002 violence – most of them organised in the Sangh parivar, with some holding official posts and none of them under prosecution – openly hailing their involvement[25]. This 'transparency' was absolutely unprecedented, compared, for instance, to Congress leaders who had done everything in their might to deny their role in orchestrating the anti-Sikh pogrom in 1984, which in scope and level of organisation comes closest to the Gujarat pogrom[26]. Many critics feared that what was meant by Tehelka to be a revealing wake-up call, re-installing a culture of accountability, might actually serve as an additional *advertisement* for Modi just before the elections, indicating the degree to which his 'dis-agreement' has found public legitimacy. Indeed, it is likely to have contributed to Modi's post-election statement that this was 'the most democratic election I have ever seen'[27] and to his continuing popularity with the communalised Hindu majority in Gujarat as India goes to the polls in 2009. What Dutt describes as the 'tragic irony of today's Gujarat' is thus in many ways the tragic irony of today's media in India, and by trying not to 'remain prisoners of the past' they seem to have become even more prisoners of the present. The media are 'free' insofar as they are in their commercial avatar legally largely unprotected and, regarding Hindutva, subject to a densely-woven net of contingencies that leaves them apparently every – but actually very little – space to manoeuvre.

It has become much harder to pronounce critique not merely because it is de-legitimised, ignored or openly attacked, but also precisely because it is allowed – and, like in any other democracy, even *needed* in order to vindicate opposition. The lack of interest of an increasingly privatised larger public to be enlightened about Hindutva's doings has in the commercial context of audience ratings and market value helped to mitigate open accusations, and in case the critical voices become too convincing there is always the option of another 'Muslim terrorist attack' that 'necessitates counter-violence' and 'security measures'. Growing evidence of bomb-manufacturing by the Sangh parivar, especially the Bajrang Dal[28], for instance, which severely questions the unambiguous four-step logic generally displayed by the Indian police of 'local Muslim militant groups' (particularly SIMI – Students' Islamic Movement of India) – 'Islamic jihadis' – 'ISI' (Inter Services Intelligence, Pakistan's intelligence service) – 'Al-Quaeda' at the swelling number of bomb attacks in India has so far failed to make a substantial impact on audiences. On the contrary, when in the course of the debate on a ban of SIMI Mulayam Singh Yadav of the Samajwadi party, former Chief Minister (CM) of Uttar Pradesh (UP), asked 'when there can be a ban on SIMI why a ban cannot be imposed on the Bajrang Dal' (Expressindia, 23 September 2008)[29], the following comment in the attached readers' forum ranked among the more harmless: 'Mulayam Singh Yadav, who killed hundreds of Hindus[30] when he was the Chief Minister of UP, will go to the extent of sympathizing with SIMI to get the minority votes. To compare SIMI with Bajrang Dal is to compare a Satan with a mischievous boy.'

Yet, equally, dissident critical voices are indispensable in their function of keeping alive 'other readings' of democracy; this remains the great strength and the weakness of every open discourse. The Indian/Gujarati case indicates the degree to which 'freedom of expression' has enhanced, rather than eased, the responsibility of journalists, artists (and scientists) to reflect critically and self-critically upon the ways in which their product might lend itself to unintended interpretations and appropriations on a (post)-global scale.

Notes

1 While the Modi-government claimed 900 dead 'on both sides', 2000 Muslim victims is a number that was given already in May 2002 in an independent Fact-Finding Report (Kamal Mitra Chenoy/S.P. Shukla/K.S. Subramanian/Achin Vanaik, *Gujarat Carnage 2002. A Report to the Nation*) and seems still a conservative estimate, given that bodies are being detected till today (Times of India (Ahmedabad), March 10, 2007: 'State dismissed mass graves as stunt: US report').
2 Barkha Dutt, 'Prisoners of the Past', in: *Hindustan Times*, 8 December 2007.
3 http://nanopolitan.blogspot.com/2007/08/burkha-dutts-secular-shrillness.html (accessed 15 July 2008).
4 http://barkhadutt.wordpress.com/ (accessed 18 July 2008).
5 See Robert Greenwald's documentary 'Outfoxed' (USA 2004) that describes the undisguised practises of political colouring in favour of the Bush government in Murdoch's US Fox News, and the Guardian Weekly, 'Speaking with their master's voice', 27 February-5 March 2003.
6 See Times of India, 24 December 2007: 'Modi shows success can attract allies'; Hindustan Times, 23 December 2007: 'Modi is king of Gujarat'; *Indian Express*, 24 December 2007: 'Modi, Modi, now Mega Modi.'
7 There have been an estimated 13 000 Hindu-Muslim riots in India since 1950. 87% of the victims were Muslims, many of them killed in police action (Dayal 2002: 36).
8 The BJP-led National Democratic Alliance had actually won the elections with a minimal margin, but oppositional parties mustered enough support to enforce its resignation after only 13 days in office.
9 See *13 Dec. A Reader*, 2006.
10 After the Bombay riots, for instance, the Congress leadership had done the same by replacing the then Chief Minister of Maharashtra Sudhakarrao Naik through Sharad Pawar.
11 This contrast became most evident from my own fieldwork, which happened to be conducted – in the context of two different projects – both in 1992/93 and in 2002, i.e. during both events of violence (see Ohm, forthcoming, *The Televised Community. Culture, Politics and the Market of Visual Representation in India*, New Delhi/London/New York: Routledge).
12 A look at the readers' comments in various newspapers online or the discussion links of TV channels, particularly NDTV, at the time gave a vivid and largely shocking picture of the main straits of accusations (most are now irretrievable in that form but very similar arguments can be found any time in comments on articles or TV reports raising 'sensitive issues').
13 See Human Rights Watch, 2004, *Discouraging Dissent: Intimidation and Harassment of Witnesses, Human Rights Activists, and Lawyers Pursuing Accountability for the 2002 Communal Violence in Gujarat*, at: http://hrw.org/backgrounder/asia/india/gujarat (accessed 6 August 2008).
14 The trigger of the violence was the burning of a coach of the Sabarmati Express outside the station of Godhra on 27 February, which killed 58 people, mainly Hindutva activists along with women and children. It was immediately declared by the Sangh parivar a pre-planned terrorist attack by Muslims, but the Justice U.C. Banerjee Committee's interim report, submitted in 2005, suggested that the fire was most likely caused by an accident inside the train. This has been heavily disputed by the Sangh parivar – in the manner of a complete interpretability of facts – after the recent publication of the report of the Nanavati Commission, which had been installed by the Modi-government in 2002 and

which comes to the conclusion that 'what was to be done was planned in advance' (p. 159). The full report has, in contrast to the final report of U.C. Banerjee – whose tabling in parliament was stalled in 2006 – been made public immediately at www.home.gujarat.gov.in/homedepartment/downloads/godharaincident.pdf. See www.expressindia.com, 25 September 2008: 'BJP hails Nanavati report, says it exposed the truth' and http://lawandotherthings.blogspot.com/2008/09/nanavati-report-on-godhra-tragedy.html (accessed 6th August 2008).
15 In *Sidhi Baat* (Tacheles Talk), a weekly interview programme on Aaj Tak (lit. 'Up until Now'), 3 April 2002.
16 Documented in: PUCL 2002.
17 Annexure 4, in: Patel/Padgaonkar/Verghese, page 36.
18 Modi in an interview with *Outlook* (weekly English language magazine), 18 March 2002.
19 See then NDTV-editor Rajdeep Sardesai, 'The Media did not Ransack Shops, take Lives, Mr. Modi', in: *Indian Express*, 7 March 2002.
20 Reporters from various national media, press and TV, have over the years gone back to Gujarat and tried to follow up the aftermath regarding the plight of the Muslims or at least to closely follow the trials of judicial cases, most prominently the Best Bakery-case. They usually did so, however, at the risk of facing hurdles in Gujarat itself or of provoking verbal attacks or, at best, ignorance on the part of their audiences. Barkha Dutt was not amongst those reporters, having concluded already in 2003 that 'the election result [in December 2002, B.O.] was so resoundingly a reminder of our impotence. [...] I think it made the media weary of treating the story the same way' (Interview with the author, 20 April 2003).
21 *The Times of India*, 5 March 2002: 'Media not playing a constructive role: PM'.
22 India First Foundation, 2002, Report on *National Seminar on Godhra and After. The Role of the Media*, New Delhi, page 35.
23 The Telegraph, 7 April 2002: 'BJP builds Bush shield for Modi'.
24 Letters to the Editor in: Hindustan Times, 24 December 2007.
25 *Tehelka* Special Issue, 3 November 2007: 'The most important story of our time – Gujarat 2002: The Truth in the words of the men who did it'.
26 See The Hindu, 10 February 2005: 'Nanavati Commission report on 1985 anti-Sikh riots submitted'. It is not devoid of irony that the same retired Supreme Court judge, G.T. Nanavati, headed both inquiry commissions on the Gujarat violence and the anti-Sikh violence 18 years earlier. See also Praful Bidwai, 'The Nanavati Report and After', in: *Kashmir Times*, 16 August 2005, at: www.countercurrents.org/comm-bidwai160805.htm (accessed 6 August 2008).
27 *The Times of India*, 24 December 2007: 'I'm jewel in India's crown: Modi'.
28 Human Rights Watch pointed out already in its 2001 World Report that 'crude bombs were set off in two churches in Karnataka. In August, police charged members of a Muslim sect, allegedly based in Pakistan, with masterminding the attacks. Human rights activists maintained that the arrests were meant to deflect attention from Hindu hardliners' campaign of anti-Christian violence' (p. 198). With regard to Muslims, these activities got more into view with the bombing of a mosque in the town of Malegaon, Maharashtra, in 2006 see 'Malegaon: The Road to Perdition', in: *The Hindu*, 9 September 2006. That bombings cannot simply be ascribed to communities by way of their targets becomes evident not merely from the fact that Islamist attackers care little whether they also kill Muslims. It also has to be seen in the dimension of the bomb explosion in the house of a prominent local Sangh parivari in Nanded, Maharashtra, which apparently happened

accidentally at manufacturing. On the spot found turbans and artificial beards at least indicate that Hindutva activists would also not refrain from feigning another identity – in this case of Sikhs – in order to manipulate prosecution (see PUCL report 2006).

29 www.expressindia.com/latest-news/If-SIMI-can-be-banned-why-not-Bajrang-Dal/364949/. expressindia is a web-portal of the newspaper Indian Express (accessed 28 July 2008).

30 Is most probably referring to the death in police firing of activists demanding a separate state of Uttarakhand in 1994, which Yadav as Chief Minister opposed. According to long-term investigations, altogether six activists were shot (see 'State of Limbo', in: *Frontline*, October 2003).

References

Ahmad, A. (2003) 'Contextualizing Conflict: The US "War on Terrorism"', in Thusu, D. and Freeman, D. (eds) *War and the Media*, London: Sage Publications, pp. 15–27.

Akbar, M. J. (2003) *Riot after Riot. Reports on Caste and Communal Violence in India*, New Delhi: Roli Books (reprint of the 1991 revised edition, originally published in 1988)

Brass, P. R. (2003) *The Production of Hindu-Muslim Violence in Contemporary India*, New Delhi: Oxford University Press

Corbridge, S. and Harriss, J. (2001) *Reinventing India. Liberalization, Hindu Nationalism and Popular Democracy*, New Delhi: Oxford University Press

Datta, P. K. (2003) '*Hindutva* and the New Indian Middle Class' in Indira Chandrasekhar/Peter C. Seel, (eds) *body.city. siting contemporary culture in India*, Berlin/Delhi: The House of World Cultures/Tulika Books, 186–197

Dayal, J. (ed.) (2002) Gujarat 2002. Untold and Re-told Stories of the Hindutva Lab, Delhi: Media House

Dembowski, H. (2001) *Taking the State to Court. Public Interest Litigation and the Public Sphere in Metropolitan India*, Asia House, online version at: www.asienhaus.de/

Dutt, N. and Girdner, E. J. (2000) 'Challenging the rise of nationalist-religious parties in India and Turkey' in *Contemporary South Asia* 9(1): 7–24

Eckert, J. (2003) *The Charisma of Direct Action: Power, Politics, and the Shiv Sena*, New Delhi: Oxford University Press

Fernandes, L. (2006) *India's New Middle Class: Democratic Politics in an Era of Economic Reform*, Minneapolis: University of Minnesota Press

Frank, T. (2001) *One Market Under God: Extreme Capitalism, Market Populism, and the End of Economic Democracy*, London: Secker&Warburg

Ghosh, P. S. (1999) *BJP and the Evolution of Hindu Nationalism: From Periphery to Centre*, New Delhi: Manohar

Hansen, T. B. (1999) *The Saffron Wave: Democracy and Hindu Nationalism in Modern India*, New Delhi: Oxford University Press

―――― (2001) *Urban Violence in India. Identity Politics, 'Bombay', and the Postcolonial City*, New Delhi: Permanent Black

Hasan, Z. (2003) 'The Changing Political Orientations of the Middle Classes in India' in: Panikkar, K.N. and Muralidharan, Sukumar (eds) *Communalism, Civil Society & The State. Ayodhya 1992 – Gujarat 2002: Reflections on a Decade of Turbulence*, New Delhi: Safdar Hashmi Memorial Trust (SAHMAT), 60–74

Imhof, K. (2006) 'Mediengesellschaft und Medialisierung' in: *Medien & Kommunikationswissenschaft* 2/2006 191–215

Iyer, V. (ed.) (2000) *Mass Media Laws and Regulations in India*, Singapore: Asian Media Information and Communication Centre (AMIC)
Krotz, F. (2001) *Die Mediatisierung des kommunikativen Handelns. Der Wandel von Alltag und sozialen Beziehungen, Kultur und Gesellschaft durch die Medien*, Opladen: Westdeutscher Verlag
Jaffrelot, C. (2001) 'Hindu Nationalism and Democracy' in Niraja Gopal Jayal (ed.) *Democracy in India*, New Delhi: Oxford University Press, 509–534
Jeffrey, R. (2000) *India's Newspaper Revolution. Capitalism, Politics and the Indian Language Press*, New Delhi: Oxford University Press
―――― (2001) 'Media Revolution & 'Hindu Politics' in North India, 1982–99', in: *Himal Southasian*, July, Volume 15, Issue 7: 32–41
McLagan, M. (2006) 'Introduction: Making Human Rights Claims Public', Section of Visual Anthropology, 'Technologies of Witnessing: The Visual Culture of Human Rights' in *American Anthropologist* 108 (1): 191–195
Ninan, S. (2007) *Headlines from the Heartland. Reinventing the Hindi Public Sphere*, New Delhi: Sage Publications
Ohm, B. (1999) 'Doordarshan: Representing the Nation's State' in Brosius, Christiane/Melissa Butcher (eds) *Image Journeys. Audio-Visual Media and Cultural Change in India*, New Delhi: Sage Publications, 69–98
――――, (2001) *Ist dies eine Invasion? Transnationale Sender und Nationales Fernsehen in Indien*, Münster/London: Lit
――――, (2007) 'Narratives of the Underbelly of Democracy' in *Economic and Political Weekly*, Dec. 8–14, Volume XLII (49): 26–31
Patel, A., Padgaonkar, D. and Verghese, B.G. (2002) *Rights and Wrongs: Ordeal by Fire in the Killing Fields of Gujarat*, New Delhi: Editors Guild Fact Finding Mission Report.
People's Union for Civil Liberties (PUCL) (2002) *The role of the media during the Gujarat carnage: A brief analysis*, at: www.pucl.org/reports (accessed 28 July 2008)
―――― (2003) *Violence in Gujarat. Reports and Analysis*, at: www.pucl.org/gujarat-index.htm (accessed 28 July 2008)
―――― (2006) *A report on bomb blast at the house of prominent RSS activist in Nanded, Maharashtra*, at: www.pucl.org/Topics/Religion-communalism/2006/nanded.htm (accessed 28 July 2008)
Rajagopal, A. (2001) *Politics after Television: Hindu Nationalism and the Reshaping of the Public in India*, Cambridge: Cambridge University Press
Rancière, J. (2002) *Das Unvernehmen. Politik und Philosophie*, Frankfurt/Main: Suhrkamp
Roy, R. and Wallace, P. (eds) (2007) *India's 2004 Elections: Grassroots and National Perspectives*, New Delhi: Sage Publications
Sontag, S. (2004) *Regarding the Pain of Others*, New York: Picador
Shani, O. (2007) *Communalism, Caste and Hindu Nationalism: The Violence in Gujarat*, New Delhi: Cambridge University Press
Varadarajan, S. (ed.) (2002) *Gujarat: The Making of a Tragedy*, New Delhi: Penguin
Vasavi, A. R. (2002) 'Gujarat's proclivity to violence' in *The Hindu* (Magazine supplement), May 2005
Without Editor, (2006) *13 Dec. The strange case of the attack on the Indian parliament A Reader*, New Delhi: Penguin
Wolf, N. (2007) *Make it Real: Documentary and other cinematic experiments by women filmmakers in India*, unpublished PhD-thesis, Europa-University, Frankfurt/Oder, Germany
Yagnik, A. and Sheth S. (2005) *The Shaping of Modern Gujarat: Plurality, Hindutva and Beyond*, New Delhi: Penguin
Zavos, J. (2000) *The Emergence of Hindu Nationalism in India*, New Delhi: Oxford University Press

Chapter Eight

MYTH – THE NATIONAL FORM: *MISSION ISTANBUL* AND MUSLIM REPRESENTATION IN HINDI POPULAR CINEMA

Noorel Mecklai

Introduction

During the course of the coverage of the attacks of 26 November 2008 in Bombay, the New Delhi TV (NDTV) anchorperson, Barkha Dutt (whose remarks also open the previous chapter by Britta Ohm) commented upon the resemblance of the events unfolding to those in a film. Another viewer interviewed by NDTV also made the same remark. Both comments expressed disbelief that these were *real* attacks suggesting that it is possible to become inured to violence and the idea of terrorism in the post 9/11 era, which has become the most represented theme in film contributing to the mythology of Islamic terrorism. In recent films from the Hindi cinema not only is the main subject about terrorism, in some cases the events are played out within the film but on television via simulations of news broadcasts. In *Mission Kashmir* (2000, dir. Vidhu Vinodh Chopra) Sufi Parvez was a television anchor; in *Fanaa* (*Destruction*, 2006 dir. Kunal Kohli) a blind woman befriends a Kashmiri terrorist; in *LOC Kargil* (2003, dir. J. P. Dutta) Preity Zinta's character became a reporter; the mission in the film *Mission Istanbul* (July 2008 dir. Apoorva Lakhia. MI hereafter) was to thwart terrorist attacks on Indian cities, with obvious reference to Bombay, a television station owner in Istanbul being identified as the mastermind. The actual reporting by NDTV jounrnalists on 26 November 2008 was no different from much that is depicted within Hindi films. Before it was clear what was happening, a diplomat from the Canadian embassy in Bombay had to point out to Barkha Dutt that the protagonists were 'perpetrators of violence' and not automatically 'terrorists' until such information was confirmed. Nevertheless, her coverage was full of speculation and conjecture (cf. Ramakrishnan 2009). The opposition Bharatiya Janata Party politician, Mr. L. K. Advani's call for war against Pakistan was heard first on New Delhi TV 24–7 several days before it was confirmed that there was any evidence that the attackers in Bombay were indeed from a terrorist cell (Lashkar-e-Toiba) based in Pakistan occupied Kashmir. Advani's party, which represents Hindu nationalist politics, and as discussed by Britta Ohm in this volume, has been instrumental in creating the most horrific riots and anti-Muslim pogroms from 1992 onwards, between Hindus and Muslims since partition (Rajagopal 2001; Bhatt 2001). A legacy of partition was the emergence of conflict based on religio-ethnic communities or communalism.

There has been recent speculation regarding the veracity of information emerging from reports of the Bombay attacks of 26 November 2008, and some doubt expressed about how the Chief of the Anti-Terrorist Squad, Hemant Karkare, was killed just as he was on the verge of a damning terrorist investigation linking Hindu rightwing groups to a series of bomb attacks. There is widespread criticism of the electronic media coverage of the events that called for war[1]. These lead one to be circumspect when assessing the news reports that emerge during conflict. What we do know is that very rarely if ever are the perpetrators of violence against Muslims in riots or pogroms brought to trial or indeed identified. This is a trend since the partition riots and each subsequent incident like Ayodhya 1992, Bombay 1993, or Gujarat 2002, the perpetrators have still not been brought before the courts[2]. The fallout of the November 2008 attacks in Bombay has been the resignation of the Home minister in the Central cabinet and the removal of the Chief (Vilasrao Deshmukh) and Deputy Chief (R. R. Patil) ministers of the State of Maharashtra. Their removal was a means to quash criticism of the failure of the state in its preparedness to combat terrorism[3]. 'The proverbial last nail in the coffin apparently was the 'conducted tour' of the Taj Mahal hotel [a terror site] that Deshmukh offered to film director Ram Gopal Varma during his official visit to the site after the 60-hour siege was over'[4]. Terrorist attacks have happened serially in Bombay in 1993, 2002, 2006 and 2008. In each instance the police have been found to be ill equipped and ill informed, the media indiscreet, but the public have demonstrated a great deal of good sense. On 26 December 2008, they marched in solidarity and called for politicians from all parties to be held to account.

A festering point of conflict surrounding this attack has been the ambivalent status of Kashmir and the betrayal of Kashmiris by the very instruments within the Indian constitution ostensibly designed to create a special status for the landlocked state. In 1947 there was an undertaking made by the Indian government to conduct a plebiscite supervised by the UN (Navlakha 1998), in Kashmir to settle the issue of independent statehood or union with India for

Kashmiris even as Pakistan forcibly occupied part of the Kashmir state. Kashmiri insurgency is a legacy of Indian and Pakistani conflict since partition. This has been met with violent suppression and human rights abuses perpetrated by Indian armed forces and Special Forces that have left a trail of bloodshed.

The subsequent inclusion of the Kashmir conflict into the 'War on Terror', unleashed by George W. Bush during his presidency of the United States has had serious consequences across South Asia. In addition, multiple pressures, like the war in Afghanistan and its bordering tribal areas, the fallout from the Iraq conflict and its relations with Iran, and the unresolved issue of a Palestinian state, have seemingly made Pakistan's territory a haven for Muslim insurgency. U.S. support has strengthened the Pakistani military and intelligence services that challenge the fragile democracy cobbled together after the assassination of Benazir Bhutto.

It is within the framework of current global geo-politics and India's history and position within it that I discuss this proliferation of films from the Bombay cinema (Sethi 2002). They could be termed ultra-nationalistic and jingoistic in that all instances of Muslim critique or militancy are constructed as terrorist. The portrayal of Muslims in Hindi cinema has not always been so extreme, so I am interested to trace the movement towards this parochialism as well as the voices which get sidelined: some members of the audiences who engage in internet reviews and comments on blog sites are rather discerning in their remarks and display a great deal of knowledge about the aesthetics and politics of Hindi cinema.

Hindi Cinema and Muslim Representation

Three general observations regarding Hindi Cinema can be drawn from the literature on the subject. First, its narratives have their origins in myth; secondly, questions of probity arise surrounding the financial dealings of this Cinema which has a nexus of interests including the Bombay underworld, and the world of state politics (Rahman and Katyar 1993)[5]; and finally, this Cinema has been identified as providing a basis for national identity (Chakravarthy 1993, 8). Hindi popular cinema has assumed a significance that is contradictory: as a vibrant expression of 'third' world cinema and national identity and as an industry that epitomises the nexus between crime, business and politics (Singh 2002). Some researchers have implicated this cinema in the construction of Hindu nationalist discourse (Zutshi 1994) because the film narratives can be traced to mythological stories, so it begs the question as to how other communities find a way to identify with the films and therefore with the nation. In this section I examine some of the ways Hindi cinema has addressed members of the subcontinent's largest religious minority: the Muslim community.

Since partition, Hindi film producers have had to tread carefully under the surveillance of the film censorship regime to ignore the subject for most of their work, or used a nuanced approach to broach relations between Hindus and Muslims. In my dissertation on the representation of the Muslims in Hindi Cinema from 1947 (2000–2006), I observed that the content of Hindi cinema has become more overtly polarised, especially in the last decade of the twentieth century and increasingly post 2000. The communal tensions sparked over the unresolved issue of Kashmir, marginalisation and victimisation of Muslim communities, the failure of the Indian state to defend Muslim communities during riots, the linkage of Indian Muslim communities to notions of global jihad, and a growing consensus amongst the ruling elite of a virulent parochial politics are suggested to be reasons for Hindi films' general partisanship (Rai 2003). Hindi cinema in the post-colonial period has been uncomfortable with the representation of Muslims and consequently there are few if any instances where a Muslim has been represented as a modern citizen. Hindi cinematic representation has generally either relegated Muslim characters to the canvas of history or framed them as 'backward' or subordinate to a macho or forgiving Hindu hero (Mecklai 2006).

Indian cinema and Indian nationalism developed synergistically when the sub-continent was still under British rule. Those aspiring to the profession of film production recognised the political value in cinema. Through the use of mythological stories based upon the Hindu epics their film projects supported the development of Indian nationalism by developing a form that privileged Hindu identity. Dadasaheb Phalke, recognised as the 'father of Indian cinema' made films like *Raja Harishchandra* (1913) a minor story from the Hindu epic *Mahabharata*. He called his efforts a 'cottage industry' in keeping with the nationalist spirit of *swadeshi*, which encouraged indigenous entrepreneurship as opposed to collaboration with British manufacture. He was part of a faction of nationalists who privileged Hindu identity and was supported by extremist politicians like Lokmanya Tilak, a well-known Freedom fighter who established a newspaper *Kesari* in Western India (Amladi 1997, 172–4).

Muslim genres developed from the Parsi theatre, which drew entertainment from Perso-Arabic themes of doomed lovers, like *Laila Majnu,* or *Ali Baba and the Forty Thieves,* or stories from the Arabian Nights. These themes were produced in many versions throughout the history of cinema. Several tropes of the Hindi popular cinema emerged from the adaptation of Parsi and Urdu theatre including the combination of song and dance sequences, which were produced under the auspices of a studio system that developed following the advent of sound and the talkies. Film inherited a steady stream of actors, technicians, artists and scriptwriters from the theatre (Garga 1996: chapter 5). Another popular genre that was mainly devoted to the representation of

Muslims was the historical film, describing the opulence of the Mughal courts or the culture of Muslim principalities that remained at the turn of the last century. This genre combined spectacle and the reconstruction of a regal past depicting Muslim kings and their courtly activities in support of the arts. *Nurjehan* (1923, dirs. J. J. Madan and Ezra Mir), the story of a Mughal princess, the wife of Humayun) inspired a remake by Mehboob Khan in 1945. He was an influential and successful Muslim director who was at the forefront of film production in Bombay who established his studio at the time of Indian independence in 1947. The famous film *Mughal-e-Azam* (1960, dir K. Asif) is a much later example of a nostalgic historical that combined elements of the 'courtesan films' that became another genre proffering a critique of gender norms and social mores. Courtesans were highly regarded prostitutes, trained in music and dance, raised in an establishment or *kotha*. They usually performed for the elite in society under the Muslim rulers of Indian states. They provide colourful narratives of unfulfilled love because of their profession and the high status of their patrons, who they were never allowed to marry even if they bore their patron a child. The child would then be raised in the profession if it was a girl, or as a musical performer if male (cf. Kesavan 1994; Kazmi 1994). *Pakeezah* (1972, dir. Kamal Amrohi) is an outstanding example of this genre of film, where the talented courtesan is exploited for her soft heart and profession.

These genres were consolidated under the term 'Muslim social' and like the *masala* film, included a mix of generic attributes including the music sequences, comedy or love story. These Muslim socials were made ostensibly to appease a large Muslim audience (Vasudevan 1996), but I see these films as a critique of Muslim mores, personal laws or *Shariat*, which concerned issues relating to marriage and divorce in particular. They showed a Muslim society of kings and their courts or harems, apparent wealth concealing the abject poverty in which the majority of Indian Muslims found themselves after partition. I find this a paradox in Hindi cinema's representations, which at times appears to desire to support the interests of this large minority, the Muslims, but most frequently seems to undermine their identity from a textual perspective.

The 1970s – especially towards the second half of the decade – introduced the criminal element into Hindi cinema, with films like Sholay (1975, dir. R. Sippy) and Muqqadar ka Sikander (1978, dir. P. Mehra). In these films, the persona of Amitabh Bachchan as the 'angry young man' is established and the lurid deeds of a growing criminal element in Bombay society are unveiled. Gold smuggling was one of the activities prevalent at the time of the gold control order, and illicit trade in this element was the prime commodity in India. Smuggling in general, of electronic equipment and consumer goods, was widespread as the Government of India had strict import controls

(Bhattacharya 2002). Some suspected that this business somehow lined the pockets of many aspiring to the world of film politics and bureaucracy.

Here, especially in low budget, 'B' grade films like *Angaar* (1992, dir. K. Shashilal Nair), Muslims were cast as the 'outsider', the miscreant, or as violent gangsters, in short as anti-national[6], despite the obvious contradictions of Muslim stars playing Hindu heroes. The most famous example is Yusuf Khan who assumed the name of Dilip Kumar in the 1950s and 1960s, and increasingly a host of contemporary heroes like Shahrukh Khan, Aamir Khan, Salman Khan and even Zayed Khan who portrays the Hindu hero of *Mission Istanbul*. A large part of cinema talent were Muslims, such as scriptwriters like Sadat Hasan Manto, Sahir Ludhianvi, Aga Hashr Kashmiri, Kamal Hasan and the Salem-Javed duo; musicians include Naushad, Ismail Darbar, Khayyam and A. S. Rehman; and production hands from the classical film carpenter turned director, S. Fattehlal, to Mehboob a bit-part actor to producer/director.

The Mythic Narratives of Hindi Popular Cinema

The discussion of the nationalist or *swadeshi* imperative in Hindi Popular Cinema began with the genre of 'mythological' films. It is within this genre of the 'neo-traditional', evoking stories from Hindu mythology, particularly the *Mahabharata* and *Ramayan*, that Phalke is credited as being the 'father of Indian Cinema' (Rajadhyaksha 1986). It is appropriate, in this context, to delineate the discussion around the use of myth as it has been described both by Kumar Shahani and Roland Barthes. The semiotic analytical frameworks used by Shahani (1986) and the work done by Barthes (1973) on representation in the context of mythology, are useful in the analysis of Hindi films, because they allow exploration of the complexity of cultural signs and their meanings in the Indian context. The critical work that surrounds films of the 1950s underscores the importance of Hindu iconography and signs in cinematic representation. Few have looked, except cursorily, at the possible repercussions of this symbolism for relations between Hindus and the minority Indian communities. Barthes defines myth and then explores its relation to semiology, ideology and history:

> Myths are nothing but this ceaseless, untiring solicitation, this insidious and inflexible demand that all men recognise themselves in this image, eternal yet bearing a date, which was built of them one day as if for all time. (Barthes 1973, 155)

Barthes' position illuminates the 'mythic-realism' of narratives in Hindi Cinema. His concept of myth forms the basis of a methodology that permits discussion of these narratives because it explains the nexus between semiology, ideology and history. This goes to the very core of the problems of identification for Muslim viewers with regard to the form of representation found in many contemporary Indian popular films. It is a scheme by which the 'imagination' of the nation state (Anderson 1983) has been read in several forms of Indian artistic and literary expression, and often continued without any reference to the reality of lived culture. Some critics call Hindi cinema 'Epic Melodrama' (Rajadhyakhsha 1993), 'socials' (Vasudevan 1996), 'feudal family romance[s]' (Prasad 1994), straightforward Melodrama[7] or as Kumar Shahani (1986, 71–78) discusses, 'Myths for Sale': basically, forms that can be read as nationalist (and homogenising) allegories.

> [M]ythology is a part both of semiology in as much as it is a formed science, and of ideology in as much as it is an historical science: it studies ideas-in-form...the form is emptied of meaning....only in its rereading in a historical context does it become 'filled' of meaning...myth is to be appropriated...(being a second order signifier), stolen and restored— the very principle of myth: it transforms history into nature... what allows the reader to consume myth innocently is that he does not see it as a semiological system but as an inductive one. (Barthes 1973, 109)

Myths can be recycled, and recognised; in this context, one school of thought 'read[s] Bombay film as a form which is homologous with the narrative paradigm established over two millennia ago in the Sanskrit epics, namely the *Mahabharat* and the *Ramayana*' (Mishra 1988).

The transformation of these 'myths' of a homogenous and devout Hindu populace, and their use as ideological tools by the Hindu nationalist political parties in their bid for wider electoral gain is an example of the way that popular media narratives can propel an absolutist view (Rajagopal 2001). Historically, 'epic' mythology has been used both consciously and unselfconsciously by members of the film industry to establish a nationalist identity. In recent times, I suggest, this has fed into the resurgence of Hindu fundamentalist politics, exponents of which have revived themes from the mythological epics to focus on a (fictitious) unbroken tradition of Hindu culture (Thapar 1989).

The narratives of Hindi cinema frequently have a predictable beginning and ending. Their unfolding, however, whilst often privileging the perspective of the North Indian Hindu male, remains a convoluted construction with detailed subplots offering points of identification for numerous subsections of its heterogeneous audience (Banaji 2006). Whilst the core story may be familiar it is the very twists and turns of the plot that are pleasurable and novel (Srinivas 2002). Some textual theorists argue that this thematic familiarity of the epics is used for social inspiration and control and mediated through a pleasurable performance (Mishra 1988). But such a perspective is far too simplistic and needs to be questioned. Indeed, Mishra's early work has already been thoroughly criticised for naturalising 'the ideal past, such that a Sanskrit Hindu past is forcibly rendered as collective memory and commonsense' (Gopalan 1993, 87). Unwittingly, then, the reading of all Hindi cinema as based on the Hindu epics rather than through its diverse interpretations by audiences or via more complex textual methods essentialises myths and *excuses* the misrepresentation and exclusion of women, lower castes and minority communities in many contemporary narratives. Although early cinema practitioners used the idea of a particular Hindu consciousness as national identity, the proliferation of iconography and narratives contributed to the development of a parochial consciousness. This is different from saying that early directors were consciously producing an ideology of religious and communal antagonism. Nevertheless, I suggest, the screening and interpretation of these film narratives at a particular political and historical juncture were such as to enhance antagonistic impressions.

Some scholars analyse different film genres, underscoring the study of Hindi cinema and the melodramatic narrative form as a mythic nationalist form (Gopalan 1993; Thomas 1995). Some define it in terms of third cinema theory; some with respect to its 'translation' of myths or as 'neo-traditionalist' texts; Jyotika Virdi (2003), argues that:

> [a] coherent national identity comes about by naturalizing a particular cultural formation; nationhood and film histories are produced by repressing internal differences among groups criss-crossed by hierarchical relationships – in terms of gender, ethnicity, community, religion and class. Nations are not a "given" but something that is gained, and cinema is one of the means by which this happens. By constructing an imaginary homogeneity, film represents the interests of one group while marginalizing others. It has been argued that national cinema is a form of "internal colonization", offering up a contradictory unity and privileging a limited range of subject positions (Virdi 2003, 35).

In this context, Virdi (2003, 34–42) cites the films *Henna* (1991, dir. Randhir Kapoor), *Roti Kapda Aur Makan* (*Bread, Clothes and a Place to Stay*, 1974, dir. Manoj Kumar) and *Amar, Akhbar and Anthony* (1977, dir. Manmohan Desai) as examples of a 'fair' representation of Muslims. She fails, however, to question the covert strands of 'racist' representation within these texts, which I argue, continue to place Muslims (and Christians) on the margins of the Indian state. In *Amar, Akhbar and Anthony*, each of these protagonists is actually born to Hindu parents, but separated at a young age. Akhbar is so named because he was brought up in a Muslim family, and Anthony by Christian parents, whilst Hindu parents raised Amar. In the resolution we are aware that they were Hindu at birth, and so the film infers that Hindus are tolerant and accepting of all religions. These films, perhaps inadvertently, take a partisan role in their representation of the construction of Indian national identity therein, resulting in racism or pro-Hindu chauvinism.

Mission Istanbul: Text, Context and Online Audience

Arguably, prejudicial representations of any group or community gain a greater valence from repetition. As discussed, although they may at times be unselfconscious, these repetitions and the construction of stereotypes are neither accidental, nor random acts; they require the efforts of a number of people towards a common – though not necessarily well-defined or clearly articulated – purpose. What could be the purpose of the negative portrayal of Muslim characters in much of commercial Hindi cinema? A number of recent films for example, *Fiza* (*1999*, dir. Khaled Mohamed), *Fanaa* (2006, dir. Kunal Kohli), *Lakshya* (2004, dir. Farhan Akhtar), *Heena* (1999, dir. Randhir Kapoor), *LOC: Kargil* (2003, dir. J. P. Dutta) and *Veer Zaara* (2004, dir. Yash Chopra), all concern the relationship between India and Pakistan but frequently touch upon Indian Muslims as key characters. The insidious on-screen association of all Muslims and Muslimness with Pakistan disregards the Indian Muslims, many of who are marginalised (as characters) or who are pushed into a position where they have to interrogate their relationship with the nation repeatedly. Some of the films mentioned further differentiate between a 'good' or patriotic Indian Muslim and a 'bad' (anti-national) alien or terrorist Muslim. These films have been aptly identified as establishing a genre of 'cine-patriotism' (Sethi 2002). In *Fiza* for example, the eponymous heroine has to pay an exacting price for the restoration of her national acceptance. She has to kill her brother, who has transgressed expectations of the Hindu community by seeking restitution for the victimization of his minority community and joining a terror outfit, after witnessing the death of his friend during anti-Muslim pogroms. In *Fanaa*, to the same end, the heroine must shoot her beloved, a 'terrorist' but also the father of her son.

In discussion boards on internet sites like 'apunkachoice.com', 'youthcurry.blogspot.com' and 'indicine.com' where these films are discussed, self-identifying Muslim participants do sometimes express their sense of marginality in the films' political narrative; but generally the discussants tend to restrict their comments to the inequities of the director, actors, and shortcomings of the script. Nevertheless, although many comments are written in a sarcastic tone, some critical comments indicate that the audience have a great interest in Hindi films as they cross-reference films and actors' repertoires of performances with familiarity. Occasionally comments reflect a political aspect to this critique of Hindi cinema[8].

In relation to *Mission Istanbul* (MI, dir. Apoorva Lakhia 2008) there are three common threads in online discussions. The first is the description of the film as within the 'action film genre, but one that lacked any logic'; the second theme was about the 'skin show', the reference to the display of men's bodies, their muscular torsos; and finally, many posts enjoyed the sequence performed by a George Bush look-a-like, played by a stand-up comedian Brent Mendenhall, who according to the director, paid a visit to the office of the then Chief Minister of Maharashtra, Vilasrao Deshmukh.[9] Another politician, now the Chief Minister of Jammu and Kashmir, Omar Abdullah was interviewed in the film, playing himself, and this was before his election to the office. The director boasts of his friendship with Omar Abdullah as they were schoolmates, and expresses the opinion that his appearance in the film really helped the film. Perhaps it helped the politician as well, even though the Internet-savvy audience disparages the film.

MI, like many other politically motivated films, has an opening disclaimer that says 'the characters are fictitious and bear no resemblance to any real people' but immediately recognisable are an Osama bin-laden character, a George Bush, and images of terrorists now stereotypically portrayed in Hindi cinema. The juxtaposition of footage from news broadcasts that introduces the film, situates the narrative within a non-fiction realm and emphasises for the audience the dire threat that Islamic militancy poses. The message is that such terrorists are planning to target India and its cities in particular. In the context of the spate of bombings in Bombay by what has become known as 'home-grown terrorists', and after the London incidents of 2005, the idea that there is a link with Middle Eastern Islamists is a confabulation that denies any logic for retributive Islamist violence in India or anywhere. With reference to Kashmir, MI makes the expedient simplification of linking all Islamist militancy under one banner – the notorious and hyped Al-Qaeda. And it is the media-technology savvy, Lawrence-school – IIT[10] educated Hindu hero who is ideally placed to deflect the threat. The reference to Kashmir has been authenticated by an interview with Omar Abdullah, grandson of the 'Lion of Kashmir', Sheikh Abdullah[11]. As the current President of the National Conference, a political party of Indian-occupied Kashmir, he denies that there is any violence in the Valley and insists that the media only hype up stories of disaster. He seems to be pushing a Congress government line, and subverts the interests of all freedom-aspiring Kashmiris.

The hero, Vikas Sagar (played by the actor Zayed Khan) decides to accept a position with Al-Johar TV in Istanbul, which is an obvious reference to the Al-Jazeera television station located in Oman. As it is the nature of journalists' work that they are too busy to fulfil the obligations of married life, even though his wife is also a journalist, Anjali (actor Shreya Saran) decides that she is prepared to leave him despite their deep and abiding love. The flashback in a romantic song sequence reveals their relationship played to a tune that is a copy of the chorus of the Cat Steven's 1970 hit 'Wild World'.

Arguably, the iconography of this film is directed towards the new elite of the 'call centres'[12] who emulate their American clientele so well, and to some of the Indians working abroad in the West, whose identity in the West is supposedly shored up by 'cool' images of 'Indianness' in such films. This observation is well supported in MI with a humorous cameo, inserted for comic relief, of a President George Bush look-alike, Brent Mendenhall, who makes deliberate reference to Indians being everywhere, and not upsetting them because if they close the call centres then US businesses would come to a standstill. Vikas stumbles upon a terrorist mastermind, Ghazni (actor Nikhitin Dheer) and his outfit, operating under the guise of the TV Channel Al-Johara from Turkey. He is alerted to the trouble when he is warned against visiting the 13th floor of the towering building where the office is located. Shadowed by a Turkish intelligence man, Rizwan (actor Vivek Oberoi), himself a target of Ghazni, Vikas is warned and rescued by Rizwan.

The choice of the name Ghazni for the terrorist mastermind is interesting because the name is of the historical figure, Mahmud of Ghazni, who invaded India in the 11th Century and whose exploits have been mythologised as being the iconoclast of Hindu gods by his desecration of temples. This story has been investigated by the historian Romila Thapar with reference to the sacking of the Hindu temple at Somnatha on the coast of modern day Gujarat (Thapar 2005). In a highly complex exposition, she identifies the story to have gained prominence with Hindu nationalists in its retelling after embellishments by Kanhaiyalal Maneklal Munshi, a scriptwriter and novelist, whose novel *Jaya Somnatha* speaks of the treachery of a Brahmin who told Mahmud of underground tunnels before he entered and destroyed the temple. Munshi, like his Indian fascist associates, was concerned with racial purity and '[H]ence the need to project a constant and visible distance between Hindus and the Muslims throughout history' (Thapar 2005: 190). As a scriptwriter, Munshi influenced a number of filmmakers who sought inspiration from early nationalist texts. Subsequently, the lives of Hindus and Muslims were rarely intertwined either through marriage or social intercourse in Hindi cinema, especially during the era of early nationhood. It is my view that Munshi was perhaps most important in circulating early ideas of religious segregation amongst those viewing and making Hindi cinema, and amongst the middle-class intelligentsia in Bombay. Thus, in MI, the use of Ghazni as the name of a ruthless terrorist mastermind raises the spectre of a continuous Muslim 'terrorist' history that has plagued the (implicitly Hindu) Indian nation. The film shows in gory detail scenes of hands being cut off, beheadings, the stoning of women, an Afghani gun market that resembles a vegetable market, bombings, torture and sadism. Each of the scenes is an embellished re-creation of images that circulate in news stories about atrocities committed by the Taliban or other militant Islamists in Afghanistan and Iraq. The curious result seems both to amplify Islamophobia and to inculcate Islamicism in the viewership. One commentator, 'bollywoodgaramasala'[13], calls the film 'a reality show' because the images are reflective of television news; his opinion was reflected in responses to the shocking events of the most recent attacks of the luxury hotels in Bombay, particularly in Barkha Dutt's coverage on Indian television (NDTV). As mentioned previously, her comment that the scenes were filmic was reiterated by an interviewee on 27 November 2008, the second day's coverage by the station. Myths are created daily in the media as they embrace a simplistic idea or concept that emerges from politics or public events.

In MI, after Vikas strays onto the quarantined 13th floor of the Al-Johora TV Channel, bashed and tortured, he is convinced that the organisation has a murky side. Rizwan then compels Vikas to join the Mission, as he is already a marked man. His only reprieve would be a photograph in the Martyr's hall where every other recalcitrant journalist ended up. Rizwan ushers him to the safety of his abode where they lay their plans for the final showdown with unexpected assistance from Ms Lobo (Divya Bhardwaj) who has betrayed them earlier and reveals that she is a RAW agent[14]. Rizwan, as a Turkish agent, has commandeered a huge arsenal, Ms Lobo, drives the indestructible Scorpio, Mahindra's SUV, and our Hindu journalist is of course, a computer whiz kid. You would be forgiven if you thought that the denouement was a slick advertising campaign. More than one product is endorsed and the language of the streets of New York used liberally. In one revealing exchange on a blog-site, the discussion is appropriately critical with speculation about which regional area in North India would have the best box office returns, UP or Bihar. The proliferation of Western images now consumed throughout India has dramatically influenced the changing language and sensibilities of metropolitan India. Scenes from several films from which snatches of scripts are serially vandalised provide ammunition for yet another anti-Muslim tirade. It is at this stage that the use of myth can be seen most clearly. How easily attitudes and cultural meanings are transported across the globe is illustrated by *Mission Istanbul*, linking a global Islamicism that has permeated media images. It is useful here to quote from Timothy Marr's Afterword from his book *The Cultural Roots of American Islamicism:*

> the Muslim world remains today a contested symbolic geography – a 'mobile sign' that can either repulse or attract depending on the nature of the engagement and the conventions employed to interpret Islam's

significance...how its protean meanings rely upon the historical circumstances, the performative situations, and the ideological intent of the different individuals who deploy its expressive grammar. (Marr 2006, 297)

In this historical period, the Indian producers and directors have chosen to align their positions clearly with an American establishment that has violated the human rights of Muslim citizens repeatedly[15] and exploited the notoriety of a small group of mis-guided Muslims who, according to the media that constructs them larger than life, seek to wreak 'global terror'.

Mission Istanbul is difficult to refer to as a 'B' movie because of its high production values and the apparent 'privilege' of a Hindi film gaining international release. The fact that it has been shot to a great extent in Turkey means that expense was not a great consideration for the director, although the share price of this company has fallen dramatically since 2006. There are three producers, Ekta Kapoor,[16] Suniel Shetty[17] and Shabbir Boxwala[18]. Ekta Kapoor, the producer of the longest running television serials in India, is a household name. Her association is with Balaji Telefilms, and the production company credited in this film is Balaji Productions[19]. In the film, Suniel Shetty acts as a good guy who dies fighting terrorists in Afghanistan, but he is also the producer of MI, and a businessman with interests in hotels and fashion. Finally Shabbir Boxwala's presence on the internet is discreet, and he has no biographic profile except credits for a few films, which he has scripted or produced. What could this successful team have felt about supporting such a flimsy film that has drawn its inspiration from media coverage, and blatantly twisted terrorist plots, to construct the centrality of India and Indians in the so-called fight against international terrorism?

Considering the recent spate of bomb blasts across the country,[20] the unresolved issue of Kashmir and its relationship to India and Pakistan, and the continuing occurrence of inter-community violence led by the fascist politics of both sides of politics in India, the issue of 'terror' is not far from front page news or television screens at any given time. This subject is addressed serially, as the director of this film has another big star cast[21] film, *Shootout at Lokhandwala* (2007), which is based on a real-life gun battle between gangsters and Bombay police in the locale of Bollywood. Perhaps because this was an actual event, Lakhia was able to control the storyline.

Mission Istanbul is an example of a recent film that is steeped in the already mediated world of 'international terrorism' and is a fanciful 'mythopractice' that has all the elements of an ideological discourse. From a neglect to represent Muslims as part of a congenial mixed society, Muslim representation in Hindi popular cinema has now created a separate genre for them and refrained from addressing issues arising from partition, pogroms or riots. This chapter has discussed how, recently, various Hindi film directors have constructed terrorism as a pathology of Muslims who must demonstrate extreme forms of personal sacrifice to be considered legitimate citizens of the Indian nation. It is, however, redeeming to read the ironic comments made by a majority of the online audience, who resist acceptance of at least part of this partisan politics, choosing to focus instead on cinematic practice and narrative issues. Full-fledged critique, however, is far more rare on these film forums. Only one member of the Internet audience, a Muslim, acknowledges that *Mission Istanbul* is '... a complete waste of three hours where I was watching nothing but a director hostile attitude towards muslims and the way they were propagating against journalism ...'[22]

Conclusion

It is within the framework of contemporary politics and history that the Hindi film should be situated and read. The discourse of 'Muslim terrorism' reverberates across media products within Indian and international politics, constructing members of this community as the perpetrators and instigators of mindless violence, which is inexplicable and lifted out of its historical and political context. The rush to convict and execute members of the Muslim community accused of these crimes, and the laxity of the judicial process to bring to book perpetrators of violence *against* Muslims whether they are Hindu fundamentalist groups, or grassroots actors operating with state sanction such as the military or police, underscores the difficulties besetting the use of negotiated means to settle communal differences. The repetition of this theme of terrorism in fiction films contributes to the construction of a contemporary myth, fuelling a culture of antagonism between the Hindu and Muslim communities in India. This chapter has argued that these factors, combined with the nexus of interests that include criminals, politicians and members of the film industry in India, are complicit either inadvertently or deliberately in constructing an ideological framework that exacerbates communal differences in real communities. These operate in the same vein as fascist politics closely allied to rightwing economic and political agendas. All of this can only be understood as a dangerous prospect for democratic governance and secularism in India.

Notes

1 http://www.samarmagazine.org/archive/article.php?id=278; (accessed 3 January 2009); http://www.aljazeera.com/news/articles/39/9_is_not_11.html# Arundati Roy.
2 The unresolved issue of two government inquiries on Godhra, and a question mark as to the authenticity of two Commisions of Inquiry has left the investigations mired in dispute.
3 http://www.samarmagazine.org/archive/article.php?id=275 'As the Fire Dies', Biju Mathew (accessed 3 January 2009).

4 Ramakrishnan, V. in New Delhi & Bavadam, L. in Bombay (2009) *Frontline Volume 25 –* Issue 26: Dec. 20, 2008–Jan. 2002 http://www.flonnet.com/fl2526/stories/20090102252601800.htm (accessed 7 January 2009).
5 One example from a number of articles published that describes the links between the Bombay film industry and crime.
6 This typecasting was especially evident in the late 1980s as politics in India became increasingly authoritarian with the rise of the Bhartiya Janata Party to power.
7 Ravi Vasudevan, Rosie Thomas, Sumita Chakravarty, among others who have described Hindi films in this vein.
8 http://hindicinema.wordpress.com/2008/07/25/mission-istanbul-movie-review/ 2 November 2008, Comment left by Junaid Farooque accuses the director of being political and just denigrating Muslims. (accessed 16 November 2008).
9 http://www.zoomtv.in/view/news/bush-laden-in-mission-istanbul-0 (accessed 16 November 2008).
10 The late Indira Gandhi's children, both Sanjay and Rajiv, were educated at the Lawrence school in Sanawar, UP. IIT is the well-known abbreviation for Indian Institute of Technology, which is the elite engineering university that has five campuses in India.
11 'Kashmir Comes Full Circle' available at http://news.bbc.co.uk/2/hi/south_asia/7806153.stm (accessed 1 January 2009). Omar Abdullah is about to become the Chief Minister of the State of Kashmir, India.
12 This terminology is used to identify a young upwardly mobile, western oriented person.
13 http://forums.glamsham.com/viewtopic.php?t=6869&highlight=mission+istanbul (accessed 2 November 2008).
14 RAW acronym for Research and Analysis Wing, Government of India's investigative experts.
15 Banner, M. (2004) 'Terror and Torture' in Meron Benvinisti et al. *Abu-Ghraib: The Politics of Torture*. Terra Nova Series. North Atlantic Bookshop, 1–16. The essay is one from a collection that details abuses by the US in Iraq. The film MI is replete with language and scenes from American films like Mission Impossible, and one instance, early in the film, soon after Vikas is introduced to his colleagues at Al-Johora TV his boss declares, "Works done, let's party!" Also, cf. Harbury, J. (2005) *Truth, Torture, and the American Way: The History and Consequences of U.S. Involvement in Torture* Beacon Press, NY. USA. Chapter one speaks of post 9/11 torture, but the rest details repeated forms of torture and interrogation endemic to US international relations.
16 http://en.wikipedia.org/wiki/Ekta_Kapoor This reference is not attributed to verified sources.
17 http://en.wikipedia.org/wiki/Sunil_Shetty
18 http://www.imdb.com/name/nm0101555/ Little information is available apart from his credits which include scriptwriting.
19 http://www.businessofcinema.com/news.php?newsid=9250 Sunjay Dutt and Balaji sign Rs. 5Bn deal to produce 9 films. http://en.wikipedia.org/wiki/Balaji_Telefilms Largely television production company grown since 2001, a family run business by yesteryear Jetendra and his wife, son and daughter Ekta.
    7:40 PM (a person identified by the nick name...) Eternal dreamer said... 'I agree wid gopal...though I'm from Delhi, yet I think pigeonholing UP & Bihar as some shit is mindless....Refrain from doing that...else d review is k..though I wud like to lable it as "worst over-hyped movie of all times". I just didn't c d logic behind making such crap....& my guess is , its not Lakhia but Balaji which is behind dis senseless piece of shit...'. http://www.indicine.com/movies/bollywood/mission-istanbul-movie-review/

20 Two incidents in very recent Bombay history relevant to the discussion are available at http://news.indiainfo.com/spotlight/Bombay_bomb_blast/ and http://timesofindia.indiatimes.com/Bombay/ATS_to_file_a_fresh_case_in_Malegaon_bomb_blast/articleshow/4003943.cms (accessed 2 January 2009)
21 http://sydney.citysearch.com.au/tv/1137609020127/Shot+in+Bombay Review of Liz Mermin's documentary on the making of 'Shot in Bombay' on the film by Apoorva Lakhia and Sanjay Dutt's involvement in the sordid politics of the Bombay blasts and his ability to juggle court rooms, jail and shooting schedules.
22 Farouque Junaid (2008) Comments re Mission Istanbul, 14 September 2008 at 8:29 pm available http://hindicinema.wordpress.com/2008/07/25/mission-istanbul-movie-review/ (accessed 2 November 2008)

References

Amladi, P. R. (1997) 'New Apprehensions: The Ambivalence of Modernity in Early Indian Cinema' unpublished PhD dissertation, New York University

Anderson, B. (1982) *Imagined Communities: Reflections on the Origin and Spread of Nationalism*, London, Verso

Banaji, S. (2006) *Reading 'Bollywood': The Young Audience and Hindi Films*, Basingstoke: Palgrave Macmillan

Barthes, R. (1973) *Mythologies*, St. Albans: Paladin

Barthes, R. (1977), 'Myth Today' in *Image, Music, Text*, trans. S. Heath London: Fontana Press, 165–169

Bhatt, C. (2001) *Hindu Nationalism: Origins, Ideologies and Modern Myths*, Oxford and New York: Berg

Bhattacharya, H. (2002) 'Deregulation of Gold in India: A Case Study in Deregulation of a Gold Market' World Gold Council Research Study No. 27: 11–12 www.thebulliondesk.com/ content/reports/temp/india1.pdf (accessed 31 January 2009)

Chakravarty, S. S. (1993) *National Identity in Indian Popular Cinema, 1947–1987*. Austin: University of Texas Press

Garga, B. D. (1996) *So Many Cinemas: The Motion Picture in India* Eminence Design Ltd. Bombay. Chapter 5

Gopalan, L. (1993) 'Coitus Interruptus: Love Story and National Identity' in *Wogs, Natives, Heroes: Examining Cinema & National Identity* Chapter two of unpublished PhD thesis University of Rochester, NY, USA. Available UMI Dissertations Services

Jameson, F. (1991) *Postmodernism or the Cultural Logic of Late Capitalism*, Durham: Duke University Press

Kazmi, F. (1994) 'The Muslim social and the Female Protagonist' in (ed.) Zoya Hasan *Forging Identities: Gender, Communities and the State*, New Delhi: Kali for Women, 226–243

—––––– (1999) *The Politics of India's Conventional Cinema: Imaging a Universe, Subverting a Multiverse*, New Delhi, Sage Publications

Kesavan, M. (1994) 'Urdu, Awadh and the Tawaif: The Islamicate Roots of Hindi Cinema', in: Zoya Hasan (ed.), *Forging Identities: Gender, Communities and the State*, New Delhi: Westview Press

Marr, T. (2006) *The Cultural Roots of American Islamicism*, Cambridge: Cambridge University Press

Mecklai, N. (2006) *Abrogated Identity: Muslim Representation in Hindi Popular Cinema 1947–2000* unpublished thesis, Edith Cowan University, Perth Western Australia

Metcalf, B. (1999) 'Nationalism, Modernity and Muslim Identity' in P. Van der Veer (ed.) *Nation and Religion: Perspectives on Europe and Asia*, Princeton, NJ, USA, Princeton University Press, 129–143

Mishra, V. (1988) 'Towards a Theoretical Critique of Bombay Cinema' *Screen*, Volume 26: 4–19.

Morcom, A. (2007) *Hindi Film Songs and the Cinema* London: Ashgate Publishing, Ltd SOAS Musicology Series

Navlakha, G. (1998) 'Invoking Union: Kashmir and Official Nationalism of "Bharat"' in (ed.) T.V. Satyamurthy, *Region, Religion, Caste. Gender and Culture in Contemporary India, Volume 3*. Oxford University Press Delhi *Series: Social Change and Political Discourse in India*, 77–79

Noorani, A. G. (1964) *The Kashmir Question*, Bombay: Manaktala Press, 40–70

Prasad, M. M. (1994) 'The State and Culture: Hindi Cinema in the "Passive Revolution". PhD Dissertation, University of Pittsburgh, PA, USA

Rai, A. S. (2003) 'Patriotism and the Muslim Citizen in Hindi Films' *Harvard Asia Quarterly*, Volume VII, No. 3. Summer 2003 available online: http://www.asiaquarterly.com/content/view/136/40/ (accessed 16 November 2008)

―――― (2008) 'First Day, First Show: The Pleasures and Politics of Hindi Film Culture' *Samar* 15: Summer/Fall, 2002 available online, http://www.samarmagazine.org/archive/article.php?id=120 (accessed 16 November 2008)

R.H. (contributor, *Samar Magazine*) 'Who Killed Hemant Karkare?' *Samar 32, 15 December 2008*, available online http://www.samarmagazine.org/archive/article.php?id_278 (accessed 15 December 2008)

Rajadhyaksha, A. (1986) 'Neo-traditionalism'– Film as Popular Art in India. *Framework*, Nos 32/33: 21–67

―――― (1993) 'The Epic Melodrama: themes of Nationality in Indian Cinema'. *Journal of Arts and Ideas* Nos. *25–26* December pp. 55–70

Rajagopal, A. (2001) *Politics After Television: Hindu Nationalism and the Reshaping of the Public in India*, Cambridge: Cambridge University Press

Rahman, M. and Katiyar, A. (1993). 'Bombay Film Industry Underworld Connections' Cover Story *India Today* Volume XVIII No. 9: 1–15

Ramakrishan, V. (2009) "Measured Steps' update regarding media 'adventurism' re Bombay attacks and government response available http://www.flonnet.com/fl2602/stories/20090130260203000.htm (accessed16 January 2009

Roy, A. (2008) '9 is not 11' available at http://www.aljazeera.com/news/articles/39/9_is_not_11.html (accessed 18 December 2008)

Sethi, M. (2002) 'Cine-Patriotism' *Samar* 15: Summer/Fall 2002, available online http://www.samarmagazine.org/archive/article.php?id_115 (accessed 12 September 2006)

Shahani, K. (1986) Dossier: Kumar Shahani 'Myths for Sale'. *Framework* Issue 31: 71–99.

Singh, J. (2002) 'Bollywood & mafia: What lies beneath' in *The Pioneer*, 19 August 2002. Record Number A0354485

Thapar, R. (1989). 'Imagined Religious Communities? Ancient History and the Modern Search for a Hindu Identity' in *Modern South Asian Studies*, Volume 23, No. 2: 209–231

―――― (2005) *Somnatha: The Many Voices of History*, London: Verso

Thomas, R. (1985) 'Indian Cinema: Pleasures and Popularity', *Screen* Volume 26 Nos. 3–4 May/Aug: 116–131

Thomas, R. (1995) 'Melodrama and the Negotiation of Morality in Mainstream Hindi Film' In Breckenbridge, C. A. (ed.) *Consuming Modernity: Public Culture in a South Asian World*, Minneapolis: University of Minnesota Press, 157–182

Vasudevan, R. (1995) Addressing the Spectator of a 'Third World' National Cinema: Bombay 'Social' Film of the 1940s and 1950s. *Screen* 36 No. 4: 305–324

Virdi, J. (2003) *The Cinematic Imagination: Indian Popular Films as Social History*, NJ USA: Rutgers University Press

Zavos, J. (2000) *The Emergence of Hindu Nationalism in India*. New Delhi: Oxford University Press

Zutshi, S. (1994) 'Woman, Nation and the Outsider in Hindi Cinema' in (eds) T. Niranjana, P. Sudhir and V. Dhareshwar *Interrogating Modernity: Culture and Colonialism in India* Calcutta: Seagull Books, 83–141

Chapter Nine

A PEACE OF SOAP: REPRESENTATIONS OF PEACE AND CONFLICT IN POPULAR TELEDRAMAS IN SRI LANKA

Neluka Silva

Introduction

It is 8.30 pm in Sri Lanka. The prime time television slot, immediately after the Sinhala News on Rupavahini, the State Television channel, is usually reserved for viewing the most popular teledramas. Families across the country sit together expecting images of 'reality' to bombard their screens. In the last twenty years, 'bombard' has taken on many connotations, as television producers/directors, actors and actresses attempt to capture the two crucial trajectories that have shaped the fabric of the nation: war and peace, that Sri Lanka has endured for the last three decades.

Although this has now broken down irrevocably in 2008–9, a de-escalation of the ethnic conflict and a temporary ceasefire agreement in 2002 between the Government of Sri Lanka (GoSL) and the Liberation Tigers of Tamil Eelam (LTTE) created a tenuous peace. After the Peace Accord, the mood of euphoria was contagious and everyone jumped on the 'peace bandwagon', including the television industry. An exploration of selected episodes from two popular teledramas that were scripted and screened during the ceasefire is a conduit to uncovering the political meanings underlying messages of peace in popular television. These messages need to be contextualised in relation to the larger discourses of nationhood within which peace is circulated and established in the public consciousness.

In this chapter, I will argue that the configurations of peace in television not only resonate closely with the dominant public and political discourses, but also invoke and are inscribed by discourses of identity, and racial and cultural purity, that have marked the ideological terrain of the ethnic conflict in Sri Lanka thus far.

Fiction Media and Social Identities in Sri Lanka

Serialised dramas or soap operas, whether as television or radio productions, are becoming increasingly regarded as a powerful medium through which social behaviours and attitudes can be purposefully informed and influenced. Social impacts related to knowledge, attitudes and behaviours are fundamental requirements in peace building and conflict transformation. In countries where conflict is complex, protracted and seemingly intractable, the fractured relationship between different groups is frequently underpinned at a community level by the narrowing of identities. This leads to a demonisation of the 'other' and the subsequent persistent failure of parties to overcome the hurt and anger of past injustices and atrocities (Lederach 1997; Rigby 2001). Lederach's (2002) assertion that there is a correlation between the transformation of conflict toward peace and the level of popular awareness or *conscientization* regarding the nature of the conflict in question, highlights the important role that popular television can play in mass social communication. As communities are often unaware of how identities and relationships have been constructed, the establishment of a cognitive knowledge base becomes an essential prerequisite for conflict transformation by providing the starting point from which stereotypes or prejudices can be challenged and dismantled. As Mary Anderson notes, in conflict-affected communities many aspects of life such as culture, values, experience and institutions 'continue to connect people rather than divide them' (1999, 24). The need to be entertained and the desire for a good story are 'connectors' that can bridge ethnic, racial, political or religious differences, and ferment local capacities for peace through a range of devices such as evoking reminiscences of inter-communal harmony in a peaceful past or exposing the agendas of conflict dividers and peace process spoilers. The careful deployment of characters in such narratives can help uncover further layers of interconnection. Anderson goes on to point out that in conflict contexts there are always some individuals or groups who refuse to demonise or stereotype the other and instead continue to express tolerance and acceptance for the other side (1999, 26). The realistic portrayal of such characters through television dramas reveals to the wider population that there are empowering alternatives besides conforming to the divisive propaganda and representations of the 'other' that are commonly found in conflict affected societies.

Analysing the content, themes and audience reactions to two teledramas in Sri Lanka is a way of determining if and how this genre has attempted to engage with the issue of peace[1]. As I will argue in this chapter, affirming the need for peace is not adequate, but it is imperative to identify how peace is configured and the obstacles to conveying a sustainable peace.

The teledramas *A9* and *Take this Road* emphasise the need for peace at the civil society level. This is crucial since, at the early stages of the peace process, the 'peace agenda' was confined to the state level. The recognition that conflict transformation includes a wide range of activities and spheres in which the functions of non-state actors are of great importance is the most difficult element of peacemaking (Liyanage 2006, 279).

For instance, differences of ethnic communities have been portrayed in simple, overarching and stereotypical ways in Sri Lanka, and in their reportage the media have contributed to constructing/reinforcing difference in xenophobic terms. For the most part, their articulation of peace has also been limited, as they have subscribed to overplaying the polarities between communities. In Thiru Kandiah's analysis of the media he reveals that

> items about peace constitute just one side of a two-sided discourse, a side which, even as it is being filled out, is being decisively undermined by what is being said on the other side. .... Clearly peace can be freely talked about, but only on terms approved of or determined by one section of one party to the conflict (2001, 14–16).

Recognising the potential of the teledrama in Sri Lanka, the signing of the peace negotiations impelled a private television network, Maharajah Television, to embark on the production of a teledrama that relayed the message of peace. *A9* charted the lives of characters in a post-conflict context, and mixed the Sinhala and Tamil languages to provide linguistic access to both communities. The Media Director of Maharajah Television in an interview said that the chairman felt that this organisation had a responsibility to reinforce the message of peace through teledrama, as it is the most powerful cultural medium in Sri Lanka. This teledrama was produced at a high cost because some of the shooting was done on location in Jaffna, which lacks infrastructure facilities for this kind of production.

A9

Sydney Chandrasekra, who was working as a director for Maharajah Television, was anxious to produce a teledrama where the concept of peace through personal relationships was brought to the forefront. He felt that audiences seek a sense of immediacy in teledrama, a sense of the here-and-now. According to him:

> People expect to see contemporary issues. Though we don't talk about the war in this teledrama, we show the present context of how to rebuild the relationships between the communities that were lost during the war. Today people are immune to war and violence. Everybody is talking about the number of lives lost, property that is destroyed and the economy. No one talks about the love that we've lost. (Interview with author, 31 March 2003)

A9 marks a departure in focus from the conventional teledrama narrative emphasising the post-conflict context. It taps into a desire for reconciliation as an important prerequisite for achieving peace expressed by the majority of viewers in their response to the question: 'What issues should be addressed to achieve sustainable peace?' When the teledrama was conceptualised and launched and the script produced, advertisers immediately responded positively seizing an opportunity to identifying themselves with promoting peace.

The teledrama deviated from the conventional teledrama formula, not only in theme, but also from the linear narrative structure, by incorporating techniques such as flashback, stream of consciousness and dream sequences. It also invoked the genre of the Hindi film (extremely popular among Sinhala and Tamil audiences) by interweaving song and dance, and its popularity can also be attributed to this factor.

The publicity material stressed the association of the teledrama with song. As Chandrasekera states 'All these years we have only seen the theme song, but now the actors themselves are singing the songs.' The image of Sinhala actors singing an old *Tamil* song *Wanga Machan* (reworked to incorporate Sinhala and Tamil) was a radical gesture and had a particular meaning for viewers. It was devised as a subliminal encoding of anti-chauvinist ideology. In a context where the actor is not just deemed to be playing a role, but is identified with/as the character, the transformative potential of this moment cannot be overlooked. Here the Sinhala or Tamil character, singing a Tamil/Sinhala song, is associated with the ethnic minority – his/her 'antagonist' – and vice versa. To be seen in a public domain singing in the language of the 'other' was a device to promote acceptance – the first step towards reconciliation. This song had wide audience appeal. The ideological purchase of the song was that it enabled viewers to break down ethnic barriers; it was resonant of an era when ethnic harmony was demonstrated through the sharing of popular songs and other popular cultural artefacts. Benedict Anderson argues that, songs, hymns, along with print capitalism, were intrinsic to, and form part of, the cultural repertoire of the modern nation. Here is an instance where the nation's modern liberal project – in this case, peace, is deliberately advanced through song. Both the producers and cast acknowledged its service in the agenda of the teledrama. Chandrasekera said: 'These days every radio station plays this song. It is also popular in pop concerts. Because of the teledrama, it became popular among all the communities' (interview with the author, 31 March 2003). The impact of the song suggests that processes of reconciliation and healing can be successfully initiated by moving beyond narrative (Kabir 2005, 29). It has been recognised that 'non-narrative cultural formations, including symbols, folk models and rituals are mobilised to inscribe, resist and heal trauma' (Robben and Suarez-Orozco 2000, 2–3). Songs have the capacity to recall other histories that circulate through and beyond narrative.

Furthermore, the song's immense popularity reveals how it separates itself from the teledrama and brings in its own market forces. Promoting a catchy song was an expedient device not solely for ideological but also for economic purposes. It was marketed independently through CDs, tapes, and promoted as being both distinctive from, and yet associated with, the teledrama.

A9 narrates the story of Siriwansa, a Sinhalese from the South – Matara – who sets up a small but lucrative bakery in Jaffna. He marries his friend's sister, Nirmala, a Tamil, but the riots of 1983 force Siri to flee Jaffna, abandoning his wife and baby son. He is unable to return to Jaffna and, subsequently, finds out that Nirmala dies in an army offensive. Siri then becomes a successful entrepreneur in Colombo, and marries a Sinhalese woman Dharmaseeli. They have a daughter. His business grows and Dharmaseeli, who is actively involved in social service projects, is approached to become a member of parliament. When the peace settlement is enforced, and the road between Jaffna and Colombo – the A9 – is opened, Siri decides to visit Jaffna. He is determined to see his son, Sunny, and then persuades him to come to live with him for a while in Colombo. He is forced to reveal the truth to his Sinhalese wife, who, albeit initially distraught, accepts the Tamil boy as a part of the family. Siri is then approached by the LTTE who know that Sunny is in Colombo, and they force him to go back with them to Jaffna. Siri falls ill, and while he is on his deathbed in hospital, Sunny is taken away. In the closing shot he swears that he will return to be with his father.

The title, which is the name of the road linking Colombo and Jaffna, evokes images of linkage because 'the A9 linked people in the south and the north. But since the road was closed, people from south and north stopped having any connection with each other. The ability to travel allowed the possibility of establishing relationships between people of the north and south. No one talks of the love that has been lost because of war. Before the war, there were only cultural differences. In those days there were no ethnic divisions,' so states Sydney Chandrasekera, whose primary aim in writing this is to emphasise the need to establish inter-ethnic relationships[2]. This comment can be construed as somewhat facile, for it places the onus for the troubles entirely on the physical rupture between the ethnic groups. Yet, Chandrasekera's admission of the elemental (lack of) understanding between communities and ethnic groups is meant to be progressive: 'We don't show a single bomb blast or a grenade. But we intend to bring back to light the love Sinhalese, Tamils and the Muslims had.'

The kind of naïveté expressed in these statements by Chandrasekera is reflected in a highly romanticised narrative. Constructions of character also veer towards one-dimensional exaggerations. Many ambiguous points in the narrative are not satisfactorily dealt with. For instance, though the protagonist emerges as a do-gooder and is portrayed as passionately fond of his son, Siri's protracted narrative of why he left Jaffna without his wife and child does not adequately vindicate him from this transgression. When he goes back after more than 15 years, he expects his Tamil wife's family to accept him without any rancour, and the fact that they do so is troubling. Likewise, the expectations placed upon Sunny by Siri and his Sinhalese family are simplistic. He is brought to Colombo from Jaffna by his father, and is situated in the household under false pretences. He is transplanted from one geographic and cultural location to another without any understanding within the narrative of his anxieties and reticence in such a situation or the underlying tensions of this context. When Sunny refuses to speak/learn Sinhala, this is also dismissed perfunctorily in the narrative by his father as 'stubbornness'. At no point in the teledrama does Siri appear to even strive to understand, let alone accept, his son's psychological state, and though narrative space is provided for Siri to articulate *his* justification for leaving his wife and child in Jaffna, Sunny is denied this privilege.

Ironically, political circumstances and the socio-historical context are entirely absent from the narrative frame and do not factor in shaping the trajectories of relationships, especially the inter-ethnic relationships. Even if one accepts Chandrasekera's argument that during the pre-conflict era ethnicity did not determine personal relationships, the configuration of relationships in the post-conflict phase cannot be made analogous to this perceived 'halcyon' era. This absence is testimony to the tension between 'reality' and desire and underscores the element of wish-fulfilment within teledramas that strive to endorse simplistic notions of harmony.

A further element of romanticising is manifest in the attitude of Siri's second wife towards Sunny. Her enthusiastic acceptance of him as a son, after the initial shock, is intended to relay a positive message about ethnic relations. But it may also be symptomatic of the positioning of woman as *inherently* peace loving within the dominant gender stereotyping across discourses of peace and conflict. As Ritu Menon insightfully notes: 'Women are generally *supposed* to be nurturing and caring, naturally maternal and, therefore, predisposed towards peace, just as men are *supposed* to be the opposite' (2004, 64: my emphases). Though Menon goes on to challenge these value systems in her essay, they are continually bolstered in popular culture, and seem to have impelled the construction of Dharmaseeli's role. Such characterisations imply that popular culture generally serves the interests of the dominant ideology, 'for it is this that provides the common ground between producers and audience-seen-as-consumers, and between different audience groups whose differences are thus minimised' (Fiske 1987, 39).

Malini Fonseka, who played the character of Dhamaseeli, is possibly the most popular film and television actress in the country, which motivated the director in casting her in this role. He said: 'I thought she is the ideal person to communicate the message woven in Dharmaseeli's character. I thought that people will accept the message if it was given through Malini.' Audience responses suggest that the strategy was regarded as 'unrealistic'. When Fonseka was asked: 'Do you think your role was a realistic one?' followed by: 'How did you feel about Dharmaseeli accepting Siri as her son?' she replied to the former: 'My character was very true to life' and to the latter: 'I had no difficulty in this role. As a woman, I might not like to accept it. But the character is such that she cannot deny accepting him as her son because she is a social worker and works with children.' Both responses fail to adequately address the motivation in the narrative. Moreover, she appears not to have perceived any complexity in the character. Her reason for taking on this role was to reinforce the message of peace.

Despite these limitations, moments in the narrative strive towards affirming the need for peace. The deployment of language merits further analysis. In *A9* three languages are used, and is a crucial determinant of the parameters of the relationships. At one level, majoritarian politics determine communication patterns, reinforcing the presupposition that the minority has to succumb to the linguistic hegemony. Sunny, who is unable to communicate in Sinhala, is marginalised and is expected to learn Sinhala. His struggle, though not intended as such, does map the hegemony of the national language. As conflict escalates, the dominant language is reinvested with power. Most teledramas are confined to the dominant language, with an occasional sprinkling of English (signifying the phenomenon of globalisation and the increasing prominence of English as a language of social mobility). In *A9* though the majority of characters comply with the orthodox linguistic hierarchy – positioning themselves vis-à-vis the dictates of the Sinhalese, another linguistic level emerges from the characters, which projects a progressive view of language as a vehicle for peace. For instance, Siri is fluent in Sinhala and Tamil and interacts easily with the Tamil community in Jaffna. This fluency enables him to forge deep, long-lasting relationships with his extended family, so that even when he returns many years later to Jaffna, he is able to resume the bonds. The breaking down of the language barrier signifies the first step to ethnic harmony.

Among the younger generation, Siri's daughter (the most positive and perhaps 'realistic' character in the teledrama) attempts to learn Tamil in order to communicate with Sunny, and symbolically enacts how reconciliation is to be envisaged in the future. She conveys the message that, as a community, there is potential to forge a bridge between the diverse ethnic and caste groups by learning each other's language and securing a fundamental need of humans – the ability to communicate. She asks Nirmal/Sunny in Tamil: '*Mr Nirmal, pasi kadi?*' (Are you hungry?). Nirmal is silent. She repeats: 'Are you *pasi kadi?*' followed by the Sinhala '*Oyata badagini nadda?*' to which he replies in English '*I am not hungry*'. It points to Chandrasekera's insight into the way in which language governs personal relationships. Though language is initially a barrier for the protagonists, what *A9* reveals is that it is not an insurmountable barrier. As the dialogue proceeds, brief though it is, the mix of all three languages portrays a reality: the common erasure of the phenomenon of the coexistence of languages, the prevalence of mixed marriages and racial and cultural intermixing. It counterbalances the threatening overtones of ethnic, cultural and linguistic exclusivity that determine the validation and legitimisation of ethno-nationalist conflict off-screen. The deployment of three languages is not simply promoting or describing 'reconciliation' but actively enacting a new scenario of hybridity. Language not only demarcates identities but also destabilises monolithic identities, and has the capacity to become an active creator of a new kind of identity, a pluralistic, inclusive identity that is denied by competing nationalisms. But language is also power, and the complexities of negotiating language in an unevenly multilingual society in *A9* is a non-idealised representation of the politics and problems of language.

Siri's daughter becomes the conduit through which another phenomenon that is suppressed in official and public discourses is unveiled – the existence of racial mixing. Her comment to Sunny that she and he are of 'one father and two mothers' is a radical avowal of this reality of Sri Lanka, and the admission of creating positive inter-ethnic relationships within the family unit metonymically captures the possibility of achieving ethnic harmony at the macro, political level. While cultural and racial syncretism is an actuality, the disjuncture between lived experience and representation – where by representation I mean, nationalism's representation of ethnic identity – is foregrounded here.

Hybridity (whether racial or cultural) as it appears and is lived is fraught with tension. This is mirrored in the anxiety that Sunny experiences about his identity. He is brought up as a Tamil (and it can be inferred that he is unaware of his Sinhala father until Siri comes to Jaffna). He joins the organisation to fight the Sinhalese, and then unexpectedly he is transplanted into an alien milieu. As a member of the minority community, he is then expected learn the dominant language, Sinhala. Only his half-sister makes an effort to make a concessionary gesture of trying to learn his language.

It is significant that both the characters of Sunny and the daughter were played by less well-known actors. In view of the politics of television such casting is significant. The teledrama world in Sri Lanka is dominated by a small coterie of actors who repeatedly get cast, or more accurately, typecast, into particular moulds. As a result, audiences have begun to associate them with particular roles, and find it difficult to accept them in other roles. This is avowed in Chandrasekera's claim that 'I thought if we can use new faces, people would accept the messages conveyed in the teledrama without any prejudice'[3]. Chandrasekera has recognised one of the constituents of soap opera relating to character portrayal as conforming to 'the representation of *real* people' (Fiske 1987, 149). The 'nowness' of television means that in soap operas, characters exist in a similar way to their audience, and so relate to characters on screen in terms of 'familiarity and identification'. As Fiske argues 'total identification' rarely occurs, but what is more appropriate is the process of implication: 'a simultaneous involvement with, and detachment from the character': implication, while extrication is 'closely connected with pleasure and unpleasure, with liking and disliking, and with the real and unreal. The real-seemingness of the character results from the viewer's projection of his/her own 'real' self into the character in the process of identification' (1987, 174). This view must be treated with a note of caution, since identification is a problematic phenomenon.

> Identification then becomes a process of imaginative wish fulfilment which can be, and is, criticised from at least two points of view. The moralists criticise it on the grounds that it is mere escapism, and in encouraging people to imagine a better existence for themselves discourages them from working to achieve it in reality. At the other end of the spectrum, the ideologists argue that identification is the process whereby the values of the dominant ideology are naturalised into the desires, almost the instincts, of the individual, and are thus endlessly reproduced and perpetuated (Fiske 1987, 170).

For *A9*, which grappled with an innovative and sensitive theme, in order to provoke the process of identification (crucial for 'liking' a character, and therefore, by extension, the message that is conveyed), the 'new faces' that the director speaks of, he felt would be more readily accepted as 'real' characters. Even if the characters were able to attract the audiences, and they had the potential to transform the dominant codes with their progressive on-screen behaviour, such moments are undermined by the denouement. Firstly, Sunny's unease about being a Tamil in a Sinhala household is dispelled without attempting to capture the complexities of his situation, and within the narrative framework no trajectory is offered to consider the process with which he reconciles himself to his mixed identity. Though this condition is valorized and promoted as the ideal, the problematic aspects of such a condition are ignored in the narrative. Secondly, though in the pre-conflict scenario (when Siri works in Jaffna) positive relationships among ethnic groups exist, during the ceasefire, efforts to ameliorate ethnic relations appear to occur only by the Sinhalese. In Siri's household, his wife, daughter and other members of the household accept Sunny, albeit on their terms. In contrast, the Tamil community – who are portrayed in the teledrama primarily as the members of the 'movement' who 'abduct' Sunny – are entrapped by racial stereotyping. They emerge as ruthless, violent and lacking any humanity. This slippage undercuts hitherto described efforts to revise received prejudice. The culmination of the teledrama, especially the final shot of the image of Sunny's helplessness in the hands of the merciless 'movement' legitimises the chauvinistic view of the Tamils as unwilling to compromise and the Sinhalese as humane, peace loving, making all the conciliatory gestures. Such polarisations of contending groups cast doubt on the teledrama's potential for establishing real ideologies of peace.

The principal limitation of this teledrama was its ineffective audience impact. It was only aired on Sirasa, a part of Maharajah Television, which does not have the wide reach that the State channel Rupavahini does. Although in interview the media director said that it had wide audience appeal, there is no structured system of programme rating to indicate its popularity. Estimations by MTV were based on conjecture. The pre-publicity was scant, and the director also conceded that a more rigorous effort should have been made to publicise this teledrama as a crucial intervention in the immediacy of the ceasefire.

Following *A9*, which has subsequently come under assault by other television companies, a more deliberate and conceptualised production of a peace-related teledrama was the collaboration between a local television network – Young Asia Television (YA TV) and the Academy of Educational Development (AED), a part of USAID.

Take this Road

Take this Road, while foregrounding the theme of reconciliation and ethnic and cultural diversity, was also designed to highlight the human cost of war. A local film and television director, Asoka Handagama, was chosen for his bold and approach and sensitive style, his perceptions of the complexities of the ethnic conflict and his technical innovations[4]. Handagama said that he accepted this project for two reasons. After the opening of the A9 road he had travelled several times to the north, and had built up relationships there, and he felt that this teledrama would enable him to express his experiences there and allay some of the fears and misconceptions that people in the south had towards Jaffna. In addition, the collaborative nature of the project, where all three communities were engaged in contributing input to the script, appealed to him. This was the first time he had participated in such a project, and he felt that the sensitivity with which the teledrama was conceptualised granted him an exceptional opportunity to use the format of teledrama for relaying a compelling message that might have a tangible effect in transforming the public imagination[5].

Recognising that the teledrama industry is Sinhala-dominated in the pre-production stage, the organisation recognised the need for adopting a process of dialogue and consultation in order to ensure that all the stakeholders in Sri Lanka's peace process were represented. Therefore, the script was developed through a collaborative, consultative process, providing these groups with the opportunity to express their views and concerns about media treatment of conflict.

The cast and crew worked in all three languages, and the series was shot primarily on location in Jaffna. It was decided to film in Jaffna because of its significance as an area which had been inaccessible to people in the south for almost 20 years. Some of the actors were chosen from Jaffna and part of the production involved several sessions of rehearsing together and a workshop for the artistes involved.

The teledrama was intended to foreground the cost of conflict on fragile community relations and to reflect the hopes and aspirations of all the communities who had faced armed conflict in one form or another. Sharmini Boyle, Editor-in-Chief, of YA TV made the following statement about the aim of this teledrama:

> It will underscore the need for dialogue and accommodation in Sri Lanka's present ethno-political context and attempt to build confidence and trust between parties through counteracting misconceptions and highlighting common ground and shared experiences and expectations.

The producers were also conscious of achieving a high standard of visual quality and sophisticated technical effects. An original sound track with a theme song was produced in the hope of maximising audience appeal. What they regarded as 'essential elements' in a plot for entertaining television – love, friendship, passion and politics were carefully interwoven.

Since the President took control of the state media in November 2003, securing airtime entailed several negotiations leading to a delay in airing the programme. *Take this Road* was broadcast in January 2004 on the State Television Corporation Rupavahini's Channel Eye. Subsequently, it was shown on other private channels. The primary broadcast of the series was complemented by a repeat telecast on Rupavahini Channel 1, but this was not aired during prime time.

The title *Take this Road* serves as a metaphor for the roads travelled by three families. It also inscribes an appeal to 'take' the road to peace. The narrative depicts the journey of a Sinhala family, the Subasinghes, on the A9 to Jaffna. They take the opportunity for Mrs Subasinghe to materialise her long-felt wish of making a pilgrimage to Nagadipa to worship in this revered sanctum on a sequestered island. A victim of a bomb explosion, Mr. Subasinghe is not keen on travelling to Jaffna, and neither is his University student daughter, Nadee, who is suspicious of the LTTE's motives. But the son Ranga, a musician, is more positive and they decide to make the journey, before it is too late and the road is closed once more. Likewise, a Muslim family, the Jamaldeens too are under pressure to return to Jaffna since the owner of a shop who gave them a place to stay in for 12 years is anxious to get back his land so that he can expand his business. They make plans to re-settle in their original home. Fathima, the wife is particularly worried as they have a young daughter, Ameera, and things are still uncertain for them in Jaffna. Meanwhile in the North, the Kanagaratnams, a Tamil family subject to trauma, is domiciled in Jaffna. They are surprised when their son Rathidharan, who they never expected to see again, comes back home. Their daughter, Gowrie, a dance teacher also lives with them.

During the journey the Sinhala family meet the Jamaldeens, and when they are in Jaffna the Kanagaratnams provide them with a place to stay. The narrative then charts their experiences in Jaffna, as each of them comes to terms with their traumas of the past. The story ends with the Subasinghes leaving for Colombo, with the foundation being laid for a growing friendship between the families, due to their new perspective on each other's communities.

The characters are sensitively portrayed and though they are representative of what Handagama calls 'real life' characters, there is a conscious attempt to eschew the kind of ethnic and gender stereotyping that have permeated the narratives of teledramas[6]. Although outward symbols of ethnic identity, such as dress (the Muslim women cover their heads, and the Tamil characters wear the 'pottu' on their foreheads) and food, align characters to particular ethnic groups, they are individualised and not simplistically drawn along the perceived 'attributes' – such as miserliness, cunning in business ventures, – that have previously marked ethnic divisions.

Nadee, the Sinhala daughter, just completed her undergraduate education; with her idealistic temperament and emergent political views she does not typify the configuration of the 'ideal, dutiful daughter'. Traditionally, the beautiful and virtuous daughter is common in teledramas. Nadee articulates her political views in a forceful manner, is unafraid of familial or public opinion, and does not seem to adhere to the expectations of a 'good daughter'. As Purnima Mankekar argues 'good daughters always [defer] to the authority of the patriarchal family' (1999, 118). In contrast Nadee, together with her brother, Ranga, make decisions for their parents. Her humanity, especially in the way that she empathises with the other characters irrespective of ethnic or religious boundaries, is empowering in that it subverts the stereotypical role of the hardline nationalist. Her relationship with Vishwa, a Tamil boy whom she meets at university, is also conducted in an open manner, making for a candid appraisal of inter-ethnic romantic relationships. However, the hint of romantic aspirations on her part and her possessiveness towards him are disappointing because they are testimony to the reluctance in South Asian cultural works to situate male-female relationships beyond the confines of a stereotypical romance paradigm. Though in teledramas the romance paradigm predominates and sustains audience interest, it is problematic in that it renders gender inequalities as 'natural' since, in most cases, the female is situated in a position of submissiveness. Though for the most part she is configured as a perceptive and sensitive character, in the scenes with Vishwa (especially when he is with Gowrie, a Tamil girl from the community), Nadee is also cast as being irrational and not in control of her emotions in her own relationship, thereby diffusing the positive impact of her role and complicating claims on the part of the teledrama's makers to new forms of characterisation.

The other characters are also configured in an evocative manner, in order to accentuate the effects of ethnic conflict on their physical and psychological being. Each character offers a different perspective, and no one community is spared. A particularly chilling moment in the narrative is the episode of the young dance pupil who becomes the victim of a landmine. The visual and auditory impact is graphically captured and the effect on the community is enacted with poignancy. The characters come together in their endeavour to rush the child to hospital. The Sinhala family who witness the incident are as traumatised as the others, revealing the indiscriminate ravages of conflict. The emotional magnitude of this experience underlines the spuriousness of boundaries drawn on the lines of ethnicity, culture, language etc, since ultimately, human suffering transcends these divisions.

A further rendition of the psychological cost of conflict is the relationship between Subasinghe, the Sinhala father, and Kanagaratnam. This is manifest in his discomfiture when he is forced to stay with the Kanagaratnams, which indicates that he is suspicious of *all* Tamils[7]. His inability to differentiate militant from civilian denotes a phenomenon that impedes forging personal relationships between ethnic groups, and the perception that all Tamils are the malevolent 'other' percolates into the larger political scenario where peace agreements cannot be transacted or maintained. As the two men embark on an acrimonious debate about the political situation, the implicit representational biases of ethnic groups surface. The oppositional views of the political situation are deeply embedded in historical (mis)representation, and add immeasurably to the nuances of the cultural and political complexities of this increasingly multi-ethnic nation. Albeit the acrimonious ending to the argument, it is enabling on many levels, since both protagonist and viewer witness a gradual shift in perspective. It acutely demonstrates the *possibility*, notwithstanding the difficulties, of initiating dialogue between political as well as civil society actors. Furthermore, it cautions against facile interpretations of historical and cultural processes established by nationalist impulses. At an ideological level, this debate raises many issues about the ethnic conflict that have been marginalised in the public domain. Sharmini Boyle of YA TV identified this as a radical moment in the series. She regards it as a moment of rupture in the genre of teledrama, affirming the possibility that 'while doing entertainment, the medium of popular television can be used to talk about something serious.' This is how civil society peace-building occurs. When two enemies truly hear and understand each other's stories, they discover their shared humanity, and convey the central message that peace will benefit everyone, not just one community.

The production process also mirrored the thematic content of *Take this Road*. The dynamics of working in Jaffna prompted compromises by both cast and crew of all ethnic groups to work together. Private houses accommodated members of the team, and there was a high level of anxiety since providing shelter to the different ethnic groups was an act of intimacy and involved contending with their fears of the 'other'. At the initial stages, the Sinhalese actors and crew were also uneasy because many had never visited or worked in Jaffna and were reluctant to speak Sinhalese there. Some of the Tamils, who were fluent in Sinhalese, were also unwilling to speak Sinhala in the north. However, after the filming started, gradual collaboration between the actors and crew was evident. This led to friendships between the Sinhala actors and actresses and the Tamil actors and actresses while on location. As Handagama observed: '[t]hat was a very significant outcome. In fact, the ordinary couriers of peace are more effective than the official, superior activators of peace'[8]. For instance, during a party for the cast and crew, one of the Tamil actors started singing a Sinhala song 'Uthuru kone numba hinahena' (You Laugh in the South Corner). Handagama had asked him whether he was aware that the Janatha Vimukthi Peramuna (JVP) had used that song in their repertoire of revolutionary anthems in the early 1970s and late 1980s. This revelation had surprised the young man, but he continued to sing it[9]. As Handagama asserts 'peace-building takes many forms.' This episode serves as a potent reverberation of a pre-ceasefire era and reiterates the urgency of peace.

Though *Take this Road* won several awards at Raigam Tele-awards 2004 for Best Director, Best Actor, Best Production, Best Script and both Handagama and YATV were satisfied with the production process, Handagama feels that the idea of peace was not communicated compellingly enough to the public and it lacked a larger impact and the transformative potential of the teledrama was not exploited by the sponsors or by the channel, Rupavahini. His disillusionment stems from the belief that if the teledrama had been marketed more aggressively by implying that the peace content was crucial at this historical juncture commercial sponsorship could have been viable, and the midway advertising would not have been an issue. He argues that the teledrama scene has reached a stage where, due to the plethora of teledramas, viewers no longer take them seriously and it is purely a vehicle for entertainment. In the past a culture of seriousness had existed and some teledramas had provoked discussions on social issues[10]. In order to create this atmosphere, the significance of *Take this Road* needed to be stressed in the preview stage with trailers to maximise its impact on the public.

The politics and particularly the political economy of television invaded the way in which the series was televised. Rupavahini, which secures commercial sponsors for their teledramas, imposed the condition that unless there was a mid-programme advertisement they could only show it on Channel Eye. In the pre-production contract Handagama had refused to allow any mid-programme advertising as he felt that this would detract the viewers from taking the message seriously and would also disrupt the flow of the narrative. Rupavahini did not budge, and it was finally aired on Channel Eye (another subsidiary channel of Rupavahini), even though it has a lower audience base and reach than Rupavahini[11]. There was no organised publicity and previews were scant. An intensive campaign to make the public aware of the objective of this teledrama and a concurrent effort to promote the 'peace dividend' were essential. Though some efforts were made to launch organised shows in selected areas and bring the communities together, it appears that this was a rather ad hoc venture and Handagama felt that this process should have been sustained over a long period of time[12].

As a narrative, *Take this Road* complies with all the constituents of the teledrama genre. It is primarily a story that relies upon the modality of creating human interest through the perspectives of different communities. The stories of daily lives, together with the tensions within the narrative framework contributed to total numbers who viewed it[13].

Conclusion: Where Do We Go From Here?

The two teledramas examined in this chapter reveal that portraying peace is not a seamless process. Even if the discursive strategies within the teledrama do not fail (as in the case of *Take this Road*), other extraneous factors such as controls imposed by the state television stations or the politics of marketing disrupt the optimal use of the medium of television for propelling the idea of peace.

As Sri Lanka has launched once again into a state of conflict with an escalation of violence and destruction, the mood in the nation has radically altered from hope to despair and the overriding concern in the public consciousness seems to be that peace can never be achieved. The political, religious and cultural diversities are being reasserted and reaffirmed through the gun. As we move into such a climate, the commitment towards peace in the media is also being diffused and overlaid by the traditional rhetoric of xenophobia.

Having experienced the dual trauma of disaster and armed conflict, we must remind ourselves that a commitment to challenging and dismantling war-making structures is demanded of popular culture, summed up in Sharmini Boyle's words.

> The transformation of a conflict-ridden society into one of sustainable peace between communities involves a process of change – changing situations characterized by mistrust, fear and bloodshed into environments in which reconciliation, respect for others and social justice can take root[14].

Even though we are engulfed by violence once again, the possibility of reinscribing discourses of peace is being reaffirmed by cultural producers. An avowal of transformation through popular culture and especially popular television is imperative in order for the minorities and warring factions to recognise that civil society is striving to achieve peace, in spite of military and political developments. One such endeavour was an exhibition of digital art entitled *Quest* which took place in early June 2006. At this exhibition, artists, academics, television and media personnel came together to espouse the need as producers of cultural capital to share in the burden of making peace work. I end this chapter with one affirmation that powerfully evokes this commitment: 'It is necessary for poets, painters, dreamers, scholars, religious re-thinkers and visionaries to raise their collective voices and jolt the public conscience, showing us the futility of the terrifying discriminations we have invented and hopefully persuading us to resurrect the gentleness. ... that many of us have suppressed. Then we can sleep'[15].

Notes

1 The period of investigation for the audience survey covered 12 months from December 2001, which was when the ceasefire was signed.
2 Chandrasekera in interview with Neluka Silva, 31 March 2003.
3 Chandrasekera, the director in interview with Neluka Silva, 31 March 2003.
4 Sharmini Boyle, producer in interview with Neluka Silva, April 2006.
5 Asoka Handagama in interview with Neluka Silva, 7 April 2006.
6 Asoka Handagama in interview with Neluka Silva, 7 April 2006.
7 The Central Bank of Sri Lanka, located at the heart of the business centre in Colombo, was blown up by a group of suicide bombers in 1996.
8 Asoka Hangama in interview with Neluka Silva, 7 April 2006.
9 The JVP, now a mainstream political party, in the 1970s and late 1980s were involved in armed anti-government insurrections.
10 For instance, *Kadulla* had engendered public debates in the newspapers and talk shows on television.
11 According to a newspaper report 'US Envoy Launches Peace-Oriented Teledrama', a total of 4.1 million people in Sri Lanka – approximately 25 percent rural viewers and 41 percent urban viewers had seen the teledrama by February 2004. Unfortunately, these figures cannot be compared with figures for other teledramas as statistics are not available, but even without them, it is a significant figure.
12 Asoka Handagama in interview with Neluka Silva, 7 April 2006.
13 *Daily News* Report. http://www.dailynews.lk/2004/02/21/new07.html (accessed August 2008).
14 Sharmini Boyle in a speech made at the launch of *Take this Road*, September 2004.
15 Interview with Gananath Obeyesekere, 2006.

References

Anderson, M. B. (1999) *Do No Harm: How Aid Can Support Peace – or War*, Lynne Rienner: London
Estes, C. (2006) 'Can Soap Operas Save the World?' http//:www.scfg.org (accessed 10 January 2009)
Fiske, J. (1987) *Television Culture*, London: Methuen
Galama, A. and Tongeren, P. V. (eds) (2002) *Towards Better Peacebuilding Practice: On Lessons Learned, Evaluation Practices and Aid and Conflict*, European Centre for Conflict Prevention: Utrecht
Kabir, A. J. (2005) 'Beyond Narrative: Song and Story in South Asia', *Moving Worlds: A Journal of Transcultural Writings*, Volume 5, No.2: 28–42
Kandiah, T. (2001) *The Media and the Ethnic Conflict in Sri Lanka*, Marga Monograph Series on Ethnic Reconciliation, No. 19, 2001, Marga Institute
Lederach, J. P. (1997) *Building Peace: Sustainable Reconciliation in Divided Societies*, Washington DC: USIP
Mankekar, P. (1999) *Screening Culture, Viewing Politics: An Ethnography of Television, Womanhood, and Nation in Postcolonial India*, Durham, North Carolina and London: Duke UP
Menon, R. (2004) 'Doing Peace: Women Resist Daily Battle in South Asia' in Coomaraswami, R. and Fonseka, D. (eds) *Peace Work: Women, Armed Conflict and Negotiation*, New Delhi: Women Unlimited

National Institute for Statistics. (2002) *Evaluation of the Radio Soap Opera Produced by the Centre for Common Ground,* Instituto Nacional de Estatisticas: Luanda

Rigby, A. (2001) *Justice and Reconciliation: After the Violence,* London: Lynne Rienner

Robben, A. C. G. M and Suarez-Orozco, M. M. (2000) *Cultures Under Siege: Collective Violence and Trauma,* Cambridge: CUP

Chapter Ten

DESTIGMATISING STAR TEXTS – HONOUR AND SHAME AMONG MUSLIM WOMEN IN PAKISTANI CINEMA

Irna Qureshi

Introduction

Lollywood is the nickname given to the Pakistani film industry, predominantly based in Lahore, one of Pakistan's most historic cultural centres[1]. A career in Lollywood is glamorous yet it lacks prestige. This chapter examines Lollywood actresses as star texts, concentrating broadly on the intersection of gender, class and ethnicity, and specifically on Reema, one of Pakistan's most famous female celebrities. Like a number of film actresses, Reema allegedly hails from the Kanjar ethnic group, a community of prostitutes and dancing girls – a detail which overshadows her public persona.

Beginning with a brief history of cinema in Pakistan, the chapter will consider notions of morality in Islam, and how these affect the Kanjar community. It will then examine the ways in which the Kanjar taboo influences how Lollywood actresses are publicly perceived, before exploring some of their strategies to 'sanitise' their own star texts. The chapter explores the extent to which financial success helps Lollywood actresses to renegotiate notions of honour, shame and morality. Given its avowed interest in public perception and the scarcity of official material, the research in this chapter concentrates on newspaper articles, internet chat room discussions, and talk show interviews from Pakistan. Pakistani cinema has received barely any attention, particularly in English publications. Only one book exists, which covers 50 years of cinema since partition (Gazdar 1997) and a handful of Urdu books written by journalists and scriptwriters may be found, featuring personal reflections rather than academic analysis. However, I draw on some of the literature on gossip and sexuality in Bollywood, given the many parallels between the popular Hindi cinema of India (Bollywood) and of Pakistan (Lollywood).

Cinema in Pakistan

Lux soap has historically been associated with film stars. Any actress lucky enough to be chosen to endorse the brand, as the 'Lux girl', quickly becomes the epitome of beauty and style[2]. It is no surprise then that the Lux Style Awards, only launched in 2002, have already become the undisputed showbiz event of the year, recognising excellence in the fields of fashion, style, music, television and film. Ironically, one might question Lollywood's relationship with the Lux Style Awards, were it not for the 'Lux girl' connection. Of the thirty or so categories, only one or two are reserved for film. Each of the other categories receives up to five nominations. The film categories receive none since standards are so poor that there is usually only one film annually that merits any critical acclaim[3].

Until the early 1990s, Pakistan was one of the world's top ten film producing countries, regularly making in excess of ninety films a year (Gazdar 1997, 239). In the late 1970s, instability created by Zia-ul-Haq's martial law intensified a downturn in Pakistani cinema. The unstable political situation influenced the rise of a new 'ghandasa' genre promoting vengeance through violence and vulgarity. Themes became so repetitive that, over a twenty-year period, one screenwriter used the same story, characters and actors in over 300 films (Gazdar 1997, 14–154). Vulgar content kept away family and middle class audiences, who began to rely on television and pirated videos for viewing the latest Indian and American films (Gazdar 1997, 175). Lollywood films are viewed by a small, local, male niche market. Poor patronage has seen cinemas reduce in number from 750 during the 1980s to just 139 in 2007. According to *Pakistan Film Magazine* only 26 Urdu and Punjabi films were made in Pakistan during 2007 (www.mazhar.dk/film). Meanwhile, Bollywood films made in Hindi, a language practically indistinguishable from Urdu at the colloquial level, remain popular across Pakistan. Lollywood must also be distinguished from Pakistan's emerging independent cinema, based predominantly in Karachi, which makes socially challenging films. *Khuda Ke Liye* ('In the Name of God', Shoaib Mansoor 2007) is one such film made about events surrounding 11 September 2001 and it became one of Pakistan's biggest international hits, receiving the Lux Style Award for best film.

Today, Pakistan's popular film industry is dominated by two actors and two actresses who have each acted in around 150 films. Shaan is the son of a film director and former Lollywood actress. Moammar Rana is the son of a former Pakistani cricketer. Since her 1990 debut, actress Reema has enjoyed sustained success and is also emerging as a talented director. Her chief rival is the reclusive Saima, wife and muse of Syed Noor, arguably Lollywood's top director.

Women and Morality in 'Lollywood'

Women make up 48 per cent of the population in the Islamic Republic of Pakistan (ESCAP 1997, 5–6). Their level of independence and mobility depends largely on their class, social origin and regional location. In tribal areas, women are largely invisible (Grima 2004), whilst visibility and opportunities are greatest in densely populated urban areas like Lahore and Karachi, the focus of this study. Particularly in rural regions, segregation remains the norm, although a shift towards de-segregation has begun as more urban women enter the office sector (Mirza 2002, 1). UN figures[4] suggest that 33 per cent of Pakistani women participate in the labour force compared to 83 per cent of men. Nevertheless, most women's lives are 'governed by the same rules of patriarchy which cut across class and regional differences to create some measure of uniformity and similarity' (Mumtaz & Shaheed 1987, 21–3).

This study focuses on the professional singers, dancers and actresses associated with Hira Mandi, Lahore's vice district. They are known as 'Kanjar' and trace their roots to the Hindu caste system, which rigidly ranked groups according to ritual purity and occupation. Centuries ago, when young girls were dedicated to Hindu temples to perform ritual dances, many also sold sex to supplement their temple income. Since social status was inherited at birth, a potter's son became a potter, and the daughter of a dancer and prostitute took on her mother's profession. As Islam spread and fused with Indian social practices, it adopted many of the values of the caste system, despite the system's incompatibility with the ethos of equality in Islam (Brown 2005, 27–8). The Kanjar now inhabit Hira Mandi (literally 'the market of diamonds'), alongside other clan-like occupational groups such as Dhobi (washermen), Mochi (cobblers) and Mirasi (musicians). Each group's rank is determined by its relationship with others. For instance, Mirasi and Kanjar are considered inferior since they are paid to perform at the weddings of the other groups. Mirasi provide musical accompaniment for Kanjar dance performances, but rank higher than Kanjar because their women are not associated with prostitution (Murphy 1996, 56–7). So despised is their occupation in Pakistan that the ethnic marker 'Kanjar' is a common term of abuse, not dissimilar to the English 'whore' (Murphy 1996, 136–137).

In this context, many Kanjar now prefer to operate from upmarket areas in Lahore. Indeed, not all Kanjar are prostitutes, with many claiming to work only as performing artists, which has resulted in the 'nexus between performing arts and prostitution' becoming 'tenuous' (Saeed 2001: Foreward). The stigma attached to acting, singing and dancing traditionally limited the choice of artists available to film makers, and created a demand for Kanjar women in the entertainment industry. Many acclaimed Lollywood actresses from the 1990s such as Neeli, Anjuman, Reema and Babra Sharif are believed to have Kanjar associations (Murphy 1996, 208) as are many famous film dancers including Amy Minwala, Ishrat Chaudhry, Meena Chaudhry, Zamarrud and Alia (Saeed 2001, 58). They were deemed to be well qualified since, from a young age, Kanjar girls are trained by Mirasi teachers in music and dance, and hone their performance skills at weddings and private parties (Saeed 2001, 62). Dance is an integral component of Pakistani cinema, so it is easy for them to make the transition to screen acting. In fact, many Kanjar women have regarded Lollywood as an escape route from Hira Mandi, like this retired film actress did at the beginning of her career, after catching the eye of a film producer:

> He took me out at night, and sometimes, he would buy me things. One day he said he had a role for me in a film. My whole family was ecstatic. He and my mother arranged the terms. I don't know much about that. He wanted me to be exclusively his, but my mother disagreed, and said that would harm my career…She said that I would be available whenever he wanted me, but I couldn't be exclusively his, unless, of course, he made a contract. You know, a marriage, with monthly payments and all (quoted in Saeed 2001, 102–3).

In Pakistan, sex is officially permitted only within marriage. Moreover, the role of women is largely determined by the close discursive relationship between morality and virginity (Walle 2004, 96). Islam considers women's sexuality to be more potent than men's, and can appear obsessed with managing it to prevent sexual chaos (fitna). One interpretation suggests, 'the woman is fitna, the epitome of the uncontrollable, a living representative of the dangers of sexuality and its rampant disruptive potential' (Mernissi 1983, 44). Such interpretations underline arguments linking female visibility with obscenity in Pakistan. 'The idea of woman as a femme fatale that makes men lose control over themselves and therefore must be made invisible from the public's male gaze is central to the rationale for purdah (veil, clothing, segregation…)' (Kothari 2005, 292). Such discursive beliefs were exemplified practically during Zia-ul-Haq's military dictatorship, when restrictions were imposed on the way women could appear on Pakistan Television. Presenters and actresses in dramas had to cover their heads and wear high-collared dresses, and a ban meant women could only appear in TV commercials to advertise 'domestic' products such as sewing machines and detergents (Kothari 2005, 290–1).

The ideal of sex within marriage is also played out on-screen. Directors prefer to cast single (and apparently) sexually inexperienced girls. They believe that a narrative depicting 'first love' can more plausibly be represented by a youthful and exuberant actress, seemingly on the cusp of marriage. For this reason veteran director Pervez Rana encourages each of his heroines to 'act like a sixteen year old virgin'[5]. Actress and director Reema promptly dropped a newly signed actress who got married because 'naturally that becomes a negative point for the film'[6]. Marriage can ruin an actress' career even in the Indian film industry because audiences are unwilling to accept a married woman in a romantic role (Dwyer 2001: 274). Internal chat room discussions also suggest that an actress perceived as sexually available is more marketable than one who is not. As one poster writes, 'actually, the top female stars always remain unmarried due to their commitment to the audiences. Our innocent audiences of the subcontinent want to see our heroines as their eternal screen girlfriends'[7].

Paradoxically, while single girls may be in demand, they are also the ones who must maintain exemplary behaviour, to help secure good marriages off-screen. Acting in Lollywood is not generally perceived as an acceptable career for chaste girls, since any perception of sexual experience (even that acquired via acting it) on the part of an actress could tarnish her family's honour (izzat).

> Any deviant behaviour is most severely punished as it brings shame and disgrace to the family, and a socially deviant girl may not find a good husband...It is the responsibility of parents to marry off a daughter with her virginity intact...Nothing can sully a family's izzat as much as the loss of virginity of an unmarried girl (Joseph 2005, 203).

Stigmatising Star Texts

Male Sphere

Many Pakistani actresses working predominantly in television dramas enjoy respectable careers. In her discussion of drama serials in Pakistan, Shuchi Kothari defines the space held by women as the 'zenaana' (women's sphere), since dramas are written by women, and perceived as belonging to women, despite having a large male audience. The leading characters are women; therefore the concept of zenaana embraces both production and reception of these stories (Kothari 2005, 292–3). Moreover, drama serials present 'melodramatic family romances rather than sexual romances' (Dwyer 2000, 188). However, for Lollywood, I argue, the concept of 'mardaana' (men's sphere) holds true, since the films are predominantly written by men, the lead characters are men, with women usually playing secondary roles. Crucially, the films are perceived as belonging to men due to their overwhelmingly male working class audience, and sexual overtures on screen which ritually attract whistles, heckles and coin-throwing in cinemas. Moreover, economic pressure to satisfy male desire means that storylines are manipulated to maximise the opportunity to present the female as an erotic spectacle (Kasbekar 2001, 290). Kasbekar's reference to Bollywood audiences in India is equally applicable to Lollywood. According to one Pakistani writer: 'Everyone is looking for guaranteed success...so, if a movie with some vulgar dances, some romance, some action, one or two rape scenes, a comedian, several flashy songs, dances, and lots of fights is successful, every film should have that' (Saeed 2001, 145). Lollywood actresses often protest that their 'dare-bare' dances are a contractual obligation and hence do not reflect their moral fibre[8], yet such scenes do inevitably shape their reputations. For instance, despite receiving death threats for allegedly filming a kiss in an Indian film, Lollywood actress Meera maintained she had 'not done anything in the movie which contravenes the norms of society I come from'[9].

Off-screen too, actresses are presumed to embrace western values and excessive freedom. Travelling overseas independently for location shoots potentially liberates them from family restrictions, and creates opportunities for mixing freely with men. The notion is further magnified by leading actresses, who are equally famous for their off-screen romances as for their on-screen work. Journalists adopt a scandalous tone when writing about actresses' relationships. One article titled 'Reema set to wed married man' reported about Reema's alleged 'four-year long affair with Saqib, a married man with three children'. The article claimed that Saqib planned to fund Reema's next production and that 'Reema told her family that she was on her way to perform Umra [lesser pilgrimage performed at Mecca] but instead she went to Switzerland with Saqib, from where she announced her wedding plans.' The article also quoted Reema protesting her innocence[10].

Lineage Stigma

Lineage has always been important in Bollywood, by lending credibility to a newcomer's star text, exemplified by the success of Raj Kapoor's grandchildren (Kareena, Karisma and Ranbir). In Pakistan too, I argue that an actress' background determines her public profile. For those with Kanjar associations, lineage becomes their downfall; they may warrant celebrity status but their negligible background prevents them from becoming real role models. This is because Kanjar is perceived to be 'an essential status, which cannot be transcended by marriage and/or a change in occupation' (Murphy 1996, 208–9). In other words, one's behaviour and occupation rather than purchasing power determine one's 'moral probity'. Thus, while a poor person can gain respectability, a rich Kanjar cannot (Murphy 1996, 73–4). This is similar to the Indian caste system, where acquisition of wealth is usually not enough to secure upward mobility. However, social rank can be improved by collectively assuming some of the fundamentals of high caste lifestyles, such as vegetarianism (Robinson 1989, 364).

Upper class/caste circles in Pakistan also use various 'measures of superiority' to determine social or political standing, such as wealth, education and ancestry (Murphy 1996, 56–7). It is common knowledge that many upper and middle class actresses, as well as some of Pakistan's top models hail from distinguished family backgrounds. Actress Zeba Bakhtiar is daughter of a former attorney general. Model turned actress Aaminah Haq belongs to one of Pakistan's most influential families, and the country's top model Vaneeza Ahmed is a diplomat's daughter. I suggest that their privileged background releases them from moral criticism: risqué roles are interpreted as challenging; their unapologetic discussion of boyfriends makes them appear liberated rather than dishonourable. Similarly, ex-model Samina Peerzada, who believes she was the first Lollywood actress from 'an educated background,' can afford to admit she enjoyed filming romantic scenes:

> Even on television when we were not allowed to touch each other, we could only look at each other, and I used to love doing [romantic] scenes and looking at the actor. And I think I was quite famous for my scenes where I said so much more with my eyes. (Interview with Samina Peerzada, 25 November 2008)

Despite such apparent orientations towards modernity, models and actresses are nevertheless keen to publicly shun any social or professional link with the Kanjar, in case they are presumed to share the same 'dishonourable' moral codes. In a magazine interview, Vaneeza Ahmed stressed that despite modelling daring outfits, models like her boast respectable backgrounds, and highlighted the hazards of being linked with Lollywood (and thus, indirectly, with the Kanjar):

> People don't realize that we are normal girls from normal families trying to make a living for ourselves. Just because I show my arms or my midriff doesn't make me corrupt...we make a decent living. Yes, there are some girls who use showbiz as their runway to fly high. Like one of the girls from Lahore during a show asked me to have coffee with someone she knew who was willing to pay heavily for it. Afterwards, I made sure that girl didn't get any show, and thankfully she hasn't. (La Dolce Vaneeza, Rewaj Online 2005)[11]

Lahore socialite Yusuf Salahuddin is the grandson of Sir Muhammad Iqbal, one of Pakistan's greatest poets and scholars. Salahuddin hosts one of the country's most anticipated parties to mark the annual kite festival, an event highly popular with celebrities. But when actress Reema attended the party in 1994, Salahuddin and his wife were unhappy. His wife admitted being 'cold' to Reema so that she would not return the following year (Murphy, 1996: 180–1). Salahuddin's reluctance to welcome Reema to his party 'illustrates the distinction between appreciating actresses on the screen and accepting them socially' (Murphy, 1996: 204) that undermines Lollywood actress' struggles to construct themselves as star texts.

Religious Hypocrisy

Many Pakistanis are uneasy about the notion that Kanjar regard themselves as religious. Lollywood actress Reema talks openly about offering prayers and reciting the Quran regularly[12], and her use of religious expressions is well known. She begins her acceptance speeches at award ceremonies with 'bismillah' (literally 'In the name of Allah'), believed to be auspicious when recited at the start of any task – although not a common practice among celebrities. Reema's religious reference was famously parodied on television by fellow actress Veena Malik. Furthermore, newspapers have accused Reema of using her faith as a ruse for a romantic liaison. *The Daily Times* (25 October 2005[13]) alleged that 'Reema told her family that she was on her way to perform Umra [the lesser pilgrimage], but instead she went to Switzerland with Saqib, from where she announced her wedding plans'. This allegation was printed despite Reema's insistence that she did perform Umra. A talk show host also criticised Lollywood actresses for their religious hypocrisy:

> Whenever I hear the likes of Reema and Resham, no matter how vulgar a film trailer is showing, no matter what sort of character, they're saying, "It's all thanks to God that I got this role" and "I'm so grateful to God that my film is a hit"... Well, if you have that much faith in God why the need to take your clothes off? In front of an audience, in a Muslim country, in front of Muslim people! Why? Do it if you fancy, but please don't bring God into it. (*Best of Nadia Khan Show*, Geo UK, 24 January 2009)

Yet, while many Pakistanis feel that Islam and immorality are incompatible, Reema does not 'see any contradiction in her religious duties and professional obligations'[14]. Actress Laila suggested on a talk show that actors are equally entitled to turn to religion for comfort, 'Why do people consider us filmi folk to be a separate breed? We belong to this world as well. So of course if I'm going through some hardship I'm going to remember my God, not my director'[15].

Destigmatising Star Texts

Lifting the Veil

The abundance of chat rooms devoted to discussing speculation surrounding the real lives of Lollywood actresses highlight the extent of interest in their lives, albeit negative. The advantage of anonymity has perhaps made chat rooms a liberating space for exchanging views on risqué topics, without the fear of negative evaluation. While their alleged Kanjar background is never acknowledged formally in the media, it remains a constant undercurrent in chat room discussions, as this typical unedited discussion, titled 'Lahore's Famous Heera Mandi (Prostitute/Sex Market)' reveals:

'Is it true that most lollywood actresses were originally from this profession? The way they act in their movies, I wouldn't be surprised'

'yeah a lot of them were..now they are high class pros...like reema, resham..reema was sheikh rasheeds' mistress.. same goes for some models and t.v. actresses in Pakistan'

'I've come across some videos on You Tube where Nargis is performing vulgarly on some indian/paki song. It's disgusting...they definately need to do something about it...shutting down the 'kotas' [brothels] including the film industry for starters. Our country has forgotten the meaning of the term 'PAK-istan''

'You should see their backrounds, where they come from before 'Lollywood'. They are hardly innocent, educated women. I could say more, but Reema's reputation says it all.'

'So all those rumors are true? They are really from hira mundi?'

'They're all brain dead. Teendabby heer mundi is OLD NEWS dammit!'

'Yup, these Lollywood actresses are all 'available' to those in Pak with the right contacts and at least 1 lakh. There is a reason they are not respected by the educated middle class'

'Real Deal, I won't be surprised if this is true, they stoop so low when making those vulgar dance moves in their movies, so it's hardly surprising.'

'i read a book once by Fouzia Saeed, TABOO: The hidden culture behind a red lite area ... it overviews lahore's redlite district ... the author asked a young 'girl' in a brothel who 'inspires' her ... and she answers ...", Reema, who's from us and has become really famous"... that says it all ...'

'yeah ... i too think that bashing reema or any other girl now is useless ... listen the media here is not as flourished as the western one and neither r our films ... there r no paparazzis ... no lawsuits and no authentic sources ... so the things v hear r results of gossips etc ... i've no definite views about other gals...but reema definitely has a very twisted history...her flings with sheikh rasheed, residents of shahi mohallah saying they know she is from us, a friend of mine has an uncle who finances these punjabi movies and he tells me that reema's secretary still 'manages' her 'customers' etc...'

(http://www.paklinks.com/gs/video-gallery/236902-lahores-famous-heera-mandi-prostitute-sex-market.html, accessed 25 November 2008)

This discussion thread is devoted to measuring the morality of Lollywood actresses. The range of sources fuelling the speculation – 'vulgar dance moves' as seen on a You Tube film clip, a book extract, as well as rumours about affairs, and the word of an uncle's friend – reveal the dearth of reliable information. Thus, contributors evaluate the conduct of Lollywood actresses according to the markers already discussed in this chapter. A reference to 'PAK-istan' (literally 'land of the pure') serves as a reminder that sexual flamboyance equated with immorality is not concordant with Islamic values. Also, Lollywood actresses and their Hira Mandi lineage are clearly distinguished from the 'innocent' and 'educated middle class'. Furthermore, it is 'vulgar' dance clips on You Tube as well as hearsay about alleged liaisons that lead contributors to presume that Lollywood actresses like Reema are 'high class pros'. Yet, there lies a tension between the way actresses are perceived and the way they would like to be perceived. What becomes important is not simply who Reema *really* is, but also who she purports to be. This creates a fascinating vicious circle – the public look for ways to 'lift the veil' to reveal the *real* actress, while the actress attempts to perpetuate her own myth which may or may not be close to the 'truth'.

Reinventing Identities

On conducting research in Hira Mandi, Brown has written about the unreliability of extracting accurate information from interviews. 'Respondents rarely say anything you could take as 'truth'. Instead their life stories were constantly shifting narratives, a way of presenting self and identity,' (Brown 2007, 414). Gazdar has also written about the way Pakistani film people perpetuate inaccuracies: '...some well-known film makers, after attending International Film Festivals as official delegates, claimed in the press and in the public that they had won awards, whereas in most cases their movies were not even screened in the competition' (Gazdar 1997, xi–xii). This vagueness makes it difficult for journalists to be certain about the 'truth'. An actress meanwhile can exploit this ambiguity – by adopting strategies to renegotiate her identity, she can sanitise or 'destigmatise' her star text. She can modify her life story, and conveniently veil any unfavourable realities.

Budding actresses in the past did their best to disassociate themselves from their origins and many moved out of the Mohalla [neighbourhood] before they became successful. They usually made up a story about their past and introduced their manager as their mother or aunt, which in many cases, was the truth. After becoming famous, whenever interviewed by the media, the actresses would totally deny their origins or any link with the Mohalla. (Saeed 2001, 142)

Others, like 1980s heroine Neeli are evasive about their past, preferring to focus on the here and now, as a way of distancing themselves from their 'lowly' roots. '...like so many other Pakistani film heroines who begin their careers in bazaars, now that she has put her past firmly behind her, her life before films is a closed chapter as far as she is concerned' (Khan 1998, 80). Similarly, very little is known about Reema's family and background. I could not ascertain her precise age or how many siblings she has. Reema's difficulty, however, is her role model status among the Kanjar due to her success and their shared background, as already witnessed in the chat room discussion (Saeed 2001, 43). While Reema may never publicly acknowledge any link with them, she cannot prevent the Kanjar from publicly associating themselves with her.

Indian film actors and actresses traditionally adopted stage names, not so much to 'conceal' their religious background since this was common knowledge anyway, but rather to have names which sounded 'modern, neutral...fashionable and less 'ethnic'' (Dwyer 2006, 134–5). In Lollywood though, actresses adopt stage names precisely to conceal their Kanjar lineage. Since name is an important marker of lineage in Pakistan, many would-be actresses begin using stage names long before becoming famous, so that they cannot be traced back to their notorious roots. 'I interviewed several dancing girls in Hira Mandi who were reluctant to give me their names on the grounds that they hoped to enter the filmi world and did not want to be associated with Hira Mandi in the public mind' (Murphy 1996, 208–9).

There is a trend in Lollywood for actresses to choose overtly Hindu or 'non-Muslim' sounding names such as Meera, Nirma and Reema. This could be seen as aspirational, given the popularity of Bollywood films in Pakistan. A more likely reason may be to distance themselves from an overtly Muslim identity, influenced perhaps by the knowledge that Pakistanis do not wish to see Muslim actresses flaunting so-called immoral values on screen. Controversial actress Meera changed her name after succumbing to family pressure: 'My mother has instructed me not to reveal my real first and second names'[16]. This is paralleled in India, where the Hindu right urge directors to use Muslim and Christian names for cutting-edge characters such as lesbians.

Just as in Bollywood's golden era, actresses using stage names do not normally apply a surname. Interestingly, Reema has just started adding the surname of 'Khan', after being known only as Reema since her 1990 debut, though even 'Reema' is alleged to be a stage name[17].

Reema's Grooming

Reema's enduring popularity means regular appearances on the various chat shows aired on Pakistan's burgeoning satellite channels. Programmes like *Good Morning Pakistan* (Bakhabar Savera), *The Nadia Khan Show* and *Brunch with Bushra* are hosted by amiable female personalities, who are quick to delve into the private lives of their celebrity guests. It is not uncommon to discuss, for instance, how a singer's parents located the bride of his dreams. Celebrities are sometimes accompanied by their (non-celebrity) spouses, so they can be introduced to viewers. The mid-morning scheduling of these programmes, broadcast on competing channels, suggests a predominantly female audience.

Evidently, Reema's presumed Kanjar lineage has been an impediment in the improvement of her social standing. In this context, she exploits other 'measures of superiority' (Murphy 1996, 56–7) to achieve upward mobility. Since her appearance as a child star in *Qismat* (Iqbal Kashmiri 1985) and subsequent 'launch' in *Bulandi* (Mohammad Javed Fazil 1990) apparently at the age of 18, Reema has had a remarkable image and personality makeover. The actress is regularly commended for working on 'her own personality, her own education, mannerisms, articulation', and applauded for grooming herself 'to international standards'[18]. Her reinvention is unusual because it goes beyond the superficiality of a name change. When she appeared on a popular breakfast show, *Good Morning Pakistan* (ARY One World, 14 February 2008) Reema used the two hour programme to discuss the usual diet and beauty tips; but, I argue, she ultimately used this appearance to manipulate her public persona. Being evasive suits an actress like Reema. Firstly, despite harmful speculation, viewers and journalists may not be entirely confident about her real background because she has never confirmed it. Secondly, Reema intentionally discloses particular details about her private life to boost her reputation – usually 'facts' which are difficult to verify. It is worth scrutinising what Reema did and did not articulate on the programme, in order to understand her strategy for status enhancement.

Reema maximised the chance to showcase respectable aspects of character. She played down her looks and dance prowess which initially brought her fame, 'I'm not the prettiest girl in the industry and I'm not the most skinny'. She also highlighted traditional moral values by distancing herself from the so-called vulgar dances that dominated her early career: 'We all had to do scenes like that, but there comes a time when enough is enough'. Reema suggested that directing films meant she could control her own career and make wiser choices.

The Valentine's Day programme invited viewers to phone in and ask Reema to read out messages to loved ones – be they parents, children or spouses. When a caller asked Reema to pass on a message of love to his girlfriend, the actress illustrated the high value she places on family approval by reminding the caller to pursue his love only 'with the blessings of your elders'. Discussing her day off 'at home with family' enabled viewers to learn that, contrary to popular perception, Reema does not live independently. Her remark also suggested that her family sanctioned her acting career, and that perhaps there is some degree of familial control, in the form of elders to whom the actress is answerable. One might have presumed that her life experience and age qualified Reema to choose her own life partner; however, her avowed preference for an 'arranged marriage' further emphasised her traditional values. Reema suggested that her family have benefited from her reputation and social status, by revealing that her sisters had no problems in attracting good marriage proposals: 'People check the character of the oldest sister to determine the character of the younger sisters'. Reema's revelations also illustrate that other families are willing to create social ties with hers.

On the programme, the actress discussed her desire to acquire knowledge informally to compensate for her lack of education. Reflecting on her motivations to learn English, she remarked: 'If you speak English, you are considered educated...If you get it wrong, people laugh at you.' Reema's attempts to illustrate her intellectual aspirations and social conscience reflected a degree of superficiality: she likes to keep up with current affairs and routinely surveys newspapers, but did not touch on issues she finds important; she writes a column called *Reema ki Baatein* (All About Reema) in an unnamed newspaper. Keen to highlight that she had been honoured internationally, Reema even brought some personal photographs to share with viewers. In the first, Reema was photographed with Bill Clinton after discovering they were staying in the same hotel. The second photograph showed Reema being honoured by a French Lord Mayor. She also revealed her pride at becoming the first actress from Pakistan to be nominated as a United Nations goodwill ambassador. Her hopes to do 'something positive for my Pakistan and my fellow countrymen' and her sense of duty to help reverse the fortunes of her country's ailing film industry, had even prompted her to reject offers from Bollywood.

One can draw parallels between Reema's 'grooming' and the cultural accomplishments of the courtesans or dancing girls, glamorised in Indian cinema classics such as *Pakeezah* (Kamal Amrohi 1971) and *Umrao Jan* (Muzaffar

Ali 1981). Dwyer suggests these films depict the courtesan as classy, and groomed in poetry, manners and etiquette, and therefore different from a common prostitute. Crucially, these films suggest that the protagonist is not responsible for her dishonourable career choice since it is usually forced upon her (Dwyer 2006, 117–8). There is a tragic air of fatalism to many such heroines. Here, I draw another parallel by arguing that Reema's discourse on *Good Morning Pakistan* alludes to her own victim narrative.

Reema's introduction to Lollywood films has a number of similarities with Nargis, one of Bollywood's finest actresses, whose mother was incidentally an accomplished courtesan. A recent book, which includes extracts from her private diary, reveals that Nargis was 'forced to be the earning member of the family from a very tender age' (Desai 2007, 222). Nargis' earnings 'went mostly into the family coffers. Some of it was invested in property and jewellery, and the rest was spent in maintaining the lifestyle the family had got used to…' (Desai 2007, 79). The book also reveals that Nargis funded the education of her brother's daughters to compensate for her own lack of formal education. In fact, their dependency on her film earnings led Nargis to believe her family were intentionally delaying her marriage. 'You see people think that I should not think of a house or of settling down – I have never heard my brother wish that I should get married, settle down and have kids' (Desai 2007, 211). Marriage would inevitably shift Nargis' priorities, meaning her siblings would no longer have a claim on her earnings. Around fifty years after Nargis retired from films, chat room discussions about Reema speculate that she also started working at a young age to support her family.

> Reema is indeed from the Heera Mandi but she left at the age of 12 and moved into a private house in Lahore. Her training however continued. Her only choice to save her sister from the same fate as hers was to perform mujras [dance recitals] and earn enough money to keep her sisters out of the business. (http://www.pakstop.com/pmforums/f87/serious-question-curiosity-purposes-78795/index3.html, accessed 25 November 2008)

During her appearance on *Good Morning Pakistan*, Reema expressed regret at not being able to follow her studies after her acting career soared. She is making up for it by supporting the education of her younger sisters. The actress proudly revealed that one of them had earned an MBA from Britain's Oxford University, presumably financed by Reema. These voluntary disclosures fuel speculation about Reema supporting her family, and may also explain why Reema is still single. Such is the importance of marriage in Pakistan that many refer to the state of being single as 'unmarried'. As television presenter Mehreen Khan remarks, 'You could say you have just won the Nobel Prize for literature, but they will still ask when you are getting married. It's like you are doing other things only as a build-up to getting married'[19]. Interest in Reema's future marriage is evident in headlines such as 'Reema Seeks Ideal' (*Pakistan Times*, 4 March 2004) and 'Reema set to wed married man' (*The Daily Times*, 25 October 2005). The notion that marriage can harm a Pakistani actress' career has already been discussed and it is possible that Reema has deliberately remained single to maintain her popularity. However, it is uncommon for Pakistani women to remain single until their late thirties (Reema was apparently born in 1971), particularly in a society where a wife's fertility is often viewed as her most precious commodity. Like Nargis though, it may be that Reema's marriage has been delayed by her family's reluctance to relinquish their claim to her income. Parents in Pakistan marry their daughters strictly by birth order, to avoid the most talented ones from being chosen at the expense of others. As the eldest of several siblings, Reema would ordinarily have been first in line for marriage, yet she admitted to being the only unmarried one. Thus conflicting discourses and motives arising from patriarchal culture, social convention, a desire for wealth and feudal as well as capitalist family relations could well have conspired to keep the actress single.

Conclusion

A complex duality of standards sees Pakistani society shifting between multiple moral perspectives. The juggling through which both actresses and audiences try to resolve fundamentally polarised interpretations, such as 'equality and inequality, virtue and corruption, honor and shame', is termed 'sleight of mind' (Murphy 1996: 16). Thus, we find a community of professional dancing girls and prostitutes in the Islamic Republic of Pakistan. Furthermore, the Kanjar trace their roots back to the Hindu caste system, which is entirely at odds with the ethos of equality in Islam. 'Sleight of mind' applies equally to Lollywood, where the country's top actresses attract celebrity status as well as moral disdain while the actresses themselves see no contradiction between their religious obligations and a career that is considered disreputable.

This chapter has focused on Reema, one of Lollywood's most enduringly popular actresses, with alleged Kanjar associations. Since Kanjar 'immorality' is deemed to be inherent (see also Sawhney's discussion of the supposed 'criminal nature' of the Chhara community, in this volume), onlookers expect it to be manifest in the behaviour of an actress. Speculation about a 'vulgar' on-screen scene or gossip about an off-screen romantic liaison act as discursive clues to a supposedly 'shameless' background, to the extent that their accumulation can stigmatise a heroine's star text. Thus, despite her celebrity status, Reema may be snubbed at a party or mocked publicly for suspected religious hypocrisy. I have demonstrated Reema's considerable efforts to counter the negative speculation about her origins. Reema strategically manipulates the media to 'destigmatise' her star text. Playing down her 'flaws' and highlighting her virtues enables Reema to emphasise her traditional moral values.

The use of standard interviewing techniques comes into question when conducting research in an environment where actresses effectively rewrite their life histories through misrepresentations. I initially set out to conduct oral history style interviews with leading actresses like Reema and Babra Sharif, in order to establish the 'real facts' about their origins and career choices. As a 'senior actress', Babra Sharif was adamant that I could establish the 'real facts' from reading previous interviews with her. It also became clear that 'personal' details would not be forthcoming. Moreover, I was wary of contributing either to Babra's own or any other actress' 'destigmatization' or, indeed, further stigmatization. Both Babra Sharif and Reema are alleged to have Kanjar links. Yet, when my plans to interview Reema emerged, Babra was quick to distance herself from Reema and her supposedly dubious origins: 'Reema is not even a real actress! Everyone knows she's just a dancer'[20]. Thus, it would seem that actresses themselves perpetuate Kanjar and gender stereotyping in Lollywood. What remains to be seen is how Reema – and others like her – can progress in a quest to attain credibility as an artist and director, as well as a dignified reputation given the social and discursive histories in which they are embedded.

Notes

1 Meanwhile, a critically acclaimed alternative cinema is gaining momentum in Karachi, Pakistan's financial capital, which also hosts the internationally recognised Kara Film Festival.
2 Interview with Lux Style Awards Spokesperson, 24 September 2008.
3 Ibid.
4 http://data.un.org/CountryProfile.aspx?crName=Pakistan (accessed 19 January 2009).
5 Interview with Pervez Rana, 18 December 2001.
6 'Rendezvous with Reema', *Rewaj Online*, 15 November 2005, http://www.rewaj.com/entertainment/rendezvous-with-reema.html
7 http://forum.kalpoint.com/celebrities/72265-sana-fakharthe-toast-tinsel-town.html (accessed 8 February 2009).
8 'Pakistani Cinema Offers Cheap Entertainment', *Daily Times*, 14 November 2002, http://www.dailytimes.com.pk/default.asp?page=story_14-11-2002_pg7_10 (accessed 6 January 2009).
9 'Meera seeks Police Protection', *Pakistan Times*, 4 March 2005, http://pakistantimes.net/2005/03/05/societal1.htm (accessed 6 January 2009).
10 'Reema Set to Wed Married Man', *The Daily Times*, 25 October 2005, http://www.dailytimes.com.pk/default.asp?page=2005%5C10%5C25%5Cstory_25-10-2005_pg7_28

11 21 January 2005, http://www.rewaj.com/entertainment/la-dolce-vaneeza.html (accessed 6 January 2009).
12 'Reema's Revelations', *Dawn*, 5 October 2003 http://www.dawn.com/weekly/images/archive/031005/images1.htm (accessed 6 January 2009).
13 'Reema Set to Wed Married Man', *The Daily Times*, 25 October 2005, http://www.dailytimes.com.pk/default.asp?page=2005%5C10%5C25%5Cstory_25-10-2005_pg7_28 (accessed 6 January 2009).
14 'Reema Searches Ideal', *Pakistan Times*, 4 March 2004, http://pakistantimes.net/2004/03/04/life.htm (accessed 25 January 2009).
15 *Best of Nadia Khan Show*, Geo UK, 24 January 2009.
16 'Actors have Done More than Politicians in Bringing India and Pakistan Together', *Tribune India*, 21 November 2004 http://www.tribuneindia.com/2004/20041121/spectrum/main5.htm (accessed 3 February 2009).
17 www.opf.org.pk/almanac/A/actorsf.htm (accessed 24 November 2008).
18 *Brunch with Bushra*, Geo UK, 25 October 2008.
19 'People Still View a Single Woman with Curiosity', *Newsline*, March 2005, http://www.newsline.com.pk/NewsMar2005/mahreen.htm (accessed 3 Febrary 2009).
20 Telephone conversation with Babra Sharif, 25 November 2008.

References

Brown, L. (2005) *The Dancing Girls of Lahore*, London: Harper Collins
―――― (2007) 'Performance, Status and Hybridity in a Pakistani Red-Light District: The Cultural Production of the Courtesan', *Sexualities*, Volume 10, No. 4: 409–23
Desai, K. (2007) *Darlingji – The True Love Story of Nargis and Sunil Dutt*, London: Harper Collins
Dwyer, R. (2000) *All You Want is Money, All You Need is Love – Sex and Romance in Modern India*, London: Cassell
―――― (2001) 'Shooting Stars', Dwyer, R. & Pinney, C. (eds): *Pleasure and the Nation: The History, Politics and Consumption of Public Culture in India*, New Delhi: Oxford University Press
―――― (2006) *Filming the Gods – Religion and Indian Cinema*, London and New York: Routledge
ESCAP (Economic and Social Commission for Asia and the Pacific), (1997) *Women in Pakistan – A Country Profile*, New York: United Nations
Gazdar, M. (1997) *Pakistan Cinema 1947–1997*, Karachi: Oxford University Press
Grima, B. (2004) *Secrets from the Field: An Ethnographer's Notes from North Western Pakistan*, AuthorHouse Press
Joseph, S. (ed.) (2005) *Encyclopaedia of Women and Islamic Culture – Family, Law and Politics*, Volume II, Brill
Kasbekar, A. (2001) 'Hidden Pleasures: Negotiating the Myth of the Female Ideal in Popular Hindi Cinema', Dwyer, R. & Pinney, C. (eds): *Pleasure and the Nation: The History, Politics and Consumption of Public Culture in India*, New Delhi, London and New York: Oxford University Press, 286–308
Khan, R. K. (1998) *Profiles: The Friday Times*, Vanguard
Kothari, S. (2005) 'From Genre to Zanaana: Urdu Television Drama Serials and Women's Culture in Pakistan', *Contemporary South Asia*, Volume 14, No. 3: 289–305
Mernissi, F. (1983) *Beyond the Veil: Male-Female Dynamics in Muslim Society*, Al Saqi Books
―――― (1993) *The Forgotten Queens of Islam*, London: Polity Press

Mirza, J. (2002) *Between Chaddor and the Market: Female Office Workers in Lahore*, Oxford: Oxford University Press

Mumtaz, K. & Shaheed, F. (1987) *Women of Pakistan: Two Steps Forward, One Step Back?* Vanguard Books

Murphy, R. M. (1996) *Space, Class and Rhetoric in Lahore*, Ph.D Thesis, University of Oxford

Robinson, F. (ed.) (1989) *The Cambridge Encyclopaedia of India, Pakistan, Bangladesh, Sri Lanka*, Cambridge University Press

Saeed, F. (2001) *Taboo! The Hidden Culture of a Red Light Area*, Karachi: Oxford University Press

Walle, T. M. (2004) 'Virginity vs. Decency: Continuity and Chance in Pakistani Men's Perception of Sexuality in Women', in Chopra, R., Osella, C., Osella, F. (eds), *South Asian Masculinities*, New Delhi: Kali for Women

Part Three

ALTERNATIVE PRODUCERS: THE ARTICULATION OF (NEW) MEDIA, POLITICS AND CIVIC PARTICIPATION

Chapter Eleven

THROUGH THE LENS OF A 'BRANDED CRIMINAL': THE POLITICS OF MARGINAL CINEMA IN INDIA[1]

Rashmi Sawhney

What I am about to narrate is the story of the Chharas, one of the communities that constitutes the sixty million 'denotified and nomadic peoples' (DNTs)[2] in India. This is not though, a 'story of the Chharas' in either a mythical or a historical sense, but is better described as an aerial shot of the media-channelled ripples effecting change in the lived conditions of the Chharas. It is centripetal to the extent that the loci of the narrative is grounded in the agency, cultural production and activism springing out of Chharanagar, a 'ghetto of Chhara DNTs'[3] in Ahmedabad, Gujarat. One must also, it seems, locate the writing of this chapter itself in the context of these mediated socio-cultural ripples and acknowledge the crass limitations of cultural theory as a guide, even an accomplice, to social activism. As Stuart Hall said, speaking on the subject of AIDS in the 1990s, 'against the urgency of people dying in the streets, what in God's name is the point of cultural studies?', adding that, at the same time, 'AIDS raises politically important cultural questions too – who gets represented and who does not – that cultural studies alone has a privileged capacity to address' (Procter 2004, 2). From this vantage point, this chapter explores the politics of Chhara cinema, deconstructing its production process, form and audience, in seeking to locate marginal cinemas within the larger discursive context of Indian media cultures. The argument developed is that in order to account for doubly marginalised cinema cultures operating in the space of a 'fourth' or 'indigenous' cinema, received theories of audience, genre and form need to transcend the fixity imposed by the 'national' framework and start engaging with the inherent openness and fluidity of film as text and practice. The chapter is structured into three parts: the first part introduces the socio-historical context of the stigmatization of the Chharas as criminals and their ongoing social activism through theatre and media production; part two focuses on Chhara film production, highlighting the politics of audience and cultural capital in the Indian film and media sphere; the final part is a discussion of *Bulldozer* (2006), emphasising the form and aesthetic of the film in offering a reading of Chhara cinema.

Chharas: History, Social Activism and Media Production

The Chharas are originally a nomadic community from the Punjab region (like the Sansis or Kanjars), and only one among about two hundred such groups, whose nomadic lifestyles were systematically obliterated by the British government in the nineteenth century[4]. British rationalism deeply shaped by the transition from feudalism to industrialism, both rooted in the value of land/capital ownership, failed to comprehend nomadism, resulting in reactionary measures, and the labelling of these communities as criminals by way of the 1871 Criminal Tribes Act. Such nomadic communities who were itinerant traders, craftsmen, or cattle-herders in pre-colonial times, had already been dealt a blow by the building of railway lines in the 1850s and the passing of the Indian Forest Act in 1865. This deprived them of their access to the forests and its resources, and transferred it instead, into the hands of British-appointed forest officers. At least 70 tribal uprisings (across nomadic and settled communities) took place in colonial India, some of which have been documented through the work of the Subaltern Studies Collective; more recently, Ghanshyam Shah's (2004) substantial chapter on tribal movements indicates the pre-eminence of the tribal's place in the imagining and shaping of modern India.

The word 'tribal' conjures up images of forest-dwelling communities; industrialisation, mining, and dams ravaging traditional ways of life and sustenance[5]. These images have been beamed into living rooms through television screens time and again, and constitute a very real tribal world. However, these imageries exclude those nomadic communities such as the Chharas, who were forcefully 'settled' in prison-like ghettos replete with high walls and barbed wire fences by the British in the 1930s, in what were largely urban areas. Such communities have, for the past 80 years or so, come to inhabit the neglected peripheries of modern Indian cities, embodying the complexities of a violent 'up-rooting' through re-settlement, and a simultaneous denial of the civil rights of settled Indian citizens. The story changes little after independence: in a magnanimous gesture by India's first Prime Minister Jawaharlal Nehru, those communities notified as 'Criminal Tribes' during colonial rule were 'denotified' in 1952; no further attempt at rehabilitation accompanied this announcement, and in 1956 the Habitual Offenders Act was brought into force. The new Act did not decry the DNTs as 'born criminal', but retained many of the provisions of the previous Act in terms of restrictions on movement and incarceration in 'corrective settlements'. This fuelled and sustained public perception of DNTs as 'criminals'. Despite the efforts of social activists in India, strong campaigns run by Resist Initiative International (RII) and the Forum for Fact-finding Documentation and Advocacy (FFDA), and appeals by the UN's Committee on Elimination of Racial Discrimination (CERD), the Habitual Offenders Act still remains to be repealed.

Irrespective of this 'radical past', to borrow the words of Nandini from Govind Nihalani's *Hazaar Chaurasi ki Maa* ('Mother of 1084', 1998, Hindi), which might 'seem fashionable', Chharanagar embodies in every sense, an ordinary and familiar setting of a lower-class urban sprawl in an up-coming metropolitan city. Narrow lanes, make-shift, half-built houses and shops made with plaster, concrete, mud, and tin, line both sides of the streets, jostling for space, cheek-by-jowl, as is the case in many parts of urban India. Residents, traders, shopkeepers, women, go about their daily chores; children run across the streets, dodging bicycles, scooters and rickshaws with some agility; music from the latest Bombay commercial film blares through a loudspeaker hidden from sight. There is a sense of quietness here despite the frenetic movement and constant buzz. It may be the demands my mind makes on my imagination in the knowledge that I share an awareness of Chhara history, but one gets the feeling that a cry of lament engulfs the area into a still silence. Some twenty thousand residents live in this three square mile area that constitutes Chharanagar, which is infamous in Gujarat, a state where the consumption of alcohol is prohibited, for the illegal brewing of liquor. Many of the residents continue to live here since 'denotification' and release from the settlement, which has over the years, become 'home'.

In August 1998, a library and community centre was established in Chharanagar by the Indian writer and activist Mahasveta Devi through the Bhasha Research and Publication Centre, Vadodara. Over time, these became focal points for the youth of Chharanagar to meet. Six months earlier, in February 1998, in another distant part of India in Purulia district of West Bengal, Budhan Sabar, a DNT man, had been killed by torture while in police custody, and the Kheria Sabar Welfare Samiti led by Mahasveta Devi had filed a petition seeking justice in the Calcutta High Court. The young boys and girls of Chharanagar decided to stage a play based on a published version of the court verdict delivered by Justice Ruma Paul of the Calcutta High Court[6]. To date, close to two hundred performances of this play have been staged across the country. This, effectively, marked the beginning of a wave of media-driven interventions by the Chharas, in some ways an expression of their

Figure 11.1. 'Entrance to Chharanagar' (courtesy of P. Kerim Friedman)

politicisation[7]. However, the Chharas' romance with theatre had begun in 1980, in a manner both symbolic and ironic: Prem Prakash, a well-known Gujarati theatre director was producing a play called 'Spartacus', and came to Chharanagar looking for actors to cast as 'slaves'. An older generation of Chharas performed this play, which became a major success in the history of

Figure 11.2. Scene from *EkAur Balcony* ('One More Balcony') (courtesy of Budhan Theatre)

Figure 11.3. Scene from *EkAur Balcony* ('One More Balcony') (courtesy of Budhan Theatre)

Gujarati stage productions, generating an interest in theatre in Chharanagar, later rekindled through the theatre group established in 1998.

To commemorate Budhan Sabar's tragic death and with the objective of speaking on behalf of the hundreds of others silenced like Budhan, the theatre group set up in Chharanagar was called 'Budhan Theatre' and over the last ten years, twenty-one different plays, including a recent adaptation of Jean Genet's

'Balcony', have dealt with issues of social injustice and stigmatization faced by tribal communities on a daily basis. The tremendous potential for impact of these productions becomes apparent when Dakxin Bajrange, Chhara filmmaker and theatre director, proudly describes how the Chharas are now perceived as 'a community of actors' as opposed to 'a community of thieves'[8].

The impact of these productions on mainstream Indian society is evident through the encouraging invitations Budhan Theatre has recieved in recent times to perform at premier locations in Ahmedabad such as Crosswords, HK Hall, City College, and the Indian Institute of Management. The plays have also attracted a good deal of media coverage across India, including in mainstream national newspapers like *The Times of India* and *The Hindu*, and magazines such as *Tehelka*. New Delhi Television (NDTV), a leading national media company, produced a special feature on Budhan Theatre in 2007. Moreover, as a site of creative struggle, Chharanagar has attracted national and international attention: in 2003, Delhi-based documentary filmmaker, Lalit Vachani, produced *The Chhara Projects* (video, 63 min, rough cut) on the use of political street theatre; Kerim Friedman and Shashwati Talukdar, ethnographic documentary filmmakers based in Taiwan and the USA co-produced *Acting Like A Thief* (2005, DVD, 15 min, DER) which is part of a larger film project entitled *Hooch and Hamlet in Chharanagar*, currently in production.

Despite such attention from both mainstream and independent media, Bajrange is firm in maintaining that 'if people really want to help the Chharas and other DNTs like us, they need to go beyond an appreciation of our plays and films and start giving us jobs in the companies they run, admissions in the educational institutes they teach in'[9]. To some extent, a few Chhara youth originally involved in the setting up of the Budhan Theatre Group have already secured jobs in mainstream media establishments. Kalpana Gagdekar has found a foothold in the commercial Gujarati film industry (which though floundering, is still recognised as an industry) and also acts in other theatre productions; Roxy Gagdekar works as a journalist and crime reporter for the newspaper DNA; Alok Gagdekar, who graduated from the National School of Drama (NSD) in Delhi works in the Bombay film industry and with Saathi, a Bombay-based NGO; Vivek Ghamande, who also graduated from the NSD too works in the Bombay film industry; Tushaar Kodekar works as a television reporter in a Gujarati channel called TV9 and hosts two popular crime shows – *Finger Print* and *Crime Diary*; Ankur Garange works with Tushaar in TV9 as a scriptwriter for the crime shows; and Dakxin Bajrange, who is at the helm of the Chhara's cultural production, is an independent documentary filmmaker and director in Gujarati film and television media. His independent documentaries include *The Lost Water* (2007), *Bulldozer* (2006), *Actors are Born Here* (2006), *Fight for Survival* (2005), *Thought for Development* (2005), and his theatrical credits as writer, director and actor include *Budhan, Pinya Hari Kale Kī Maut, Encounter, Majhab Hameen Sikhata Aapas Mein Bair Rakhna, Bhoma, Khoj, Ulgulan,* and *Muje Mat Maro...Saab*. He is currently working as associate director on a Gujarat film series with the acclaimed documentary filmmaker Rakesh Sharma. Despite their individual commitments, those Chharas still based in Ahmedabad, regularly train younger artists and media producers shaping a new generation of cultural activists, ensuring for them a creative voice and space and potentially a livelihood in the years to come. Notwithstanding this considerable success, Chharas are still refused bank loans, and as Sonia Faleiro writes, 'the back seat of the police van is a place every adult Chhara is acquainted with' (*Tehelka*, 2005).

The picture painted above may lead one into thinking of Budhan Theatre as a representative voice for the Chharas and hence symbolic of the larger sentiment of 'progress' in Chharanagar. Rather, it represents a counter-voice, oppositional because its key rationale is to stop the tracks of history, to free the Chharas from the historical burden of being branded as criminals, and to nurture younger generations as artists, preventing the earlier complicity established between Chhara liqueur brewers, petty thieves and the police: 'we want a Chharanagar where words like thief and alcohol have no place. Where children don't know what these words mean' (Bajrange in *Tehelka*, 2005)[10]. Thus, the creative outputs of the Chharas need to be seen as embodying precisely the zone in and through which an older history of marginalisation and abuse of the Chhara people by the colonial government and the Indian state is being actively contested.

It is clear that the Chharas' use of media as a vehicle to carry their stories is rather unusually focussed, almost strategically so, one might suggest. In very few other tribal communities, whether denotified, nomadic or settled, does one encounter such extensive and single-minded emphasis on modern media as a way of addressing popular misperceptions. It could be argued, as Bajrange himself suggests in the film *Acting Like A Thief* (2005), that the Chharas have always had an acumen for the performative, and hence by extrapolation, theatre, cinema and television present a natural attraction. Indeed, the kind of media programming the Chhara youth are involved in certainly suggests a tendency towards the spectacular and folk dimensions of performance: crime-based shows on television, Gujarati commercial cinema, and a theatre group whose plays don't shy from melodrama, for example. Given the absolutely low production costs of Budhan Theatre plays, and considering that this is street theatre at its political best, the productions of the group rely extensively on strong, dramatic scripts, evocative body language, the optimum and creative use of space, and nominal props. To an extent, this already defines and restricts the form of the plays.

It would be an interesting exercise to map the aesthetic characteristics of these plays in the context of wider street theatre or commercial theatre representing a more middle-class ethos; or to study the form and content of the television stories on crime, or the newspaper reports on crime, in relation to this kind of reportage originating from mainstream Indian society. However, I would like to focus here on the cinema, and to look more closely at the kinds of films emerging from Chharanagar, within the wider framework of debates on mainstream Indian cinema. The reasons for focusing on cinema, rather than a general 'media culture' demand some elaboration. Firstly, there is the obvious limitation of treating theatre, cinema, television, and print journalism as a single cross-platform media culture whereby the specificities of form and the production politics of each of these mediums would be compromised. Secondly, the aesthetic style evidenced in Chhara cinema references a wider history of Indian film and film-related discourses that can be drawn upon to signal the challenges to documentary filmmakers working from the margins. The production processes associated with the aesthetics of Chhara cinema also allows an interrogation of the place of this cinema within a larger Indian film culture – how can doubly marginalised films and filmmakers be accounted for in film theory? – a question taken up in section three of this chapter. And finally, the material quality of a DVD, a VCD, or a film print lends itself to constituting a mobile archive – accessible across time and space – for understanding the processes that shape historical narration, revisions, re-presentations, and indeed communal mobilisation through the media. Cinema thus, by virtue of being able to transgress spatio-temporal and cultural boundaries constitutes the most critical creative expression through which the Chharas can aspire to influence social perception.

The Politics of Production: Genre, Audience and Cultural Capital

My sole intention in making films is to effect *change*. Where I or my theatre cannot reach, there my films should be able to reach. They should be able to sensitise the audience to the voices and issues of the most marginalised communities.

(Dakxin Bajrange, Chhara theatre producer and filmmaker)

The films produced by the Chharas are documentaries. Following on from John Grierson's use of the term 'documentary' for the first time in relation to Robert Flaherty's film *Moana* in 1936, the conventions that are assumed to generally characterise documentary films include a distinctive viewpoint and approach to form and production method, along with some sort of expectation in terms of an audience response (Ellis 2005). Through interviews and a wider critical engagement with film theory, this section highlights some of the key challenges involved in the production of documentary film for the Chharas: a reading that could be extrapolated to represent the situation of other marginalised communities, particularly DNTs, in urban India. The Chhara films, mainly produced by Bajrange, are made from an advocacy point of view, with the objective, at the very minimum, to generate an awareness of the history of the Chharas and their everyday troubles. This indicates that form and audience are crucial to Chhara films; their objective would lie unrealised without an effective language of cinema or without spectators. This is true for any film and filmmaker, but what is crucial in the Chhara case is that cinema is much more than an artistic expression: it is a 'fight for survival'.

Audiences

I begin with the issue of audiences, and this involves a necessary digression from the Chharas to debates within film studies. As it stands, the Chharas don't have any mechanism for distribution and exhibition of their films, other than an ad hoc 'handing out' of DVDs, free of cost, to anyone remotely interested in listening or viewing. Only recently have Documentary Educational Resources (DER) taken up distribution for *The Lost Water*. Indian audiences don't pay to watch documentaries, and hence, independent documentaries seldom get screened in cinema halls, or outside film festivals, film clubs and the university circuit. There are various reasons for this lack of interest in documentary (both among spectators and film theorists, whose focus of attention has been popular cinema). These include: firstly, that, the disproportionate anthropological interest in India, and the large number of anthropological films made about Indian, and particularly tribal communities, have frequently failed to disassociate themselves from a colonial viewing-position and perspective. The key problem with such films is that the text functions as a invisibly encoded whole – using conventions at variance from those outlined by Colin MacCabe (1974) in the context of classical realism in Hollywood cinema, but ironically, functioning to the same effect – where the observer/filmmaker captures an endangered, pre-modern, pure cultural 'other', at best, under threat from the ravaging forces of modernisation, and at worst, in idyllic isolation. Secondly, among the various genres of cinema that gained ground in post-independence India, the documentary was most aligned with, and supportive of, a state-driven agenda for several decades.[11] This meant that the genre became something of a straitjacketed propaganda format; film form took a backseat to the subject, becoming a medium through which crude government policies were communicated to a captive, albeit grudging audience. But the most crucial reason for the low interest in documentary is, apparently, the tremendous force exerted by popular Indian cinema (mainly that from Bombay, but also from Chennai) on what one might call the Indian imaginary, and the associated ease for researchers of 'accessing India', or at least parts of it, through the 'Bollywood' cultural idiom.

The key difference is that documentary cinema demands from its audience, a certain locus of believability, distinct from that of melodrama/fiction. 'Believability' is shaped by characteristics of the film text – narrative, editing, characterisation, mise-en-scène and so on – but also by the place occupied by the film's subject ('nation', star, theme) in the spectator's imaginary. And conversely, as some film theorists would have one believe, by the spectator's socio-economic coordinates. I will not rehearse the outlines of the contested 'national history' of Indian cinemas here, but simply allude to the fact that the spectator has been key to theorising Indian cinemas, and also, that the tension between 'nation' and 'state' has shaped much of this discourse[12]. For example, it is suggested that the 'national imaginary' represented by and through popular cinema is at odds with the state's attempt, to instil through its ancillaries (National Film Development Corporation, Films Division, FTII, NFAI), a sense of aesthetic and ideological values through another 'socially sympathetic', 'progressive' or 'parallel' cinema[13]. The debate between the kinds of audience 'parallel' cinema has catered to, in comparison to the more popular variety has been intensely played out, among other places, in the pages of the film journal *Deep Focus*. George Kutty, editor of *Deep Focus* has critiqued the Indian New Wave (which included parallel cinema) for catering to the cultural sensibilities of a middle-class audience which itself was subjugated to a western consciousness[14]. In a country where details of realism failed to capture the dominant literary imagination (Mukherjee 1985), Sumita Chakravarty suggests that the general support for cinematic realism in the early post-independence era was linked to 'the intelligentsia's feelings of being alien in their own environment and of their search for a "real" India' (1993, 85). She thereby argues that 'one of the anomalies contained in the demand for realism in cinema is that the concept itself is alien to Indian philosophic and aesthetic traditions. . .but it was taken as a transparent means whereby "Indian reality" could be revealed' (1993, 85). This line of reasoning suggests little hope, or scope, for documentary filmmakers, who by virtue of their chosen genre necessarily engage with a larger social reality, in cultivating an audience. The situation is particularly damning for communities such as the Chharas, for whom survival itself is contingent on dispelling public misperceptions, and contesting representation in the media and cultural sphere. It also seems to elide any openness to inhabiting multiple subject-positions as spectators – any potential movement across audience for popular, parallel, and documentary films – fuelling the myth of 'nation-making' in terms of texts and audiences neatly categorised as Indian/western, traditional/modern, rural/urban, working-class/middle-class. The reality is that despite the cinematic techniques of closure, film almost always eludes fixity, making the exercise of reading audience through text vacuous. Ironically, in an article titled 'Fragmenting the Nation', Chakravarty quotes Stam and Shohat (1996) in defence of the 'multiaccentual and polyvocal' nature of film, and credits to this fluidity the gap in critical and public readings/responses to Mani Rathnam's *Terror Trilogy*, thus reinforcing the critical investment in reading film through the framework of nation (2000, 233). The tenacity of such arguments is put to test by examples such as that of Chhara cinema, which, not only represents the subaltern, but is also the product of a subaltern labour and imagination. Let me cite an example of the unpredictability of audience response here: the Madari's, a DNT community that perform as snake-charmers, have lost their means to livelihood since animal rights activists launched a campaign to seize their snakes. Not only this, the activists were so enraged that they put some Madaris into a dog-cage to drive their point home. Bajrange made a short film, *Fight for Survival*, on this episode to put forward the Madaris' view-point explaining that they did not remove the fangs or venom glands of the snakes, and in fact, did not treat them with cruelty. The film was screened at the Jeevika Film Festival in Delhi (2006) where it won an award. Bajrange also showed it to the Madaris, which he says was a very pathetic and humiliating experience for them[15]. The interesting episode regarding audiences took place when he showed the film to a group of animal rights activists in Rajkot; following a heated discussion about the future of the Madari community, many activists decided to adopt Madari children and provide them a quality education. Thus, film can sometimes elicit the most unexpected audience response from the least expected quarters. The pleasures and mercies of such fluidity would be wasted and lost if the debate on audiences, genres, and aesthetics is not dislodged from its current ideological home on to a new terrain exploring the material conditions of cinematic production and form in India.

To spell out the implications of such a shift in no uncertain terms, this means that educators and film theorists will need to bear a greater responsibility towards creating spaces within public and academic discourse to find a language for documentary and marginal film cultures. As documentary filmmaker Paromita Vohra wryly states, 'academics and critics develop increasingly sophisticated ways of talking about mainstream culture but a language and framework to assess the contemporary alternative culture seems not to coalesce' (December 2008, *Pratilipi*). It is telling that there is not a single text available so far that provides an overview of the documentary tradition in India, let alone a comprehensive history of Indian documentary[16]. As has been the case historically in Indian cinema, greater visibility for documentary in the public domain through film journals, festivals, film societies, and the media, should gradually lead to enhancing the culture of documentary viewing and production, a process that has already begun.

Cultural Capital

In contrast to the impoverished condition of critical discourse on documentary is the fact that documentary film production has been thriving over the last two decades, and invoking an articulate sense of the social and political[17]. This raises an interesting aside on the relationship between theory and praxis in India, as well as that between script and orality in some sense – issues that have long been debated in the field of Indian literature. Whatever the significance of the written word or theory for practice, it is certainly true that an absence of engagement with documentary film leaves the theorising of 'Indian cinemas' amiss. However, what this *does* imply for aspiring documentary filmmakers, is a longer, and perhaps harder struggle to gain access to resources for production, distribution, exhibition and training, independent of a systematic facilitation/ process, which is the second key issue that needs to be addressed in speaking of Chhara filmmakers. It could be argued that those with an interest in films can avail of the NFAI's film appreciation courses, or join the FTII and other private film education institutes that are mushrooming around India: the determined will find a way out, in other words. But in truth, these are beyond the reach of a substantial part of Indian society, and particularly so for DNTs and tribal communities. One, it brings up the issue of literacy, which itself cannot be taken for granted in India; two, it poses the challenge of financial resources to support an education; and three, it raises the vexed question of 'fair' competition for scarce resources (jobs, seats in educational institutes) by historically disadvantaged groups such as the DNTs, Scheduled Tribes (ST), Scheduled Castes (SC) and Other Backward Classes (OBCs). It is no surprise that Bajrange and some of the other Chhara youth learnt filmmaking by experimenting with excess video tapes, leftovers from recording local weddings in the late 1980s, filmed during the brief half-hours snatched before rented video cameras needed to be returned to their owners. Bajrange narrates:

> I have no godfather in the film industry and neither did I learn filmmaking from any institute ... As a child I often used to miss school to watch films. I have watched *Sholay* at least sixty-five times. And I used to wonder how these characters came on the big screen ... There is a lot of pain, sorrow, problems and stories around me to be able to live life with great enjoyment ... it is my childhood enthusiasm that set me off on this creative journey[18].

Eventually he did manage to attend a film appreciation course at the NFAI through the Bhasha Research and Publication Centre, but only after having first made films independently. The double marginalisation of DNTs from the public sphere also means that it is much more difficult to gain access to the financing, distribution and exhibition networks critical to film practice: since DNTs are still refused bank loans and credit cards, financing for independent cinema becomes a very crucial challenge. As modern day bureaucracy involves the writing of lengthy and sophisticated proposals (usually in English) for any funding application, this automatically disadvantages DNTs and other communities whose historical and material circumstances have restricted access to formal education. Besides, stigmatization as criminals continues to haunt them wherever they go in the film industry: 'there are a few filmmakers in the Chhara community, but due to the stigma, I was never accepted or employed by any producer while I was struggling to get work in the Gujarati film industry. When someone came to know about our identity, immediately they turned their face'.[19] On a sad note, Bajrange mentions that working with Rakesh Sharma on a film about the Gujarat riots in 2002 was an especially harrowing experience, as the police had implicated the Chharas as one of the rioting communities; thus, every time a Muslim interviewee learned of his Chhara identity, their expression and response immediately changed. Rather an unfortunate and deeply saddening episode this, but nothing new to the Chharas, who everyday face persecution by the police, the public, and the state, and have done so for centuries. As the only possible entry-genre for emerging filmmakers, particularly those representing marginalised voices, and perhaps those too who do not see an alternative to 'documenting' through film a larger social struggle, and in the context of the challenges and circumstances outlined here, the absence of a critical engagement with documentary on the part of academics and film educators seems not to present an option any longer.

Theorising Chhara/Marginal Cinema

How does one then begin to theorise such a marginal cinema as that of the Chharas? And what value would such a theorising offer? To start with, and reverting to Hall's notion of cultural theory cited earlier in the chapter, unravelling the received master narrative about film and media cultures in India, which emphasises a rather distinct role and place for the popular, the folk and the elite (within the 'national'), would expose the myopic vision of such a position. Fortunately or unfortunately, the capacity for artistic cross-fertilisation is higher than everyday human engagement with 'difference' and the 'other'. While exercising caution about the possibility of cultural commodification this creates, art, performance and the media provides a chance to transcend comfort zones, and understand diversity and difference in all its embodied-ness. I will speak through the example of a Chhara film, *Bulldozer* (2006), which uniquely captures India's contemporary urban predicament, navigating the politics of the production and form of the film, in offering a theoretical reading of Chhara cinema.

In recent years, demolition of residential and commercial property has become a major source of anxiety in less prosperous urban locations in India: a panic that has spread across the country irrespective of the party-politics of regional governments. *Bulldozer* is a film that addresses this issue by representing the plight of people made 'homeless' through the Ahmedabad Municipal Corporation's 'sanitizing' drive. Positioned as a 'mega-city in the making', the Ahmedabadi middle-classes are in a hurry to dispose off the seeming squalor of its underbelly. Many tribal and DNT communities, such as the Sansi, Vaghari, Bairagi, Jogi, and Rajbhoi, who settled down several decades ago in parts of Ahmedabad, particularly in the locality of Maninagar, are now being asked by the Corporation to produce documents that prove their land rights. Papers which, not surprisingly, they don't possess. The film was conceptualised in response to this harassment of such displaced communities; an angry response, when Bajrange found a homeless girl dead on the footpath outside one of India's premier educational institutes, the Indian Institute of Management (IIMA). On watching the film, the spectator learns that several children had succumbed to the cold and died, when the Municipal Corporation broke down their make-shift homes with bulldozers; the homes of some families had been destroyed up to ten times. The youngest child who died was seventeen days old. At the other extreme, two women, one aged 116, the other 106, barely able to sit up, had to be relocated by their families during the demolitions. The interviewees explain that no notice is provided by the Corporation, and no new land is allocated for resettlement; if any opposition is voiced, the police who accompany the demolition squad, use physical force to silence them. Demolitions are particularly savage when dignitaries and political figures are slated to visit the IIMA.

Filmed entirely on location, involving a cast which is made up of non-professional actors (and occasionally actors from the Budhan Theatre group), the form of this film represents something between observational cinema (in the vérité tradition) and what Solanas and Getino termed as 'interventionist cinema' (Nichols 1976). Excerpts from interviews reproduced below describe this approach more adequately:

> I started shooting *Bulldozer* on a handycam, interviewing affected people at IIMA and Maninagar basti.... . different perspectives of the issue emerged as I filmed.... . I shot several times.... . there was no specific structure in my mind for this film.... . whenever demolitions occurred

I returned to film, sometimes after some days as I didn't want to shoot like news bites'[20].

I never prepare a script first and shoot accordingly. I always shoot on the spur of the moment, collect the footage keeping the issue in mind and then finally put the entire footage on a time line to make sequences.... While shooting I just keep the camera rolling most of time because I don't want to lose any momentum. My independent documentary film making style is to catch the moment and that should come out in the film.... I generally avoid interviews of experts. I don't want the views of experts or my self in the film. It is better that to bring out something one talks with affected people; captures their emotions, thoughts, and problems. According of me that is a true documentary film'[21].

From this description it is clear that many of the conventions of observational cinema – the desire to 'capture the moment', long takes and little or no cutting while filming, representing 'voices from below' – are systematically adhered to. Yet, the films also transgress the norms of observation – as observation requires the presence of a literal or symbolic 'other' who can be inscribed in a partial truth (recognising that the kino-eye is always ideological and selective) through filmic revelation – by imposing a structural coherence through extensive editing[22]. Interestingly, Bajrange does not use sync sound: 'I don't like commentary. Testimonies should speak for themselves, not the director's or researcher's text'[23]. A problem he highlights in post-production is finding an editor who is sensitive to the issue and the footage; thus he often finds himself sitting with the editor to cut shot by shot.

The film uses an *ensemble* approach, juxtaposing stylised shots of daily-use objects, bulldozers, archival footage of activist meetings, interviews, scenes from the Budhan Theatre street play 'Bhoma', interspersed with a voice-over narration of moving prose by Bajrange. Narrativity is constructed episodically by linking socio-political context (symbolised through material objects), testimony/ interview, performance ('Bhoma'), and voice-over in this order. Each episode of the film (not demarcated as an episode) reveals the tremendous influence of the performative on the film's aesthetic. Contrary to the feigned 'transparent' reality of many interview-based documentaries, or the extreme non-interventionist ideals of some observational cinema, *Bulldozer* (and other Chhara films) accentuates social reality through staged performance. The film's sentiment is fierce, youthful, and resilient, and although reminiscent of Third Cinema as theorized by Solanas and Getino (1976), it moves beyond its emphasis on the 'national', towards a Fourth Cinema (indigenous cinema) that demystifies the myth of the nation as a totality[24]. *Bulldozer* forebodes a public outcry against oppressive powers, most poignantly in the concluding scene, an extra-diegetic narration in Hindi superimposed on a frozen still from the play 'Bhoma'.

> Loha jab pighalta hai to bhaap nahin uthti
> Par kothali uthane wale ke dil se bhaap uthti hai, to loha bhi pighal jata hai
> Pighle hue lohe ko kisi bhi aakar mein dhala ja sakta hai
> Kothali ki aakar mein is desh ki takdeer dhali hui hai
> Aap lohe ki baat karte ho? Hamne loha khaya hai.

'No vapour is generated when iron melts. But the steam generated from the hearts of those picking up the axe melts iron too. Molten iron can be given any shape. The destiny of this nation is shaped as an axe. You talk of iron? We have eaten iron'[25].

It could be argued that the in-between-ness of form (between observation and intervention) is moulded by the filmmakers' and texts' embededness within Chhara history; it is thus a historiography that writes itself through cinema as opposed to a film historiography shaped through textual strategy. And while these films could be interventionist, the films produced so far seem less concerned with historiography than with history itself.

What Solanas and Getino meant by a cinema that intervenes in history is classically demonstrated by a film such as *The Battle of Chile* (Guzmán 1973, Argentina) where considerable pre-production preparation is invested in the analysis of the socio-political situation to shape a script[26]. Film theorist Ana Lopez argues that such films represent a self-reflexive, analytical cinema, akin to 'historiography in the scripting' (1990, 274). In so far as the writing of the narrative and its form must distil the essence of a historical period/ journey in this kind of interventionist process, it remains distant to Chhara films thus far. The reason for this, I suggest, is that more often than not, historiographical writing (or scripting for cinema) is deployed with the objective of, and to serve the purpose of, rescuing the past and reinstating a un/known version of it. It resembles an inscription of memory: the text/film becoming a receptacle to hold individual and collective utterances of remembrance. The Chhara youth and media producers are working against the grain of history, to distance themselves from the past (not necessarily to forget it, but to move away from its circumstances); the creation of each Chhara film exists as a record of the erasure of the past and present. Each film becomes thus, a receptacle of death, what Susan Sontag (1977) identifies in the photographic record as the 'act of aggression'. As the axis of image production increases, there is a converse decrease in the social historical subject of the image. The act of memorialisation takes place here not within individual film texts, but across and along the range of films, collectively marking a passage of time. Even though the subject matter of each film is different, and in this sense Chhara film production doesn't offer any sort of serialised comment, the films function as a chronicler of time, telling stories of the wider change in Chharanagar and other DNT localities brought about through advocacy, and media cultures over a length of time. Metaphorically speaking, it is a sort of invisible ink, whose writing can be revealed only after the act of writing is complete.

Rather than draw a conclusion, it seems more appropriate to emphasise that a silent turmoil seems to be brewing in the marginal cultures inhabiting the peripheries of modern India's consciousness; some like the Chharas are expressing this through creative media cultures, others through more aggressive means. Unless the sweeping strokes of South Asian film and media studies are recalibrated away from the 'national' focal point to zero in on the margins, the risk of missing the larger picture runs high. It seems timely thus, to lay down the flags and, as the Chharas say, pick up the axe instead.

Notes

1 I am grateful to Brian Coates, Alan Grossman, Aine O'Brien, Ganesh Devy and Shakuntala Banaji for their careful reading of the initial draft of this chapter. Their questions, suggestions and critiques have made the process of writing that much more enriching. More so, the residents of Chharanagar, and Dakxin Bajrange in particular, need to be thanked for responding to my incessant correspondence despite the demands of life in Chharanagar.
2 Mahasveta Devi, tribal rights activist and novelist explains the position of denotified tribes, or DNTs thus: 'In 1871, the British Government of India "notified" certain tribes as "criminals". The logic was simple. These people lived in forests, or were nomads. Only the criminals would do this. As Indians follow caste professions, these mysterious (to the British) people too are hereditary criminals. Thus history's most heinous crime was perpetuated in the 1871 Criminal Tribes Act'. (March 2002, *Budhan*)
3 Devy, G.N. (2002) *Painted Words*, pg. 259.
4 Kasturi, K. (2 November 2007) 'Forever Stigmatised: Denotified Tribes', *OneWorld.Net* Accessed 20 Jan 2009 at http://archive.oneworld.net/article/view/154795.
5 Tribal communities in India are commonly referred to as *adivasis* or *janajatis*. The term 'tribal' will be used in this essay, as it more easily translates the discourse about de-notified communities.
6 The Bhasha Research and Publication Centre along with Mahasveta Devi and Lakshman Gaiekwad established a DNT Rights Action Group (DNT-RAG) in 1998 to mobilise denotified communities, and had started publishing a monthly magazine entitled *Budhan* to keep the members and volunteers of DNT-RAG informed of developments. The story of Budhan Sabar and the Calcutta High Court's ruling in this case had been published in the inaugural issue of *Budhan* (1998); it is also reproduced in *Painted Words*.
7 Even though theatre is not a part of the discourse of/on media, in the case of the Chharas, it becomes necessary to treat the emergence of a theatre group as the starting point for exploring the media cultures originating in this area and community. It indicates too, on

the one hand, the relative power of theatre as a form of political communication and social activism in comparison to (technologically) mediated forms such as TV, radio, or cinema by way of lower barriers and costs of entry. On the other hand, the groundedness of theatre in the here and now, the attachment of a performance to a locale, necessarily restricts the spread and reach of the theatre, and the possibility of creating an archive or record that can be reinvoked/ re-accessed at another time and place.

8 Interview with Bajrange, Ahmedabad, 6 January 2009.
9 Ibid.
10 Faleiro, S. (26 November 2005) 'Theives Who Steal A Chance in Life', *Tehelka*. In addition, Bajrange says, 'the Chharas can never be afraid of the police, they are regarded as friends. . .the police collect substantial bribes from Chharanagar, and hence, development of the Chharas undermines the vested interests of the police' (Interview, 6 January 2009).
11 For an excellent discussion of the role of the Films Division and its documentaries in substantiating the discourse of postcolonial 'nationhood' see 'Moving Pictures: the Films Division of India and the Visual Practices of the Nation-State' in Srirupa Roy's (2007) *Beyond Belief: India and the Politics of Postcolonial Nationalism*.
12 For discussions of 'national cinema' see Jyotika Virdi (2003) *The Cinematic ImagiNation: Indian Popular Films as Social History*; Madhava Prasad (1998) *Ideology of the Hindi Film*; Sumita Chakravarty (1993) *National Identity and Indian Popular Cinema*. Also relevant is Valentina Vitali's (2006) critique of Indian film historiography 'Not A Biography of the "Indian Cinema": Historiography and the Question of National Cinema in India'. The 'national' history of Indian cinemas has also been contested in more specific works on regional-language film industries. Moreover, a large part of the New Wave itself did not speak on behalf of the nation as a monolithic entity, and it encompassed films in several different languages. All these discourses do not even begin to take into account the immense documentary production that has taken place in the last two or three decades.
13 This argument has been reiterated in various texts on Indian cinema, and possibly most forcefully by Madhava Prasad (1998) in the chapter on 'Developmental Aesthetics' in his book *The Ideology of the Hindi Film: A Historical Reconstruction*.
14 See issues 1 (2) June 1988; 4 (2) 1992 of *Deep Focus* in particular.
15 Correspondence, 5 April 2009.
16 The small amount of existing scholarship on Indian documentaries falls within two categories: the first, is the body of material represented by publications like Indian Panorama, listing profiles of IIFT films included in the annual showcase or monographs on documentaries published by the Films Division under the Ministry of Information and Broadcasting; the other are stand-alone essays in books and journals from within the humanities and social sciences framework. For example: Vinay Lal (2005) 'Travails of the Nation' in *Third Text*; Monteiro and Jayashankar (2001) 'Documentary and Ethnographic Film' in *Elsevier Encyclopaedia of Social and Behavioural Sciences*; Paromita Vohra (2008) 'Knowing for Sure Without Knowing for Certain' in *Pratilipi*; Surabhi Sharma (2008) 'Songs of the Ship' in *Pratilipi*; Butler and Mirza (2006) *Cinema of Prayoga: Indian Experimental Film and Video*; Srirupa Roy's (2007) chapter on the Films Division although very informative, excludes independent documentaries and others not funded by the Films Division; some essays and interviews with documentary filmmakers have been published in *Deep Focus* too.
17 Vinay Lal's (2005) 'Travails of a Nation: Some Notes on Indian Documentaries' discusses some documentary films on the theme of communal violence in Gujarat, and provides an optimistic comment on new emerging work in this area. In addition to the filmmakers

discussed in Lal's essay (Anand Patwardhan, Suma Josson, Rakesh Sharma and Gopal Menon), several documentary filmmakers including Madhushree Dutta, Paramita Vohra, Sanjay Kak, Anjali Monteiro and KP Jayashankar, Anjali Panjabi, Manjira Datta, Sabe Dewanand Shohini Ghosh have addressed serious, often difficult, socio-political issues through their films.
18 Correspondence, 5 April 2009.
19 Ibid.
20 Ibid.
21 Correspondence, 6 March 2009.
22 This is a rather simplified view of observational cinema. Lucien Taylor's foreword to MacDougall's (1998) *Transcultural Cinema* teases out the complexities of observational cinema and its development over the years. It is impossible to engage with this material within the scope of this essay, but nonetheless, it is worth pointing out that accessing memory and violating the subject in scenes that the camera-eye cannot be privy to have been identified as serious limitations of observational cinema; docudrama and the autobiographical documentary offer two possible alternatives in redressing this limitation. Hence, once again, it is either the interiority of the speaker-subject (who is positioned as insider/outsider/or both) and fiction, which get called upon to validate the truth element of documentary.
23 Correspondence, 5 April 2009.
24 See Sawhney, R. (2009) 'Cinema and the Adivasis of India' in *Moving Worlds: A Journal of Transcultural Writing*, Volume 9, No. 1.
25 An approximate translation of the Hindi voice-over narration in the film's last scene as used in the subtitles.
26 In *The Battle of Chile*, the distance between reality and representation is deliberately collapsed – not through an appeal to the viewer to take a leap of faith and believe the pro-filmic frame – by making transparent the scripting of the conflation of reality and its referent. Leonardo Henrickson, the Argentinean cameraman of the film, shoots the scene of his own death, when he refuses to abandon filming at the orders of an army officer, a scene which is also captured by an Equipo cinematographer, and relayed to the spectator in another part of the plot.

References

Butler, B. and Mirza, K. ed. (2006) *Cinema of Prayoga: Indian Experimental Film and Video*, London: no.w.here

Chakravarty, S. (1993) *National Identity in Indian Popular Cinema*, Austin: University of Texas Press

―――― (2000) 'Fragmenting the Nation: Images of Terrorism in Indian Popular Cinema in *Terrorism, Media, Liberation* Slocham, D. (ed.), NJ: Rutgers University Press, 232–247

Devy, G.N. (2002) *Painted Words: An Anthology of Tribal Literature*, Delhi: Penguin Books

Ellis, J. (2005) 'Documentary and Truth in Television: the Crisis of 1999' in *New Challenges for Documentary* (ed. Rosenthal, A. and Corner, J.), Manchester: Manchester University Press

Kasturi, K. (2 Nov 2007) 'Forever Stigmatised: Denotified Tribes', *OneWorld.Net* Accessed 20 Jan 2009, at http://archive.oneworld.net/article/view/154795)

Kutty, G. (June 1988) 'New Cinema: A Legitimisation Crisis?', *Deep Focus* Volume 1. No. 2: 44–49

———— (1992) 'Popular Indian Cinema: Overcoming Prejudices', *Deep Focus*, Volume 4. No. 2: 34–43
Faleiro, S. (2005) 'Thieves Who Steal A Chance in Life', *Tehelka*. 26 November 2006 Available http://www.tehelka.com/story_main15.asp?filename=hub112605thieves_who.asp (accessed 1 March 2009)
Lal, V. (2005) 'Travails of a Nation: Some Notes on Indian Documentaries', *Third Text*, Volume 19. No. 2: 177–187
López, A. (1990) 'At the Limits of Documentary. Hypertextual Transformation and the New Latin American Cinema', *The Social Documentary in Latin America* Burton, J. (ed.), Pittsburgh: University of Pittsburgh Press: 403–432
MacCabe, C. (1974) 'Realism and the Cinema: Notes on Some Brechtian Theses', *Screen*, Volume 15. No. 2: 7–27
MacDougall, D. (1998) *Transcultural Cinema*, New Jersey: Princeton University Press
Monteiro, A. and Jayashankar, K. P. (2001) 'Documentary and Ethnographic Film' in *Elsevier Encyclopaedia of Social and Behavioural Sciences*, Oxford: Elsevier Science Ltd.
Mukheerjee, M. (1985) *Realism and Reality: The Novel and Society in India*, NY; Oxford: OUP
Nichols, B. (1976) 'The Voice of Documentary' in *Movies and Methods, Volume II* Nichols, B. (ed.), Berkeley: University of California Press: pp. 258–273
Prasad, M. (1998) *The Ideology of the Hindi Film: A Historical Reconstruction*, New Delhi: OUP
Procter, J. (2004) *Stuart Hall: Routledge Critical Thinkers*, London: Routledge
Roy, S. (2007) *Beyond Belief: India and the Politics of Postcolonial Nationalism*, Durham: Duke University Press
Sawhney, R. (2009) 'Cinema and the Adivasis of India', *Moving Worlds: A Journal of Transcultural Writing*, Volume 9. No. 1:102–115
Shah, G., (2004) *Social Movements in India: A Review of Literature*, New Delhi: Sage Publishers
Sharma, S. (October 2008) 'Songs of the Ship', *Pratilipi*. Available http://pratilipi.in/2008/10/songs-of-the-ship-surabhi-sharma/ (accessed 20 March 2009)
Solanas, F. and Getino, O. (1969/1976) 'Towards A Third Cinema' *in Movies and Methods: An Anthology*, Volume I (ed. Nichols, B.). Berkeley: University of California Press, 44–64
Sontag, S. (1977) *On Photography*, London: Penguin
Virdi, J. (2003) *The Cinematic ImagiNation: Indian Popular Films as Social History*, New Jersey: Rutgers University Press
Vitali, V. (2006) 'Not A Biography of the "Indian Cinema": Historiography and the Question of National Cinema in India' in *Theorising National Cinemas* Vitali and Willemen, P. (eds), London: BFI
Vohra, P. (2008) 'Knowing for Sure Without Knowing for Certain', *Pratilipi*. October 2008. Available http://pratilipi.in/2008/10/knowing-for-sure-without-knowing-for-certain-paromita-vohra/ (accessed 20 March 2009)

Chapter Twelve

PAKISTANI STUDENTS' USES OF NEW MEDIA TO CONSTRUCT A NARRATIVE OF DISSENT

Saman Talib

Introduction

4 November 2007 was witness to a very unusual sight in Pakistan: hundreds of students marching in a political protest. The protest was launched at a small, elite university, LUMS, and the students were protesting the arrest of faculty members in the aftermath of the emergency declared in Pakistan on 3 November. The sight of students protesting was to become increasingly familiar as the weeks of emergency dragged on. Initially, the movement seemed to be composed of a number of independent and unrelated individuals. However, over time, certain foci of attention emerged and eventually led to the formation of SACs, student action committees, at different colleges and universities.

These SACs worked in conjunction and individually on political agendas that continued to evolve over time. The students were faced with many challenges: the authoritarian response of the government to any public dissent; the mass-media blackout imposed by the regime; a need for anonymity; and the need to organise rapidly. The most logical solution turned out to be the personal new media these students had access to, particularly mobile phones and the World Wide Web. They used these media to piece together a discourse that quickly found its way into local media discussions as well as the international media.

The theoretical framework for this chapter will be drawn from concepts of youth political activism, particularly in urban areas, and the impacts of new media on civic engagement amongst young people. This study takes place against the backdrop of a constant narrative of youth political disengagement and apathy (Delli Carpini, 2000). However, previous studies on youth activism and new media have suggested that certain strategies are more conducive to engagement and motivation than others (CIRCLE 2006). In addition, Bennet has suggested that certain conditions are more suitable to the use of new media by activists (2003). Finally, the narratives created by different youth movements have been shown to have various functions: motivation, community building, framing, and identity formation. This chapter focuses on the discourse strategies of the Pakistani youth involved in the pro-democracy movement and reflects on the response to this narrative of both local and international media. Consideration is also given to the innovative use of new media to bypass a controlling regime to create a counter-narrative that seemed, for a time, to overpower even the government's voice.

The Immediate Political Context

President Musharraf's move to impose a state of emergency in Pakistan in the latter months of 2007 was not an unexpected event. His continuing clash with the Supreme Court Chief Justice as well as his bid to be re-elected had created a downward spiral as far as public perception was concerned. It was with much trepidation that the nation watched the burgeoning news channels in anticipation of the inevitable. When the inevitable did arrive, it was still a shock to many Pakistanis. On 3 November 2007, a state of emergency was announced. This was all talking place against the backdrop of an upcoming national election, which had brought into play democratic leaders and parties who had been absent for eight years. The presidential election was to be held in November 2007 and the general elections were to follow in early 2008. Musharraf was supported by the Pakistan Muslim League Quaid-e-Azam (PMLQ). The other main players were the Pakistan People's Party (PPP) headed by Benazir Bhutto and the Pakistan Muslim League Nawaz Sharif (PMLN) (John 2007). Quite prominent on the political scene was the lawyers' movement born in the wake of the deposing of the Chief Justice of Pakistan, Iftikhar Muhammad Chaudry[1].

What made the emergency all the more unnerving was that in previous months the airwaves had been replete with rhetoric about how Pakistan had changed under Musharraf, particularly when it came to freedom of expression. Private news channels were routinely airing talk shows openly criticising the government, and street protests were becoming a commonplace sight[2]. The government even seemed to be tolerating a particularly vigorous resistance movement by the lawyers community in the populous state of Punjab. So, the one thing that took many by surprise was the blocking of all news channels with the exception of the state-run *Pakistan Television*. The move made sense from the government's point of view: if they could control the information and control the positioning of that information, any resistance could be contained. But the strategy backfired.

For some days people across Pakistan did seem to submit to this new regime. Privately, many turned to the internet in the hopes of finding any independent information through international broadcasters. Others called relatives in the US, England, and other countries to see if they were still receiving international feeds from banned local news channels. So, it was obvious from this period of time that there were holes in the information firewall that the government had sought to throw up around the citizens of Pakistan. The permeability of this wall was to be sorely tested in the following months by members of the media, citizens, and, particularly, students across the country.

3 November 2007 was also witness to a coincidence of events on the campus of a small, elite university in the ancient city of Lahore. Concerned by the political situation in Pakistan and the apparent lack of youth voices in the political arena, the Law and Politics Society students at the Lahore University of Management Sciences (LUMS) had invited Imran Khan to give a talk. Imran Khan, a well-known figure in South Asia from his days as a cricket star, is much liked by some members of the younger generation for his fiery candour. It was during his speech to an overflowing crowd of students and faculty that he learnt of the Emergency. It was Imran Khan who announced this news to the majority of the student population of LUMS and exhorted them to actively protest against the President's action. After Khan's departure, the faculty and students were left to discuss their own reactions and responses to the development. This gathering provided an opportunity to the students and faculty to discuss their views and share information.

The Lahore University of Management Sciences (LUMS) is considered to be one of the best universities of Pakistan. It was created as 'an institution, which would provide rigorous academic and intellectual training and a viable alternative to education comparable to leading universities across the world' (LUMS Website 2009). Based on its reputation LUMS attracts the best students from around the country who go through a rigorous testing and selection process to gain admission to the University. The students themselves are characterised as being 'of diverse backgrounds, perceptions and interests, and the brightest minds of Pakistan attend this institution' (LUMS LUMUN 2009).

It was a common misconception in the media, both local and international, that the student movement that emerged out of LUMS was sparked initially by defiance of the emergency. However, the student march on 4 November 2007 that became the starting point of this anti-emergency movement was actually incited by events much more personal to the students, as is often the case. Some students and faculty decided to join the lawyers' community as well as civil society organizations protesting the Emergency. Since the Emergency forbade all forms of protest, the police attacked and arrested thousands of protestors, including several LUMS faculty. It was the arrest and incarceration of their faculty engaged in peaceful protest that sparked outrage amongst students and led to the first protest march specifically by the LUMS students. It was the videos and images of this march that ended up on *Youtube*, *CNN*, in newpapers and on cellphones and became the face of the movement.

In conducting this study, several types of data were collected. The main informants were the students who were at the core of the LUMS movement. To protect the identity of these students, their names have been changed to aliases in this chapter. Interviews were conducted with a key member of the Law and Politics Society (LPS, the society that was seen as a key motivator behind the student movement); he will be called Ahmad. Two female students, Sana and Asma, who formed the core of the SAC media team were also interviewed. A young blogger, Saima, was interviewed in an attempt to understand the role of students outside the SAC itself. An interview was also conducted with one of the publishers of *The Emergency Times*. Additional data was gathered by collecting, archiving and organising different kinds of new media material. This included emails sent out by the SAC LUMS to the faculty, students and staff mailing lists of LUMS. Emails that were sent by SAC to a larger audience were also accessed. Major blogs[3] have also been used, with particular attention paid to *The Emergency Times*. *Youtube* videos and *Youtube* channels maintained by students have also contributed to the formulation of the ideas in this chapter.

Forming the Resistance

The initial response of the students to the imposition of the emergency and the resulting media blackout was quite interesting. The fact that all the news channels had be pulled off air meant that there was a wide hole in current information for Pakistani audiences. A particularly noticeable feature of the Pakistani media landscape in recent years has been the overabundance of 24 hour news channels (see also the chapter by Tahir Naqvi in this volume). The effect of having so many news channels was twofold: first, there was intense competition between the channels leading to a focus on breaking news and uncovering scandal; second, Pakistani audiences, at least those connected to cable television, had become accustomed to this profusion of news and analysis. In addition to the increasing penetration of cable television, internet access and cellphones grew exponentially in the Pakistani market. Internet subscribers were at 3.5 million in 2007, up from 2 million in 2004. Actual internet user figures were placed at 17.5 million in 2007, an increase of 7 million users in only three years (ITU 2009). Pakistan is also one of the fastest growing markets in the world for cellphones. The number of cellphone subscribers exploded from 1.7 million to almost 63 million subscribers between 2002 and 2007 (ITU, 2009).

Lazarsfeld and Merton (1948) have identified a tendency in mass media audiences they called 'narcotizing dysfunction'. The gist of the theory is that an abundance of mass media can have a narcotic effect on audiences, where the audience, by merely listening and discussing the news, feels as if they have participated in the public sphere. This, say Lazarsfeld and Merton, leads to a passive polity. So, when the lights were turned off on the above mentioned news channels, Pakistani audiences had no option but to switch gears from being passive recipients of prepackaged news to active seekers of information if they were interested in events in the public sphere in Pakistan. This was quite a significant transformation, both because events were developing and changing quickly and also because it forced many people to engage in information gathering and sharing that they had never undertaken previously. Another development was that many citizens began to use new media to take on the role of news reporters.

An early example of this phenomenon was the arrest of the LUMS faculty and how the news spread. In one instance, a faculty member as he was being arrested at the offices of a human rights organisation, sent out an email from his Blackberry to the LUMS faculty mailing list informing them of the arrest. This email was then forwarded to the student mailing list. This news was then further texted through cell phones. The result was that, while the state media were proclaiming that the country was running smoothly, people knew that citizens were being incarcerated. This kind of viral news proliferation became the mainstay of the student movement. One of the main reasons for this was the hostile atmosphere in which the students were organising. Arrest warrants were issued for faculty members and students. Activists around the country were being arrested and held in droves[4]. Closer to home, a permanent police presence was maintained outside the main gate of the university. The students were also informed that if they tried to take a protest demonstration out of the university grounds, they would all be arrested immediately for disturbing the peace.

In addition, the very media the students were using to spread their messages, images and videos were also a source of insecurity. While initial videos and images of students organising showed faces, students were later cautioned to tape videos and take images only from behind or to blur the images before release. This cautious attitude also manifested itself in the organisational structure of the student movement.

No single person or group was assigned to any leadership positions. Students sought to take cooperative and proactive action and to protect each other from the backlash in the process. It was, nonetheless, the activities of the students and, especially, the skill with which they used online and offline organising that led to the quick recognition and acceptance of the movement by a wider public and the international media. In his interview, Ahmad narrates the case of the first group of text messages sent out by students regarding the emergency. The network effect was so strong and the need to share any information was so great that by the following morning, Ahmad was receiving back texts that he himself had sent out the previous night.

Another quick and highly effective way of informing others of the existence of the student resistance was Youtube. Students were already familiar with this website, which was regularly used to share viral videos for entertainment and do research for academic purposes. In the wake of the Emergency in 2007, YouTube became something akin to a personal news channel for the students. Within minutes of its occurrence, several individuals posted images of the first student protest. Slide shows of images quickly followed the videos. Students also used interactive sections of international news websites to put themselves on the political map. A very popular example is that of LUMS student Zahra Sabri, who uploaded a video of the protest to the CNN I-Report Section. Within hours Zahra was contacted by CNN for an interview. This was a pivotal moment for the students, because they were able to see one of their peers on an international stage, voicing opinions not too dissimilar to theirs.

Creating an Identity

Local and international attention to the movement was almost instantaneous. Very early on the University and its students were recognised as a part of some kind of student movement. This, however, brought as many challenges as opportunities. One of the primary challenges facing the students was the attempt by various political personalities to capitalise on the students' resistance. The students were approached by politicians such as Benazir Bhutto and Nawaz Sharif with requests to meet with them. However, the students were very aware of the danger of their being linked to one political party or another. While students might have sympathised with different political parties, they were quite cognisant of the fact that they wanted their voice to be distinctly their own. So, the students had to formulate a way of not only reaching a consensus amongst themselves on various issues, but also of conveying their own independent position to others.

To this end, the students created an organisation called the SAC, Student Action Committee. This SAC originally started off at LUMS. However, soon there were SACs representing entire cities. The initial LUMS SAC was composed of students who wanted to be actively involved in the propagation of the nascent student movement. The SAC LUMS was a training ground for the young people wishing to resist the authoritarian imposition of state control. As with all movements, the driving force behind the SAC was a core group of highly motivated students. However, the challenge for the students was to remain democratic, have a clear voice, and to maintain anonymity. Additionally, to fulfil their aim of giving all students an equal voice in the daily decision making, the SAC held open meetings for all. However, the motivation level of the students greatly varied within the student body and much of the organising fell to a few individuals. One way of allowing the diversity of the student body to show through was the creation of online forums via which individuals were able to express opinions. This meant that the SAC started blogs and email lists. Unofficially, SAC members were connected through their cell phones and text messaging. These blogs, lists and online discussion groups also served to create an identity for the SAC[5]. When you received an email from their email address, you knew that it was created as an outcome of the consensus of the students that the SAC represented. The blogs and discussion groups on the other hand allowed the students to share opinions, ideas, and information on the latest developments in the movement. However, the fact that these texts existed on forums authorised by the SAC LUMS meant that there was an authenticity attached to their expression.

One of the methods used for organising the SAC was its email list. However, as the movement grew and its requirements spiralled, the emails themselves went through a transformation. Initially, SAC emails were sent out using the Student Council email address to the general email lists created for different populations in the university. However, as the movement widened and came to the notice of the government, a special, anonymous email address titled Student Action Committee (sac.lums@gmail.com) had to be used. Due to privacy concerns this email was again changed to SAC LUMS Lahore (saclhrlums@lists.hcs.harvard.edu).

The Emergency Times[6] was another good tool for disseminating and debating information and political positions. Students and other citizens were able to send in a range of texts and visual media to share. There was also an evolution in *The Emergency Times* as the students became more experienced. Initially, *The Emergency Times*, created by the SAC LUMS, was delivered in three formats: print, email, and blog. However, the print version was discontinued within the first month because by then it had become widely recognised and people were routinely reading it in one of its online versions. Over time, the email version was also discontinued, with its publishers only sending out weekly notifications regarding a new edition on the blog.

In conjunction with the email list, interested readers were able to get a holistic view of the activities of the SAC. The email lists would often update and inform students about upcoming pro-democracy activities, talks and events. After the events, one could usually visit the emergency blog to watch videos of the event, look at pictures, and read reports and other sorts of feedback on the event. The result was that even if the mass media chose to ignore the movement, there was a source for one to get information on ongoing activities.

Getting Organised

A crucial feature of the structuration and blossoming of the student movement was the use of informal social networks by students to get the word out as well as to draw in participants and information. While LUMS is a small, academically elite university, the students were able to extend their campaign both physically and virtually through the social connections of the students, alumni and faculty. Social network research in relation to civic organisation distinguishes between at least two kinds of relationships between people: strong ties and weak ties. Strong ties are said to be those relationships characterised by frequent contact and high levels of intimacy, such as close friends and family members. The term weak ties describes those relationships where interaction is occasional and consists of superficial information exchanges, such as with acquaintances and co-workers (Haythornthwaite 2007).

Networking theory suggests that, while strong ties are important for garnering resources in people's daily lives, it is the weak ties that extend an individual's network into the world. Weak ties can be seen to connect an individual to other people outside his or her immediate social circle. It was these weak ties that turned out to be pivotal for the students in Pakistan to reach out to other like-minded individuals within and outside their campus and start shaping an anti-authoritarian student movement[7]. An example of this was the active role that alumni of the college played in connecting the students with people known to the alumni. Many alumni, who had moved to other universities, organised student protests around the world in coordination with the local SACs. Others provided referrals to media people, intellectuals and media outlets. On the ground and offline, the realities of keeping the student movement focused and organised turned out to be a little more problematic. All of those interviewed, with the exception of Ahmad, complained about the lack of motivation of other students in LUMS. The interviewees said that, while the students would show up in large numbers to join protests, few people were willing to put in the time and effort to do the hard work of organising and maintenance. As a consequence, the burden of creating an ongoing sequence of offline and online actions, of informing everyone of the selected time and date, and of ensuring the safety of those involved fell on the shoulders of a much smaller number of engaged students. There was also the question of coordination between the various Student Action Committees (SAC) that had sprung up in colleges around the country. Someone had to take the time to organise meetings for students located in various campuses in different locations. This, of course, had to be done entirely via text messages, because email was felt to be an insecure medium, prone to state abuse and censorship.

The student movement was, of course, not above criticism. Internally, Sana and Asma were quite critical in their interviews about the organisation and commitment of students to the SAC. They felt that there was a general lack of commitment to the daily and time-consuming tasks of organizing by other students. Both eventually left the organisation within a few months of the beginning of the movement. As to external criticism, there was also no shortage of that. The students were criticised in online and offline media as being misguided, elitist and self-indulgent. The YouTube channel created by the media arm of SAC, LUMS anonymous, routinely received comments – such as the one below – disparaging both the students and the movement:

silentvoiceeee

Just chanting slogans because major businesses/board members affiliated did not get some subsidy or maj govt contract and just exploiting the situation! Musharraf would anyways be ousted or killed, look at ur own lifestyle and univ culture to see how much adherent to islam ??? does lums looks like university in islamic rep of pakistan? cont ...[8].

Building a Narrative

One of the most significant purposes of this Pakistani students' movement was to create a counter narrative to the stance of the Pervez Musharraf regime. Since the government had effectively shut down all the broadcast media, and since the print media was not taking an activist stance, the students took it upon themselves to set the agenda for this alternative public conversation. The posted materials within this counter-narrative constituted a wide variety of forms from online videos and images of protests to opinion pieces, articles and even poetry. It was not only that the students in this movement sent out press releases or stood on podiums to make speeches. They were actively able to counter the frames created by the government and to create an online public sphere for their conversation. Also, the students decided for themselves what counted as news or even what the latest news was. Through the skilful use of the internet and its capacity for storing and sharing multimedia content, the students were able to garner local as well international media attention. Through this coverage the students put forth their own points of views and perspectives. In addition, they were able to inform each other and to motivate each other.

In the field of mass communications, the Spiral of Silence theory (Noelle-Neumann 1984) contends that people will tend to remain silent if they believe that their views are in the minority. One of the greatest dangers in the hours following the declaration of emergency and blackout of news media in any country is the silencing of any counter-arguments and dissenting voices to the government's actions. The students in the Pakistani case-study examined in this chapter were able to counter this by speaking out themselves and creating forums where other dissenting voices could join them. In creating this alternate narrative the students were faced with a dual challenge. On the one hand, they were forced to become citizen journalists to get their message of resistance out to various audiences. On the other hand, they were faced by a government crackdown on any expression of dissent. The solution to this problem was to be found in the increasingly knowledgeable and skilful use of new media tools by these students.

The individuals in the thick of organising the movement resorted to using untrackable SIM cards for their cell phones; they created anonymous email accounts from which to send out messages. Eventually, all official email and online discussion within the SAC was moved to a Harvard University account. Thus the students at LUMS used all the resources of the internet and mobile communications networks to create and sustain a conversation about their views on the emergency and desire for a return to democratic governance. The major objective of all of this work by the students was to counter the official position of the Pakistani government both locally and abroad. Much of the daily energy of the students was spent, therefore, in tracking the events and views of the government and in countering them with a different frame. This was particularly true with the media wing of the SAC LUMS, which put out daily press releases as well as position statements[9]. Students would post on the internet and they would in turn receive comments from both international and local audiences.

The students interviewed for this chapter were quite aware of the fact that their purpose was not only to report on daily developments and counter government media, but also to actually set the agenda for the conversation surrounding the emergency within any existing mainstream media. To achieve this purpose, they created daily press releases that were distributed to local media. They also became the source for images and videos depicting and recording the actions taken for the movement and against it. In addition, the students involved in the media council of the SAC became spokespeople for the student movement and gave interviews to local as well as international media outlets regarding their motivations and goals. In this manner, another form of public sphere was created around comments and responses to the media posted on the World Wide Web and to the stories printed by mainstream local media.

It must be emphasised, of course, that all the comments and articles were not positive or supportive of the students' democratic goals; nevertheless, they did allow those most involved in the resistance to gauge how their efforts were being received and perceived outside the active students' circles.

Conclusion

That a small group of students at a small university in a city of Pakistan were able not only to counter the narrative of a government but were actually able to instigate a countermovement that spread throughout the country has been characterised as an unusual event[10]. However, in today's highly mediated age, 'social movements rarely actively engage more than a small fraction of the population, although their efforts can have consequences for everyone' (Meyer 2007: 44). Such was the case with these students. However, while the core of the students' movement was comprised of a handful of politically knowledgeable and socially motivated individuals with highly proactive personalities, they themselves are quick to acknowledge that they could not have mobilised so many unless there was a genuine current of discontent in the larger population. In this context, new media from cell phones and digital cameras to the internet became the bridge between these few motivated students and the many willing to show up at protests and demonstrations. New media was also the means through which the students organised themselves, kept in touch and reached out to people around the world, thus effectively sidestepping any possibility of a 'spiral of silence'.

The events themselves, and the key role played by cell phones, emails, blogs and other internet tools have become significant on the global political landscape. Crucially, in these circumstances, the ease of communication, immediacy and compression of space offered by these new media were skilfully harnessed by a few young people to stand up for ideals held not just by themselves but millions of others. The movement, though short-lived and subject to many criticisms, was able to put a new face on the youth of Pakistan as intelligent, courageous and media savvy.

Notes

1 Some lessons from the lawyers' struggle : http://www.dawn.com/wps/wcm/connect/dawn-content-library/dawn/in-paper-magazine/encounter/some-lessons-from-the-lawyers-struggle
2 PML-N to hold protest demo outside EC office: http://www.dawn.com/2007/09/26/nat2.htm (accessed 28 March 2009).
   KARACHI: Protests by lawyers, parties today: http://www.dawn.com/2007/04/24/local3.htm

Missing people's families stage demo outside SC: http://www.dailytimes.com.pk/default.asp?page=2007\04\19\story_19-4-2007_pg7_15 (accessed 29 March 2009).
3 Blogs that originated during the emergency (all accessed 29 March-22 April 2009):
http://emergencymediaarchive.blogspot.com/
http://pakistanmartiallaw.blogspot.com/
http://www.naitazi.com/
http://riseofpakistan.blogspot.com/
http://emergencypk.blogspot.com/
http://pakistan-blackout.blogspot.com/
http://emergency2007.blogspot.com/
http://academicsforfreedom.blogspot.com/
4 Students shout loud: http://www.dailytimes.com.pk/default.asp?page=2007\11\08\story_8-11-2007_pg13_1 (accessed 29 March 2009).

KARACHI: Lawyers step up anti-govt drive despite arrests: http://www.dawn.com/2007/11/06/local1.htm (accessed 22 April 2009).

KARACHI: Journalists reject media curbs: http://www.dawn.com/2007/11/06/local2.htm (accessed 22 April 2009).
5 SAC Blogs: Emergency Times: http://emergencymediaarchive.blogspot.com/ (accessed 29 March 2009).

SAC Press Release: http://www.dailytimes.com.pk/default.asp?page=2008\02\04\story_4-2-2008_pg7_34 (accessed 29 March 2009).
6 http://pakistanmartiallaw.blogspot.com/ (accessed 15 April 2009).
7 In one press release, the students demanded 'the reinstatement of the judiciary and the restoration of the Constitution and of basic civil rights, the release of illegally detained prisoners and an end to preposterous curbs on the media,' LUMS students movement Press Release: http://lahore.metblogs.com/2007/11/18/students-movement-at-lums-press-release/ (accessed 15 April 2009).
8 http://www.youtube.com/watch?v=pRaTbDR-PeM (accessed 15 April 2009).
9 Student Action Committee takes to the streets for judiciary again: http://pakistanmartiallaw.blogspot.com/2008/05/students-take-to-streets-for-judiciary.html (accessed 23 April 2009).
10 Editorial: Rebirth of democratic student power!: http://www.dailytimes.com.pk/default.asp?page=2007\11\21\story_21-11-2007_pg3_1 (accessed 15 April 2009).

References

Bennett, L. W. (2003) 'New Media Power: the Internet and Global Activism' in Nick Couldry & James Curran (eds) *Contesting Media Power: Alternative Media in a Networked World*, Oxford: Rowman & Littlefield, 17–38

CIRCLE, '*Young Voters Guide*,' http://www.civicyouth.org//?p=211 (accessed 22 April 2009).

Delli Carpini, M. (2000) '*Gen.com: Youth, Civic Engagement, and the New Information Environment*,' *Political Communication*, Volume 17: 341–349

Haythornthwaite, C. (2007) "Social networks and online community," in A. Joinson, K. McKenna, U. Reips and T. Postmes (eds) *Oxford Handbook of Internet Psychology*, Oxford: Oxford University Press, pp. 121–136

International Telecommunication Union (ITU), http://www.itu.int/ITU-D/icteye/Indicators/Indicators.aspx# (accessed on 22 April 2009)

John, W., (2007) *'Pakistan Elections 2007–2008: Key Players,' ORF Issue Brief*, Brief 8. India: Observer Research Foundation

LUMS Website, http://www.lums.edu.pk/the_university/history.php (accessed 22 April 2009)

LUMS LUMUN, http://www.lumun.org/interdel/lums.html (accessed 22 April 2009)

Lazarsfeld, P. and Merton, R.K. (1948) 'Mass Communication, Popular Taste, and Organized Social Action' in Lyman Bryson, (ed.) *Communication of Ideas*, New York: Harper & Brothers, 95–118

Meyer, D. (2007) *The Politics of Protest*, New York: Oxford University Press

Noelle-Neumann, E. (1984) *The Spiral of Silence*, Chicago: University of Chicago Press

Chapter Thirteen

EXPANDING THE ART OF THE POSSIBLE: LEVERAGING CITIZEN JOURNALISM AND USER GENERATED CONTENT (USG) FOR PEACE IN SRI LANKA

Sanjana Hattotuwa

At first blush, the media in Sri Lanka is diverse and multilingual with distribution and consumption of traditional media (e.g. TV, radio, print) spread over the island. Further examination reveals serious and growing challenges to impartial, accurate and responsible journalism. Journalists themselves rarely adhere to professional standards and ethics, or are often violently coerced into supine, submissive agents of government propaganda. There is not a single newspaper in Sri Lanka that is in Sinhala and Tamil. Journalists themselves tend to be monolingual. Lack of access to the embattled North and East and the stereotypes of the other result in biased, unprofessional reporting that fuels war (Deshapriya and Hattotuwa 2003 and 2005). The overarching problems of a state riven by violent conflict, corruption, nepotism and the significant breakdown of democratic governance and human rights, especially in recent years, deeply inform the timbre of traditional media. It is a vicious symbiosis – traditional media is both shaped by and shapes a violent public imagination[1]. The potential of web 2.0 and new media in general and citizen journalism, mobile phones and USG in particular (e.g. *YouTube* videos, blogs, SMS and mobile sites) suggests that content that critiques the *status quo*, authored by civil society, can play a constructive and increasingly significant role in peacebuilding and stronger democratic governance in Sri Lanka. Through the example of *Groundviews*, Sri Lanka's first citizen journalism website, this chapter will interrogate the potentials and pitfalls of web and Internet activism in a country where political violence is an everyday reality. In this chapter, I argue that the greatest challenge lies not in the technology of new media itself, but in the creation of a social and political movement – one fostered by citizen journalism and mediated through new media and new technology – that is able to maintain, in some small way, the hope of a just and lasting peace in Sri Lanka.

The Current Situation

The current situation in Sri Lanka is one in which intense hostilities between the Sri Lankan military and the Tamil Tigers have resulted in a humanitarian and human rights crisis. All out war has already had significantly adverse repercussions for democratic governance and especially the protection of human rights – the violations of which are at crisis proportions at present[2]. Civil society will have to be proactively engaged through local and international advocacy to strengthen democratic governance even during violent conflict. International influence, pressure and assistance will have to be employed in the absence of credible and independent local institutions and procedures and pending the political commitment to the restoration of their integrity and effectiveness. As military hostilities are currently at their height and the costs of war escalate both in human and financial terms, there is an urgency with regard to strengthening the institutions and processes in civil society to deal with this serious erosion of rights, political responsibility and democratic governance.

While the current focus of military operations is the Northern Province, incidents of violence have been recorded in other parts of the country including in the East and North Central Provinces in the recent months. The violence has incurred the loss of life, exacerbated a range of human rights violations and led to the brutalisation of communities, mass displacement, destruction of property and infrastructure, loss of livelihoods and mobility and an increase in militarization. Given the number of reports on the intimidation and harassment of journalists, it is apparent that the Cabinet Subcommittee appointed in 2008[3] by the government to look into the grievances of the media community is powerless to foster media freedom and the freedom of expression in Sri Lanka or investigate meaningfully the violence directed against journalists. Civil society actors and NGOs have also come under increasing pressure due to a number of factors including rising public support in the South for the war, political intolerance for dissent and the intimidation of actors calling for the restoration of the rule of law, democratic governance and human rights. According to major local and international press freedom groups, 14 journalists/media workers have been killed since 2005. 7 have been abducted. More than 25 have been forced to leave Sri Lanka.

There are disturbing reports of torture and psychological abuse of journalists detained by the Police. Ironically, instead of investigating and preventing attacks against journalists, the Police have themselves attempted to abduct journalists. Several journalists live in fear of their lives and have been forced to bunker in safe houses. Tellingly, the Chairman of the State controlled Sri Lanka Broadcasting Corporation (SLBC) openly called for the death of a senior journalist in June 2008[4]. The Army Commander Major Gen. Sarath Fonseka has repeatedly made incredibly racist comments in the media and tellingly, no State or Private media have asked him to be accountable or to resign forthwith[5]. Several journalists have been repeatedly named and shamed by the Ministry of Defence website as traitors and enemies of the State. The Defence Secretary and brother of the President Gotabaya Rajapakse, named by *Reporters Without Borders* (RSF) as a media predator in its Annual Report for 2008, has repeatedly and viciously threatened senior journalists and editors with complete impunity[6]. In late October 2008, a letter was posted to leading Human Rights defenders and lawyers, as well as given to all Court Registrars to be handed over to lawyers who appear for human rights cases. The letter, in Sinhala, from a group that called itself the '*Mahason Balakaya*' ('Mahason Regiment') clearly states that lawyers who defend human rights cases will be summarily killed or will receive life-threatening injuries[7].

Fundamentally, the question is this in a country and context such as Sri Lanka today: Can Citizen Journalism and User Generated Content (USG) in particular, and Information and Communications Technologies (ICTs) in general, help transform violent conflict and strengthen democracy?

New Technology, Civil Society and Authoritarian Regimes

Stafford Beer's socialist information and communications network – Cybersyn – in Allende's Chile (Beckett 2003) and the use of computers and modems in Operation Vula, the ANC's underground communications network against apartheid,[8] are two pertinent examples in this regard. New Media – media that uses ICTs and particularly digital technologies to produce, archive and disseminate information and knowledge – follows in a similar vein today. Yet, does it meaningfully strengthen human security when a language of hate and harm, pervasive violence, a culture of impunity and an illiberal regime have a vicelike grip on both polity and society? On the one hand, a growing number of examples from countries with repressive regimes suggest that even when civil society and the Fourth Estate are co-opted or severely vitiated, new media increasingly play a vital role in strengthening human security, rights and democracy[9]. On the other hand, illiberal regimes also now use new media and ICTs for their own parochial ends and propaganda and actively impede their use by civil society[10]. The recent cases of Egypt[11] and Myanmar[12] demonstrate the overwhelming power of highly authoritarian regimes to clamp down on pro-democracy communications as well as to jail, torture and kill civil rights activists, including bloggers. Though, increasingly, the strongest and most open voices of dissent within repressive regimes are found in new media[13], it is argued by some that media mediated through the Internet and web are still too diffused and exceptional to effectively secure and strengthen human security, democratic institutions and processes (O'Hara 2001: NP). In this chapter, I suggest the value of a perspective that looks at new media and the social and political movements they create, strengthen and complement as those that can widen as well as deepen democracy over the longer term. The impact of new media, the authors submit, is in its ability to strengthen contemporary events and processes, to strengthen democratic governance and also to record with great detail a violent *zeitgeist* for posterity. Quite simply, it holds up to public scrutiny those responsible for the breakdown in democracy and governance in ways otherwise impossible to engineer. Arguably new media enables a permanent record that can be contested but is almost impossible to erase or block.

As the Berkman Center for Internet and Society recently notes with regard to Iran, '[g]iven the repressive media environment... blogs may represent the most open public communications platform for political discourse. The peer-to-peer architecture of the blogosphere is more resistant to capture or control by the state than the older, hub and spoke architecture of the mass media model' (Kelly and Etling 2008). Events since the Iranian elections in 2009 have proven this point. This mirrors the conditions in many other countries with similar regimes. New media is mobile, decentralised, two-way, adaptive, resilient and pervasive with content in the *swabhasha* as well as English. Web and internet access are often no longer tethered to wires. As discussed by Saman Talib in the previous chapter, the myriad technologies to bear witness, produce and disseminate information have exponentially increased in number, expanded in footprint and declined in cost. Citizens with mobile phones are redefining our understanding of journalists and journalism[14] or at the very least causing traditional journalism to take serious stock. Shut or block one website, a dozen others spring up – many with information on how to by-pass such censorship. Jail a blogger and, arguably, many more will cover the same events and processes with more vigour and scrutiny, despite the creation of a culture of fear. Attempt to cull an entire village and the world may be a witness, thanks to initiatives such as Amnesty's *Eyes on Darfur*[15]. There is now talk of a 'mobile democracy' and 'm-government' – in the Philippines, large scale demonstrations organized via cell phones and text messaging (SMS) were a major factor in forcing President Joseph Estrada to resign, thus bringing about change without large-scale violence[16]. From Zimbabwe[17] and Kenya[18] to China and Kuwait[19], from electoral processes and women's suffrage to voicing dissent against oppression, new media is already revolutionising our approach to and understanding of political and social activism.

There are important market and technological factors propelling this growth and influence of new media in South Asia. In general, SAARC member states and least developed countries show the highest growth for mobile phone subscribers in the Asia-Pacific, as noted by a recent UN report[20]. Sri Lanka in particular already has more mobile subscribers than fixed line subscribers including significant mobile phone ownership and use amongst the lowest economic groups, a vast and expanding wireless broadband footprint, low costs of Internet access and text messaging (SMS), low prices of new mobile devices (including the latest 3rd generation handsets), a thriving black market for mobile devices, significant increases in broadband connectivity (wired and wireless) and a healthy growth in PC sales. Yet it is not simply the case that ICTs strengthen civic consciousness. Commercial and purely personal promotions and use of new media abound, but leveraging them for political and social activism is another matter. This is linked to the phenomenon that in Sri Lanka, voters often make poor citizens. The exercise of one's franchise at elections is all that most see as their fullest participation in and contribution to the mechanisms of democratic governance. The potential of new media to transform, to reform, to make transparent and to hold accountable is simply lost to those who do not see the need to participate actively in the change that they all acknowledge, privately, is necessary and urgent.

On the other hand, a central feature of internet and new media has been noted to be its uniquely open two-way communicative architecture (Bentivegna 2002). Traditional communications media, such as television and radio, might be said to fail to enable full democratic participation partly due to lack of two-way communication. For example, online message boards and chat rooms allow people to exchange opinions and even pose questions to candidates and elected officials in a way that broadcast television cannot support. The Internet provides any electorate with the possibility of a pervasive voice. Studies argue that people feel more connected when they are able to participate in dialogue, instead of to be idle recipients of information doled out to them. The Internet's structure allows for a diversity of views and exchange of information that is impossible, currently, in any other communications medium. The key to this communication is the decentralization of the information; no source has near exclusive control on the diffusion of information, as is the case with television and radio. On the other hand, technology itself redefines control. A mobile phone in the hands of a knowing and active citizen can subvert the blanket censorship of governments. A blog is a powerful medium through which the ground realities of conflict may be communicated to counter the propaganda of the antagonists. Picture phones can monitor ground conditions and generate real-time images that might be used to influence key policy decisions in support of peace. New technologies that mix satellite imagery with Geographical Information Systems (GIS) are able to monitor movements of Internally Displaced Persons and refugees and are able to counter false statistics given out by various actors with vested interests in keeping the numbers low. The key in all these cases is the *potential* of these new media technologies for peace-building and undermining authoritarian regimes.

Finally, new media and citizen journalism is also not to be confused with traditional e-government initiatives. The emphasis of new media is on information produced by citizens for their own benefit – empowerment from within, as opposed to empowerment facilitated by the mercurial and often parochial largesse of a ruling elite. While many e-government initiatives seek to open up information within government to citizens, new media often works the other way, promoting citizen driven content to a larger audience that includes government. In this paradigm, control of information can rest with the citizens themselves, with the technologies of access almost impossible to control, at least at present. With the introduction of vernacular language capable mobile phone handsets and the increasing affordability of multimedia mobile devices, it is difficult, though not impossible, for governments to stifle voices from the ground giving a picture radically different to that which the government seeks to promote[21].

Citizen Journalism and User Generated Content

Whether we like it or not, new technologies are changing the manner in which we gather, store, disseminate, consume and comment on news. The overall experience after the tsunami in Sri Lanka and the subsequent design of ICTs for humanitarian aid suggests that ordinary citizens can play a pivotal role in facilitating the flow of information in relief and conflict management mechanisms. Today, professional photographers still take celebrated images, but now have to compete with citizens with digital cameras in their mobile phones who are often the first to arrive, or already present at the scene. We could call this victim journalism. The first images of the London bombings (7 July 2005) were not from broadcast quality video cameras of TV networks or the high-end cameras of photojournalists. They were grainy, jittery images and videos taken from mobile phones by citizens, many of whom were victims of the bombings. For hours after the bombings, this visceral footage was shown repeatedly on the BBC as well as other news networks globally.

Citizen journalism is also known as participatory journalism, which ideally allows for the strengthening of democracy through the dissemination of information that is accurate and wide-ranging as interpreted by the citizens of that country. In addition, the advantages it presents, the most important of which is the strengthening of democratic values through the freedom of expression and encouraging dialogue, have been recognised as one of its most positive attributes. In some contexts, citizen journalism can help mitigate violence. With new Internet and web based technologies that are revolutionising communications even over vast distances, citizens in Sri Lanka who have been effectively cut off from mainstream media have found new ways of expressing themselves, their concerns, their aspirations and their ideas for conflict transformation. Often, this new age of citizen journalism lacks the grammar of age-old diplomacy and socio-political norms – the conversation is raw, visceral, impatient, irreverent, pithy, provocative and sometimes confusing. In Sri Lanka, it is a conversation that's largely still in English, and also limited to urban centres. The potential of citizen journalism, however, is that in giving a foundation for all citizens – literate, illiterate, male and female, of all ethnicities, castes, classes and religions – to risk expressing themselves, the transformation of polity and society to accommodate ideas and measures that facilitate conflict transformation and engender peace also occurs apace. The web is littered with examples of how SMS (Short Message Service, often called text messages) helped in the immediate aftermath of the tsunami in Indonesia and Sri Lanka[22]. An enduring lesson in this regard was that since SMS is more resilient to mass scale destruction of telecoms infrastructure[23], it can be the foundation for early warning systems[24] and a key alerting tool for communities at risk[25].

Bearing Witness

In Sri Lanka, citizen journalism initiatives feature content from ordinary citizens with little or no training in journalism. The contributors attempt to humanise violent conflict, support peace and reconciliation and expose the growing divide between that which the Government and other warring parties promise and actually do. In fact, citizen journalists are increasingly playing a major role in meaningfully reporting deaths, the humanitarian fallout and hidden social costs of violent conflict, often glossed over or sensationalised by traditional media. The Human Rights Video Hub[26], run by WITNESS and Global Voices, is a powerful example in this regard. Another is how Nepali citizens used blogs to restore democracy from the disastrous rule of the Monarchy that led to hundreds of deaths and gross human rights abuses[27]. Such initiatives – simple yet effective – can help strengthen accountability, expose corruption, help in the restoration of democracy and support governance mechanisms responsive to the needs of citizens. For example, an author from the embattled North of Sri Lanka wrote in May 2008[28],

> An armed group abducted my younger brother this month. He was 25 years old. They came in a van in early February at around 8.30 in the night.

I am the eldest son in my family and I returned to Mannar after my marriage. After one year I told my parents to come down to Sri Lanka since a ceasefire agreement was signed between LTTE and the government. They returned to Mannar after 12 years from India.

As soon as he was abducted I informed the ICRC, FCE, Citizen Committees and CHA. My abducted brother is the youngest in our family. He neither knows nor has any connection with any militant group.

Yet he was abducted.

We searched all over but we could not find him. In early March I suddenly got an anonymous call. The person one who spoke to me over the phone did not tell me his name or address. He just said, "Your brother is in the Colombo National Hospital".

The following day we went to the hospital where we found my brother, lying on a bed. He was senseless and restless. We could see that he had gone through a lot of pain.

The doctors advised us to not ask him anything until he fully recovers.

That may be a long wait.

A year earlier, another voice from Jaffna (a key city in the North of the country) noted that[29] '[t]raders on Jaffna Stanley Road are badly affected by the closure of the road. The road is closed for public usage for security reasons and only pedestrians are allowed to use it. Even bicycles are not allowed by forces.' On other occasions, citizen journalists have also alerted the rest of Sri Lanka and the world about communications blackouts in the region[30], violence that often goes underreported in mainstream, Colombo-centric media[31], local political developments[32], narratives of IDPs[33] and war refugees[34], issues of marginalization in education[35] and humanitarian conditions in theatres of war[36].

Mainstream news organizations are taking note – today, citizens across the world are actively encouraged to submit their 'palm-grown' content through dedicated portals on Reuters, AP, BBC, CNN, Al-Jazeera and many other major networks[37]. New media through ICTs have also given rise to new ways of visualising disasters – activists now use tools such as Google Earth to highlight the enormity of human tragedy in places such as Darfur[38]. The emergence of Sri Lankan bloggers on the Blogosphere is also a form of citizen journalism, as events are analysed and information disseminated from and to the public. For example, the analysis of events from popular bloggers like Deane's Dimension[39], Indi[40] and Dinidu De Alwis[41] to name a few, have become a daily read for many involved and tuning into the blogosphere. Many of these blogs are read by those within the country as well as Sri Lankans and others in the diaspora and internationally. Some blogs of Sri Lankans in the diaspora are extremely popular in the blogosphere in Sri Lanka – e.g http://londonlanka.blogspot.com/. While there is no censorship of blogs, over personal interactions with the author, some bloggers who are overtly critical of government and governance have confessed that they are increasingly worried over their personal safety and security. The blog aggregator, Kottu.org, has over 300 Sri Lankan blogs which address political, economic, entertainment, security and technology topics related to the country, and thus has created a public forum for the collection of news and the re-interpretation as well as deconstruction of such news through the individual dogmatic blogger[42]. Some bloggers are well-known (e.g. David Blacker who is a prize winning author in Sri Lanka), others are anonymous. Although contested as a positive attribute, by encouraging discussion and formulating ideas it allows for expression and narrows at some level the democratic deficit. This is particularly evident in sites such as *Beyond Borders*[43] and *In Mutiny*[44], featuring high quality (English) content and debate, by youth, for youth[45]. *Kottu*, for example, features daily rants on theatre, art, poetry, IT, higher studies, puberty, pre-puberty blues, post-puberty blues, love, lack of love, social revolutions, peace, media, democracy, fascism, liberty, religion, music, ear rings, tattoos, books, reviews and a huge array of photos from Flickr that capture moments both private and public of the varied lives of bloggers. Blogs like *Dare to be Different* (run by a politician)[46] jostle for attention with *Voices in My Head*[47]. From personal rants on the top 10 Extremists in Sri Lanka[48] to more thoughtful analyses of Sri Lanka's socio-political dynamics[49], *Kottu's* collective voices offer far more food for thought than most mainstream media today. The key voices in the Sri Lankan blogosphere with whom the author is familiar are overwhelmingly vibrant and passionate and, generally, young. As Electra[50], a regular and one of the more eloquent bloggers in Sri Lanka points out:

> …for what it's worth, our opinions need to be out there, reaching out to a community larger than that which has access to and interest in the Sri Lankan blogosphere. More people need to see this. More people need to hear us.

Groundviews: A Case Study

Cognisant of the context outlined above and interested in the subversive nature of what we can characterize as 'professional' citizen journalism to effect progressive conflict transformation in Sri Lanka through a space simply not available in other media, *Groundviews* – www.groundviews.org – was launched in December 2006 as the first tri-lingual citizen journalism initiative in Sri Lanka. It is to date the only such initiative. In December 2007 the site was awarded an

Award of Excellence in New Communications from the Society for New Communications Research (SNCR) based in Boston. Content from *Groundviews* is regularly featured on other news aggregation sites as well as media reports. 'For ongoing analysis of the conflict, the citizen journalism site groundviews.org provides interesting and often tragic reporting', says the renowned press freedom organisation Freedom House of *Groundviews* on its blog[51]. Over the course of 2008, *Groundviews* published over 250 compelling contributions from ordinary Sri Lankans, award winning poets and authors, renowned academics, diplomats, civil servants, leading civil society activists and others. Operating without any donor funding, content from *Groundviews* is consistently republished in mainstream media, academic journals, books, other leading news websites and blogs and widely quoted in presentations at leading workshops and conferences locally and internationally. Content published in 2008 ranged from essays to poetry, photos to videos, serialised narratives to academic papers and unique perspectives of life on the ground from embattled cities in the North and the 'liberated' Eastern Province. The site welcomed well over 2,30,000 readers in 2008 with over 3,400 substantive comments by readers. Technically, the site features the most secure and sophisticated commenting system on any media website in Sri Lanka (including mainstream media sites)[52] and offers content over email, mobiles and news feeds. *Groundviews* is also the first and to date only citizen journalism website from Sri Lanka to be featured and fully indexed on Google News.

Content published on *Groundviews* since its launch in 2006 demonstrates how professional web based citizen journalism can strengthen progressive, civil dialogues on highly complex and inflammatory issues and topics[53]. The site regularly publishes content that will not and cannot be published in mainstream / traditional media in Sri Lanka today. In doing so, it shows that web based citizen journalism and media can meaningfully foster vital debates on war, peace, human rights and democracy even within violent conflict.

The author is completely cognisant that far more than technological impediments, deeply entrenched cultures of secrecy, anxiety and fear deeply influence the creation and dissemination of information and opinions via new media. On the other hand, analysis of the narratives engendered by *Groundviews* suggests that many perspectives, events, processes, needs and aspirations of those most affected by the conflict and living in the embattled North and East find expression and engagement on the site. Ordinary citizens, weary of violence, write them. Artists, human rights and media activists, academics, young bloggers and thinkers – few of them with any background or training in journalism – write them. Some write under their real names, others under pen names. Many say that to write is cathartic and an act of defiance against violence with impunity. Bloggers are increasingly concerned about their safety and security, but see the medium as one essentially more secure than other media in terms of identity protection and more open than mainstream media in terms of the ideas that can be flagged for public debate and scrutiny. A comparison with reportage in mainstream media since *Groundviews* was launched sharply highlights the contrast in content: the Fourth Estate, under unprecedented levels of state and self-censorship, has largely failed to articulate the voices of those fearful of both war and the lack of any meaningful steps taken to foster peace. A significant challenge in this regard has been to leverage and experiment with new media *within* violent conflict and a rapidly eroding human rights context. Funding for *Groundviews* ended in February 2007, three months after the site was launched. Through personal and professional relationships, significant content was attracted to the site in these early days when it was still relatively unknown. A model of paid submissions was eschewed save for two organisations with links on the ground to the North and the East from where information would otherwise have been impossible to get. The technologies used by *Groundviews* also evolved in line with its expanding reach and influence amongst local and international stakeholders, including the Sri Lankan diaspora. *Groundviews* began to aggregate full length videos from BBC, Al Jazeera and others on Sri Lanka and cross-featured content from its *swabhasha* equivalent Vikalpa as well as from the *YouTube* Video Channel and podcasts from VOR Radio. This allowed text, photos, audio and video to be employed to strengthen advocacy for human security. Coupled with regular email updates and the use of other technologies inherently part of the new media architecture, one measure of the success of *Groundviews* to date in bringing to light issues, events and processes vital to the democratic fabric is the fact that this site has riled the State and supporters of the LTTE in equal measure!

A usually hidden metric that is particularly revealing of the two-way nature of communications on *Groundviews* is the number of comments received to date on the site to all its posts – over 3,500 by over 2,000 unique authors. Indeed, some of these comments have been as probing and incisive as the original posts they were responding to and have been penned by young people in the Sri Lankan diaspora and members of Sri Lanka's diplomatic corps. The Centre for Policy Alternatives (CPA) itself and other leading NGOs and mainstream print media have even republished some comments in other publications – such has been their value in pushing forward the debate on issues related to power-sharing and human rights. Having set out to humanise the conflict, *Groundviews* evolved into a site for interrogation, contestation and civil debate based on Sri Lanka's first editorial policy and guidelines for citizen journalism as enumerated on the site[54]. It is unique in this respect even today – two years after its launch. Issues now flagged on the site have a ripple effect globally and in this respect it is as influential as the websites of traditional print and electronic media in Sri Lanka to galvanise the limited interest of the International Community to urgent and significant developments and processes in ordinary citizens' lives. Further, *Groundviews* has critiqued the standards of traditional media on more than one occasion[55], helping thereby to highlight significant fault lines of the Fourth Estate. Further, the diffusion of majoritarian, state-centred conceptions of national security, democracy, rights and human security on *Groundviews* provide valuable perspectives that are markers of significant challenges facing the country on a number of fronts.

Yet *Groundviews* is not just for the amplification of the local to the global, or about the reduction of the rich texture of peacebuilding in Sri Lanka to only that which is published on the site. It does not and cannot replace traditional media or courageous individuals in civil society who stand up, when few dare to, against the egregious violations of human rights and the erosion of human security. We see *Groundviews* as a force multiplier, able to strengthen the work of CPA and civil society in the advocacy for and the protection of rights and human security. That begs the question as to whether the increasing visibility of the site and its content creates its own security concerns for those associated with it and whether this in turns vitiates its sustainability. The technology employed on the site is itself a line of defence – selected and maintained to a high degree of resilience, redundancy and easily replicated in case of attempts to block, shut it down or hack into it. No efforts are foolproof, but it is a guarantee that such attempts will not go unnoticed by the international community – visibility, in this sense, is its own deterrent to attacks. Those who provide the content are also protected, by their anonymity or in most cases an identity only known to the Editor of the site[56].

Clearly, *Groundviews* needs to be located in the larger framework of new media growth in Sri Lanka. *Swabhasha* (vernacular) blogging has grown in the past two years alongside English language blogging. The geographical footprint of bloggers has widened and now extends to non-urban areas and non-elite groups. With this growth one sees the diversity of conversation on blogs sorely lacking in the Fourth Estate. On the other hand, the regime and its proxies – both locally and internationally – are also using the web and new media for propaganda. The Ministry of Defence website, for example, regularly spews hate speech against independent and investigative journalists, CSOs and NGOs working on power-sharing and peacebuilding as well as individual media and human rights activists. This content is regurgitated elsewhere on blogs and social networking sites (e.g. Facebook groups) and mirrors the pro-LTTE Tamil diaspora's expertise and experience in using the Internet and web for propaganda and financing (Enteen 2006). This contestation of ideas and opinions on the web, sometimes violently at odds with each other, will continue to be a feature of content on democracy, war and peace in Sri Lanka on the Internet. For example, one of the most commented on authors on *Groundviews* is Sri Lanka's Ambassador to the United Nations in Geneva, Dayan Jayatilleka. What is interesting is not only the fact that

Ambassador Jayatilleka writes to *Groundviews* regularly, but that he is quick and committed to engaging with responses submitted by others to his articles. Voices featured on *Groundviews* are thus clearly pro-Government, pro-LTTE, pro-Sinhala Buddhist and pro every political leaning – liberal, communist, anarchist and more. Yet, *Groundviews* is unique amongst similar web initiatives in (or on) Sri Lanka in that it is a moderated site[57], with site content submission guidelines that clearly note what's permissible on the site and the tone of discussion that will be encouraged. These guidelines, *sui generis* in the Sri Lankan blogosphere, have inspired others to follow suit and have, over time, become a *de facto* standard for high quality citizen journalism in Sri Lanka[58].

The Challenges of New Media and Citizen Journalism

The simple fact that most of us now have access to a hundred times more content on a disaster than before does not mean that we get any closer to understanding it or responding to it. Information overload is a real problem, as is the subjectivity of citizens, who only capture what they feel is important and often ignore aspects to a disaster beyond their own comfort zone and prejudices. There is still no widely accepted standard for citizen journalists, though organizations such as the Centre for Citizen Media are actively working towards such standards[59]. There are other challenges associated with citizen journalism, especially in a context of violent conflict. Not all citizens, even when they can do so and have access to digital devices, record disasters or human rights abuses – especially when their own security could be compromised for having done so. Indeed, governments can also clamp down hard on citizen journalism. The French Constitutional Council approved a law in early 2007 that criminalizes the filming or broadcasting of acts of violence by people other than professional journalists. The law could lead to the imprisonment of eyewitnesses who film acts of police violence, or operators of Web sites publishing the images[60]. Sri Lanka unofficially banned a pro-Tamil nationalist website[61] in 2007 and regularly cuts off mobile phone and Internet services in the North and East of the country[62]. Scared by the potential for embarrassment, political debacles and popular uprisings, countries such as Egypt, Iran, Cuba, North Korea and China vigorously censor and monitor content on blogs and exchanges through SMS, prompting Julien Pain, head of the Internet freedom desk at *Reporters Without Borders* (RSF) to note[63]:

> ... all authoritarian regimes are now working to censor the Web, even countries in sub-Saharan Africa. The Ethiopian regime of Prime Minister Meles Zenawi has blocked openly critical Web sites and blogs since May 2006, and President Robert Mugabe of Zimbabwe is considering a law

allowing security forces to intercept online messages without reference to the courts. One of the first moves by Thailand's military rulers after their September (2006) coup was to censor news Web sites, even foreign ones that criticized the takeover.

It is a significant challenge for citizen journalists to cover disasters and conflict in such contexts. What is essential here is to identify the social and organisational contexts in which the technology is implemented. It is true that the evidence of the use of ICTs in disaster management and early warning is growing[64]. It is also true that mobile devices are increasingly powerful because they are pervasive, personal and capable of authoring content[65]. However, like any other tool, they can lie unused, be used for purposes they were not intended for, be misused or only used for personal gain. There is no guarantee that images and photos from disasters produced by victims in the thick of it will galvanise attention and support. ICTs can also merely serve to strengthen hierarchies and bureaucracy that impede accountability and responsive aid delivery. In Sri Lanka, the significant deterioration of democracy in 2006–2007 has resulted in a country where anxiety and fear overwhelm a sense of civic duty to bear witness to so much of what is wrong. No amount of mobile phones and PCs is going to magically erase this deep-rooted fear of harm for speaking one's mind.

If it doesn't foster measurable and tangible change for citizens facing the brunt of violence and conflict, citizen journalism in Sri Lanka could fall by the wayside as a fad or worse, as something that reinforces the traditional political divisions. The conversations on citizen journalist websites and blogs can be trivial and silly or even racist and deeply divisive. It should not be assumed that *more* communication automatically brings with it *greater understanding*. It may well be the case that terrorists (and sections of the State interested in the perpetuating of war that brings with it huge material wealth for a coterie deeply uninterested in peace) mould the basic technologies and frameworks of citizens journalism to spread hate and violence. New media may foster new perspectives, but the old problem of dealing with an intolerant and violent State or intolerant and violent civil society groups does not simply vanish by the mere introduction of ICTs. Thirdly and finally, I question the extent to which new media does and can make a difference in a context such as we find in Sri Lanka today. For example, though censorship of media and cultural production in Sri Lanka isn't new[66], the Rajapakse regime has taken it a step further by promulgating a new set of regulations through a gazette notification, called the Private Television Broadcasting Station Regulations. These wide-reaching and ill-defined regulations, in parts copied and pasted verbatim from Indian Cable TV and IP TV regulations, were a measure to further undermine independent media in Sri Lanka. On 14th November 2008, the Supreme Court, issuing a stay order suspending the operation of these regulations[67], granted a case lodged by the Sri Lanka Working Journalists Association and others who opposed the proposed regulations as an affront to the freedom of expression leave to proceed. The case is to be heard on 26 January 2009. Disturbingly, the proposed regulations are a significant challenge to all bloggers in Sri Lanka, since they seek to hold accountable all ISPs for the qualitative nature of the content transmitted, accessed and produced using their service.[68] As the author has noted elsewhere[69],

> I would be elated to realise political change on account of the content featured on say Groundviews, but I would not be disappointed if this does not happen any time soon. The content on the site and the larger content on the SL blogosphere, including all of that which I don't agree with, are deeply valuable in a country precisely for the reason that they offer a greater spectrum of opinion than what I find in traditional media today – which is silent by fear or coercion.

Final Thoughts

This discussion on the potential of new media, the web and internet platforms to transform policies and practices of illiberal democracy isn't, as yet, one that has traction amongst many people in Sri Lanka. Millions of people live without any awareness of the Internet or its potential for social change. There are arguably more pressing social issues in some regions than the digital divide – including the ravages of terrorism. However, the terrains of violence and conflict also hold within them the possibilities of democratic dialogue mediated through the Internet and mobile phones in particular. Three ideas, amongst many others, that can help capture the potential of new media for peace-building are:

- Creating new media based initiatives that amplify community aspirations for peace while at the same time being sensitive to the fragile and complex web of socio-political relations in the context of on-going peace processes;
- Expanding a community's social and knowledge capital through enhanced access to the Internet through mobile phones, while eschewing the facile notion that access to the internet based information itself is indicative of community empowerment;
- Using the internet and in particular the interactive potential of the world wide web to devise communities of practice that transform information to trusted and verifiable knowledge that aids conflict transformation within and between communities.

Animating the potential of new media and the internet in South Asia and worldwide is the promise of a vibrant democracy. A vibrant democracy in turn is nourished by a culture of open discussion on core issues of governance and as they are felt by citizens in all regions of a country. This symbiosis between democracy and dialogue, between new media and its influence on progressive social policy, between the promise of the internet to empower communities and the appropriation of ICT by communities to strengthen their engagement with justice and peace, is a qualitative and quantitative measurement of the health of democracy in Sri Lanka.

Notes

1 *Sri Lanka – how conflict drives information*, http://ivonotes.wordpress.com/2008/05/14/sri-lanka-how-conflict-drives-information/ (accessed 13 January 2009).
2 *War, Peace and Governance in Sri Lanka Overview and Trends 2006: An annual report of key trends affecting the peace process*, Centre for Policy Alternatives, January 2007, http://www.cpalanka.org/research_papers/War_Peace_Governance.pdf (accessed 13 January 2009).
Trapped and Mistreated: LTTE Abuses against Civilians in the Vanni, Human Rights Watch, 2008, http://www.hrw.org/en/reports/2008/12/15/trapped-and-mistreated-0 (accessed 13 January 2009).
Recurring Nightmare: State Responsibility for "Disappearances" and Abductions in Sri Lanka, Human Rights Watch, 2008, http://www.hrw.org/en/reports/2008/03/05/recurring-nightmare-0 (accessed 13 January 2009).
3 *Ministerial Committee to look into journalists' grievances commenced duties*, http://www.lankamission.org/content/view/439/9/ (accessed 13 January 2009).
4 *Sri Lankan State Media Chairman Threatens Journalists' Leader*, International Federation of Journalists (IFJ), http://freemediasrilanka.wordpress.com/2008/06/13/sri-lankan-state-media-chairman-threatens-journalists'-leader/ (accessed 13 January 2009).
5 *CPA Statement On The Recent Comments By General Sarath Fonseka In Canada's National Post*, http://transcurrents.com/tc/2008/09/cpa_statement_on_the_recent_co.html, (accessed 13 January 2009).
6 *Sri Lanka's Defence Secretary threatens Editor*, Free Media Movement (FMM), http://www.freemediasrilanka.org/English/news.php?id=523&section=news (accessed 13 January 2009).
7 *The implications of the death threat from Mahason Balakaya to lawyers, judges and the public*, Asian Human Rights Commission, http://www.ahrchk.net/statements/mainfile.php/2008statements/1753/ (accessed 13 January 2009).
8 *Operation Vula: ICT vs Apartheid*, http://fl3tch3r.wordpress.com/2008/04/02/operation-vula-ict-vs-apartheid/ (accessed 13 January 2009).
9 *Defeating repressive regimes*, http://ict4peace.wordpress.com/2006/05/10/defeating-repressive-regimes/ (accessed 13 January 2009).
10 *Dictatorships catching up with Web 2.0*, http://www.news.com/2010-1028_3-6155582.html?part=rss&tag=2547-1_3-0-20&subj=news (accessed 13 January 2009).
11 *Why Egypt Is Cracking Down on Bloggers*, http://www.time.com/time/world/article/0,8599,1199896,00.html (accessed 13 January 2009).

12 *Myanmar's sad lesson – Internet censorship still rules*, http://ict4peace.wordpress.com/2007/10/05/myanmars-sad-lesson-internet-censorship-still-rules/ (accessed 13 January 2009).
13 *Blogging the Coup*, http://www.cjr.org/short_takes/blogging_the_coup_1.php (accessed 13 January 2009).
14 *Endangered: Our right to 'shoot' in public*, http://www.groundviews.org/2008/02/14/endangered-our-right-to-shoot-in-public/
15 http://www.eyesondarfur.org/ (accessed 13 January 2009).
16 *Political Texting: SMS and Elections*, http://www.thefeaturearchives.com/topic/Culture/Political_Texting__SMS_and_Elections.html (accessed 13 January 2009).
17 *Kubatana reaches out with FrontlineSMS in Zimbabwe*, http://www.blogspot.kiwanja.net/2008/04/kubatana-reaches-out-with-frontlinesms.html (accessed 13 January 2009).
18 *Kenya in crisis*, http://news.bbc.co.uk/2/hi/technology/6241603.stm (accessed 13 January 2009).
19 *New political tool: text messaging*, http://www.usatoday.com/tech/news/2005-06-30-politics-text-tool_x.htm?csp=34 (accessed 14 January 2009).
20 *Asia-Pacific tops in various telecom sectors: UN report*, Thaindian News, http://www.thaindian.com/newsportal/uncategorized/asia-pacific-tops-in-various-telecom-sectors-un-report_10091104.html (accessed 12 January 2009).
21 *Ushahidi – Testimonies of violence in Kenya on the web*, http://ict4peace.wordpress.com/2008/01/16/ushahidi-testimonies-of-violence-in-kenya-on-the-web/ (accessed 12 January 2009).
22 http://www.boingboing.net/2004/12/27/smses_from_sri_lanka.html and http://www.boingboing.net/2005/01/01/nyt_sms_as_warning_s.html (accessed 14 January 2009).
23 http://www.lirneasia.net/2007/08/another-instance-of-voice-failing-and-sms-triumphing-during-disasters/ (accessed 14 January 2009).
24 http://www.lirneasia.net/2005/01/sms-as-part-of-early-warning-system (and also the interesting comments that follow the original post) (accessed 14 January 2009).
25 http://www.textually.org/textually/archives/2005/01/006698.htm (accessed 14 January 2009).
26 http://globalvoicesonline.org/-/human-rights-video/ (accessed 14 January 2009).
27 http://www.asiamedia.ucla.edu/article.asp?parentid=21285 (accessed 14 January 2009).
28 http://www.groundviews.org/2008/03/28/my-abducted-brother-found-in-colombo-national-hospital/ (accessed 12 January 2009).
29 http://www.groundviews.org/2007/07/30/stanley-rd-closure-hits-traders-in-jaffna/ (accessed 12 January 2009).
30 http://www.groundviews.org/2007/05/10/mobile-phones-connections-cut-in-jaffna/ (accessed 12 January 2009).
31 http://www.groundviews.org/2007/02/04/popular-activist-in-oddamavadi-targeted/ (accessed 12 January 2009).
32 http://www.groundviews.org/2007/12/31/alliance-of-parties-in-the-east/ (accessed 12 January 2009).
33 http://www.groundviews.org/2008/05/09/fate-of-the-displaced-mannar/ (accessed 12 January 2009).
34 http://www.groundviews.org/2008/06/09/war-idps/ (accessed 12 January 2009).
35 http://www.groundviews.org/2007/01/01/discrimination-in-law-college-entrance/ (accessed 12 January 2009).
36 http://www.groundviews.org/2006/11/28/situation-in-vakarai/ (accessed 12 January 2009).

37 http://ict4peace.wordpress.com/2006/12/07/new-media-in-cycles-of-violence-using-technology-for-new-voices/ (accessed 14 January 2009).
38 http://ict4peace.wordpress.com/2007/04/12/darfur-through-google-earth-the-reality-of-conflict-through-crisis-in-darfur/ is one example, of a growing number, of the use of multimedia rich mapping tools such as Google Earth to help visualise the otherwise difficult to comprehend enormity of humanitarian crises such as Darfur (accessed 14 January 2009).
39 http://deaned.blogspot.com/ (accessed 14 January 2009).
40 http://www.indi.ca/ (accessed 14 January 2009).
41 http://dinidudealwis.com/ (accessed 14 January 2009).
42 Kottu.org generated 19,096 page loads in December 2008. *Groundviews* alone generated 19,188 readers in December 2008.
43 http://beyondborders.wordpress.com/ (accessed 14 January 2009).
44 http://inmutiny.wordpress.com/ (accessed 14 January 2009).
45 See What makes a Sri Lankan Blogger?, http://londonlanka.blogspot.com/2007/06/what-makes-sri-lankan-blogger.html (accessed 12 January 2009).
46 http://bandaragama.wordpress.com (accessed 12 January 2009).
47 http://caffeinaholic.blogspot.com/ (accessed 12 January 2009).
48 http://landlikenoother.blogspot.com/2006/07/top-10-extremist-of-sri-lanka.html (accessed 12 January 2009).
49 http://transcurrents.com/tamiliana/ (accessed 12 January 2009).
50 http://electra.blogsome.com/ (accessed 12 January 2009).
51 http://blog.freedomhouse.org/weblog/2008/02/weekly-governan.html (accessed 12 January 2009).
52 The site commenting system is based on the IntenseDebate plugin for Wordpress – see www.intensedebate.com (accessed 12 January 2009).
53 E.g. Articles written to remember the anti-Tamil riots of July 1983 and 1958, http://www.groundviews.org/remember/ (accessed 12 January 2009).
54 http://www.groundviews.org/submission-guidelines (accessed 12 January 2009).
55 *Rajpal Abeynaike, Editor of Lakbima, offers exceptional responses to story on Groundviews*, http://www.groundviews.org/2007/07/12/rajpal-abeynaike-editor-of-lakbima-offers-exceptional-responses-to-story-on-groundviews/ (accessed 12 January 2009).
56 *Groundviews* in November 2008 completely revamped its comments architecture and at the time of writing features the most sophisticated and secure platform for comments on any blog in Sri Lanka. Using a plug-in for Wordpress (a blogging platform that *Groundviews* runs on) called IntenseDebate, commentators can choose to be anonymous or create an online identity, that cannot be traced back to them, that allows them to safely and securely engage with the content on the site.
57 Disclosure: The author is the Editor of *Groundviews* and is solely responsible for the site's content management, technical upgrades and maintenance, marketing and development.
58 The full guidelines can be read here – http://www.groundviews.org/submission-guidelines/
59 http://www.citmedia.org/principles (accessed 12 January 2009).
60 http://www.macworld.com/news/2007/03/06/franceban/index.php?lsrc=mwrss (accessed 12 January 2009).
61 http://freemediasrilanka.org/index.php?action=con_news_full&id=625&section=news (accessed 12 January 2009).

12 *Myanmar's sad lesson – Internet censorship still rules*, http://ict4peace.wordpress.com/2007/10/05/myanmars-sad-lesson-internet-censorship-still-rules/ (accessed 13 January 2009).
13 *Blogging the Coup*, http://www.cjr.org/short_takes/blogging_the_coup_1.php (accessed 13 January 2009).
14 *Endangered: Our right to 'shoot' in public*, http://www.groundviews.org/2008/02/14/endangered-our-right-to-shoot-in-public/
15 http://www.eyesondarfur.org/ (accessed 13 January 2009).
16 *Political Texting: SMS and Elections*, http://www.thefeaturearchives.com/topic/Culture/Political_Texting__SMS_and_Elections.html (accessed 13 January 2009).
17 *Kubatana reaches out with FrontlineSMS in Zimbabwe*, http://www.blogspot.kiwanja.net/2008/04/kubatana-reaches-out-with-frontlinesms.html (accessed 13 January 2009).
18 *Kenya in crisis*, http://news.bbc.co.uk/2/hi/technology/6241603.stm (accessed 13 January 2009).
19 *New political tool: text messaging*, http://www.usatoday.com/tech/news/2005-06-30-politics-text-tool_x.htm?csp = 34 (accessed 14 January 2009).
20 *Asia-Pacific tops in various telecom sectors: UN report*, Thaindian News, http://www.thaindian.com/newsportal/uncategorized/asia-pacific-tops-in-various-telecom-sectors-un-report_10091104.html (accessed 12 January 2009).
21 *Ushahidi – Testimonies of violence in Kenya on the web*, http://ict4peace.wordpress.com/2008/01/16/ushahidi-testimonies-of-violence-in-kenya-on-the-web/ (accessed 12 January 2009).
22 http://www.boingboing.net/2004/12/27/smses_from_sri_lanka.html and http://www.boingboing.net/2005/01/01/nyt_sms_as_warning_s.html (accessed 14 January 2009).
23 http://www.lirneasia.net/2007/08/another-instance-of-voice-failing-and-sms-triumphing-during-disasters/ (accessed 14 January 2009).
24 http://www.lirneasia.net/2005/01/sms-as-part-of-early-warning-system (and also the interesting comments that follow the original post) (accessed 14 January 2009).
25 http://www.textually.org/textually/archives/2005/01/006698.htm (accessed 14 January 2009).
26 http://globalvoicesonline.org/-/human-rights-video/ (accessed 14 January 2009).
27 http://www.asiamedia.ucla.edu/article.asp?parentid=21285 (accessed 14 January 2009).
28 http://www.groundviews.org/2008/03/28/my-abducted-brother-found-in-colombo-national-hospital/ (accessed 12 January 2009).
29 http://www.groundviews.org/2007/07/30/stanley-rd-closure-hits-traders-in-jaffna/ (accessed 12 January 2009).
30 http://www.groundviews.org/2007/05/10/mobile-phones-connections-cut-in-jaffna/ (accessed 12 January 2009).
31 http://www.groundviews.org/2007/02/04/popular-activist-in-oddamavadi-targeted/ (accessed 12 January 2009).
32 http://www.groundviews.org/2007/12/31/alliance-of-parties-in-the-east/ (accessed 12 January 2009).
33 http://www.groundviews.org/2008/05/09/fate-of-the-displaced-mannar/ (accessed 12 January 2009).
34 http://www.groundviews.org/2008/06/09/war-idps/ (accessed 12 January 2009).
35 http://www.groundviews.org/2007/01/01/discrimination-in-law-college-entrance/ (accessed 12 January 2009).
36 http://www.groundviews.org/2006/11/28/situation-in-vakarai/ (accessed 12 January 2009).

37 http://ict4peace.wordpress.com/2006/12/07/new-media-in-cycles-of-violence-using-technology-for-new-voices/ (accessed 14 January 2009).
38 http://ict4peace.wordpress.com/2007/04/12/darfur-through-google-earth-the-reality-of-conflict-through-crisis-in-darfur/ is one example, of a growing number, of the use of multimedia rich mapping tools such as Google Earth to help visualise the otherwise difficult to comprehend enormity of humanitarian crises such as Darfur (accessed 14 January 2009).
39 http://deaned.blogspot.com/ (accessed 14 January 2009).
40 http://www.indi.ca/ (accessed 14 January 2009).
41 http://dinidudealwis.com/ (accessed 14 January 2009).
42 Kottu.org generated 19,096 page loads in December 2008. *Groundviews* alone generated 19,188 readers in December 2008.
43 http://beyondborders.wordpress.com/ (accessed 14 January 2009).
44 http://inmutiny.wordpress.com/ (accessed 14 January 2009).
45 See What makes a Sri Lankan Blogger?, http://londonlanka.blogspot.com/2007/06/what-makes-sri-lankan-blogger.html (accessed 12 January 2009).
46 http://bandaragama.wordpress.com (accessed 12 January 2009).
47 http://caffeinaholic.blogspot.com/ (accessed 12 January 2009).
48 http://landlikenoother.blogspot.com/2006/07/top-10-extremist-of-sri-lanka.html (accessed 12 January 2009).
49 http://transcurrents.com/tamiliana/ (accessed 12 January 2009).
50 http://electra.blogsome.com/ (accessed 12 January 2009).
51 http://blog.freedomhouse.org/weblog/2008/02/weekly-governan.html (accessed 12 January 2009).
52 The site commenting system is based on the IntenseDebate plugin for Wordpress – see www.intensedebate.com (accessed 12 January 2009).
53 E.g. Articles written to remember the anti-Tamil riots of July 1983 and 1958, http://www.groundviews.org/remember/ (accessed 12 January 2009).
54 http://www.groundviews.org/submission-guidelines (accessed 12 January 2009).
55 *Rajpal Abeynaike, Editor of Lakbima, offers exceptional responses to story on Groundviews*, http://www.groundviews.org/2007/07/12/rajpal-abeynaike-editor-of-lakbima-offers-exceptional-responses-to-story-on-groundviews/ (accessed 12 January 2009).
56 *Groundviews* in November 2008 completely revamped its comments architecture and at the time of writing features the most sophisticated and secure platform for comments on any blog in Sri Lanka. Using a plug-in for Wordpress (a blogging platform that *Groundviews* runs on) called IntenseDebate, commentators can choose to be anonymous or create an online identity, that cannot be traced back to them, that allows them to safely and securely engage with the content on the site.
57 Disclosure: The author is the Editor of *Groundviews* and is solely responsible for the site's content management, technical upgrades and maintenance, marketing and development.
58 The full guidelines can be read here – http://www.groundviews.org/submission-guidelines/
59 http://www.citmedia.org/principles (accessed 12 January 2009).
60 http://www.macworld.com/news/2007/03/06/franceban/index.php?lsrc=mwrss (accessed 12 January 2009).
61 http://freemediasrilanka.org/index.php?action=con_news_full&id=625&section=news (accessed 12 January 2009).

62 http://freemediasrilanka.org/index.php?action=con_news_full&id=443&section=news (accessed 12 January 2009).
63 http://news.com.com/2010-1028_3-6155582.html?part=rss&tag=2547-1_3-0-20&subj=news (accessed 13 January 2009).
64 http://ict4peace.pbwiki.com/ (accessed 12 January 2009).
65 http://www.worldchanging.com/archives/006458.html (accessed 12 January 2009).
66 http://ict4peace.wordpress.com/2008/11/13/censored-forum-theatre-on-freedom-of-expression-at-a-time-of-war/ (accessed 12 January 2009).
67 http://freemediasrilanka.wordpress.com/2008/11/15/supreme-court's-grant-of-leave-to-proceed-and-interim-relief-in-challenges-to-new-television-regulations/ (accessed 12 January 2009).
68 See http://ict4peace.wordpress.com/2008/11/16/gagging-the-web-and-internet-implications-of-the-proposed-private-tv-broadcasting-regulations-in-sri-lanka/ for a deeper analysis of this issue (accessed 12 January 2009).
69 http://ict4peace.wordpress.com/2008/07/13/mass-audiences-and-citizen-journalism/ (accessed 12 January 2009).

References

Beckett, A. (2003) 'Santiago Dreaming: The forgotten story of Chile's 'socialist internet', *The Guardian*, Monday 8 September 2003 on page 2 of the Technology News & Features section, (accessed January 9 2009) http://www.guardian.co.uk/technology/2003/sep/08/sciencenews.chile

Bentivegna, S. (2002) 'Politics and New Media', in L.A. Lievrouw and S. Livingstone (eds) *Handbook of New Media: Social Shaping and Consequences of ICTs*, London and Thousand Oaks: Sage: 50–61

Deshapriya, S. and Hattotuwa, S. (2003) *A study of Media in the North-East of Sri Lanka*, Centre for Policy Alternatives, 2003

――― (2005) *A Study of Media in Sri Lanka (excluding North and East)*, Centre for Policy Alternatives, Sri Lanka

Enteen, J. (2006) 'Spatial Conceptions of URLS: Tamil Ealam networks on the world wide web', *New Media and Society*, Volume 8. No. 2: 229–249

Kelly, J. and Etling, B. (2008) 'Mapping Iran's Online Public: Politics and Culture in the Persian Bloggosphere', Internet and Democracy Case Study Series, available at http://cyber.law.harvard.edu/publications/2008/Mapping_Irans_Online_Public (accessed 12 January 2009)

O'Hara, K. (2001) 'Democracy and the Internet' http://www.abdn.ac.uk/philosophy/endsandmeans/vol4no3/ohara.shtml, (accessed 13 January 2009): NP

Chapter Fourteen

CONCLUSION

Shakuntala Banaji

Jump Cuts and Unusual Angles

In looking across histories, national borders, urban and rural regions, social classes, genders, ethnicities, cultural practices and political traditions in the South Asian region to give a sense of the contexts in which media producers and audiences make meaning and texts are formed and used, the contributors in this volume have not taken a uniform approach. Herein lies the richness of this collection, but also the difficulty in drawing conclusions that are in agreement with all chapters' findings and orientations. I do not, therefore, intend to restate the complex findings of individual chapters but simply to draw out common theoretical strands, questions and absences.

Reading through the collection, it becomes apparent that *the* South Asian audience, singular, does not exist. Nor does *the* Indian or *the* Sri Lankan audience. Nor does the *child* audience or the *rural* audience, per se. There is also no overarching, publicly funded, government-controlled national media framework in any of the countries that has not, by 2011, been compelled to interact with and cede much of its market to local and international commercial media interests. Nevertheless, all the variety of media interests in each of the countries included in this collection clearly operate within and against the backdrop of the existing cultural ideologies of various civil society actors *and* national, regional or state political regimes. There can be no doubt, therefore, about the very political nature of the processes surrounding and inflecting all production and consumption of media across the subcontinent. And, as each contributor has shown here, even media practices that seem the most individual or detached from wider politics, such as families watching vernacular serials or talk shows with no explicit aim other than entertainment and relaxation, may be contributions to the discursive construction of national or ethnic identities, gender, age or class power blocs. Further, the idea that fiction media texts do not contribute to debates in the civic public sphere, or that all non-fiction texts are treated with the same seriousness and respect is conclusively rejected. As Liesbet van Zoonen has noted, 'popular fictions of politics enable people to perform as citizens' (205, 150).

As most of the contributors pay attention to the subtle permutations of representation and discourse in media formats, their discussions of culture and politics are frequently refracted via textual narratives and via interviews with media users and producers. People's *representations* of their experiences of media-making or meaning-making are neither straightforward correlates of their 'real' feelings nor precise maps of the media content they refer to (Buckingham 1993: 210). Across the collection, the variety of contexts and the focus on constructed and constructive uses of language in representing individual and collective identities militates against simplistic attributions of totalising power to audiences, texts or producers.

In chapters by Lotte Hoek, Daisy Hasan, Noorel Mecklai, Irna Qureshi and Rashmi Sawhney, the topic of cinema was approached from five totally different theoretical and empirical standpoints. Based on these, mainstream and alternative cinemas are displayed embedded in a multiplicity of ways, in a diversity of contexts and playing different roles in the maintenance and/or construction of intersecting class, religious, gender and ethnic identities. From internet film-fan discussions about nation and religion, through the historical encodings of cinema halls, the ethnicisation of gender discourse in relation to lower caste actresses and lack of popular engagement with documentary film, to the appropriation of Bollywood narratives and sensibilities by Manipuri directors and audiences, these writers have urged a reconsideration of taken-for-granted academic and common-sense positions on national cinematic traditions. In their chapters, Mecklai, Qureshi and Sawhney grappled with a series of questions about representation and self-representation through media. They looked at the ways in which stigma (framed by gender, religion or ethnicity) attaches to particular sections of the public off-screen, inflecting both their representation onscreen and the reception of their on-screen work. Sawhney, saliently, described both despised communities and debates around hierarchies of value in relation to different cinematic traditions in India. Crucially, she pointed out that the divide between the South Asian intelligentsia's approval of 'art' and 'realist' cinema and their rejection of popular [Hindi] film has done little to make a wider spectrum of viewers literate about documentary. This leaves marginalized communities working with undervalued media formats at a double remove from equality and opportunity.

Through her vivid and exhaustive attention to the detail of cinema halls in a small Bangladeshi town and the weaving together of narratives about history and audiences from the points of view of theatre staff, workers and owners, Hoek drew attention to the deep-seated nostalgia and snobbery governing cinephile and academic accounts of popular cinema in the country. She underlined questions that, I suggest, any of us interested in South Asian media cultures need to ask: who controls the value ascribed to media products and viewing contexts across the subcontinent? How can the tensions between the need for commercial success/survival of media cultural spaces or forms and the maintenance of 'standards', 'traditions' and artistic integrity be reconciled in places where different classes have distinct and entrenched regimes of taste? Hasan's chapter, likewise, drew attention to the counterintuitive ways in which seemingly 'imposed' or threatening cultural forms (such as western popular culture in South Asia, or Indian commercial film in non-Hindi speaking areas) can be adopted and adapted critically and playfully, and incorporated into local and regional media rather than totally disavowed or completely accepted. All five chapters raised important questions about the ways in which mainstream and marginal, documentary and fiction, critical and popular, not-for-profit and commercial films are inscribed with multiple layers of political culture and cultural politics.

The Shaping and Expression of Identities and Aspirations

In relation to mainstream television, the significance of intersecting identities of class, gender and ethnicity for viewing is even more striking. In a Sri Lanka indelibly marked by decades of ethnic discrimination, state repression and civil war, Neluka Silva pointed us towards the complex interplay of commercial forces and social ideologies in the representations, successes or failures of several contemporary teledramas. Like my own findings in relation to Hindi films that deal with religious 'riots' in supposedly liberal and 'neutral' ways (Banaji 2006), Silva's chapter teased out the problematic misrepresentation and possibly inadvertent re-stereotyping of Tamil characters and women characters even in teledramas that purport to be about cross-cultural understanding and reconciliation. In an urban Pakistani context, Tahir Naqvi analysed the shifting discursive references to religion, sexuality, gender, corruption and the state that make the rhetoric of new daytime talk-shows so compelling for those who tread a fine line between nationalist and international, religious and secular identifications. He pointed out that the orientation of most of Pakistan's large private broadcasters towards moderate Islam and middleclass identities under the Musharraf regime led to the cautious reconfiguration of religious content as a 'consumer good' on all channels. This finding speaks directly to persistent debates about the reshaping of the media sphere in South Asia by different financial, ideological and political alliances.

Britta Ohm's chapter on Indian broadcast news media and Hindu-chauvinist politics made connections between a refutation of independent journalism by a communalised middleclass Hindu public and the painful erasure of Muslim voices, subjectivities and rights taking place in Gujarat. Her analysis of the curiously paradoxical relationship between the media, an elected populist far-Right Hindu chauvinist government and the fascist policing of the public sphere by civil society actors directs us to think in new and complicated ways about the construction, representation and meaning of democracy. One of her key questions will not be entirely new to those who have worked in Europe, Australia and North America, especially in relation to the propaganda that surrounded wars in Afghanistan and Iraq: what do we do when the language we use to discuss and describe democracy – 'equality', 'freedom of expression', 'community', 'justice' and 'rights' – has been colonised and appropriated, almost imperceptibly, by an exclusive totalitarian narrative? In this sense, the psychic and material repercussions of meanings and uses made from South Asian cultural products are a central focus in much of this collection.

Cautions against both textual and contextual determinism notwithstanding, contributors show little hesitation in pushing us towards readings and conceptualisations that see situated social phenomena – exceptional and mundane, positive and negative – as having been inflected by media cultures. Paul Greene pointed us towards the ways in which young people's social identities, their aspirations and social options in contemporary Nepal are reflected in their articulation of international and local, mainstream and traditional idioms in Nepali pop music. His analysis focuses attention on a peculiarly South Asian cultural hierarchy, wherein Western formats, Indian popular culture, modern synergies and local traditional cultures vie for position in local imaginaries. He emphasised that they are taken up differentially in different eras or political contexts as expressions of resistant or nostalgic personal and group identity. Concerned, like Greene, with an age-specific segment of the media public, my research indicates that the pedagogic achievements, aspirations, pleasures and social autonomy of vast numbers of children across India may be intimately bound up with their access to and use of media. In this instance, it is not only the amount and quality of media access that is significant but the social standing of media within families and communities and the amount of personal control children are given over media technologies and leisure time. The pedagogic and educational stress put on curtailing children's enjoyment of media has wide-reaching implications for all kinds of learning, including media literacy and traditional print literacy, multilingualism and understandings of health, sex and relationships. The restriction of rural and small-town children's representations on television and in the movies, and, off-screen, of most children's leisure time and pleasure in media, alongside adult insistence on constant 'productive', 'developmental' and/or 'safe' activities may also be read as a metaphor for children's collective and persistent disenfranchisement within most South Asian public spheres.

Both chapters indicated clearly that framing debates as if western or commercial media forms/narratives are all that need to be resisted or censored to maintain local and national identities and traditions can work to further disadvantage the least powerful groups within South Asian societies. As in several of the other contributions, these two chapters suggested the importance for media research of paying attention to regimes of power *amongst* audiences and *between* members of particular media cultures rather than simply between some amorphous group of 'producers' and the mass of 'consumers' of media products. While examining the creative and resistant uses to which some people choose to put their media viewing and participation, the descriptions of media use by young people in Nepal and children in India also highlight what David Buckingham (1993) has called the casual, uncommitted and 'routinised nature' of much cultural activity. Oddly, this knowledge might prove *comforting* in some contexts, especially those where a huge *commitment* to xenophobic, inflammatory, discriminatory rhetorics – examined, for instance, by Hattotuwa, Ohm, Mecklai and Qureshi in this volume – might be destructive of communities, people and relationships in the real world.

Top-Down or Bottom-Up? The Case for Civic (New) Media

The notion of an ideological separation between the interests of civil society and those of the state and elite groups was a running theme in several of the contributions. Saman Talib and Sanjana Hattotuwa used case studies to describe the affordances of new media platforms such as blogs and mobile phones for the pursuit of egalitarian and democratic goals by civil society groups in situations where the mainstream media has succumbed to censorship, state propaganda and violent repression. Talib's piece, built around a student campaign for democracy and restoration of civil liberties, concluded that in Pakistan, in the particular context of *young people*, new media platforms allow openings to sidestep traditional political alliances and create alternative political narratives to those of the governing elites. Acknowledging both the vulnerability of those attempting to develop peaceful debates about or responses to ethnic/political conflict *and* the participation of various sections of civil society in the violent imaginaries sustaining conflict, Hattotuwa remains hopeful about the role that online citizen-controlled spaces can play. Hattotuwa and Talib explicitly contrasted the realm of top-down 'mass' media to that of alternative production enabled by the internet and mobile communication technologies. Where dissenting mainstream journalists are being censored, physically intimidated and murdered by the state and by violent non-state actors, new media platforms do still offer a modicum of safety and security. Where getting across views which challenge government agendas in the mainstream press is all but impossible for ordinary citizens in the most volatile South Asian areas across all five countries, the anonymity and low cost of new media platforms can enable a far greater number to venture opinions, offer solutions and criticise those in power. Overall, however, given the short-lived nature of the student movement in Pakistan and the variety of views being expressed on the 'alternative' civic web, these chapters still leave open questions about the wider and longer-term political impact of citizen-driven media initiatives in South Asia.

Despite the key role that new and alternative media circuits have been shown to play by some of the contributors in this volume, democracy and democratisation of the public/media sphere in South Asia cannot be left to rest with this realm alone. After all, both authoritarian/exclusionary and pro-democratic/egalitarian 'civic' agendas can and do gain expression over the internet (Banaji 2008), and mobile phones and digital videos have also been implicated in the mobilisation of fascist cadres to kill Christians and Muslims in India, Tamils in Sri Lanka and Hindus and Christians in Bangladesh and Pakistan. At the same time, all popular film, television and newspapers should surely not be ceded to corrupt, non-secular, authoritarian political formations or entirely commercial interests. Forms of representation and circuits of finance and distribution alike need to be challenged, consistently and repeatedly, across South Asia. Concomitantly, personal empowerment through media viewing, media use and media making is not synonymous with political empowerment or with greater collective visibility in the public sphere. The children in my research, the Chharas in Rashmi Sawhney's, the Kanjar actresses and their families in Irna Qureshi's, the various peoples and producers of North-East India in Daisy Hasan's work and the multitudes of Indian Muslims who participate in Hindi film fandom (as well as those who do not), continue to be cast in stereotypical and/or discriminatory ways in wider cultural and political life. Middle and uppermiddle-class power seems, at one level, to be the only guarantee of access to personal safety and security if you happen to belong to a 'stigmatizied' group in South Asia, and this in itself does not guarantee that you can control most or even any of the representations of your group in the media and in the wider public imagination.

Hegemony, Meaning and Cultural Agency

Finally, when it comes to the Gramscian notion of *hegemony*, the non-coerced acceptance by a majority of the population of ideological principles and systems supporting elite interests and inequitable social relationships (1971), contributors do not necessarily agree with each other or even attempt to take up conclusive positions. Mecklai, for instance, writing specifically about cinematic representations of Muslims and the possible repercussions such representations have in authoritarian and conflict-ridden social and political settings, argued that hegemonic myths serving the interests of particular sections of ruling elites in India exist and are perpetuated by Hindi films. Arguments about dominant or hegemonic ideologies and discourses have evidently dominated textual studies of media in South Asia for decades, notably influencing discussions about commercial Hindi and Tamil cinema (cf. Prasad 1998; Kazmi 1999; Gopalan 2002; Virdi 2003 to name but a few) and their audiences (Dickey 1993; Derne 2000). Although these readings may miss some of the complexity of meaning, and some of the texture of everyday viewing pleasure, I have argued elsewhere (Banaji 2006) that while there may be a temptation to 'redeem' audiences by asserting their autonomy and activity, the attribution of vast numbers of completely unpredictable 'negotiated' meanings to media texts is also problematic. Texts and textual structures may always only be part of a wider symbolic and material context, but these texts still *initiate* discussion about or *invite* collusion with and *participation* in a limited range of discourses belonging to recognisable ideological frameworks. The fact that texts are internally inconsistent and fragmentary, or that media viewers, users, audiences and producers 'read' from individual perspectives, contradict themselves, misinterpret and misremember when describing texts might create a greater range of potential meanings and undermine the singularity of some critical interpretations of media texts, but it hardly indicates that texts are now insignificant. Consequently, contributors in this collection have consistently resisted both the assertion of unproblematic causal relationships between media use and social behaviour *and* the attribution of infinite numbers of meanings and interpretations to media texts. They focused, rather, on the ways in which history and context in South Asia can inspire meaning-making and cultural production. Similarly, most contributors have also been wary of suggesting that textual representations and media pleasures push audiences into an ideological position from which there is no escape, that films, news programmes, dramas or blogs surreptitiously *compel* psychic agreement or material action. In this manner, writers in this collection have provided evidence for and urged a distinction between different *sets* of media meanings, pleasures and uses that are individual and/or context-specific in South Asia. In particular, this distinction has been drawn between media meanings that suggest pre-existing coherent ideological frameworks or group perceptions and those that are deliberately constructed to disrupt these. Pushing these issues further, it would be productive to see future studies of South Asian media cultures digging deeper into the realms of experience, learning and action that surround media production and use, trying to tease out the spaces where explicit financial or moral support would strengthen and sustain interesting, egalitarian, peaceful and internationalist media cultures and practices. Studies combining carefully theorised survey research in the realms of media and politics with complex observational and interview data would also be a welcome addition to the field.

References

Banaji, S. (2006) *Reading 'Bollywood': The Young Audience and Hindi Film*, Basingstoke: Palgrave Macmillan

───── (2008) 'The Trouble with Civic: A Snapshot of Young People's Civic and Political Engagements in Twenty-first Century Democracies' in *Journal of Youth Studies*, Volume 11, No. 5, October 2008: 543–60

Buckingham, D. (1993) *Reading Audiences: Young People and the Media*, Manchester: Manchester University Press

Derne, S. (2000) *Movies, Masculinity and Modernity: An Ethnography of Men's Film-going in India*, Westport Ct. and London: Greenwood Press

Dickey, S. (1993) *Cinema and the Urban Poor in South India*, Cambridge, MA.: Cambridge University Press

Gopalan, L. (2002) *Cinema of Interruptions: Action Genres in Contemporary Indian Cinema*, London: BFI Publishing

Gramsci, A. (1971) *Selections from the Prison Notebooks*, London: Lawrence and Wishart.

Kazmi, F. (1999) *The Politics of India's Commercial Cinema: Imaging a Universe, Subverting a Multiverse*, New Delhi: Sage

Prasad, M. M. (1998) *Ideology of the Hindi Film: A Historical Construction*, New Delhi/Thousand Oaks/London: Oxford University Press

Van Zoonen, L. (2005) *Entertaining the Citizen: When Politics and Popular Culture Converge*, New York/Toronto/Oxford: Rowman and Littlefield Publishers Ltd.

Virdi, J. (2003) *The Cinematic Imagination*, New Jersey and London: Rutgers University Press

LIST OF CONTRIBUTORS

Shakuntala Banaji, PhD, is a lecturer in the Department of Media and Communications at the London School of Economics. She teaches courses on international media and the global south, world cinema, visual analysis and film theory. She has previously lectured and researched at the Centre for the Study of Children, Youth and Media at the Institute of Education and taught English and media in London schools. She retains a strong interest in young people, critical education and pedagogy at all levels. Her writing on Hindi cinema, news, audiences, children, young people and media, online civic cultures and creativity has been widely published. She is currently researching children's media cultures in India and representations of children, childhood and child labour in South Asian media. The second edition of her book *Reading 'Bollywood': The Young Audience and Hindi Films* will be out in paperback in 2012, and another book, co-authored with David Buckingham, *The Civic Web: Young People, the Internet and Civic Life* is forthcoming from MIT Press in 2012.

Paul D. Greene is an associate professor of ethnomusicology and integrative arts at Pennsylvania State University, Brandywine Campus. His research focuses on music, technology, and Buddhism in Nepal and India.

Daisy Hasan has completed a PhD in media cultures of North East India from Swansea University and id a former senior media fellow of the Public Service Broadcasting Trust, New Delhi. She has worked in both the state-owned and independent sectors of the Indian media and is currently a postdoctoral research assistant at the School of English, University of Leeds where she is working on a multifaceted programme looking at artwork by women artists in the context of 'conflict' in South Asia.

Sanjana Hattotuwa is a senior researcher at the Centre for Policy Alternatives and an Ashoka Foundation News & Knowledge Entrepreneur. He is the founder and editor of *Groundviews* (www.groundviews.org), an international award-winning web based citizen journalism initiative in Sri Lanka.

Lotte Hoek is a lecturer in social anthropology at the University of Edinburgh and is affiliated to the Centre for South Asian Studies there. Lotte has a longstanding interest in visual culture in Bangladesh and has done ethnographic fieldwork relating to photography, cinema and television in Dhaka. She received her PhD in anthropology at the University of Amsterdam in 2008. Her doctoral dissertation "Cut-Pieces: Obscenity and the Cinema in Bangladesh" is an ethnography of the Bangladesh film industry and focuses on the common practice of inserting sexually explicit imagery into B-quality action movies.

Noorel Mecklai completed her PhD in media studies from Edith Cowan University in Perth, Australia, with a substantial study of films of the Hindi popular cinema between 1947–2000 that contain a Muslim character or theme. During this period she has also undertaken a comparative study of the existing literature on Hindi popular cinema and modern Indian history, nationalism and communalism. Her further interests lie in teaching and writing on 'Islam in the Media' and in producing both features and documentaries on her subject.

Tahir Naqvi is assistant professor of sociology and anthropology at Trinity University, San Antonio, Texas. He has also worked as visiting assistant professor of anthropology at Reed College, Portland Oregon. He received his PhD in anthropology from the University of California Berkeley. His ongoing research deals with the effects of military rule by emergency on urban political space and culture.

Britta Ohm holds a PhD in social and cultural anthropology from the European University Viadrina, Frankfurt/Oder, Germany. Her thesis is on *The Televised Community: Culture, Politics and the Market of Visual Representation in India*. She is co-author of documentaries and a feature film and has worked as a journalist, screenplay consultant and cutter for German public TV. Currently she is pursuing postdoctoral research on negotiations between the secular and the Islamic on commercial television in Turkey.

Irna Qureshi is a writer and oral historian specialising in British Asian and Muslim heritage. She has collaborated on several exhibitions and books on this theme. She holds an MA in social anthropology from the School of Oriental and African Studies, University of London, and regularly conducts fieldwork in Pakistan.

Rashmi Sawhney, PhD, is a lecturer in visual cultural studies at the Centre for Transcultural Research and Media Practice, Dublin Institute of

Technology, where she teaches postgraduate and undergraduate courses in the area of film and visual culture. She is an affiliate faculty at Trinity College, Dublin, teaching on the MPhil in Ethnic and Racial Studies programme. Her publications have been in the areas of film studies, postcolonial studies and gender studies. Recent publications include an article on 'Adivasi cinema' in a special issue of *Moving Worlds* (2009); a chapter on marginal cinemas in *Indigeneity: Culture and Representation* (eds Devy, Davis, Chakravorty, 2009); an article on 'modernity and film spectatorship' in *Interventions: International Journal of Postcolonial Studies* (ed Lynne Pierce, forthcoming). She is currently working on a book-length manuscript on Indian women filmmakers.

Neluka Silva, PhD, is professor of English and the head of the Department of English at the University of Colombo, Sri Lanka. Her research interests include nationalism and gender issues in cultural production in South Asia, Sri Lankan teledrama and theatre. She is the co-editor of a book on women in the conflict zones in Sri Lanka and the post-Yugoslav states, as well as *Cross Cultural Identities: Contemporary Sri Lankan and British Writing and The Hybrid Island: Culture Crossings and the Invention of Identities in Sri Lanka*. She has been involved in Sri Lankan theatre for over fifteen years, and has published two collections of short stories and a novel.

Saman Talib, PhD, is assistant professor at Beaconhouse National University, Pakistan. She previously worked as assistant professor at the School of Management Sciences, Lahore University. She has also worked at publishing houses, broadcast networks, radio stations, and digital news organizations. Her scholarship considers the conjunctions of media and politics. She is particularly interested in researching the effective use of new media to foster knowledge, literacy and participation in civil society. She has presented her work at conferences and has been invited to contribute articles to the forthcoming *Routledge Encyclopaedia of American Journalism History*.

www.ingramcontent.com/pod-product-compliance
Lightning Source LLC
Chambersburg PA
CBHW021822300426
44114CB00009BA/280